Action on Racial Harassment: Legal Remedies and Local Authorities

Action on Racial Harassment: Legal Remedies and Local Authorities

Duncan Forbes, solicitor

Published by Legal Action Group and London Housing Unit
May 1988

Duncan Forbes is a solicitor. For five years he worked in law centres where he specialised in housing law and was adviser to many clients suffering racial harassment. Since January 1987, he has been teaching, writing and undertaking consultancy and private practice casework for a wide variety of clients and organisations throughout the country in the fields of housing, racial harassment and disability rights. He also specialises in acting as legal adviser to many voluntary organisations. He has contributed regularly to *LEGAL ACTION* and is a joint author of the 1988 edition of *Voluntary But Not Amateur, a guide to the law for voluntary organisations and community groups* published by the London Voluntary Service Council.

Phototypeset by Kerrypress Ltd, Luton, Beds
Printed by Dotesios (Printers) Ltd

ISBN 0 905099 18 4

Acknowledgements

The author would like to thank Ged Curran, Terry Dean, Robert Latham, Mike O'Dwyer, Marie Rosenthal and Clare Shirtcliff for their valuable comments and suggestions on drafts; Sheron Hamilton-Pearson for typing the manuscript; Cynthia Alleyne, Galba Bright, Sue Wolk and the other London Housing Unit staff for their assistance during the production; Ros O'Brien and the LAG staff for their work on the manuscript, indices and tables and Clare Shirtcliff for her encouragement and support. Responsibility for the contents rests with the author.

This book was initiated and funded by the London Housing Unit to whom the author expresses his thanks.

The law is stated as at 1 December 1987. Developments up to 1 March 1988 are dealt with in the Stop Press p vi.

Readers' comments and any experiences of using legal remedies discussed in the text, whether or not successfully, are warmly welcomed and should be sent to the author c/o LAG.

Cover picture courtesy of David Hoffman.

Stop press

Stop press to 1 March 1988

Chapter 2 p11 and Chapter 13 p224	See now also the judgment of the Divisional Court in *R v LB Lewisham ex p Shell UK Ltd* (1987) *Times* 22 December.
Chapter 2 pp13 and 16	The Local Government Bill passing through its final stages in Parliament will restrict the ability of local authorities to operate contract compliance.
Chapter 6 p106	The Government has published a consultation paper entitled "Home Improvement Policy: The Government's Proposals" which proposes changes to the system of housing grants.
Chapter 7 p134	The Court of Appeal began hearing the appeal against the decision of the Divisional Court in *R v LB Tower Hamlets ex p Monaf* on 29 February 1988.
Chapter 10 p166	Clause 93 of the Criminal Justice Bill would require a court to give reasons why no compensation order has been made whenever there is a victim who could be compensated.
Chapter 10 p167	Clause 113 and Schedule 7 of the Criminal Justice Bill contain amendments to the provisions relating to supervision orders.
Chapter 10 p181 and Chapter 12 p204	The Criminal Justice Bill clause 34 contains proposals to amend the rules relating to common assault to make it an ordinary summary offence with no special provisions about prosecution by victims.
Chapter 14 p243	The Criminal Justice Bill contains proposals to amend the rules relating to the giving of evidence by children.
Appendix 6 p305	The Criminal Justice Bill clause 33 proposes that criminal damage be triable only summarily where the value of the property damaged is up to £2,000 rather than the present £400.

Forewords

TONY GIFFORD QC, Chairman of the Broadwater Farm Inquiry, writes:

Racism remains rife in British society. Black and ethnic minority people know it from bitter experience. Its expression ranges from a cold stare and patronising attitude, to filthy abuse, bricks through the window, petrol through the letter-box, and knives in the heart. Many white people who would recoil from such abuse and violence are still perversely unaware and inactive about an issue which blights the lives of their fellow citizens. Others who have the power to take action against the perpetrators of racist crimes respond with culpable weakness to the pleas of the victims.

Much of the criticism about the failure to deal with racist attacks has been directed at the police. In *Policing Against Black People*, published by the Institute of Race Relations in 1987, there is a devastating compilation of cases which police officers have failed to pursue, advised the victims to take out private prosecutions, and even blamed victims for inflicting the damage or injury to themselves. Two cases are illustrative:

" • Years of harassment suffered by the Singh family of Battersea, south London, since July 1980, during which their windows were broken, they were assaulted and stones were thrown at their children, were treated by police as a civil matter. Ironically, the Singhs, who live in a neighbourhood watch area, were forced to take out a private prosecution.

• Over a six-month period in 1981 a black family living in Warrington suffered persistent harassment, including letters covered with swastikas, and threatening violence. The police told them that they could do nothing and advised the family to ignore the attacks."

But it is not just the police who should shoulder the blame. The police, even though imperfectly accountable to the public, have eventually to respond to the voices of the communities which they serve. In recent years, there has been some evidence of a greater sense of urgency from police forces towards tackling racist attacks—a response, though belated, to the public's concern. The more vocal we are in demanding action and the more other agencies themselves show an example, then the more real progress will be made by the whole community—including the police—in stamping out the evil. If we sit back and do nothing, there will not only be more victims but more self-defence and more conflict, leading ultimately to race warfare on our streets. For that is the price to be paid for the toleration of bigotry and racial oppression.

The enormous value of this book is that it challenges councillors and local authority officials to play their active part in combating racial harassment. The book sets out the wide range of legal powers available to local authorities: their housing, education and social services functions; their statutory right to prosecute or appear in any legal proceedings; their legal duty under the Race Relations Act; their powers to give assistance to victims and many more. Both practical and legal difficulties are accurately and thoroughly explained.

With this book on the shelf, no local authority official should ever have to say to the victim of racial harassment, "We're so sorry but there's nothing we can do about it". This is a rare phenomenon: a law book which could do great good for our society.

BHIKU PAREKH, Acting Chairman, Commission for Racial Equality, writes:

Racial attacks and harassment are a growing and worrying phenomenon in our society. The number of attacks, often unreported, has been steadily increasing, and they range from verbal abuse and graffiti to physical attack and arson. While they are more marked in inner-city areas, where large numbers of ethnic minority people live, they are also common in areas with relatively small ethnic minority populations. The fear of attack is now a daily experience for many ethnic minority people as they go about their normal business.

The response of the police and local authorities to the problem has sometimes been dismissive; and where sensible policies have been introduced, they have often not been properly implemented. However, as some local authorities, voluntary agencies and police forces have shown, there are practical steps that can be taken, both in support of the victim and against the perpetrator. The recent report of the Commission for Racial Equality, *Living in Terror*, summarised some of these steps and provided a series of recommendations for local authorities and the voluntary housing sector. It also emphasised the importance of using the law as far as possible in devising strategies on racial harassment.

This book is concerned solely with the law. It is a comprehensive review of the way in which the law can be used by organisations such as local authorities in countering racial harassment. It can be used as a reference book when individual problems are presented, but, just as important, it can also provide a framework for constructing a legal strategy on a systematic basis to deal with racial harassment. The tone of the book is positive, not defeatist. It argues that the law can be used both practically and imaginatively to combat racial harassment. It is an important contribution to the work of combating racial violence, and the Commission welcomes its publication.

Contents

	page
Table of Statutes	xxii
Table of Rules, Regulations and Circulars	xxxiii
Table of Cases	xxxiv
How to Use this Book	xxxix

One: Introduction   1
- A   Racial harassment   1
  - What is "racial harassment"?   1
    - A legal definition of "racial harassment"   1
  - Why racial harassment is important   2
    - 1 How do crimes amounting to racial harassment differ?   2
    - 2 Racial harassment, nuisance and neighbour disputes   3
    - 3 Racial harassment is more widespread than records suggest   4
- B   Why should local authorities be responsible for tackling racial harassment?   4
  - Why take action against perpetrators?   5

Two: General Factors Affecting all Local Authority Decisions   6
- General principles of administrative law   6
  - 1 The authority must have legal power to make the decision   6
  - 2 The authority must have understood correctly the applicable legal powers and given effect to them   7
  - 3 The authority must act so as to promote and not frustrate the policy and objects of the statute   7
  - 4 The authority must take into account all relevant matters   7
  - 5 The authority must disregard all irrelevant matters   8
  - 6 The decision must not be made in bad faith or be dishonest   8
  - 7 The facts must be correct and provide a basis for the decision   8
  - 8 The authority must not delegate decision making   8
  - 9 The decision must be reached fairly   9
  - 10 Authorisation of decision makers   9
  - 11 Any statutory procedural requirements must be followed   9
  - 12 The authority must not fetter its discretion   9
  - 13 The decision must not be one to which no reasonable authority could come   10
  - 14 Authorities must apply their policies consistently   10
- The general duty under Race Relations Act 1976 s 71   11

x Contents

    1 The scope of the duty   11
    2 Sanctions against organisations   13
    3 Sanctions against individual perpetrators   14
    Subsidiary powers of all local authorities   15
        Scope of the power   15

Three: Local Authority Court Proceedings   18
    The legal basis for a particular purpose   18
    Express power to take proceedings for a particular purpose   18
    Implied power in Local Government Act 1972 s111   19
    Express general power in Local Government Act 1972 s222   19
    1 The conditions for using s222   20
    2 Criminal proceedings   21
    3 Injunctions to prevent a criminal offence   23
    4 Injunctions to prevent a public nuisance   25
    5 Injunctions to prevent obstruction of the authority's statutory duty   26
    6 Appearing in proceedings   27

Four: Powers and Duties of all Local Authorities   30
  A Duties applying to all authorities and departments   30
    The general duty under Race Relations Act 1976 s71   30
    Discrimination in the provision of goods, facilities and services   31
    1 Better services to racial harassment victims   31
    2 The exception allowed by Race Relations Act 1976 s35   32
    3 Poorer service to racial harassment victims   32
    Discrimination against job applicants and employees   32
    1 Racial harassment of staff by other staff   33
    2 Positive action   33
    Health and Safety at Work Act 1974 s2   34
  B Powers available to all authorities and departments   34
    Employment of staff   34
    Power to second staff to other authorities and organisations   35
    Publicity   35
    Local Government Act 1972 s137   36
    Complaints against the police   37
  C Assistance to victims   37
    Inhabitants from the Commonwealth   37
    Discretionary facilities to individual victims   38
    Discretionary facilities for organisations and groups   38
  D Action against perpetrators   39
    Power to obtain details of the occupier and owner of land   39
    Resources for identifying perpetrators   39
    Protecting council property   40
    1 Preventative practical steps   40
    2 Legal action   40

	3 Private nuisance	41
	4 Trespass	42
	Claiming compensation in criminal proceedings	43
	Public nuisances	43
	Highways Act 1980 s130	44
	Power to make byelaws	45
	Destruction of dogs	46
	Withholding discretionary facilities	46
	Use of suppliers of goods and services	48
E	Intervention in the private sector	48
	Conditions on the use of land	48
	Consultation	49
	Grants and grant conditions	50
	Works on derelict land	50
	1 Land owned by the local authority	51
	2 Land previously owned by the authority	51
	3 Other land	52
	Works on any land	53
	Licensing	53
	1 Pub licences	53
	2 Licences for drinking at football clubs	54
	3 Music and dance licences	54

Five: Civil Proceedings 57
A	The tenancy agreement	57
	The status of the tenancy agreement	57
	The terms of the tenancy agreement	57
	Additional clauses to be considered	57
	1 Prohibiting nuisance or annoyance	57
	2 Prohibiting racial harassment	58
	3 Covering nuisance by dogs	58
	4 Making the tenant expressly responsible for acts of others	59
	5 Covering nuisance or harassment from people attending parties	59
	6 Covering breach of byelaws	59
	7 Prohibiting graffiti or damage to council property	59
	8 Covering the use of common parts	60
	9 Other rights associated with the tenancy	60
	10 Stating what sanctions will be imposed for breach	60
	The advantages and disadvantages of clauses on racial harassment	60
	Variation of tenancy terms	61
	1 Points to watch	61
	2 Proof of service	62
B	Possession proceedings	62
	Breach of the tenancy agreement	63

xii Contents

	Nuisance or annoyance	63
	Waste	63
	Reasonableness	64
	Reasonableness when the nuisance has ceased	66
	Choosing the grounds and method of presentation	66
	1 Protecting the victim or potential victims	67
	2 Housing management grounds	67
	3 Punishing individual perpetrators	68
	4 Acting against racism	68
	5 Grounds for claiming possession	68
C	Injunctions	68
	Grounds on which a court will grant an injunction	70
	1 Perpetual injunctions	70
	2 Interlocutory injunctions	71
	The merits of injunctions	72
	1 The advantages	72
	2 Disadvantages and limitations of injunctions	73
D	Procedure	73
	Legal aid	73
	Procedure in possession proceedings	73
	1 The notice of intention to seek possession	73
	2 Starting possession proceedings	75
	3 Speeding up the process	77
	4 The court's powers in possession proceedings	79
	Procedure on applications for injunctions	79
	1 Interlocutory injunctions	80
	2 Perpetual injunctions	83

Six: Housing Authorities and Departments   86

A	The duties of housing authorities	86
	Preference in housing allocations	86
	1 Unsatisfactory living conditions	87
	2 Homeless	87
	3 Reasonable preference	87
	The duty towards the homeless	88
	1 Racial harassment victims	88
	2 Perpetrators of racial harassment	90
	Duty not to discriminate in housing allocation	92
	Rehousing families in housing vacated by victims	92
	Contractual duty to repair	93
	Duty to take action against perpetrators	94
	1 Circumstances in which a duty may arise	94
	2 Action by a victim against the authority for nuisance	95
	3 Action by a victim enforcing the tenancy agreement	96
	The duty to consult tenants on housing management issues	96
B	Powers to assist victims with rehousing	98

	Rehousing by an authority in its own accommodation	98
	Payment of removal costs	99
	Other financial assistance to victims being transferred to other council accommodation	99
	Provision of furniture and fittings in housing	101
	Rehousing in accommodation managed by other organisations	101
	Rehousing by other authorities	102
	Assisting victims to buy their own homes	102
	1 Loans for the purchase of homes	102
	2 Guaranteeing mortgages	103
	3 Assistance for council tenants with legal costs of purchase	103
	4 Assistance with legal costs of obtaining mortgage	103
C	Powers to protect and assist victims in their homes	104
	General powers to manage the housing stock	104
	1 Power to provide security devices and improvements to security	105
	2 Power to provide communication equipment for victims to raise the alarm	105
	3 Power to provide staff to increase security on an estate	105
	4 Power to give loans or grants to tenants to allow them to install security devices and to carry out improvements	105
	Power to give victims permission to carry out their own improvements and to reimburse tenants when they move	106
	Improvement grants	106
	Loans for improvements in owner-occupied housing	107
	Allocation of flats to tenants who will provide support to victims	108
	Allocation of grants, facilities and premises to support groups	109
	1 Grants and facilities	109
	2 Premises	109
D	Powers to deter and punish perpetrators on council estates	110
	General powers to manage, regulate and control housing stock	111
	Tenants' associations	111
	1 Conditions on the use of land	111
	2 Discretionary facilities	111
	3 Consultation	112
	4 Grants and grant conditions	112
	Other community groups on housing estates	112
	Byelaws on council estates	112
	Trespass	113
	Tenants, their resident family members and visitors	114
	Action to prevent pressure on an authority to discriminate	115
E	Powers to act against perpetrators in the private sector	116
	Former council tenants who have bought their homes	116
	1 Restrictive covenants in leases and transfers	116

xiv Contents

2 Restrictions on the right to use the common parts	117
Housing associations	117
Management co-operatives and other managers of local authority housing	118
Bed and breakfast accommodation	119
1 The management practice of the owner	119
2 Other measures to deal with racial harassment	120
3 Procedures for dealing with racial harassment in bed and breakfast accommodation	122
Houses in multiple occupation	123
1 What is a house in multiple occupation?	123
2 Registration	124
3 Control orders	125
Compulsory purchase of rented housing	126
Voluntary organisations providing temporary accommodation for the homeless	127
Squatters	127
1 Action against perpetrators who are squatters	127
2 Action to protect victims who are squatting	127
Local authority hostels	127
1 Action against perpetrators	128
2 Action to protect the victim	128
Byelaws for lodging houses	128
Common lodging houses	128
1 Registration	128
2 Byelaws	129

Seven: Social Services Authorities and Departments — 133

A The duties of social services authorities	133
Duty to promote the welfare of children	134
1 Assistance to the victim	135
2 Assistance to the perpetrator	135
Duty to co-operate with housing authorities	136
Duty to make enquiries and take care proceedings	136
1 The grounds for care proceedings	137
2 When does the duty to make enquiries arise?	137
3 When does the duty to take care proceedings arise?	138
Duty to provide court reports	139
B The powers of social services authorities	140
Powers to assist victims	140
1 The provision of facilities	140
2 Provision for parents and children	140
3 Provision for elderly and sick people	140
4 People with disabilities	140
Powers to act against perpetrators	141
1 The power to take wardship proceedings	141

	2 Powers under supervision orders	142
	3 The power to withhold discretionary facilities from perpetrators	142
	4 Powers to manage residential accommodation	143
	Intervention in the private sector	143
	1 Private residential homes	143
	2 Grants, facilities and premises to voluntary organisations	143
	3 Private nurseries and child minders	144

Eight: Education Authorities and Departments — 146
- A Duties of education authorities and departments — 146
  - The duty under Race Relations Act 1976 s71 — 146
  - Duty to provide transport to and from school and further education — 147
- B Powers of education authorities and departments — 147
  - Powers to assist victims — 147
    - 1 Powers under Local Government Act 1972 s111 — 147
    - 2 Appointment of special staff — 148
  - Powers to act against perpetrators — 148
    - 1 Power to suspend or to expel children — 148
    - 2 Protecting school premises — 148
    - 3 Public nuisance — 149
    - 4 Prosecutions for causing or permitting nuisance or disturbance on school premises — 149
  - Intervention in the private sector — 150
    - 1 Protection of pupils at schools not owned or managed by the authority — 150
    - 2 Other powers in the private sector — 151

Nine: Other Powers and Duties of Local Authorities — 153
- A Duties of local authorities — 153
  - Duty to inspect the area for nuisances — 153
  - Duty to act to abate statutory nuisances — 153
    - 1 Procedure — 154
    - 2 Injunctions — 154
    - 3 Recurring nuisances — 154
    - 4 Racial harassment amounting to statutory nuisance — 155
  - Duty to inspect the district to detect noise nuisance — 155
  - Duty to abate noise nuisance — 155
    - 1 Procedure — 156
    - 2 Injunctions — 156
    - 3 Powers relating to noise nuisance — 157
    - 4 Racial harassment constituting noise nuisance — 157
- B Powers of local authorities — 157
  - Powers to protect and assist victims — 157
    - 1 Land adversely affecting the amenity of the neighbourhood — 158

xvi Contents

	2 Street lighting	158
	3 Removal of waste	158
	Powers to act against perpetrators	158
	1 Powers in relation to collection of rubbish	158
	2 Powers in relation to rubbish dumping	159
	3 Byelaws for the prevention of nuisances	159

Ten: Criminal Proceedings   161
- A   An outline of criminal procedure   161
  - Powers of arrest for criminal offences   161
    - Arrestable offences   161
  - The criminal courts   162
    - 1 The adult courts   162
    - 2 The juvenile court   163
    - 3 Starting criminal proceedings   164
    - 4 Adjournments and remands   164
    - 5 Relevant court sentencing powers   166
    - 6 Bind overs   168
    - 7 Action against parents for their children's criminal activities   168
    - 8 Practical considerations on the use of criminal proceedings   168
    - 9 Presentation of the case   171
- B   Offences for which local authorities have power to prosecute   173
  - The Protection from Eviction Act 1977   173
    - 1 Definitions   173
    - 2 Use of the provision   174
    - 3 Proving the intent behind the acts   175
  - Public Health Act 1936 and Control of Pollution Act 1974   175
    - 1 Breach of notices   175
    - 2 Dumping rubbish   175
  - The Highways Act 1980   176
  - Leaving litter   177
  - Breach of byelaws   177
  - Public nuisance   177
  - Causing or permitting a nuisance or disturbance on school premises   178
- C   Powers of authorities under Local Government Act 1972 s222   178
  - Criminal damage   178
  - Affray   179
  - Incitement to racial harassment   180
  - Common assault and assault occasioning actual bodily harm   180
    - 1 Matters common to both offences   180
    - 2 Common assault   181
    - 3 Assault occasioning actual bodily harm   181
  - Burglary   182
  - Intimidation, persistent following or watching and besetting premises   182

1 The intention		183
2 The acts		183
False imprisonment		183

Eleven: Police and Crown Prosecution Service Powers and Duties   186

A	Police powers to investigate crime	186
	Stop and search	186
	Entry and search of premises	187
	1 With a search warrant issued by a magistrate under a particular statutory power	187
	2 With a search warrant issued by a magistrate under PACE 1984	187
	3 Without a search warrant in certain circumstances	188
	Seizure of property found	188
	Arrest	188
	1 Arrest with a warrant	188
	2 Arrest without a warrant	189
	Detention	190
	Questioning	190
	Samples and fingerprints	191
	1 Fingerprints	191
	2 Intimate samples	191
	3 Non-intimate samples	191
	Identification parades and identification by witnesses	192
	1 Identification parades	192
	2 Group identification	192
	3 Confrontation	192
	4 Photographs	192
	Police bail	192
	Tracing telephone calls	193
	Other police powers	194
	1 Power to apply to magistrates' court to destroy a dog	194
	2 Power to impose conditions or ban marches and assemblies	194
	3 Prosecuting for common assault	194
	4 Power to remove persons from school premises	194
B	The duties of the police	194
	The Town Police Clauses Act 1847	194
	The duty to preserve the peace and prevent offences	196
	The duty to enforce the law	196
C	Legal remedies for police failure to tackle racial harassment	196
	Requesting reports to the police authority	197
	Making representations through the police consultative process	197
	By-passing the police and using the Crown Prosecution Service	197

xviii Contents

		Liability for failure to arrest a criminal	197
		Prosecution for misconduct in public office	198
		Submissions to the Inspector of Constabulary	198
		Complaints against police officers	198
	D	The Crown Prosecution Service	198
		Referring cases to the Crown Prosecution Service	198

Twelve: Remedies Available to Victims 201
- A Paying for legal help 201
  - Legal aid 201
  - Legal representation in court proceedings 201
  - 1 The proceedings covered by legal aid 201
  - 2 Financial eligibility for legal aid 202
- B Direct action 202
  - Self defence 202
  - Making an arrest or preventing crime 203
  - Removing a trespasser 293
  - Retaking goods that have been stolen 203
- C Action in the criminal courts 204
  - Costs in criminal cases 204
  - Common assault and aggravated assault 204
  - Obtaining a bind over of the perpetrator 205
  - Action to prevent statutory nuisances 205
  - Noise nuisances 206
  - Compensation in criminal proceedings 206
- D Action in the civil courts 207
  - The liability of children and their parents 207
  - 1 Action against the parent 208
  - 2 Criminal compensation orders 208
  - Injunctions 208
  - Damages 209
  - The types of civil action available 209
  - 1 Unreasonable harassment 209
  - 2 Assault and battery 210
  - 3 Trespass to land 211
  - 4 Private nuisance 211
  - 5 False imprisonment 211
  - 6 Interference with goods 211
  - 7 Public nuisance 211
  - 8 Breach of Control of Pollution Act 1974 212
- E Other remedies 212
  - The Criminal Injuries Compensation Scheme 212
  - Rating revaluation 213
  - Referring papers to the Crown Prosecution Service for prosecution 213
  - Preventing abusive phone calls 214

	1 Arranging interception of calls by the operator	214
	2 Changing the phone number	214
	3 Ex-directory	214
	Obtaining a mutual exchange	214
	Opposing pub licences and music and dance licences	215
F	Assistance from local authorities with court proceedings	215
	Funding court action by an individual victim	215
	Funding a voluntary organisation to act for victims	215
	Appearing in proceedings brought by victims	215
	Seconding staff to organisations assisting victims	215
G	Remedies against local authorities or the police for failure to act	216
	Remedies against the local authority	216
	1 Judicial review	216
	2 Action for discrimination	217
	3 Complaint to the Commission for Racial Equality	217
	4 Action for breach of covenant to repair	217
	5 Action against the authority for nuisance	218
	6 Complaint to the Secretary of State	218
	Remedies against the police	218
	1 Individual complaints against the police	218
	2 Other methods of complaint	218

Thirteen: Local Authority Policies and Practices — 220

A	Departmental organisation	220
	Developing a comprehensive policy	220
	1 Long-term measures	221
	2 The protection of victims	221
	3 Allocation procedures	221
	4 Procedures for taking legal action	221
	Co-ordination of policy	222
	1 The role of the legal department	222
	2 Resolving conflicts between departments	225
	Legal action against perpetrators	225
	1 Speed	226
	2 The role of the legal department	227
	3 Deciding strategies in legal action	229
	4 Liaison with the voluntary sector and support groups	230
	5 Investigation team	230
	6 Publicity	230
	7 Record-keeping	231
	8 Expert witnesses	231
B	Summary of recommendations	232

Fourteen: Collecting Evidence and Interviewing — 236

A	Rules of evidence	236

xx *Contents*

	Types of evidence and requirements for their use	236
	1 Oral evidence (civil and criminal)	236
	2 The hearsay rule (civil and criminal)	237
	3 Situations where the hearsay rule does not apply	237
	4 Real evidence (civil and criminal)	242
	5 Evidence of criminal convictions (civil only)	242
	6 Previous harassment by the perpetrator (criminal only)	242
	7 Other evidence (civil and criminal)	243
	Children as witnesses	243
	1 In civil proceedings	243
	2 In criminal proceedings	243
	Witnesses using notes when giving evidence (civil and criminal)	244
	Practical points of evidence	244
	1 Choice of witnesses and type of evidence to be produced	244
	2 Evidence from witnesses who cannot give evidence in English	248
	3 Protection and assistance for witnesses	250
	4 Children	253
	5 Summonsing witnesses	254
	6 Preventing witnesses attending	254
	7 Witness expenses	254
B	Recording and preserving evidence	254
	Keeping notes of incidents and observations	254
	1 The form of notes	255
	2 Safe-keeping of notes	255
	3 Use of notes	255
	4 What to record	256
	5 Practical steps	256
	Preserving evidence	256
C	Interviewing	257
	Preparing for an interview	257
	Preliminaries	257
	Illiciting relevant information	258
	Jogging the memory	258
	Testing the evidence	259
	1 Inconsistencies in a statement	259
	2 Conflict with other evidence	259
	3 Facts that belie common sense	260
	Explaining the procedure and future intentions	260
D	Summary of recommendations	261

Fifteen: Proposals for Change — 263
A	General powers and duties	264
B	Housing	267
	Powers and duties	267
	Grounds for possession	270

C	Planning	271
D	Education	271
E	Crime	271
F	Police powers and duties	275
G	Other changes in the civil law	277
H	Court procedure	277

Appendices

One:	Suggested Clauses for Tenancy Agreements	279
Two:	Notices Required to Vary a Tenancy Agreement	282
Three:	Sample Case Studies	285
Four:	Documents for Civil Proceedings	291
Five:	Case Reports on Possession Proceedings Involving Racial Harassment	299
Six:	Criminal Offences	305
Seven:	A Specimen Information	309
Eight:	Suggested Format for Keeping Contemporaneous Notes	310

Index 311

Table of Statutes

                                                                                              page

Bail Act 1976
    s 3(6) .... 166[19]
       (7) .... 166[21]
      6 .... 165[18]
      7 .... 166[20]
    Sch 1 .... 165[17]
Child Care Act 1980 224
    s 1 .... 105, 107, 134[1]
      (4) .... 134[2]
    2(1)(b) .... 134[5]
Children and Young Persons Act 1933
    s 55 .... 168[25]
Children and Young Persons Act 1969
    s 1 .... 135[6], 137[8]
      (2) .... 137[12]
      (5) .... 137[11]
    2(1) .... 137[9]
      (2) .... 137[10]
    3 .... 137[13]
    9 .... 139[14]
    11 .... 142[16]
    12 .... 142[17]
      (2) .... 142[18]
    37 .... 252[22]
    38(1) .... 243[14]
    39 .... 251[21]
    42(1) .... 242[9,10]
    43 .... 242[11]
    70(1) .... 137[11]
Civil Evidence Act 1968
    s 2 .... 239[5]
    4 .... 238[3]
    5 .... 240[6]
    8 .... 239[4]
    11 .... 242[12]
Conspiracy and Protection of Property Act 1875 .... 44[45]
    s 7 .... 182[64,65]
Contempt of Court Act 1981 277
    s 11 .... 251[20]

Control of Pollution Act 1974 . . . . 175, 209, 212, 218
  s 3(1)(a) . . . . 175[35]
    (2) . . . . 176[36]
    (3) . . . . 176[37]
  12 . . . . 158[36]
  13 . . . . 158[37]
    (3) . . . . 159[39]
    (7) . . . . 158[38]
  16(1) . . . . 158[34], 159[40]
    (2), (3) . . . . 159[40]
    (4) . . . . 159[42]
    (5) . . . . 158[33], 159[43]
    (6) . . . . 158[35]
  30 . . . . 158[34], 175[35]
  57 . . . . 155[15]
  58(1) . . . . 156[16]
    (8) . . . . 156[21]
  59 . . . . 206[15]
    (2) . . . . 156[18], 206[17]
    (3) . . . . 206[16]
    (4) . . . . 206[18]
  70 . . . . 156[19]
  73(1) . . . . 155[15]
  74 . . . . 156[20]
  88 . . . . 212[27]
  91 . . . . 156[22]
    (2) . . . . 156[23]
  93 . . . . 156[24]
  97 . . . . 218[35]
County Courts Act 1984 276
  s 22 . . . . 80[42]
Criminal Attempts Act 1981
  s 1 308
Criminal Damage Act 1971 305
  s 1(1), (2) 305
  ss 2, 3 305
  s 6(1) . . . . 187[2]
Criminal Evidence Act 1965
  s 1 . . . . 238[3], 239[4]
Criminal Justice Act 1967
  s 3 . . . . 203[4]
    9 . . . . 241[8]
Criminal Justice Act 1982 . . . . 168[25]
Criminal Law Act 1977
  s 1 308
    6 . . . . 174[31], 188, 204

ss 6, 8..307
Derelict Land Act 1982
  s 3..51[56]
Dogs Act 1871 ....46, 46[51]
Education Act 1944
  s 39(2)(c) ....147[2]
     (5)...147[1]
     55..147[2]
     (2)...147[3]
Explosive Substances Act 1883
  ss 2, 3, 4 307
Firearms Act 1968
  s 47...186[1]
Health and Safety at Work Act 1974
  s 2..34
Highways Act 1980 ....25, 26, 44, 176, 178, 195
  s 97...158[31]
    130..44
       (1)..44[40]
       (2)..44[41]
       (3)..44[42]
       (5)..44[44]
    137..176
    263..43[37]
    328..158[32]
Housing Act 1980 176
Housing Act 1985 ....7, 9, 15, 19, 51, 58, 61, 75, 76, 79,
                          89, 91, 97, 100, 106, 107, 113, 267, 268, 269, 270
  ss 8, 9..126[116]
  s 10 ....101[36]
  s 12 ....113[78]
     (1)(c)..110[72]
     15..102[40]
     17..126[116]
     21....................................57[3], 99[35], 104[50], 105, 111[73], 224
     22..87[1,7,8]
     23..112[74]
       (2)..112[76]
       (3)..128[21]
     26(1)(a)..99[34]
         (b)..103[44]
     27..118[89]
       (1)(a)...101[38]
       (4)..119[90]
     32..110[71]
     56....................................112[75], 113[77], 126[116], 128[121]

Table of Statutes xxv

58	88[11]
59	88[12]
60	89[13]
(1)	121[92]
(4)	89[14]
63	88[10]
65	26[28], 87[7], 88[9], 98
(3)	91[19]
(b)	91[20]
68	87[7]
69(1)	26[29]
(4)	89[14]
70	89[15]
72(b)	136[7]
73	101[39], 127[119]
80	57[1], 117[86], 214[32]
82	74[33]
84(2)	63[8]
(3)	75[35]
85	76[38]
92	214[31]
97	106[52]
100	106[53]
ss 102, 103	61[4]
s 105	96, 96[29]
(2)	97[30]
(5)	97[31]
(6)	97[32]
106(1)	87[2]
(2)	87[3]
(4)	87[4]
109	97[33]
116	65[19]
139	116[81]
345	123[94]
346	124[102]
(6)	124[103]
347	124[104]
348(1)(b)	124[105]
350	124[106]
352	125[106A]
354	125[108]
370	125[109]
372	125[107]
379	87[5], 125[110]
381	125[112]

382 .... 125[113]
401 .... 128[122]
402 .... 128[123]
404 .... 129[124]
   (5) .... 129[125]
405 .... 129[126]
406 .... 129[127]
429A .... 119[91]
435 .... 102[41]
435(1)(d) .... 107[67]
   (3) .... 102[42]
436 .... 107[68]
437 .... 102[41]
439 .... 107[69]
442 .... 103[43]
443 .... 103[45]
462(1)(b) .... 106[60]
463 .... 106[55]
464 .... 107[62]
   (4) .... 107[63]
467 .... 106[56]
468 .... 107[65]
   (4) .... 107[66]
469 .... 107[64]
470 .... 106[59]
473 .... 106[61]
525 .... 106[58]
Sch 1 para 4 .... 108[70]
      2 75
      2 ground 1 .... 63[5]
              2 .... 63[6], 270
              3 .... 63[7]
      6 paras 2, 3 .... 117[84]
          para 5 .... 116[81]
      13 .... 126[117]
Housing Associations Act 1985 269
   s 1 .... 117[85]
     58 .... 101[37], 118[87]
     69 .... 118[88]
Housing and Planning Act 1986 269
   s 10 .... 118[89]
     14 .... 88[11]
       (3) .... 26[29]
     16 .... 119[91]
     46 .... 157[26]
Interception of Communications Act 1985 193

Table of Statutes   xxvii

s 2 .... 193[28]
ss 2(2)(b), 10(3) .... 193[29]
Land Compensation Act 1973 .... 223, 224
Landlord and Tenant Act 1985 271
   s 11 .... 57[2], 93[22]
      (6) .... 51[58]
   17 .... 94[24]
Law of Property Act 1925
   s 146 .... 116[82]
      (2) .... 116[83]
Licensing Act 1964 .... 53[61]
   s 7 .... 54[63]
   77 .... 54[68]
   Sch 2 para 1 .... 54[62]
Litter Act 1983
   s 1 .... 177[41]
      (2) .... 177[42]
      (3) .... 177[43]
      (4) .... 177[44]
Local Authorities (Goods and Services) Act 1970 .... 38, 38[28], 109
   s 2 53
Local Government Act 1933
   s 276 22
Local Government Act 1966
   s 11 .... 37, 37[25], 148
Local Government Act 1972 .... 23, 26, 27, 39, 40, 45, 265, 266
   s 101 .... 9[11]
   111 .... 6, 7, 15, 18, 19, 20, 35, 46, 48, 49, 54,
                    56, 99, 104, 105, 147, 150, 161, 177, 178, 224
   112 .... 34[16], 104[51]
   137 .... 34, 36, 50, 104, 109, 215, 216, 266
      (1) .... 36[20]
      (2), (3) .... 36[21]
   142 .... 35[18], 36[22,23], 50, 98
      (2) .... 35[19]
   222 .... 7, 18, 19, 20, 21, 22, 23, 24, 25, 26, 27
                    28, 43, 44, 54, 161, 174, 178, 215, 265
   223(1) .... 28[31]
   235 45
      (3) .... 45[49]
   236 .... 45[47], 113
Local Government Act 1985
   Sch 8 para 1 .... 54[66]
      12 .... 54[66,67]
Local Government (Miscellaneous Provisions) Act 1982
   s 1 .... 54[6]

16	39[29], 52, 123[93]
33	48[54], 51[59]
40	149[8]
(2)	150[10]
(3)	149[9], 150[11,12]
(4)	151[13]
(5), (8)	151[14]
Sch 1	54[67]
para 4(4)	55[69]

Magistrates' Courts Act 1980

s 1	164[15], 309
ss 1, 2	164[12]
s 6	163[4]
13	165[16]
17	163[5]
19	163[6]
(2)	163[7]
20	163[9]
21	163[8]
32	163[11]
38	163[10]

Metropolitan Police Act 1839 .... 176, 195
  s 54 .... 195, 308

National Parks and Access to the Countryside Act 1949
  s 89(2) .... 51[56]

Nurseries and Child Minders Regulation Act 1948
  s 1 .... 144[24]

Obscene Publications Act 1959
  s 2 307

Offences Against the Person Act 1861 .... 205[7]

ss 16, 18, 20, 29	306
s 42	181
ss 42–47	180[59]
s 43	205[8]
45	205[10]
46	205[6], 210[24]
47	181[62], 205[9]
65	187[3]

Open Spaces Act 1906 12
Police Act 1964 275

ss 2, 2A	197[37]
s 12(1)	197[38]
(3)	197[39]
18	196[33]
38(2)	198[44]
Sch	196[33]

Table of Statutes xxix

Police and Criminal Evidence Act 1984 .... 196, 276
   s 1 .... 186[1]
      8 .... 187[5]
      17(1) .... 188[9]
          (c) .... 188[10]
      18 .... 188[11]
      19 .... 188[12]
      24 .... 189[13]
          (4) .... 162[1]
          (5) .... 162[2]
      25 .... 189[14]
      37(2) .... 190[17]
          (7) .... 190[19]
      38 .... 193[26]
   ss 40–44 .... 190[18]
   s 47 .... 164[13], 193[27]
   ss 56–58 .... 190[21]
   s 61 .... 191[22]
      62 .... 191[23]
      63 .... 191[24]
      84 .... 218[36]
          (4) .... 37[24]
          (5) .... 218[37]
      106 197
      116 .... 187[6]
          (4) .... 188[8]
          (6) .... 187[7]
   Code of Guidance issued under PCEA 1984 Pt D .... 192[25]
   Code of Guidance issued under PCEA 1984 para 11.3 .... 190[20]
Post Office Act 1969
   ss 11(a), (b), 78 307
Powers of Criminal Courts Act 1973 .... 272, 274
   s 35 43
Prevention of Crimes Act 1953
   s 1 306
Prosecution of Offences Act 1985 .... 204, 275, 276
   s 3 .... 198[45]
      6(2) .... 199[46]
      8 275
      17 .... 21[9], 204[5]
Protection from Eviction Act 1977 .... 1, 7, 16, 120, 122, 169,
                                                 174, 174[31], 224, 273
   s 1 .... 172, 173
      (3) .... 173[27], 273, 309
      6 .... 7[5], 173[28]

Protection of Animals Act 1911
  s 1...308
Public Health Act 1936......................8, 175, 218
  s 1..153[1]
    81...159[44]
    91..153[1]
    92..153[2]
      (1)(b) ....155[14]
    93 ....154[3,5], 205[12]
    94 ....154[6,7], 206[13]
      (3)...206[14]
    95(1)..154[8]
      (2)..154[9]
    99 ....205[11]
    100 ....154[4,10], 266
    287 ....155[13]
    322 ....218[35]
Public Health (Recurring Nuisances) Act 1969
  s 1..154[11]
    2..155[12]
Public Order Act 1986 ....1, 272, 273, 274
  s 1(4)(b)..306
    (5)(a),(b) 306
  ss 1, 2, 3 305
  s 3...179
    (1) ....179[47]
    (2) ....179[50]
    (3) ....179[48]
    (4) ....179[49]
    (5) ....179[51]
    4 ....188, 272
      (1)(a) 305
    5 ....189, 272
    12 ....194[30]
    13 ....194[31]
    14 ....194[30]
  Pt III......................................180, 273
  s 17 ....180[56]
    18 ....180[53]
      (1) ....180[57]
      (3) ....180[52]
    19 ....180[54]
      (1) ....180[57]
    23 ....180[55]
      (1) ....180[57]
    27 ....180[58]

Table of Statutes xxxi

Race Relations Act 1976 ....7, 15, 31, 32, 111, 115,
148, 217, 263, 264, 265, 267
  s 1(1)(a) ....31[3]
     (b)..31[4], 93[21]
    3(1)..32[5]
     (2)..32[6]
    4..32, 32[7]
    5(2)(d) ....33[10]
     (4) ....33[11]
    18 ....148[6]
    20...31
     (1)..31[2]
    21..92
    31 ....115[79]
    32 ....31[1], 33[8]
    35 ....32, 33[12], 93, 148[6]
    38 ....33[13]
     (2) ....33[14]
    43 ....217[33]
    53 ....115[80]
    71 ....6, 7, 8, 11, 12, 13, 14, 15, 17, 27,
30, 48, 50, 55, 94, 97, 104, 119, 133, 146, 216, 217, 224
Rates Act 1984
  s 13 ....49[55]
Registered Homes Act 1984
  s 1 ....143[19]
    9(a) ....143[20]
     (b)...143[21]
    10(a) ....143[22]
    11 ....143[23]
Rent Act 1977 ....64[15], 106, 117
  s 15 ....117[86]
    390...126[115]
  Sch 13 ....126[115]
    15 ground 2 ....126[114]
Representation of the People Act 1983
  s 95 ....48[53]
Sexual Offences Act 1956
  s 1...307
Sporting Events (Control of Alcohol etc) Act 1985
  s 3(5) ....54[65]
    (6) ....54[64]
Supreme Court Act 1981....................................276
Theft Act 1968
  ss 8, 10, 21, 25 307
  s 26 ....187[4]

Town and Country Planning Act 1971 271
　s 1(1) .... 157[26]
　　 65 .... 52, 157[26]
　　 104 .... 157[29]
　　 105 .... 158[30]
　　 107 .... 157[28]
　　 290 .... 157[27]
Town Police Clauses Act 1847 .... 176, 194, 195
　s 28 .... 195[32], 308

Table of Rules, Regulations and Circulars

Control of Noise (Appeal) Regulations 1975 SI No 2116 ....156[19]
County Court Rules 1981 SI No 1687
  Ord 5 r2 292
      6 r3 ....76[36]
      4 ....83[49]
      7 r10(5) ....76[37]
    13 r3 ....76[38], 78[40]
    20 Pt II..240[7]
    24 ....127[120]
    29 r1(2) ....82[44]
       (3) ....81[43]
       (6) ....83[46]
Grants by Local Housing Authorities (Appropriate Percentage and Exchequer Contributions) Order 1987 SI No 1379 ....106[61]
Improvement Grants (Rateable Value Limits) Order 1977 SI No 1213 ....107[64]
Legal Aid (General) Regulations 1980 SI No 1894
  reg 19..78[39]
Local Authorities (Goods and Services) Public Body Order 1972 SI No 852 ....38[28]
Magistrates' Courts Rules 1981 SI No 552.......................309
  r4 ....164[14]
Pupils Registration Regulations 1956 SI No 357
  reg 4 ....148[7]
Rules of the Supreme Court 1965 SI No 1776
  Ord 41 ....240[7]
      r1 ....250[16]
      90..141[15]
      113..127[120]
Secure Tenancies (Notices) Regulations 1987 SI No 755 ....74[33]
  Pt I...291
Sports Grounds and Sporting Events (Designation) Order 1985 SI No 1151 ....54[64]

Department of the Environment Circular 21/80 ....106[57]
Department of the Environment Circular 12/86
  para 3.9.2......................................87[6], 125[111]
Department of the Environment Circular 72/86...................37[26]
  para 21 ....37[27]

Table of Cases

page

Acrow Automation v Rex Chainbelt Inc [1971] 1 WLR 1676; [1971] 3 All ER 1175, CA...82[45]
Adams v Adams (A-G intervening) [1970] 3 WLR 934; [1970] 3 All ER 572..27[30]
Allan v Liverpool Overseers (1874) LR 9 QB ....219[25]
American Cyanamid Co v Ethicon [1975] AC 396; [1975] 1 All ER 504, HL...71[30]
Arrowsmith v Jenkins [1963] 2 WLR 856; [1963] 2 All ER 210, DC ....176[40]
Associated Provincial Picture Houses v Wednesbury Corp [1948] 1 KB 223; [1947] 2 All ER 680, CA ....8[7], 10[14]
Attorney-General v Chaudry [1971] 1 WLR 1614; [1971] 3 All ER 938, CA ....24[16], 25[23]
Attorney-General v Leveller Magazine [1979] AC 440; [1979] 1 All ER 745, HL ....251[17,19], 252[23]
Attorney-General v PYA Quarries [1957] 2 QB 169; [1957] 1 All ER 894, CA ....43[39], 178[46]
Attorney-General ex rel Tilley v LB Wandsworth [1981] 1 WLR 854; [1981] 1 All ER 1162, CA ....134[3]
Balgobin and Francis v LB Tower Hamlets [1987] IRLR 401.........33[9]
Battlespring Ltd v Gates (1983) 268 EG 355; (1983) 11 HLR 6, CA ....65[21]
Bentley v Brudzinski (1982) 75 Cr App R 217 ....181[61]
Black v Oliver [1978] QB 870; [1978] 3 All ER 408, CA............213[30]
Bond v Chief Constable of Kent [1983] 1 WLR 40; [1983] 1 All ER 456, DC ....166[23], 207[19,20]
British Oxygen Co Ltd v Minister of Technology [1970] 3 All ER 165, HL ....9[13]
Bromley LBC v Greater London Council and Another [1983] 1 AC 768; [1982] 1 All ER 153, HL ....8[8]
LB Camden v Hawkins (1986) 6 November (unreported), Clerkenwell County Court 64, 301
LB Camden v Walsh (1986) 10 April (unreported), Bloomsbury and Marylebone County Court ....10[16], 300
Chapman v Honig [1963] 2 QB 502; [1963] 2 All ER 513, CA ....250[15], 254[24]
Chiltern DC v Keane [1985] 1 WLR 619; [1985] 2 All ER 118, CA ....83[48]

Christie v Davey [1893] 1 Ch 316 ....41^{32}
Council of Civil Service Unions and Others v Minister for Civil
  Service [1984] 1 WLR 1174; [1984] 3 All ER 935, HL ....6^2, 7^2, 9^{12}
Cobstone Investments v Maxim [1984] 2 All ER 635; (1984) 15 HLR
  113, CA ....64^{13,15}
Coventry CC v Cartwright [1975] 1 WLR 845; [1975] 2 All
  ER 99, DC ....155^{14}
Cresswell v Hodgson [1951] 2 KB 92; [1951] 1 All ER 710, CA ......65^{21}
Cumming v Danson [1942] 2 All ER 653..........................65^{21}
Devenport v Salford Corp (1983) 8 HLR 54, CA...................90^{17}
DPP v Boardman [1975] AC 421; [1974] 3 All ER 887, HL.........242^{13}
Doherty v Allmann (1878) 3 App Cas 709........................70^{23}
Ealing Family Housing Association v Taylor (1987) 17 March
  (unreported), Brentford County Court 302
Esso Petroleum Co Ltd v Southport Corp [1956] AC 218; [1955]
  3 All ER 864, HL ....41^{34}
Florent v Horez (1983) 268 EG 807; (1983) 12 HLR 1, CA .....64^{14}, 65^{22}
Giles v Fox [1987] 7 CL 317 ....250^{15}, 254^{24}
Gill & Carson v Nield [1917] 2 KB 674..........................176^{39}
Goldman v Hargrave [1967] 1 AC 645; [1966] 2 All ER 989 ....41^{35}
Gorely v Codd [1967] 1 WLR 19; [1966] 3 All ER 891.............208^{21}
Gouriet v Union of Post Office Workers [1978] AC 435; [1977]
  3 All ER 70, HL...24^{16,19}
Guppys (Bridport) Ltd v Brookling (1984) 269 EG 846; (1983)
  14 HLR 1, CA ....209^{22}
LB Hackney v Towart (1987) 27 August (unreported), Shoreditch
  County Court 304
LB Hammersmith v Magnum Automated Forecourts Ltd [1978]
  1 WLR 50; [1978] 1 All ER 401, CA ....156^{21}
Hampstead and Suburban Properties Ltd v Diomedous [1969]
  1 Ch 248; [1968] 3 All ER 545..............................71^{31}
Harmsworth v Harmsworth [1987] 1 WLR 1676 ....83^{48}
Hill v Chief Constable of West Yorkshire [1987]
  1 All ER 1173, CA..197^{41}
Hillen and Pettigrew v ICI (Alkali) Ltd [1936] AC 65 ....42^{36}
HK, re [1967] 2 QB 617; [1967] 1 All ER 226, DC ....9^{10}
Hollywood Silver Fox Farm v Emmett [1936] 2 KB 468; [1936]
  1 All ER 825 ....41^{32}, 70^{25}
Hooper v Rogers [1975] Ch 43; [1974] All ER 417, CA ....41^{30}
Hubbard v Pitt [1976] QB 142; [1975] 3 All ER 1, CA ....41^{34}, 44^{45}
Hubbard v Vosper [1972] 2 QB 84; [1972] 1 All ER 1023, CA ....71^{26}
Hughes and Others v LB Hackney (1986) 6 February (unreported),
  ITT case 15898/85/LC/B ....33^{15}
LB Islington v Connor (1987) 25 March (unreported), Westminster
  County Court 303

LB Islington v Isherwood (1987) February (unreported), Clerkenwell
County Court 302
Jacobs v London County Council [1950] AC 361; [1950]
1 All ER 737, HL ....44[43]
Kent CC v Batchelor (No 2) [1979] 1 WLR 213; [1978]
3 All ER 980 ....21[7]
Kruse v Johnson [1898] 2 QB 91 ....45[48,90]
Lee v Walker [1985] QB 1191; [1985] 1 All ER 781, CA ....83[47]
Liverpool CC v Irwin [1977] AC 239; (1976) 13 HLR 38, HL ....93[23]
London and Blackwall Railway v Cross (1886) 31 ChD 354 ....70[24]
London County Council v South Metropolitan Gas Co [1904]
1 Ch 76 ....26[27]
J Lyons and Sons Ltd v Wilkins [1899] 1 Ch 255, CA ....182[66]
McGreal v Wake (1984) 13 HLR 107; (1984) 269 EG 1254, CA ......94[24]
Masters v Brent LBC [1978] QB 841; [1978] 2 All ER 664 ....211[25]
Miller v Jackson [1977] QB 966; [1977] 3 All ER 338, CA ....71[27]
Morrissey v Galer [1955] 1 WLR 110 ....45[49], 155[14]
Nagy v Weston [1965] 1 WLR 280; [1965] 1 All ER 78, DC ....176[38]
LB Newham v McDonnell (1984) 23 November (unreported),
Bow County Court 299
Newton v Edgerley [1959] 1 WLR 1031; [1959] 3 All ER 337 ......208[21]
O'Brien v Robinson [1973] AC 912; [1973] 1 All ER 583, HL........93[22]
Okereke v LB Brent [1967] 1 QB 42; [1966] 1 All ER 150, CA ......124[96]
O'Leary v LB Islington (1983) 9 HLR 83, CA ....95[25,27]
Padfield v Minister of Agriculture, Fisheries and Food [1968] AC 997;
[1968] 1 All ER 694, HL ....7[3]
Page Motors v Epsom and Ewell BC (1982) 80 LGR 337, CA........95[27]
Palmer v Loder [1962] CLY 2233; (1962) *Times* 21 December 41
Palmer v Reginam [1971] 1 All ER 1077 ....202[2]
Palmer v Sandwell MBC (1987) *Times* 12 October ....61[4]
Patel v Patel (1987) *Times* 21 August, CA ....210[23A]
Patel v WH Smith (Eziot) Ltd [1987] 2 All ER 569, CA ....71[29]
Prestatyn UDC v Prestatyn Raceway Ltd [1970] 1 WLR 33; [1969]
3 All ER 1573 ....23[11], 26[25]
Proctor v Bayley (1889) 42 ChD 390 ....71[28]
R v AMK (Property Management) Ltd [1985] Crim
LR 600, CA..174[33], 175[34]
R v Andrews [1987] 1 All ER 513, HL ....238[1,2]
R v LB Camden ex p Rowton (Camden Town) Ltd (1983) 10
HLR 30 ....124[95,100]
R v Dytham [1979] 3 WLR 467; [1979] 3 All
ER 641, CA ....196[34], 198[42,43]
R v East Hertfordshire DC ex p Bannon (1986) 18
HLR 515 ....64[17], 90[16]
R v Evangelos Polycarpou (1978) 9 HLR 129, CA ....174[32]
R v Evesham Justices ex p McDonagh (1987) 137 NLJ 757.........251[18]

R v Finnerty (1987) February (unreported), Highbury Corner
Magistrates' Court .... 170[26]
R v Harrow Justices ex p Osaseri [1986] QB 589; [1985] 3 All
ER 185 .... 180[61]
R v Howell [1982] QB 416; [1981] 3 All ER 383, CA .... 190[15,16]
R v McInnes [1971] 1 WLR 1600; [1971] 3 All
ER 295, CA .... 202[1,2], 203[3]
R v Malvern Justices ex p Evans (1987) 137 NLJ 757 .... 251[17]
R v Metropolitan Police Commr ex p Blackburn [1968] 1 All
ER 763, CA .... 196[34,35]
R v Miller [1954] 2 WLR 138; [1954] 2 All ER 529 .... 181[63]
R v Moloney [1985] AC 905; [1985] 1 All ER 1025, HL .... 175[34]
R v North Devon DC ex p Lewis [1981] 1 WLR 328 .... 90[16]
R v Reading Crown Court ex p Hutchinson (1987)
Independent 5 August .... 177[45]
R v Secretary of State for Environment ex p RB Kensington and
Chelsea (1987) 19 HLR 161 .... 126, 126[118]
R v Secretary of State for Home Department ex p Ruddock [1987]
2 All ER 518 .... 10[15]
R v Swansea CC ex p John (1982) 9 HLR 56 .... 90[18]
R v Swansea CC ex p Thomas (1983) 9 HLR 64 .... 90[16]
R v LB Tower Hamlets ex p Monaf and Others (1987) *Times* 6 August;
(1987) 19 HLR 577 .... 134[4], 224[3]
Redland Bricks Ltd v Morris [1970] AC 652; [1969] 2 All
ER 576, HL .... 72[32]
Reed v Hastings Corp (1964) 62 LGR 588, CA .... 124[97]
Rogers v Essex CC [1986] 3 WLR 689; [1986] 3 All ER 321, HL ... 147[4,5]
Rowden v Universities Co-operative Association Ltd
(1881) 71 LT 373 .... 250[15], 254[24]
Runnymede BC v Ball [1986] 1 WLR 353; [1986] 1 All
ER 629, CA .... 21[7], 24[15,17,19], 25[24]
Scott v Scott [1913] AC 417, HL .... 252[23]
Seaward v Paterson [1897] 1 Ch 545 .... 82[45]
Secretary of State for Education and Science v MB Tameside [1976]
3 All ER 665, HL .... 8[9]
Sedleigh Denfield v O'Callaghan [1940] AC 880, HL .... 95[27]
Silbers v LB Southwark (1977) 76 LGR 421, CA .... 124[98,99]
Simmons v Pizzey [1979] AC 37; [1977] 2 All ER 432, HL .... 124[98,99]
Smeaton v Ilford Corp [1954] Ch 450; [1954] 1 All ER 923 .... 41[35]
Smith v Bristol CC (1981) *LAG Bulletin* 287 .... 90[18]
Smith v Scott [1972] 3 WLR 783; [1972] 3 All ER 645 .... 95[25,26,27]
Solihull MBC v Maxfern [1977] 1 WLR 127; [1977]
2 All ER 177 .... 20[3], 22[10]
Stafford BC v Elkenford Ltd [1977] 2 All ER 519, CA .... 24[18]
Stoke-on-Trent CC v B & Q (Retail) Ltd [1983] 3 WLR 78; [1983]
2 All ER 787, CA .... 6[1], 10[16], 20[2,4], 21[5,6,7,8], 24[15,18]

xxxviii Table of Cases

Stoke-on-Trent CC v B & Q (Retail) Ltd [1984] AC 754; [1984]
  2 All ER 332, HL .... 24[13,14,16,18], 26[26]
Strathclyde RC v Porcelli [1986] IRLR 134, Ct of Session .... 33[9]
Surrey CC v Ministry of Education [1953] 1 WLR 516; [1953]
  1 All ER 705 .... 147[2]
Thanet DC v Ninedrive Ltd [1978] 1 All ER 703 .... 24[18]
Thomas v National Union of Mineworkers (South Wales Area) [1985]
  2 WLR 1081; [1985] 2 All ER 1 .... 182[66], 210
Thrasyvoulou v LB Hackney (1986) 18 HLR 370, CA............. 124[101]
Tithe Redemption Commission v Runcorn UDC [1954] Ch 383; [1954]
  1 All ER 653, CA.. 48[37]
Tod-Heatley v Benham (1888) 40 ChD 80......................... 63[11]
Torridge DC v Jones (1985) 18 HLR 107; (1985) 276
  EG 1253, CA .... 74[34]
Tower Hamlets LBC v Manzoni and Walder [1984] JPL 436 .... 156[17]
Walter v Selfe (1851) 4 De G & S 315............................ 157[25]
Walters v W H Smith & Sons Ltd [1914] 1 KB 595................ 162[3]
Wandsworth LBC v Winder [1985] AC 461; [1984]
  3 All ER 976, HL .... 6[1], 20[1]
Ward Lock & Co Ltd v Operative Printers' Assistants' Society (1906)
  22 TLR 327 .... 182[66]
West Glamorgan CC v Rafferty and Others [1987]
  1 All ER 1005, CA .... 6[1]
Westminster CC v Jones (1982) 80 LGR 241 .... 21[7], 24[18]
Wheeler v Leicester CC [1985] AC 1054; [1985]
  2 All ER 1106, HL .... 10, 11, 12, 14, 16[19], 68
Yates v Morris [1951] 1 KB 77; [1950] 2 All ER 577, CA .... 79[41]

How to Use this Book

This is a book of ideas. It is intended to generate thought and discussion.

It is written primarily for local authority officers, both lawyers and non-lawyers. It should, however, also be useful to any other individual or agency involved in tackling racial harassment.

It has been written because local authorities have been so slow to use the law effectively to tackle racial harassment. It is intended to encourage authorities to engage in some creative thinking when developing their strategies and to break out of their departmental strait jackets. It should also encourage authorities to recognise the crucial role of their legal departments in any attempts to implement strategies for tackling racial harassment and to investigate whether they are able to fulfil that role.

Much of the discussion about the powers of local authorities to tackle racial harassment in the past has centred on possession proceedings and the use of s222 of the Local Government Act 1972. Possession proceedings provide a powerful weapon in the hands of local authorities for tackling racial harassment on their estates. Section 222, on the other hand, is not a particularly useful provision and most of its uses are available to local authorities by other means which would avoid its limitations. Section 222 is discussed in Chapter 3.

Before discussing how best to use this book, a word of caution. None of the legal powers and duties referred to here were designed for tackling racial harassment. Many are untried and untested even in the fields for which they were intended. About six cases involving legal action for racial harassment have been attempted by local authorities. One has been attempted by a housing association. The law is not an exact science; it is full of uncertainties. This is compounded when the courts are given considerable discretion. The interpretation of statutory powers and responsibilities or the effect of previous court decisions is a matter of opinion, initially for an authority's legal advisers and perhaps ultimately for judges.

The book is not designed to be read from beginning to end, although anyone responsible for providing legal advice to an authority or for developing a multi-departmental strategy will wish to do so. In most cases, the chapter headings will indicate where the answer to a particular enquiry may be found. If not, there is a complete index at the back of the book, and cross-references to other relevant sections are given in the text.

The table below shows other chapters that should always be read in addition to the chapter being consulted. Until those using the book are familiar with its contents, these chapters should all be read in their entirety.

How to Use this Book

Chapter being consulted	Other chapters that should be read
1	None
2	None
3	1 and 2
4	1 and 2
5	1, 2, 3, 6 and 14
6	1–5
7	1–4
8	1–4
9	1–4
10	1, 2, 3 and 14
11	1
12	1
13	All chapters
14	1, 5 and 10
15	All chapters

CHAPTER ONE
Introduction

What is racial harassment? Is there a legal definition? In what way is it different from other crimes? Are local authorities the most appropriate agency to tackle racial harassment? This chapter explores the answers to these questions.

Tackling racial harassment is about providing equal opportunities. It is about providing equal opportunities to walk the streets without fear and to relax in the home without the constant threat of violence.

A. RACIAL HARASSMENT

What is "racial harassment"?

This book is about practicalities not semantics. Debates about the precise meaning of the words "racial harassment" are therefore not within its scope. This book is about murders, rapes, arson, assaults, criminal damage, thefts, robberies, burglaries, abuse, threats, insults, intimidation, nuisance and other criminal acts committed generally by white people against black people which are motivated wholly or partly by racism. In a nutshell, it is about crimes which are having a devastating effect on people's lives and which represent a serious public order problem which is either not being addressed at all or is being inadequately addressed by agencies that have powers to take steps to prevent or stop it.

A legal definition of "racial harassment"

Racial harassment is not recognised by the existing law. "Harassment" is a criminal offence in certain circumstances defined by the Protection from Eviction Act 1977. It is also a very minor offence newly introduced by the Public Order Act 1986. "Incitement to racial hatred" is an offence under the Public Order Act 1986 but cannot be prosecuted without the consent of the Attorney-General.

Nowhere in the law are the two aspects of racial harassment brought together, nor is harassment motivated by racism recognised or defined. Suggestions for how the words "racial harassment" might be defined in the criminal and civil law context are made in Chapter 15.

Why racial harassment is important

1 How do crimes amounting to racial harassment differ from other crimes?

Racial harassment victims are likely to be victims again
Many people are afraid of becoming victims of crime. The statistical chance of becoming one depends on such factors as age, sex and location. However, it still remains true that in most cases there is a large selection of possible victims and whether a particular person is chosen by a particular criminal will depend on chance. The chance of being the victim of a second crime by the same criminal is no greater than the chance of being victim of the first crime.

Crimes which form part of a campaign of racial harassment can be quite different. The motive for the crime is not money, but racism. The victims are chosen because of their racial origin or that of some member of their family. Where the racial harassment is being committed against one family, the members of that family are 100 per cent likely to be the next victims of a criminal offence committed by that perpetrator.

Even home is unsafe
Although many people fear crime, they often feel safe somewhere or with some people. For example, those who have a fear of mugging may feel completely safe at home. Elderly people who feel insecure at home may feel completely safe when their children stay the night.

Racial harassment victims may have no such security. Often, home is the most insecure place to be. At all hours of day and night there is a risk of attack, perhaps an attempt at murder. School, playgroups, shopping, travelling to work; all may result in an attack or other harassment. This is in addition to worrying about the safety of those left at home. Insecurity at home can result in a constant state of watchfulness and an inability to sleep.

The effect on the victim
Individual crimes can have a devastating psychological effect on the victim. Racial harassment often consists of a series of crimes, each of which can have an overwhelming effect on the victim and his or her family. Cumulatively, the effect of the crimes is likely to be even greater than the effect of each crime committed in isolation. When combined with the real and reasonable fear of the next crime, and the effects of sleep deprivation that this can cause, it is no surprise that racial harassment is destroying the lives of some families who are its victims.

The motive of the perpetrator may be more serious than at first appears
The intention of the perpetrator of a criminal act which is part of a campaign of racial harassment may be far more serious than the crime which at first

sight appears to have been committed. This may mean that the offence committed is far more serious. For example, suppose some petrol is poured through a letter-box onto a doormat. The mat is ruined and costs £5 to replace. This evidence could suggest several offences including minor criminal damage triable only in the magistrates' court and punishable by a fine or short term of imprisonment; attempted arson triable only in the Crown Court and punishable by a sentence of imprisonment; or attempted murder punishable by life imprisonment.

Unless investigations are carried out to identify the perpetrator and s/he is interrogated to establish the motive, it is not sufficient to dismiss the offence as minor criminal damage. The investigation should be treated as an enquiry into an attempted murder until that motive has been discounted.

2   Racial harassment, nuisance and neighbour disputes

Racial harassment and nuisance
All racial harassment is a nuisance but very little nuisance amounts to racial harassment. There is no comparison between racial harassment and most acts of nuisance, which is usually anti-social behaviour committed by people who do not care who suffers. Racial harassment is behaviour committed by people who want a particular family or person to suffer.

Nuisance is caused by a lack of consideration and motivated by various factors. For example, a dog may be allowed to urinate outside a door because of laziness; the owner cannot be bothered to take the dog to an exercise area. Late-night parties are motivated by a desire to have a good time. Racial harassment is committed by people who may spend considerable time devising the best way of causing suffering. The owner may go out of his or her way to take the dog to the door to urinate; the noise nuisance is committed with the deliberate attempt of stopping the victim watching television or sleeping.

Racial harassment and neighbour disputes
Racial harassment may be committed by a neighbour. To that extent alone, it could be classified as a "neighbour dispute". Where it is committed by a neighbour, this should make any crime involved easier to solve because the range of possible suspects is limited.

However, the classification "neighbour dispute", like that of "domestic dispute", is an artificial one, sometimes used by the police, local authorities and solicitors to justify a failure to take any action, either because the problem is seen as an isolated one arising between two individuals or families which causes no serious harm, or because it is assumed that both parties are partly to blame. A wide variety of grievances go unacknowledged by being labelled as "neighbour disputes", but racial harassment should not fall into that category as it is presently used. For the reasons given above, racial harassment is a serious problem and a failure to act against it cannot be justified.

3 Racial harassment is more widespread than official records suggest

The police and many local authorities keep records of incidents which may amount to racial harassment. Evidence suggests that the figures produced from such records drastically underestimate the level of racial harassment. For example:
— the 1981 Home Office report *Racial Attacks* concluded that Asians were 50 times and West Indians 36 times more likely to be the victims of racially motivated crimes than whites;
— a report by the Policy Studies Institute in 1984[1] suggested that the actual number of racial attacks could be ten times higher than that estimated in the Home Office report;
— a small survey in Glasgow found that 48 per cent of Pakistanis and 58 per cent of Indians had suffered physical attack and 88 per cent and 100 per cent respectively had suffered racial abuse;[2]
— a survey of black residents in Newham carried out in the summer of 1986 interviewed 116 victims of racial harassment who reported 1,550 incidents in the previous year.[3] In 1985 the Metropolitan police recorded only 1,877 racial incidents in the whole of the London area.[4]

B. WHY SHOULD LOCAL AUTHORITIES BE RESPONSIBLE FOR TACKLING RACIAL HARASSMENT?

The fact that this book is primarily about local authorities' powers and obligations to tackle racial harassment does not imply that they are solely responsible or the most appropriate agencies for doing so. The most useful resources and powers in relation to dealing with individual acts of racial harassment relate to the powers of investigation. The powers that the police have to investigate crime far outweigh any possessed by a local authority. For that reason, the police are an equally, if not more important, agency for dealing with racial harassment.

Much of the work being done by local authorities is to fill a perceived gap in law enforcement left by the failure of the police in some areas to take effective action against those responsible for racial harassment. Local authorities should use whatever powers they possess against racial harassment because it is in the interests of their inhabitants to do so. Racial harassment is pernicious behaviour and all agencies should use what powers they have to assist the process of its eradication. A long-term strategy to this end cannot succeed without community support and local authorities are ideally placed to build that support on a local basis.

Why take action against perpetrators?

Legal action is not an end in itself. It is a tool which should be used, in conjunction with other measures discussed in Chapter 5, primarily to provide protection for the victims of racial harassment. Until some action is taken, a perpetrator is in an extremely powerful position. S/he can commit further acts at any time and probably considers him or herself immune from any retaliation. Inaction by an authority or the police might be taken by the perpetrator as implying that his or her acts are publicly acceptable and condoned by those in authority. Immediately court action is taken, a perpetrator is put on the defensive. S/he stands to lose his or her liberty or home: the scales are tipped. The local authority is in a powerful position vis à vis the perpetrator. If, in addition, an injunction or remand on strict bail conditions is obtained, this further implies an element of disapproval from the courts. If legal action is combined effectively with work by community groups in the locality, the message conveyed to the perpetrator and others is that racial harassment is unacceptable and will not be tolerated.

1 *Black and White Britain* 3rd PSI report, 1984.
2 Third report of the Home Affairs Sub-Committee on Race Relations and Immigration 1986 para 4 and Appendix 7. For more examples of under-reporting see *Living in Terror* Commission for Racial Equality, September 1987.
3 *Report of a Survey of Crime and Racial Harassment in Newham* London Borough of Newham, 1987.
4 Metropolitan Police evidence to the Home Affairs Sub-Committee on Race Relations and Immigration 1986 Appendix 1.

CHAPTER TWO

General Factors Affecting all Local Authority Decisions

There are legal constraints on local authority decision-making, which must be observed if those decisions are to be upheld by the courts. Here they are examined in relation to tackling racial harassment.

There are three matters that all authorities should consider whenever they develop policy or make decisions:
— the general principles of administrative law;
— the duty imposed by the Race Relations Act (RRA) 1976 s71; and
— the subsidiary powers provided by the Local Government Act (LGA) 1972 s111.

General principles of administrative law

All decisions of local authorities must be made in accordance with the general principles of administrative law. If not, decisions may be open to challenge by judicial review, or the invalidity of the decision may be used as a defence.[1] It is particularly important that the requirements of administrative law are satisfied where statutory powers are being used in an imaginative and developmental way using new and untried methods. It is in precisely these sorts of situation where policies or decisions are most likely to be challenged by the perpetrators of racial harassment or others who wish to undermine or frustrate an authority's policy on racial harassment.

The courts have identified three heads under which they will control the administrative acts of public bodies including local authorities. These are:
— illegality;
— irrationality; and
— procedural impropriety.[2]

For a decision of a local authority to be immune from legal challenge it must be made in accordance with the following general principles (which frequently overlap in practice). Each is illustrated in the context of a racial harassment policy.

1 The authority must have legal power to make the decision[2]

   Example: *A decision to make payments for removal expenses to owner* *occupiers who were victims of racial harassment would be invalid because there is no legal power available to local authorities to make such payments. Payments of removal expenses to council tenants can be made (see p99).*

2 The authority must have understood correctly the applicable legal powers and given effect to them[2]

It is important that an authority uses the correct statutory power to justify its decision. For a decision to be valid the authority must have considered the requirements of the particular power used.

A decision to take court proceedings could be made using either the powers under the LGA 1972 s222 or the powers under s111. To justify proceedings under s222 the authority must consider proceedings to be "expedient for the promotion of the interests of the inhabitants of their area". Under s111 the authority must consider proceedings to be "calculated to facilitate or be conducive or incidental to" the discharge of one of the authority's functions. These are different requirements which must be understood by the authority when deciding to take court proceedings.

> **Example:** *If an authority attempted to obtain an injunction to prevent a criminal offence being committed without considering whether the proceedings were "expedient for the promotion of the interests of the inhabitants of their area" then the decision would be invalid and the proceedings could be defended on that basis.*

3 The authority must act so as to promote and not to frustrate the policy and objects of the statute under which the decision is made[3]

Authorities must be wary of this point when developing racial harassment policies. There are only two Acts whose main object and policy relate to race and harassment. The RRA 1976 is concerned with eliminating race discrimination and promoting good relations between racial groups[4] and the Protection from Eviction Act 1977 allows authorities to prosecute for harassment.[5] Where powers are exercised under other statutes the elimination of racial harassment cannot be the dominant consideration. This is discussed further in the context of the RRA 1976 s71 below.

> **Example:** *It would not be justifiable for a housing authority to arrange a transport system for children to school under the powers in the Housing Act (HA) 1985 which does not relate to education at all. Such a scheme could, however, be set up under the Education Acts.*[6]

4 The authority must take into account all relevant matters before reaching a decision[7]

The duty under the RRA 1976 s71 and the fiduciary duty to the ratepayers are both factors that are relevant to all decisions of a local authority (see below).

5 The authority must disregard all irrelevant matters when making a decision[7]

An authority must not take into account factors which it may consider relevant, but in law are irrelevant. The racial motive behind a perpetrator's acts are often an irrelevant factor when the local authority considers whether to use many of the powers referred to in this book.

While an authority may be guided by commitments made in a party manifesto this will not validate a decision that has no legal basis.[8]

Example: *The purpose of the Public Health Act 1936 is to eradicate nuisances, not racism. The perpetrator's racial motive is irrelevant when the authority decides whether to exercise its powers under the Public Health Act. What is relevant is the effect on the victim of the nuisances covered by the Act.*

How far the obligation to disregard all irrelevant factors is affected by s71 of the RRA 1976 is considered below.

6 The decision must not be made in bad faith or be dishonest[7]

Example: *A decision made by a local authority officer which was motivated by a personal dislike of an individual would be a decision taken in bad faith.*

7 The facts which form the basis of the decision must be correct and must provide a basis for the decision[9]

Example: *An authority might have a policy that it refuses to recognise any tenants' association which was shown to be condoning racial harassment on its estate. If the local authority then refused to recognise a tenants' association in line with its policy when there was no evidence that the association had condoned racial harassment, then that decision would be open to challenge on the basis that it had not been reached in accordance with the facts.*

8 The authority must not delegate decision making[7]

The authority must make the decision itself and not merely adopt the decision of another body without considering the facts on which that decision was based and whether it was correct. It is the local authority which is given power by statute to make a decision, therefore it cannot adopt automatically the decision of some other person or body. It is perfectly legitimate to take a particular person's or organisation's views into account provided the final decision rests with the authority.

Example: *A local authority could not lawfully have a policy that it would take court proceedings against the perpetrators of racial harassment in all cases where the victim requested it. This would effectively be passing the responsibility for the decision to the victim and would be unlawful. It would, however, be legitimate for an authority to adopt a policy that the victim's* *views should be taken into account and be a dominant factor in any decision to take court proceedings so that, in practice, it is the victim who has the major role in deciding whether action should be taken.*

9 The decision must be reached fairly in accordance with natural justice[10]

Whenever a decision is made as to the manner in which a particular person or organisation is to be dealt with, the person or organisation must be given an opportunity to explain their position and challenge the facts.

Example: *Perpetrators who have been evicted for racial harassment may apply for rehousing under the homelessness provisions of the HA 1985. To act fairly, the authority will have to give the perpetrators an opportunity to give reasons why they should not be considered intentionally homeless.*

10 Authorisation of decision makers

The decision must be made either by the full council or by properly authorised committees, sub-committees or officers within the scope of their delegated authority.[11] The vast majority of powers are delegated to committees, sub-committees and officers of the council. A single councillor cannot be given delegated authority to do anything.

Example: *If the Head of Legal Services alone has been authorised to issue a notice of intention to seek possession, then a notice issued by the Director of Housing would be invalid.*

In some authorities, standing orders will contain a reference to delegation powers. Urgency sub-committees or chief officers may have powers to make decisions in an emergency and report back to full committee.

11 Any statutory procedural requirements must be followed[12]

Example: *Before an authority can change the terms of a tenant's secure tenancy, it must serve a preliminary notice and invite comments. Those comments must then be considered before a final decision to vary the terms is made. If these requirements are not followed, then the decision is invalid. For further details see Chapter 5.*

12 The authority must not fetter its discretion

It must not refuse to exercise a discretion in an individual case by adopting and rigidly following a blanket policy.[13] An authority may adopt a policy to be followed in all save exceptional circumstances, as a guideline for the use of its discretion.

Authorities should be seen to be considering all the relevant facts and making an individual decision in each case.

Example: *Many authorities would like to have a policy that all perpetrators evicted for racial harassment should be considered intentionally homeless. Any policy to this effect would be unlawful because it would fetter the discretion of the local authority which must be exercised in each individual case, taking into account the relevant circumstances of the family and the eviction. The fact that a perpetrator has been evicted for racial harassment can still be a dominant factor affecting the final decision.*

13 The decision must not be one to which no reasonable authority could come[14]

The more radical and imaginative the use of statutory powers by authorities, and the more politically controversial the policies adopted, the greater the likelihood that the courts will uphold a challenge to the use of powers on the basis that no reasonable authority could reach the decision.

Example: *The decision in* Wheeler *was overturned on the basis that no reasonable authority could have reached it. The facts are described in detail below. One of the grounds for the ruling was that it was not open to the authority to require the rugby club, an independent organisation, to agree with it politically.*

14 Authorities must apply their policies consistently

Where the local authority has created a legitimate expectation that it will apply certain criteria or follow certain procedures in reaching a decision it must follow those criteria or procedures.[15]

Example: *If an authority adopts a particular procedure for considering whether homeless applicants are intentionally homeless which was made publicly available, it cannot then consider an application from a perpetrator who is evicted for racial harassment by a different, unpublished procedure.*

Practical application

These principles show how important it is for authorities to ensure that, before any decision is reached, legal advice is sought that gives the legal basis for the decision, the relevant factors that must be taken into account and the extent of delegated authority for making the decision, and a full briefing is obtained from officers on the relevant factors.

If these precautions are not taken, a racial harassment policy may be undermined by legal challenges and court actions may be lost because of irregularities in the decision-making process rather than on consideration of the merits of the case. Examples of situations where local authorities were unsuccessful in court proceedings wholly or partly because of defects in their decision-making process can be found in the cases referred to in Chapter 3 and Appendix 5.[16]

The general duty under the Race Relations Act 1976 s71

In this section, general points regarding the use of s71 powers to authorise the withholding of discretionary facilities to both organisations and individuals are considered. Examples of the application of these points to particular functions of local authorities occur throughout the following chapters.

The RRA 1976 s71 imposes a duty on all authorities:

> "to make appropriate arrangements with a view to securing that their various functions are carried out with due regard to the need—
> (a) to eliminate unlawful racial discrimination; and
> (b) to promote equality of opportunity, and good relations, between persons of different racial groups".

1 Scope of the duty

There has been one reported case which assists with the interpretation of the effect of s71, *Wheeler v Leicester City Council*.[17] The case was not concerned with the duties imposed on local authorities by s71 but with the extra powers given to authorities by the provision. However, the judgment in the House of Lords gives some guidance on the extent of the duty imposed by s71.

Because of the important effect of the decision it is dealt with in some detail.

The facts of the case
Three players from Leicester Football Club were invited to join the English rugby team to tour South Africa. Leicester City Council wrote to the club asking it to reply to four questions:
(a) Did the club support the Government opposition to the tour?
(b) Did the club agree that the tour was an insult to a large proportion of the Leicester population?
(c) Will the club press the Rugby Football Union to call off the tour?
(d) Will the club press the players to pull out of the tour?

The club replied that it agreed with the council in condemning apartheid in South Africa, but that its role in relation to its members was advisory and it was not unlawful for any member to join the tour. It did not answer any of the questions posed.

The council then passed a resolution banning the club from using a council-owned recreation ground for a period of 12 months. The rugby club applied to overturn the decision of the council. Both the High Court and Court of Appeal dismissed the club's application.

The ruling
The House of Lords unanimously allowed the appeal and agreed the following propositions:

(a) The whole purpose of s71 was to see that, in relation to all their various functions, local authorities must make appropriate arrangements to secure that those functions are carried out with due regard to the need mentioned in the section.

(b) The council was therefore fully entitled, when exercising its discretion under the Open Spaces Act 1906, to pay regard to what it thought was in the best interest of race relations.

(c) However, the manner in which the council had reached its decision was unfair. Having received a reply from the club, the council did not consider whether it was satisfactory, but instead passed a resolution banning the use of the recreation ground because affirmative answers had not been received to all four questions posed.

(d) Since the club had done nothing unlawful, the council could not use its statutory powers in order to punish the club.

(e) This did not mean that the council was bound to allow its property to be used by a racist organisation, or by any organisation which, by its actions or its words, infringed the letter or spirit of the 1976 Act.

Effect of the decision

The main effect of the decision in *Wheeler* appears to be that the need to eliminate unlawful racial discrimination, to promote equality of opportunity and to promote good relations between different racial groups will be relevant factors which must be taken into account under the principles described above, whenever an authority is making a decision. The word "arrangements" in s71 suggests that authorities must have some policy or practice for ensuring that these factors are considered when decisions are reached.

If an authority completely fails to take account of the need described in s71 when reaching a decision and has no mechanism for doing so, then the decision could probably be successfully challenged in the courts.

What *Wheeler* does not decide and what has not yet been considered by the courts is the extent to which decisions of local authorities may be challenged when they have given some consideration to the need in s71 but have given insufficient weight to it. There will be some cases where the particular function being considered has no implications in the field of race relations. There will be many others where there are implications and the need referred to in s71 will be important. Administrative law allows authorities considerable leeway in the weight given to any particular factor when reaching a decision. The extent to which s71 may impose a duty on authorities to develop a policy for dealing with racial harassment is considered further in Chapter 4, p30.

Wheeler also suggests that an authority cannot use s71 as a justification for attempting to force other individuals or organisations to agree with its political stance on race matters. It probably can use s71 to justify action against organisations which are engaged in acts that are in some way unlawful.

2 Sanctions against organisations

Actions probably authorised by s71:

(a) withholding or withdrawing grants and discretionary facilities from organisations which are known to pursue unlawful practices including discrimination in employment or in the delivery of services under the RRA 1976;

(b) withholding or withdrawing grants and discretionary facilities from organisations which cannot show that they are taking reasonable steps to ensure that they do not discriminate or that racial harassment does not occur during activities or functions over which they have some control;

(c) imposing conditions on grants to voluntary organisations requiring them to establish equal opportunities policies and policies for dealing with racial harassment;

(d) obtaining goods and services only from individuals or organisations which operate satisfactory systems for preventing discrimination (contract compliance);[18]

(e) making use of residential facilities (eg hostels, bed and breakfast accommodation, private nursing homes) only where the owners operate a satisfactory system for preventing discrimination and for dealing with racial harassment;

(f) consulting only those organisations which can show that they operate policies for dealing with discrimination and are truly representative of all racial groups in the community;

(g) withholding or withdrawing grants and discretionary facilities from organisations whose members or staff are responsible for unlawful acts of racial harassment within the organisation and which take no steps to impose sanctions; and

(h) withholding or withdrawing grants and discretionary facilities from organisations whose members are responsible for unlawful acts of racial harassment outside the organisation and which actively condone the acts.

Actions possibly authorised by s71:

(a) withholding grants and discretionary facilities from organisations whose members are responsible for unlawful acts of racial harassment outside the organisation and which take no steps to impose sanctions or which have no policy for dealing with such incidents; and

(b) withholding grants and discretionary facilities from an organisation that refuses to condemn acts of racial harassment.

Actions probably not authorised by s71:

(a) withdrawing grants and discretionary facilities from organisations whose

members are responsible for unlawful acts of racial harassment outside the organisation and which take no steps to impose sanctions; and
(b) withdrawing grants and discretionary facilities from organisations that refuse to comply with a council request to condemn racist views.

The significant difference between those actions possibly authorised and those which probably are not is that in the former the grants and discretionary facilities have never been provided. In the latter, the grant or use of the discretionary facility is being withdrawn as a sanction against the organisation when it has done nothing unlawful. It was precisely this action which the Wheeler case decided was not authorised by s71.

The sorts of organisation on which authorities are likely to wish to impose sanctions are those which generally have no policy on equal opportunities in employment or service delivery. They will probably have made little attempt either to involve people from all racial groups in their activities or to be representative of the community which they serve. Withdrawing or withholding facilities and grants can therefore be justified on legitimate grounds, using s71, and it will not be necessary for authorities to use grounds that are likely to be rejected by the courts.

3 Sanctions against individual perpetrators

Providing discretionary services to individuals
Whether sanctions against individual perpetrators can be authorised by s71 requires consideration of different factors from those relating to organisations.

Services to individual perpetrators may be provided under an authority's statutory duty. In that case, the services cannot be withheld unless the statute allows the conduct of the perpetrator to be taken into account (as is the case where a perpetrator is homeless and applies for rehousing). Where services are discretionary, the need referred to in s71 *must* be taken into account by an authority when it decides whether or not to provide those services to a perpetrator. However, as has been explained above, the authority must make a decision which promotes and does not frustrate the policy and objects of the statute under which the decision is made. In practice, there may frequently be a conflict between these two requirements, which is difficult to resolve.

The authority must consider each case on its own merits and not have a blanket policy to withhold discretionary facilities from perpetrators in all circumstances. Where withholding facilities promotes the objects of a statute, there will be no difficulty. This will apply when, for example, it can be justified on the ground of good management of a function of the authority, eg housing management or management of schools, social services children's homes, playgroups or day centres. The authority will be obliged to provide alternative facilities if the facilities are provided under a statutory duty. It will also apply when withholding facilities can be justified in the interests of other people receiving the same or some other, similar service, eg racial harassment of home helps or those delivering meals on wheels may result in recruitment difficulties in the future and consequently a cut in service generally.

Where action against perpetrators will conflict with the policy and objects of an Act, and no basis exists for arguing that the policy and objects are being promoted, it seems likely that the courts will be unsympathetic to any action, as they will take the view that the policy and objects of the Act must take priority over the need referred to in s71.

Example: *A local authority would not be able to justify punishing a perpetrator by banning him or her from public swimming pools because of acts of racial harassment against a neighbour on a housing estate.*

The duty under s71 does not override equivalent duties in the earlier parts of the RRA 1976 in relation to non-discrimination in employment or in the provision of goods and services.

Subsidiary powers of all local authorities

Authorities have power to do "anything which is calculated to facilitate, or is conducive or incidental to the discharge of any of their functions". (LGA 1972 s111).

Scope of the power

The section specifically includes the power to do things which involve spending or lending money, or disposing of property. The exact scope of the power will depend upon the particular function of the authority which is being discharged.

The power provided by s111 is extremely wide and there is no limit to the activities that could be carried out and decisions that could be made by an authority, provided that they can be supported under the general principles referred to above. When using the authority of s111 for any action, an authority should make a specific decision that the act in question is calculated to facilitate or is conducive or incidental to the discharge of its functions. The information on which the decision is based, contained in committee papers, should provide the factual basis for the decision.

Examples

Examples of the use of the powers contained in LGA 1972 s111 in the context of a racial harassment policy occur throughout the following chapters. They include:

(a) Measures to protect council property. These cover:
 — imposing conditions in tenancy agreements, licences of council property, leases of council property and transfers to tenants who purchase under the "right to buy" provisions of the HA 1985;
 — enforcing the conditions by court action where necessary;

- taking actions in tort to protect property eg trespass, nuisance, interference with goods; and
- carrying out investigations to establish who is responsible for damage to council property.

(b) Measures to ensure that other organisations or individuals assist the discharge of functions. These will include:
- imposing conditions on grants to voluntary organisations including housing associations; and
- secondment of staff to voluntary organisations.

(c) Measures to consult sections of the community before decisions are made.

(d) Measures to assist the authority in detecting breaches of the law where the authority has a duty or power. These will include taking steps to identify those responsible for breaches of byelaws, nuisances, harassment under the Protection from Eviction Act 1977 or breaches of tenancy agreements.

(e) Choosing suppliers of goods and services so as to ensure that the authority's functions are assisted. This will include:
- contract compliance clauses on equal opportunities;[19] and
- imposing conditions requiring prompt action from the managers of residential accommodation to deal with racial harassment and ceasing to use those facilities if the conditions are not fully complied with.

Whenever an authority enters into some kind of legal relationship with another individual or organisation it has the opportunity to influence the conduct of that other. It is important to remember that an authority always has a legal relationship with:
- its tenants;
- the licensees in its hostels;
- people or organisations which hire its premises, eg tenants' associations, playgroups, political parties and trade unions;
- those from whom it obtains goods and services;
- those to whom it gives grants;
- its employees;
- to an extent, the unions representing its employees;
- many of those to whom it provides goods and services;
- those from whom and to whom it leases premises, eg housing associations;
- those who purchase their own homes under the "right to buy" provisions and, in some cases, their successors in title.

1 *Wandsworth LBC v Winder* [1985] AC 461; *West Glamorgan CC v Rafferty and Others* [1987] 1 All ER 1005, CA and see also *Stoke-on-Trent CC v B & Q (Retail) Ltd* [1983] 2 All ER 787, CA.
2 *Council of Civil Service Unions and Others v Minister for Civil Service* [1984] 3 All ER 935, HL.

3 *Padfield v Minister of Agriculture, Fisheries and Food* [1968] AC 997, HL.
4 See below, RRA 1976 s71.
5 Protection from Eviction Act 1977 s6 see p173.
6 See Chapter 8.
7 *Associated Provincial Picture Houses v Wednesbury Corp* [1947] 2 All ER 680, CA.
8 *Bromley LBC v GLC and Another* [1982] 1 All ER 153, HL.
9 *Sec State Education and Science v MB Tameside* [1976] 3 All ER 665, HL per Lord Wilberforce at 671.
10 *Re HK* [1967] 1 All ER 226.
11 Local Government Act 1972 s101 and see Chapter 4.
12 N2.
13 *British Oxygen Co Ltd v Minister of Technology* [1970] 3 All ER 165.
14 N7.
15 *R v Sec State Home Dept ex p Ruddock and Others* [1987] 2 All ER 518.
16 See *Stoke-on-Trent CC v B & Q (Retail) Ltd* n1 and *LB Camden v Walsh* (1986) 10 April, Bloomsbury and Marylebone County Court.
17 [1985] 2 All ER 1106, HL.
18 At the time of writing, the Local Government Bill 1987 contains provisions which will restrict the ability of local authorities to operate contract compliance. The Government's final views on this point are not yet clear but when the Bill is enacted it seems likely it will contain some provisions restricting local authorities' powers.
19 *Wheeler v Leicester CC* n17.

CHAPTER THREE
Local Authority Court Proceedings

The general legal basis of local authorities' powers to take court proceedings against those guilty of racial harassment is examined — both the general and specific powers, the express and the implied, in civil and criminal courts.

Court proceedings may be civil or criminal. Possession proceedings are one form of civil proceedings.

In the context of a racial harassment policy, civil proceedings in the county court or High Court will usually involve a local authority seeking an injunction against a perpetrator in an attempt to prevent further harassment, linked, in some cases, with a claim for damages. Injunctions and the procedure of civil proceedings are dealt with in Chapter 5 and the evidential requirements in Chapter 14. Care and wardship proceedings are a different type of civil proceedings and are covered in Chapter 7.

Criminal proceedings in the magistrates' court and Crown Court involve punishment for past offences but provide no long-term protection for a victim. The procedure and evidential requirements of criminal proceedings are discussed in Chapters 10 and 14.

The legal basis for court proceedings

There are three ways in which the law gives authorities power to take court proceedings:
— where statute expressly gives a local authority power to take proceedings for a particular purpose;
— by the Local Government Act 1972 s111; and
— by the Local Government Act 1972 s222.

Express power to take proceedings for a particular purpose

Examples exist throughout this book of instances where authorities are given express power to take proceedings. Examples of powers to take criminal proceedings are to be found in Chapter 10 section B. Examples of powers to take civil proceedings are found on pp44 and 136.

The scope of each of these express powers will be covered in the appropriate section and it is not proposed to deal further with these here.

Implied power in Local Government Act 1972 s111

The extent of the powers provided by LGA 1972 s111 were dealt with in the previous chapter. There is no limit to the activities that might be authorised by s111 provided that such activity can be justified under the general principles of administrative law as being "calculated to facilitate" or "conducive or incidental" to one of the authority's functions. In the context of court proceedings, a further limitation to the use of s111 is that an authority can only take legal action in the same circumstances as a private individual.

A local authority may therefore be able to justify court proceedings against perpetrators of racial harassment using the powers provided by LGA 1972 s111 in the following circumstances:

(a) a criminal prosecution for any offence (unless a statute specifically prohibits a private prosecution or requires the consent of the Director of Public Prosecutions or Attorney-General, eg offences relating to incitement to racial hatred: see Appendix 6), regardless of whether or not the offence is committed against the local authority;

(b) possession proceedings against a tenant who has rented a local authority house or flat (subject to the provisions of the HA 1985);

(c) an action for breach of a contract to which the authority is a party, eg a tenancy agreement or a lease;

(d) proceedings for trespass or nuisance against anyone responsible for interference with land owned or occupied by an authority including the highway, the surface of which is vested in the highway authority;

(e) proceedings for any tort committed against the authority, eg damage to property by graffiti;

(f) wardship proceedings to protect a child;

(g) proceedings for a public nuisance but only where the local authority has suffered special damage as a result of the nuisance.

Two types of proceedings that are used by local authorities on a regular basis throughout the country appear to be authorised by s111 — wardship and possession proceedings. Neither is specifically authorised by statute. The latter is ancillary to a housing authority's power to manage its housing stock, the former is ancillary to the social services' duties towards children.

Express general power in Local Government Act 1972 s222

The LGA 1972 s222 provides:

> "Where a local authority consider it expedient for the promotion or protection of the interests of the inhabitants of their area they may prosecute or defend or appear in any legal proceedings and, in the case of civil proceedings, may institute them in their own name."

This section applies to every local authority but does not apply to the Inner London Education Authority.

In the context of a racial harassment policy there are at least five separate uses of s222 that might be considered by local authorities. These are dealt with in turn below. They are:
— prosecuting in criminal proceedings;
— obtaining injunctions to prevent the commission of criminal offences;
— obtaining injunctions to prevent public nuisances;
— obtaining injunctions to prevent the obstruction of an authority's statutory duties; and
— appearing in proceedings brought by others.

Of these five uses, only injunctions to prevent criminal offences have been attempted and all the reported cases on s222 therefore centre on this use of the provision. In these cases, some guidance is provided on the use of s222 to authorise proceedings for injunctions to prevent public nuisances. No guidance is available from the courts on the use of s222 for the other three purposes mentioned above.

1 The conditions for using s222

Before making use of s222, the conditions for its use must be satisfied. It is convenient to break these conditions into two components:
— proceedings must be considered by the authority to be "expedient for the promotion or protection of the inhabitants of their area" (the statutory requirement); and
— the authority must be able to justify its decision on administrative law principles (the administrative law requirement).

Most decisions of local authorities are never reviewed by a court, but all decisions to use s222 are likely to be reviewed by the courts since a defendant is entitled to defend the proceedings or seek to have them struck out on the ground that the authority had no legal power to bring the proceedings at all.[1] In one of the leading cases on s222, proceedings by one local authority were unsuccessful for this reason. The decision had not been properly reached, taking into account the statutory requirements.[2]

The statutory requirement

Several of the cases involving the powers of authorities under s222 have considered the meaning of "promotion or protection of the interests of the inhabitants". From these cases the following points emerge:

(a) Section 222 probably allows an authority to take proceedings for the promotion or protection of the interests of its inhabitants even though the inhabitants of other authorities may also benefit.[3]

(b) The authority must consider the interests of its inhabitants generally and not just a section of the community.[4]

(c) The authority should look for a general interest common to its inhabitants as a whole, even though it may not be in the interests of particular individuals or groups of individuals.[5]

Two general factors have been considered by the courts to support a local authority's decision that proceedings are justified:
— the fact that it is in everyone's interests, particularly in urban areas, that a local authority should do what it can to establish and maintain the ambience of a law-abiding community;[6]
— the fact that the proceedings are within an area of local authority responsibility where the authority has statutory duties either to enforce the law or to preserve the public interest.[7]

The administrative law requirements
The requirements of a valid decision under the principles of administrative law were dealt with in Chapter 2. Applying those principles to the use of s222, an authority should be able to show it has properly considered the requirements of s222 before it started the proceedings.[8] Relevant factors that an authority must take into account before deciding to take proceedings include:

(a) the likelihood of success, taking into account the strength of the evidence;

(b) the likelihood that a successful result will have the desired practical effect (eg is an injunction likely to stop the racial harassment?);

(c) the availability of any alternative long-term remedies;

(d) the cost of the proceedings and whether any costs might be recovered from the defendant (local authorities can no longer recover costs from public funds if they prosecute in criminal proceedings[9]);

(e) whether any other person or authority has power and resources to take proceedings which might be more effective, and whether such person or authority is likely to do so or has good reasons not to (eg the victim, the police or the Crown Prosecution Service could prosecute for the criminal offences committed in many instances of racial harassment. It is most unlikely the victim will prosecute since legal aid is not available. The police may be the most appropriate agency to prosecute (see below under criminal proceedings)).

Finally, before a local authority starts s222 proceedings, there must be some evidence to support the authority's decision that the proceedings will promote or protect the interests of its inhabitants.

2 Criminal proceedings
Section 222 includes the words "a local authority . . . may prosecute . . . in any legal proceedings". Many authorities have sought legal advice as to whether this provision authorises a criminal prosecution. There is no report of any case on the use of s222 for these purposes, but there is no reason

to believe that it could not be done, provided that the requirements of the provision can be satisfied.

Can a criminal prosecution be taken in the name of the authority?
Section 222 specifically provides that civil proceedings may be taken in the authority's own name but makes no such reference to criminal proceedings. This has led some legal advisers to conclude that authorities can only take criminal proceedings in the name of an officer.

This view appears incorrect, and is based on a misunderstanding of the historical basis for s222. The section replaced the LGA 1933 s276, which did not contain the words "may institute [civil proceedings] in their own name". As a result, several court cases[10] decided that local authorities were not authorised by s276 to seek an injunction to prevent the commission of a criminal offence in their own name. If they wished to obtain such an injunction, they had to obtain the permission of the Attorney-General for a relator action. They had no powers over and above those possessed by every other individual. The words "take [civil proceedings] in their own name" were thus added to reverse the decisions of the courts and give local authorities an additional power above that enjoyed by individuals, who have always had power to take a private prosecution. No additional words were needed in s222 to give authorities power to prosecute in their own name. The absence of words specifically authorising criminal proceedings in the authority's own name is merely because such words are unnecessary and not because it is intended that proceedings should be taken in the name of an officer.

By way of comparison, it has never been suggested that wardship proceedings should be taken in the name of an officer of a local authority. This is because every individual has power to take wardship proceedings and no express power is needed to allow an authority to take wardship proceedings in its own name.

Satisfying the statutory requirement
The purpose of the criminal law is to protect the public interest and most criminal prosecutions are by the Crown representing the public interest. It is considered to be in the public interest that a criminal offender should be brought to justice and punished. It can also be argued that taking criminal proceedings to punish racial harassment is in the interests of good race relations.

On these bases, an authority should be able to justify a criminal prosecution as being for the promotion or protection of the interests of the inhabitants of its area, and that one way to maintain the ambience of a law-abiding community is to prosecute those who commit criminal acts.

Satisfying the administrative law requirements
Since it is primarily the duty of the police to enforce the criminal law in the public interest, an authority must have good reasons for proceeding

where the police do not, since otherwise the authority may be failing in its duties to the ratepayers. Initially, it will usually be necessary for the authority to ask the police to act in each case and to provide them with the available evidence. Having given every assistance to the police, examples of good reasons justifying a prosecution by a local authority include:

(a) the police not investigating the crime;
(b) the police saying that they have inadequate resources to investigate;
(c) the police saying that they have insufficient evidence, when the authority's legal advice clearly states that there is ample evidence;
(d) the police deciding merely to warn the perpetrator and not prosecute;
(e) the police not prosecuting when asked to do so by the authority unless an individual local authority officer is named on the charge sheet;
(f) the police charging a minor offence when the authority has been clearly advised that there is evidence to charge a more serious offence. (Note that the authority will be unable to prosecute a more serious offence if the perpetrator has already been convicted of a minor offence based on the same facts.)

If statistical records show that over a period of time the police do not prosecute certain sorts of offences even where ample evidence exists or do not investigate such offences, an authority might be justified in taking criminal proceedings without inviting the police to do so first. Similarly, when the offence falls within one of the authority's areas of responsibility; examples of situations where this might arise include:
— offences which regularly occur on council housing estates;
— offences against children in the authority's schools or in the care of the local authority; and
— offences against the authority's staff or premises.

Perhaps the most likely situation where an authority might be in a position to prosecute but the police decide not to do so, is when the offence has been witnessed by a local authority officer. Examples might include offences of assault, criminal damage or watching and besetting the victim's home (see Chapter 10).

3 Injunctions to prevent the commission of a criminal offence

Authorities are given a power by LGA s222 to apply for an injunction to prevent the commission of criminal offences in limited circumstances.

Prior to the LGA 1972, local authorities, like other individuals and organisations, could only obtain an injunction to prevent the commission of a criminal offence by obtaining the consent of the Attorney-General to take proceedings in his name.[11] The Attorney-General ensured that the proceedings were in the public interest. Local authorities may now use s222 to take proceedings to promote or protect the interests of their inhabitants.

The circumstances in which local authorities can obtain injunctions to prevent criminal offences have been considered in several cases since 1974 from which the following principles emerge.

(a) To date, all the cases in which s222 has been successfully used by local authorities have involved applications for injunctions to restrain criminal offences in areas in which authorities have regulatory powers and duties, eg planning, Sunday trading, tree preservation orders, street trading.[12]

(b) The courts will be very cautious about granting an injunction since it might lead to harsher penalties being imposed on the offender than s/he would receive in the criminal courts.[13]

(c) The court always has a discretion whether or not to issue an injunction.[14]

(d) Authorities can seek an injunction to prevent the commission of a criminal offence where the offender is deliberately and flagrantly flouting the law.[15]

(e) Authorities can seek an injunction to prevent the commission of a criminal offence in an emergency where it is necessary to prevent dire danger or grave and irreparable harm.[16]

(f) Authorities can seek an injunction where there may be irreparable damage if they await the outcome of criminal proceedings.[17]

(g) In most cases, criminal proceedings should be attempted before an injunction is sought, but this is not essential.[18]

(h) The categories of circumstances in which authorities may be able to obtain injunctions may not be closed.[19]

(i) The statutory duties of local authorities may mean that they have wider powers than the Attorney-General to seek injunctions to restrain criminal offences in the interests of their inhabitants.[20]

The practical use of injunctions to prevent criminal offences
The above principles reveal two, or possibly three, bases on which injunctions can be sought:
— where there is a deliberate and flagrant flouting of the law;
— in cases of emergency;
— where there is likely to be irreparable damage unless an injunction is granted.

Deliberate and flagrant flouting of the law This basis requires an obvious intention to ignore the criminal penalties. It has been used by authorities to stop companies making huge profits from Sunday trading where they would only receive small fines, and evidence of repeated criminal offences was readily available and not disputed.

The remedy is unlikely to be useful where the offences involved in a campaign of racial harassment are serious, and substantial penalties can be imposed. It is most unlikely that evidence will be available of a succession of such offences, eg assault, criminal damage etc. It is more probable that evidence will be available of only one or two offences and it may be better to prosecute for the criminal offences themselves, using the evidence that exists. It may also be difficult to obtain evidence that the perpetrator intends to repeat the offence.

This basis will be most useful for minor persistent offenders. An example of one such offence is obstruction of the highway which can include some acts of racial harassment, eg against owner occupiers and private tenants or against school children.[21] It should be remembered that authorities are given express power to seek injunctions to prevent statutory nuisances and noise nuisances and therefore do not need to use s222 for these purposes.[22]

Emergency There has only been one reported case where an injunction has been granted because of emergency.[23] That case was brought by the Attorney-General before local authorities had powers under s222.

It is this basis that provides scope for authorities to develop the remedy in the context of action against racial harassment. In the one reported case, there was a risk to life and the courts can be expected to restrict the remedy to cases where there is a serious risk of some form of bodily harm. Such risk exists in many cases of racial harassment.

As with all other action against perpetrators, the main problem will be proof. When using this basis, proof of a future intention to commit criminal acts will be necessary. Written or verbal threats, perhaps coupled with proof that previous threats have been carried out, should be sufficient for these purposes.

Irreparable damage The leading case on this basis involved physical damage to the environment.[24] In racial harassment cases, the main irreparable damage will be psychological damage or physical harm to the victim. This therefore probably adds little to the previous basis.

Choice of remedy
Because of the serious limitations and the degree of uncertainty in this area, other powers should be used by authorities to obtain injunctions, where possible. These include the power to obtain injunctions to restrain a breach of contract, trespass, nuisance, public nuisance (see below), statutory nuisance, noise nuisance and in wardship proceedings. Injunctions to prevent criminal offences using s222 should be considered only as a last resort. In most cases some other legal basis will exist for obtaining an injunction.

4 Injunctions to prevent a public nuisance

The definition of a public nuisance is given on p43 where examples are given of the use that might be made of this remedy.

Where a public nuisance involves some interference with the highway, the use of the powers under s222 will be unnecessary, since the Highways Act gives authorities specific powers to take action to protect and assert the public's right to use the highway (see p44).

Although there has been no reported case in which it has been necessary to decide whether s222 gives authorities powers to obtain an injunction to prevent a public nuisance, there seems no doubt that it does. Prior to the 1972 Act the courts had decided that local authorities could not take proceedings in their own name for public nuisances unless they had suffered special damage from the nuisance.[25] Comments made in cases involving s222 since 1974, interpret the section as reversing the effect of the previous law.[26]

Public nuisances are, by their nature, usually matters which affect only one locality and are therefore exactly the kind of matters for which the powers under s222 are particularly appropriate. It should be noted that a public nuisance is a criminal offence as well as a civil matter and the local authority may additionally be able to use its powers under s222 to prosecute.

5 Injunctions to prevent obstruction of the authority's statutory duty

Prior to the 1972 Act, there was a court decision which suggested that a local authority could seek an injunction against an individual whose action was preventing the authority fulfilling a positive statutory duty.[27] The duty obstructed in that case was an obligation to carry out inspections on a daily basis. The decision appeared to be based upon the fact that the authority's own interests were being obstructed.

Section 222 now provides an additional argument that proceedings of this nature should be available to local authorities, although the point has never been tested. It is arguable that this principle should be extended to allow authorities to seek injunctions under s222 when they are being forced to breach their statutory duty, even where this is a negative duty, eg the duty not to discriminate. It might even be argued that the principle should extend to allowing injunctions to be sought when individuals prevent authorities exercising their statutory powers, eg to manage their housing stock.

Example: *The authority is unable to rehouse black homeless families because of racial harassment on an estate.*

Action could be justified on three grounds:

(a) Where homeless people are in priority need and are not intentionally homeless, an authority has a positive duty to secure accommodation for their occupation.[28] Since January 1987 that accommodation must be "suitable".[29] Council dwellings where tenants will be subjected to racial harassment are unlikely to be suitable, so the effect of the racial harassment is to obstruct the authority in the discharge of its positive statutory duty to rehouse the homeless.

(b) An authority is also under a duty not to discriminate on racial grounds in the allocation of its housing (see Chapter 6). The effect of racial harassment on a particular estate is that black tenants may feel unable to accept housing in that area. In practice, certain areas of council accommodation will become unavailable for black tenants and a discriminatory system of housing allocation will operate, however well-meaning the local authority.

(c) The positive duty to eliminate unlawful racial discrimination and promote equality of opportunity in RRA 1976 s71 can be used to support any action by an authority to prevent racial harassment in these circumstances. In practice, the racial harassment will be preventing the authority from fulfilling its statutory duty under the RRA 1976 when allocating its housing.

6 Appearing in proceedings

Section 222 states that a local authority "may . . . appear in any legal proceedings".
There are two possible interpretations of this phrase:
— that an authority can take a part in proceedings in the same way as an individual, eg when joined as a third party in civil proceedings; or
— that an authority may appear in any proceedings to represent the local public interest.
The phrase has not been considered or commented upon in any of the decisions on the extent of s222 and it remains to be decided which of the two interpretations is correct.

The first interpretation would mean that an authority is only in the same position as any private individual and can only appear in proceedings in which it is interested. The second interpretation would mean that s222 gives authorities powers which are far more extensive. The Attorney-General may appear in any proceedings with leave of the court to put forward the Government's views on public policy.[30] If this latter interpretation of s222 is correct, local authorities have similar powers to appear in proceedings between other individuals to represent the interests of their own inhabitants.

Arguments for the second interpretation
The court decisions and the 1972 Act give no clue as to why the word "appear" was included in the 1972 Act when it had not been included in the 1933 Act from which s222 originated. There is no doubt that s222 gives local authorities powers additional to those enjoyed by private citizens and similar to those enjoyed by the Attorney-General in respect of actions for injunctions to restrain criminal offences and for public nuisance. It is therefore arguable that it was intended that a local authority's powers to intervene in other proceedings are greater than those of other individuals by virtue of s222.

If the wider interpretation were adopted, then it would be possible for an authority to appear in a private prosecution brought by an individual against a perpetrator of racial harassment. Similarly, an authority could appear in any prosecution brought by the police against a perpetrator of racial harassment or in civil proceedings brought by a victim directly against the perpetrator.

The advantage of appearing in proceedings to represent the local public interest is that an authority would then be able to ask questions of witnesses and make submissions to the court, and its representative could help to ensure that the prosecution and court deal with the matter appropriately. In the case of a private prosecution for common assault, the presence of a local authority representative might ensure that the court proceeds with the criminal trial rather than binding over both parties, as is usually the case.

Since a local authority is entitled to authorise any officer to represent it in the magistrates' court, it might authorise a housing officer to represent it in criminal proceedings between tenants, provided that its appearance in such proceedings satisfies the requirements of s222.[31]

1 *Wandsworth LBC v Winder* [1985] AC 461.
2 See the decision of the Court of Appeal in relation to the proceedings by LB Barking in *Stoke-on-Trent CC v B & Q (Retail) Ltd* [1983] 2 All ER 787, CA.
3 *Supreme Court Practice* 1988 p207 para 15/11/5 cited with approval by Oliver J in *Solihull MBC v Maxfern* [1977] 2 All ER 177 at 181.
4 *Stoke-on-Trent CC v B & Q (Retail) Ltd* n2.
5 Ibid.
6 Ibid at 797 per Lawton LJ.
7 See *Kent CC v Batchelor (No 2)* [1978] 3 All ER 980; *Westminster CC v Jones* (1982) 80 LGR 241; *Stoke-on-Trent CC v B & Q (Retail) Ltd* n2 and *Runnymede BC v Ball* [1986] 1 WLR 353, CA.
8 Otherwise the proceedings could fail, see *Stoke-on-Trent* n2.
9 Prosecution of Offences Act 1985 s17.
10 See *Solihull MBC v Maxfern* n3 per Oliver J at 178–181 where he deals with these cases and the reasons for the wording in s222.
11 See, eg, *Prestatyn UDC v Prestatyn Raceway Ltd* [1969] 3 All ER 1573.
12 See the cases listed in the notes to this chapter.
13 *Stoke-on-Trent CC v B & Q (Retail) Ltd* [1984] 2 All ER 332, HL.
14 See, eg, *Stoke-on-Trent CC v B & Q (Retail) Ltd* in the House of Lords n13 per Lord Templeman at 341.
15 See the Court of Appeal decision in *Stoke-on-Trent CC v B & Q (Retail) Ltd* n2 and *Runnymede BC v Ball* n7.
16 N14 citing *Gouriet v UPOW* [1977] 3 All ER 70, HL and see *A-G v Chaudry* [1971] 3 All ER 938, CA.
17 *Runnymede BC v Ball* n7 per Purchas LJ.
18 See *Stafford BC v Elkenford Ltd* [1977] 2 All ER 519, CA; *Stoke-on-Trent CC v B & Q (Retail) Ltd* n2; *Thanet DC v Ninedrive Ltd* [1978] 1 All ER 703; *Westminster CC v Jones* n7 and *Stoke-on-Trent CC v B & Q (Retail) Ltd* in the House of Lords n13 per Lord Templeman at 342.
19 See *Gouriet v UPOW* n16 per Viscount Dilhorne at 92; contrary Lord Diplock at 99 and see *Runnymede CC v Ball* n7 per Purchas LJ at 363.
20 N7.
21 See p44 and Chapter 10.
22 See Chapter 9.
23 *A-G v Chaudry* n16.
24 *Runnymede BC v Ball* n7.

25 *Prestatyn UDC v Prestatyn Raceway Ltd* n11.
26 See, eg, the leading judgment of Lord Templeman in *Stoke-on-Trent CC v B & Q (Retail) Ltd* in the House of Lords n13 at 339j with which all the other Law Lords agreed.
27 *London CC v South Metropolitan Gas Co* [1904] 1 Ch 76.
28 HA 1985 s65 and see Chapter 6.
29 Ibid s69(1) as amended by the Housing and Planning Act 1986 s14(3).
30 *Adams v Adams (Attorney-General intervening)* [1970] 3 All ER 572.
31 LGA 1972 s223(1).

CHAPTER FOUR

Powers and Duties of all Local Authorities

All local authorities and departments have statutory obligations and powers for use in tackling racial harassment. The diverse ways in which these can be employed in assistance to victims, action against perpetrators and intervention in the private sector are explained and considered.

Certain powers and duties apply to all local authorities, ie London borough councils, the Common Council of the City of London, county councils, district councils and metropolitan borough councils. In some circumstances powers and duties may also apply to community and parish councils, but it is not proposed to cover these in this book.

All the powers and duties mentioned in this chapter apply to every department within each authority although, as a matter of day-to-day practice, the use of certain powers may be delegated to particular departments.

A. DUTIES APPLYING TO ALL AUTHORITIES AND DEPARTMENTS

The general duty under the Race Relations Act 1976 s71

Some of the effects of the general duty under the RRA 1976 s71 have been dealt with in detail in Chapter 2. Particular examples of its use are dealt with in separate sections.

Whether there is a duty to develop a policy on racial harassment is an extremely difficult question to answer and the only correct response at present is that it is impossible to say for certain. It can, however, be argued that a failure by an authority to develop a policy on racial harassment may be unlawful under s71 in two circumstances:

(a) where the absence of any policy means that, in practice, the authority completely disregards the need mentioned in s71 when carrying out its functions;

(b) where racial harassment is so widespread in the authority's area in a particular context, eg in schools, on the highway or on the authority's estates, that a failure to develop a policy to deal with it amounts to a complete failure to consider the need referred to in s71 (ie the problem is so acute that no reasonable authority could fail to have a racial harassment policy).

Thus, in an area in which racial harassment is prevalent, there may be a mandatory duty on the local authority to develop a policy for tackling it, which covers all departments.

Discrimination in the provision of goods, facilities and services: Race Relations Act 1976 s20

Where an authority provides goods, facilities or services to the public or a section of the public it must not discriminate on racial grounds. Discrimination by any member of staff will amount to discrimination by the authority as the employer.[1]

Discrimination against a person entails refusing or deliberately omitting to provide goods, facilities or services, either:
— at all; or
— of the same quality, in the same manner or on the same terms as they are normally provided by the authority to other members of the public or a section of the public.[2]

Direct discrimination against a person occurs when that person is treated less favourably than another person is treated or would be treated on racial grounds.[3] Indirect discrimination against a person occurs when:

(a) a condition or requirement is applied to that person which is applied equally to people of different racial groups but with which a considerably smaller proportion of that person's racial group are able to comply than the proportion of people not of that racial group; and

(b) which cannot be shown to be justifiable irrespective of the colour, race, nationality or ethnic or national origins of the person to whom it is applied; and

(c) which is detrimental to the person to whom it is applied, because s/he cannot comply with it.[4]

In the context of a racial harassment policy there are two ways in which the responsibility under s20 will affect an authority:
— where an authority intends to deliver or delivers a better service to the victims of racial harassment than to other residents; and
— where an authority intends to deliver or delivers a poorer service to the victims of racial harassment than to other residents.

1 Better service to racial harassment victims

If an authority has a policy on harassment which is not restricted to racial harassment then there will be no discrimination.

If an authority defines and operates a policy which allows any racial group to be classified as victims of racial harassment there will be no discrimination under the RRA 1976, even though the service to victims may be quicker and more satisfactory than to other residents, eg quicker repairs. Those who wished to undermine the policy might argue that it was indirectly discriminatory because the victims of nuisance or damage to property occurring as a result of racial harassment were receiving a better service than other victims of nuisance or damage to property. Authorities should have no difficulty in successfully defending the policy on the basis that it is justifiable.

If an authority either defines or operates a policy or practice which restricts racial harassment to acts committed by white people against black people, then this will amount to discrimination under the RRA 1976 unless the policy falls within the exception allowed by RRA 1976 s35 (see below).

2 The exception allowed by Race Relations Act 1976 s35

Section 35 allows authorities to provide access to facilities or services to meet the special needs of persons of a particular racial group in regard to their welfare. There can be little doubt that a racial harassment policy operates to meet special needs of racial groups. However, in order to make use of the exception, an authority must define the racial groups to whom the policy will apply and the facilities and services which are to be provided.

Racial group is defined in the RRA 1976 as "a group of persons defined by reference to colour, race, nationality or ethnic or national origins".[5] The manner in which racial groups is defined means that a person may fall into several racial groups and one racial group may comprise several other racial groups.[6] For example, "British" is a racial group defined by reference to nationality. It includes black and white people of many different ethnic origins.

3 Poorer service to racial harassment victims

Some authorities may provide a poorer service to the victims of racial harassment than to victims of nuisance or annoyance. For example, an authority may have a very clear policy on dealing with nuisances or intimidation by dogs, but it may be established that where the complainants are black, no action is taken by the authority in accordance with its policy. In these circumstances, the authority would be unlawfully discriminating under the RRA 1976 and action could be taken either by the Commission for Racial Equality or the victim. There would be no basis for arguing justification or the exception under s35.

Discrimination against job applicants and employees: Race Relations Act 1976 s4

It is unlawful for an authority to discriminate:
— in the recruitment, promotion, transfer or training of staff;
— in the way staff are offered access to benefits, facilities or services; and
— by dismissing staff or subjecting them to any other detriment.[7]

Authorities should already be wholly familiar with the requirements of the Act in relation to employment. In the racial harassment context there are two areas to be considered.

1 Racial harassment of staff by other staff

An employer is legally responsible for the acts of any members of staff within the course of their employment.[8] Where an employee is subjected to racial harassment by a colleague, the employer may therefore be discriminating against the victim.[9]

As a matter of good practice and to comply with its duty to eliminate unlawful discrimination under RRA 1976 s71 an authority must therefore have policies and procedures for preventing and dealing with racial harassment by members of its staff.

2 Positive action

The RRA 1976 allows authorities to adopt a programme of positive action in recruitment, training etc without unlawfully discriminating. This can be done in the following ways:

Genuine occupational qualifications[10]
Where the holder of a job provides persons of a racial group, with personal services promoting their welfare, and those services can most effectively be provided by a person of that racial group, then membership of that racial group will be a genuine occupational qualification for that job. The authority can discriminate in favour of a person of that racial group unless the authority already has employees of that racial group who could reasonably perform the duties of that job.[11]

Special needs: education, training or welfare[12]
Authorities may provide special facilities or services to meet the special needs of persons of a particular racial group with regard to their education, training or welfare or any ancillary benefits. This provision can justify special facilities being provided to employees from a particular racial group.

Other discriminatory training[13]
Authorities may provide special training facilities to existing employees from particular racial groups in specified jobs and at specified workplaces or encourage only employees from particular racial groups to take advantage of opportunities for doing particular work at specified workplaces.

At any time within the previous 12 months there must either have been no staff of that racial group working at the specified workplace or the number must have been small in comparison with the proportion of staff of that racial group employed by the authority or in proportion to that racial group amongst the population from which the authority normally recruits at that workplace.[14]

This provision does not allow recruitment of staff for training.[15]

The positive action provisions of the RRA 1976 can be used by authorities as follows:

(a) To recruit staff of a particular racial group to provide personal services to victims of racial harassment, eg social workers for victim support, housing welfare officers, race officers. If legal services are to be provided, it is important that they are provided directly to the individual concerned and not to the authority, since otherwise the services would not be "personal" to the victim. Legal posts involving direct advice to victims could be established under LGA 1972 s137. However, authorities might consider it more appropriate to fund a voluntary organisation to provide such services.

(b) To provide training to existing staff from particular racial groups to enable them to obtain jobs requiring particular experience or qualifications which will assist the authority in the implementation of its racial harassment policy, eg training programmes for employees to become qualified as lawyers, social workers or housing officers who will then have direct contact with victims from their own racial group.

(c) To provide training to members of particular racial groups within the area to enable them to provide services to their own community, eg in counselling or advice skills.

Health and Safety at Work Act 1974 s2

As an employer, an authority has a general duty to ensure, so far as is reasonably practicable, the health, safety and welfare at work of all its employees.

In the context of racial harassment, where perpetrators are prepared to commit acts of violence against victims, they may be prepared to act similarly against local authority officers, particularly if they perceive them as responsible for court action against them. Appropriate precautions must therefore be taken whenever members of staff are required to interview perpetrators or visit estates, to ensure that those staff are reasonably safe.

B. POWERS AVAILABLE TO ALL AUTHORITIES AND DEPARTMENTS

Employment of staff

Authorities have power to appoint "such officers as they think necessary for the proper discharge by the Authority of such of their functions as fall to be discharged by them".[16] This power needs no explanation. Essentially an authority can appoint staff to do anything which it can justify doing under its statutory powers or duties.

In the context of a racial harassment policy, additional staff can be appointed to implement some of the powers referred to in this book. For example, it might be possible to appoint:

— dog patrol officers;
— security officers;
— investigators;
— additional legal workers;
— additional caretakers; or
— additional staff for repair teams.

Power to second staff to other authorities and organisations

Staff may be seconded to other local authorities by agreement.[17] While there is no express power to second staff to other organisations, there seems little doubt that secondment can be authorised under LGA 1972 s111 if it assists the discharge of any of the authority's functions (see p15).

Staff seconded to voluntary organisations would have to be carrying out functions that they would otherwise be able to carry out directly for the authority. Two ways in which this could be funded are discussed on pp36 and 37 below.

This power is of most use when the authority has employees with particular skills whom it would be difficult for a voluntary organisation to recruit directly, eg, a social worker who could be seconded to a victim support scheme. Where the voluntary organisation can recruit employees itself with the necessary skills it can be provided with grant aid to do so (see p36).

Secondment between authorities may be useful when different authorities are responsible for different functions within the same area, eg district councils and county councils or inner London boroughs and ILEA.

Publicity (Local Government Act 1972 s142)

Authorities can make arrangements for the public to obtain information about:
— the services provided by the authority;
— the services provided by any other authority, charities, or voluntary organisations;[18] and
— the functions of the authority.

Special information centres can be set up and run by the authority or authorities can make grants to voluntary organisations to provide such information. Publicity can be produced about the services provided by the authority or other authorities and the authority can hold lectures or discussions, arrange displays or exhibitions and show films or contribute to the cost of these activities.[19]

The main use of this provision, in the context of racial harassment, is to enable an authority to publicise its racial harassment policy. This should allow the victims to find out what protection they can gain from the authority and potential perpetrators to be aware of the sanctions that the authority will use against them.

Most voluntary organisations dealing with the victims of racial harassment will provide information and part of their funding can therefore be justified under this power. It may also be possible to justify holding lectures and exhibitions and showing films as part of the housing management functions if they are aimed at discouraging tenants from committing racial harassment.

Local Government Act 1972 s137

Local authorities may incur expenditure "which in their opinion is in the interest of their area or any part of it or all or some of its inhabitants".[20] They can contribute towards expenditure by another authority under this power or make grants to any charity or voluntary organisation.[21] Expenditure cannot be made under this provision for any purpose which is authorised under any other statutory power, and the maximum expenditure under this provision is the product of a 2p rate.

The main use of s137 is in grants to voluntary organisations. Authorities can either grant aid voluntary organisations themselves or share funding with another authority. Some of the funding can be provided under other statutory powers.[22] Voluntary organisations have a key part to play in the struggle against racial harassment. Authorities can consider the use of grants under s137 for:

— self-defence and community support groups;
— victim support schemes;
— home security schemes;
— law centres, to enable them to appoint particular staff to act for victims in private prosecutions, injunctions etc;
— police monitoring groups to monitor the effect of police practices in combating racial harassment;
— organisers of volunteer minders to sit in with victims;
— escort services for victims;
— investigation groups with facilities such as video cameras, walkie-talkies, infra-red cameras etc.

Some authorities use s137 to authorise grants to individual victims for private prosecutions. This is considered further in Chapter 12. While this use can probably be justified, there are a number of points that should be made about this practice:

(a) it may be less easy to justify as being in the interests of some of the inhabitants of the area than a grant to a voluntary organisation;

(b) a grant to a voluntary organisation for the employment of a member of staff to act for victims in private prosecutions will probably be a far more economic and efficient use of resources than grants to individual victims for the use of legal services at commercial rates;

(c) if a grant is made to a voluntary organisation some of the funding may be justified using other statutory powers.[22-23]

Complaints against the police

Complaints can be made against individual police officers by any member of the public or on behalf of a member of the public with written consent.[24]

There is no statutory provision which allows a local authority to complain about police policy or practice. Authorities are also excluded from making complaints about individual police officers on their own behalf. They can only complain on behalf of a specific member of the public with that person's written consent.

Remedies against the police available to local authorities are considered further in Chapter 11.

C. ASSISTANCE TO VICTIMS

Inhabitants from the Commonwealth: Local Government Act 1966 s11

Authorities can apply to the Home Office for assistance with funding certain posts, under this provision. The Home Secretary can make payments to

> "local authorities who in his opinion are required to make special provision in the exercise of any of their functions in consequence of the presence within their areas of substantial numbers of immigrants from the Commonwealth whose language or customs differ from those of the community".[25]

The grant is 75 per cent of approved expenditure. Where only part of a post involves special provision, only a proportion of the costs of the post can be funded. The grant is only available for posts not yet filled and must involve special provision of services. Authorities can make joint applications with neighbouring authorities.

The Home Office has issued a circular which sets out the terms and conditions on which grants can be obtained.[26] Applications must contain an analysis of the need the authority intends to meet through the post. Grants can only be obtained to assist with the employment of local authority employees, but the Home Office will allow staff to be seconded to other organisations.[27]

In the context of a racial harassment policy "section 11 posts", as they are known colloquially, could include:
— racial harassment officers within a housing department;
— social workers providing victim support;
— housing welfare officers providing services to ethnic minority communities;
— interpreters;
— race advisers;
— possibly, additional lawyers appointed to process racial harassment cases.

When making an application for funding for one of such posts, statistics on the number of racial harassment cases reported to the authority and the police provide useful evidence.

Discretionary facilities to individual victims

Many of the services and facilities provided by a local authority are discretionary. Access to such services may be limited by strict criteria or by waiting lists because demand exceeds supply.

Examples are listed in later chapters of ways in which departments can assist victims with the provision of discretionary facilities. This may require a review of the way in which the resources are allocated to ensure that those suffering from racial harassment are given sufficient priority to gain access to the services. The sorts of services and facilities that might assist individual victims could include:
— after-school activites for children;
— playgroups, nurseries, parent-and-toddler groups etc during the day for pre-school children;
— drop-ins, lunch clubs etc during the day;
— youth clubs or other activities during the evenings;
— leisure or training facilities for disabled family members.

Discretionary facilities for organisations and groups

Authorities can provide a wide range of discretionary facilities to voluntary organisations and community groups. Grants and premises often form the most useful assistance. In addition, authorities have power under the Local Authorities (Goods and Services) Act 1970 to enter into agreements with Community Relations Councils, Citizens Advice Bureaux and "community associations" for:

(a) the supply of goods and materials;

(b) the provision of administrative, professional or technical services;

(c) carrying out maintenance in connection with land and buildings; and

(d) providing a driver with any vehicle provided to the organisation by the authority.[28]

Examples occur throughout the following chapters and on p36 of ways in which authorities can assist voluntary organisations. The sorts of services authorities might provide under the 1970 Act include:
— maintaining premises;
— supplying office materials;
— allowing access to printing facilities;
— connecting to one of the authority's telephone switchboards;
— providing legal advice to the organisation (but probably not to its clients);
— providing vehicles and drivers.

D. ACTION AGAINST PERPETRATORS

Power to obtain details of the occupier and owner of land

An authority may serve a notice on the occupier, owner or lessee of land or on the person who manages the land or receives any rent, requiring him or her to provide the name and address of the owner, occupier and manager within fourteen days if the authority requires the information to carry out any of its functions.[29] Failure to comply with a notice is an offence punishable by a fine of up to £2,000.

The information required by a notice under this provision will be of use to an authority to enable it to identify the person on whom notices would be served dealing with such matters as:
— removal of graffiti (see p157);
— management of houses in multiple occupation (see p123); and
— removal of rubbish (see p159).

In addition, notices could be served to help make use of the power to carry out works of graffiti removal on private land (see p51).

Resources for identifying perpetrators

It appears possible to justify devoting resources to identifying perpetrators under LGA 1972 in three ways:

(a)   when it is exercised to protect authority property;

(b)   when it is exercised to enable an authority to use one of its express powers to prosecute for a criminal offence (see Chapter 10);

(c)   when it is otherwise ancillary to one of the authority's functions.

If a policy to take action against perpetrators of racial harassment is to be effective, it is crucial that perpetrators are identified. At present this is often left to chance and the bravery of individual victims who may be prepared to give evidence. However, authorities might be able to take steps themselves to help identify the perpetrators. There are several points that must be considered:

(a)   The police are the best agency for this kind of detective work since they have the appropriate equipment and expertise. They will go to very great lengths to identify those committing crimes which they consider important.

(b)   Some private detective agencies possess similar appropriate equipment and often employ ex-police officers.

(c) The expense: this is particularly high because identifying perpetrators is inevitably a labour-intensive exercise.

The large expense coupled with the uncertainty of success, and the availability of conventional police powers and expertise, mean that authorities must be careful about devoting too many resources to the task of identifying perpetrators. Such action is easier to justify where special problems exist in one area which need to be overcome or when significant damage is being done to council property.

Circumstances where identifying perpetrators may be ancillary to one of the authority's functions include harassment:
— on the highway;
— which prevents or deters children from attending school;
— of children for whom the social services are responsible;
— on housing estates which results in increasing management problems.

The power to identify perpetrators could be used in some of the following ways:
- 24-hour watch of premises, perhaps using empty, neighbouring council premises;
- installation of video cameras;
- provision of infra-red cameras which can film at night;
- provision of tape recorders to victims, eg for telephone calls or abuse from neighbours.

Protecting council property

The Local Government Act 1972 allows authorities to take steps to protect their own property like other owners and occupiers. There are two ways in which this power might be used: preventative practical steps and legal action.

1 Preventative practical steps

Like any sensible owner or occupier of property a local authority will be justified in making alterations or improvements to increase security to its property and decrease the likelihood of damage. Replacement doors, windows, vandal-proof paint, anti-climb paint and other similar works can be carried out if racial harassment involves damage to council property.

2 Legal action

Legal action to protect council property may be justified in the following circumstances:
— action by the authority for public or private nuisance as the occupier or owner of land; and
— action for trespass as the owner of land.

Both nuisance and trespass are civil wrongs. In these cases, a claim for damages and an application for an injunction to prevent further recurrence may be made. In some circumstances it may be possible to obtain an injunction before any nuisance or trespass has occurred.[30]

In all cases it will be necessary to identify at least one perpetrator before any legal action can be taken. The effect of an injunction against individuals not named in the court action is considered on p82.

3 Private nuisance

A private nuisance is defined as an "unlawful interference with a person's use or enjoyment of land or of some right connected with the land".[31] Not every interference with use or enjoyment will be nuisance. Whether or not a court holds a particular act to be nuisance will depend upon all the circumstances including:

(a) the time at which it occurs, eg playing loud music at 3am will cause greater interference than at 3pm;

(b) where it occurs, eg playing loud music on waste land will cause less interference than in the middle of a housing estate;

(c) the manner in which it occurs, eg playing loud music may be justified for a short period when there is a party but may not if the only purpose of playing the music is to stop the neighbours sleeping;

(d) the effect of the acts on the reasonable individual, eg loud music once a year may be justified but every night until 2am would not.

In the context of racial harassment, the acts will usually be deliberate and there will be a malicious motive behind them. This is clearly a relevant factor and where interference is deliberate, a lesser degree of interference will probably qualify as a tort of nuisance.[32] In *Palmar v Loder* a perpetual injunction was granted against a person who deliberately caused a noise nuisance by shouting, banging, laughing and ringing door bells.[33]

Who is liable for a private nuisance?
The extent to which a landlord is liable for nuisance committed by its tenants is considered in Chapter 6. The person committing a nuisance is liable for it. It appears that it does not matter where the nuisance originates from, eg it can be committed from the street or from the common parts of a housing estate.[34]

When the nuisance originates from private premises, it seems likely that the occupier is liable for nuisance committed by any visitors, guests, lodgers or family members in the premises unless s/he takes reasonable steps to prevent the nuisance occurring once s/he has knowledge of it.[35] A tenant, sub-tenant or owner occupier will be the occupier for these purposes.

When can the authority take action?
The authority can take action when it is the occupier of premises and suffers some damage from a nuisance being committed from outside the premises. For example, the education authority is the occupier of school premises

and can take action for nuisance committed from neighbouring premises or the highway, eg harassment of pupils entering or leaving school. Similarly, the housing authority is the occupier of the common parts of any housing estate or block of local authority flats and can take action for nuisances committed either from one of the tenanted flats or from the highway adjoining the estate or block, eg the dumping of rubbish or excreta on the stairs from a flat.

Where the authority owns but does not occupy premises, it can take action only when some damage is done to its own interest in the property. This will arise when there is some physical damage to the structure of the building, eg putting burning paper through the letter-box of a council flat, as this could cause major damage to the structure.

4 Trespass

To damage property, to enter without authority or to exceed the authority to enter is a trespass.[36] Action may be taken by the authority when it is the occupier of land or the owner of a building when there is some physical damage to the structure. By restricting or withholding the permission given to a person to enter its premises, an authority may obtain a right to take legal action for trespass.

Generally a person has no right to enter private property unless s/he has permission. Implied permission may exist in practice, eg to the common parts of a housing estate. Tenants and visitors to tenants are in a special position which is considered in Chapter 6. The phrase "the public" is intended to exclude such people.

Authorities can restrict the extent of implied permission to enter their property either by informing a particular individual that s/he has no permission to enter or by informing the public at large that permission to enter is for particular purposes only. An authority could therefore erect notices around housing estates stating that the estate's common parts could only be used by the public for particular purposes, eg visiting tenants, and that any officer of the authority can require any member of the public to leave at any time. Furthermore, the notice could state that the permission to enter does not extend to committing any act of racial harassment and any person doing so is trespassing.

An example of the use of the law of trespass to obtain an injunction against a perpetrator of racial harassment is in Appendix 4.

The law of trespass could be used in the following ways:
— keeping members of the public, who come only to racially harass tenants, off housing estates;
— taking action against perpetrators for damage to authority property, eg graffiti or broken doors or glass of victims' homes;
— preventing harassment by trespassers on school premises including driveways, playing fields and other areas owned by the education authority.

Trespass to the highway
The public right to use the highway is a right to use it in a reasonable manner. Any other use may amount to a trespass against the owner. The surface of almost all highways, with the exception of trunk roads, is owned by the local highway authority,[37] which can therefore take action for trespass when the use of the highway is unreasonable. Unreasonable use will include any meeting or group of people collecting in order to harass other people, or individuals throwing stones from the highway.

Other powers in relation to unreasonable use of the highway are considered below.

Claiming compensation in criminal proceedings

Under the Powers of Criminal Courts Act 1973 s35, authorities can seek compensation orders from the magistrates' or Crown Courts for any property damaged as a result of criminal damage or arson for which a perpetrator is convicted. Details of the loss must be provided to the prosecution who should be asked to inform the court of the authority's request for compensation.

See p166 for further details.

Public nuisances

It has already been said that an authority has power to apply for an injunction to prevent the commission of a public nuisance. It may also prosecute using the powers provided by s222 if the conditions discussed in Chapter 3 are satisfied, since any public nuisance is a crime.

A public nuisance has been defined as a nuisance which inflicts damage, injury or inconvenience on all the members of a class of people who come within the sphere or neighbourhood of its operation.[38] The essential element of a public nuisance is that a class of people rather than an individual is affected.

It is not possible to quantify the number of individuals that must be affected to constitute a public nuisance, and this will be a question of fact in each case. It has been suggested that a public nuisance exists where the number of people affected is so wide that it would not be reasonable to expect one person, in the absence of special damage, to take responsibility for taking proceedings. A single act may amount to a public nuisance in some cases.[39]

Examples of acts which might be public nuisances provided they are directed at a number of people and not just at one or two are:
— intimidation of children leaving school on their way home;
— intimidation of adults or children leaving a housing estate, including spitting, shouting, abuse, stone-throwing;
— use of a dog against those on a housing estate.

Highways Act 1980 s130

The highway authorities have a duty "to assert and protect the rights of the public to the use and enjoyment of any highway for which they are the highway authority".[40] In addition, all local authorities have the power to assert and protect the right of the public to the use and enjoyment of any highway in their area, even if they are not the highway authority[41] and a duty to prevent any obstruction of the highway which is prejudicial to their area.[42] This will include the ability to act to prevent a public nuisance on the highway.

Obstruction of the highway is not necessarily limited to a fixed physical obstruction, but extends to any unreasonable use of the highway. Public nuisance on the highway has been defined as "any wrongful act or ommission upon or near a highway, whereby the public are prevented from freely, safely and conveniently passing along the highway".[43] Because of the public interest in maintaining safe passage along the highway it does not appear to be necessary for a class of people to be affected.

The reported cases on public nuisance relating to the highway have been limited to situations where the highway has been obstructed in some way. These usually amount to physical obstructions, such as parked vehicles, scaffolding or holes in the road. There does not appear to have been a reported case as to whether acts such as spitting, insults, jostling, following and general intimidation can amount to a public nuisance, but if the definition referred to above, involving the prevention of the public from "freely safely and conveniently passing along the highway", is adopted, then it should be possible to argue that racial harassment of the nature described would amount to a public nuisance and therefore be actionable.

Whatever the position under s222, all local authorities have powers under the Highways Act 1980 to take proceedings to protect the public right to use the highway.[44] ILEA is not a local authority for these purposes and has no powers to take action to protect the right to use the highway. It may, however, be able to take action in private nuisance if a school is affected by acts committed on the adjacent highway (see p41).

In addition to the power to take civil action, there are many offences relating to improper use of the highway, most of which are arrestable (see Chapter 11 and Appendix 6).

In the following instances, action by a local authority might be justified, even though only one or two people are affected by them:

— attacks from the highway against homes including those which are owner occupied, eg dumping excreta, stone-throwing, abuse or simply gathering outside in an intimidatory fashion;[45]
— intimidation of school children on their way to and from school along the highway, eg bullying, insulting, spitting;
— intimidation of adults using shops or other communal facilities;
— standing outside schools issuing racist leaflets.

The powers relating to highways can be used to protect owner occupiers and private tenants, who almost always live immediately adjoining the highway.

In the case of council tenants living on estates the local authority is usually the owner of the land forming the estate roadways and walkways which are not public highways. The authority therefore has powers in relation to an action for trespass and is in a contractual relationship with perpetrators if they live on the same housing estate. Where harassment is carried out from the highway there may be a public nuisance for which the authority can take action.

Power to make byelaws

There are many statutory powers to make byelaws.[46] London borough councils and district councils may make byelaws "for the good rule and government of the whole or any part of the district or borough as the case may be and for the prevention and suppression of nuisances" under LGA 1972 s235.

Other powers to make byelaws depend on the particular function of the authority in question and will not be considered here. The most important in the context of racial harassment are those relating to open spaces and housing. For byelaws covering open spaces the same points as are made below will apply to byelaws made under these other powers. Byelaws relating to housing are dealt with in Chapter 6.

All byelaws must be confirmed by the Secretary of State for the Environment. Model byelaws are published by the Department of the Environment (DoE). Although authorities are not obliged to adopt or use the model, any new or additional byelaws will need the Secretary of State's consent, which is not automatically given. It is therefore probably more appropriate for amendments to byelaws to be drawn up by local authority associations in conjunction with the DoE. The procedure for making all byelaws is the same and is set out in the LGA 1972.[47]

The courts have set down certain criteria which must be satisfied if byelaws are to be held valid:

(a) they must be reasonable;[48]

(b) they must be consistent with the general law and must not cover an area already precisely covered by statute;[49]

(c) they must be certain;[50]

(d) it must be within the powers of the authority to make the byelaw (see p6).

Breach of byelaws is a criminal offence. The penalties are not very great and only involve small fines (see p177). In cases of emergency or where there is deliberate and flagrant flouting of the law, or there is likely to be irreparable damage, an authority can consider seeking an injunction to prevent a breach of byelaws (see p23).

Consideration could be given to including the following matters in any byelaws made by an authority or in widening the existing byelaws used by many local authorities:
— the control of dogs;
— the dumping of rubbish;
— the control of children;
— shouting, racist abuse, throwing of stones, spitting and fouling by dogs.

A byelaw prohibiting racial harassment would be invalid due to uncertainty unless a detailed definition of racial harassment were included. Since byelaws are generally reserved for minor breaches of the law, a byelaw to prohibit racial harassment would be inappropriate as it would suggest that racial harassment is a trivial matter. It is probably therefore more desirable to consider additional byelaws only to cover some of the less serious acts which might form part of a campaign of racial harassment.

Destruction of dogs: Dogs Act 1871 s2

Any person can make a complaint to a magistrates' court that a dog is dangerous and is not kept under proper control.[51] There is no express power given to an authority to make an application under the Act. However, such a power would be conferred by LGA 1972 s111 where a dog is:
— causing a general nuisance to tenants and represents a housing management problem;
— attacking children at one of the authority's schools;
— attacking the employees of the authority.

The court has power to order that the dog should be destroyed or be kept under proper control. If it is not then kept under control a further application can be made for it to be destroyed.

Dogs are often used as an instrument of harassment. An application to destroy a dog has been successfully used by one local authority; the owner controlled the dog which was not destroyed.

Two points should be borne in mind:

(a) The fact that a family runs the risk of losing a pet may be an extremely powerful weapon in the fight to prevent racial harassment by that family. Warnings which might otherwise be ignored may be effective if a dog's destruction is threatened.

(b) An authority must be wary of negative publicity generated by dog-owners within the borough and must not be seen to be persecuting dogs when it is the owners who are to blame.

Withholding discretionary facilities

The extent to which authorities may withhold discretionary facilities from organisations which do not comply with certain requirements and from individual perpetrators was discussed in Chapter 2. Most departments and authorities provide discretionary facilities in addition to services which they are obliged to provide by statute. The points made in Chapter 2 and below will therefore be of general application.

As well as their power to withhold facilities completely, authorities have power to impose conditions on grants or permission to use their premises.[52] These powers can be used to exert additional control.

In practice, most authorities wish to keep their powers in reserve and try to persuade all those organisations that use their facilities that every possible step must be taken to ensure that groups provide facilities to all and take active steps to prevent racial harassment. Genuine commitment to these principles will be far more effective than reluctant agreement under pressure.

General requirements applicable to all organisations receiving authority services may be easier to justify than attempts to take action against particular organisations. For example, a general policy might be adopted that tenants' associations will not be provided with facilities unless:

(a) their membership is open to all;
(b) they genuinely encourage all tenants to take part in their activities; and
(c) they can show that the committee is truly representative of the estate as a whole.

Employees may be responsible for racial harassment. Authorities should persuade their staff-side that the commitment of the union branch to combating racial harassment is crucial to the effectiveness of their policy. Where branches refuse to acknowledge the problem, or are positively antagonistic, the authority may wish to consider its position in relation to recognition of that branch for negotiating purposes.

Facilities for individuals
It has already been explained in Chapter 2 that powers are not given to authorities as a method of social control. Withholding facilities from an individual as a form of punishment may therefore not be justified. In addition, an authority may have a duty to provide alternative facilities.

Examples of facilities to individuals that might be withheld on the grounds suggested in Chapter 2 are:

(a) Facilities for playgroups, parent-and-toddler groups, day centres or creches run by the authority. If the facilities require active involvement by an adult then the authority may decide it is in the interests of others using the service that any adult perpetrator of racial harassment be barred. Where appropriate, consideration should probably still be given to whether the child can attend without the parent.

(b) Home help or meals on wheels services to perpetrators where black staff are racially harassed while carrying out their duties.
(c) Suspending or expelling a pupil from school or youth group because s/he is reponsible for racial harassment within the school or group. This would be in the interests of discipline.
(d) Removing residents from hostels provided by the authority who are licensees and are perpetrating racial harassment.

Authorities cannot refuse to make meeting halls available to political parties fielding candidates at an election whatever the policies promoted by that political party.[53]

Use of suppliers of goods and services

All authorities are major customers for services and goods supplied by others. They therefore have considerable financial muscle available to persuade suppliers to adopt policies that will discourage discrimination and tackle racial harassment.

Authorities may make use only of suppliers of goods and services who operate equal opportunities employment policies. This appears justified by RRA 1976 s71 though Government proposals in the Local Government Bill before Parliament in late 1987 will restrict the ability of local authorities to use these criteria when choosing suppliers of goods and services.

However, where the services concerned are provided for individuals who are placed with an organisation by the authority, it is legitimate, as part of the discharge of the authority's function, to ensure that the individuals concerned will not become the victims of racial harassment. It is legitimate to choose facilities where the authority is satisfied that the management will take action to prevent racial harassment.

E. INTERVENTION IN THE PRIVATE SECTOR

Conditions on the use of land

Whenever an authority sells or allows the use of its land it may impose conditions on future use. This power is provided by LGA 1972 s111 and the use of the authority's discretion must be exercised, bearing in mind the need referred to in RRA 1976 s71.

Authorities have powers to bind future owners of property which they sell in addition to those possessed by other organisations and individuals. As a general rule, a positive covenant by a purchaser will be unenforceable against any subsequent owner, but local authorities can enforce positive covenants against all future owners.[54] A negative or restrictive covenant imposes an obligation on an owner not to do certain things, eg commit a nuisance. A positive covenant imposes an obligation to do certain things, eg remove graffiti within 24 hours.

A list of those with whom authorities are likely to enter into a legal relationship was given in Chapter 2 on p16. Many of those will be renting, buying or hiring land or premises owned by the authority. In Chapter 5 detailed consideration is given to conditions in tenancy agreements issued by housing departments and in Chapter 6 to the imposition of covenants in transfers under the "right to buy".

It is not only the housing department which allows the use of its land; contracts and leases will be entered into by an authority carrying out a variety of functions involving every department. It is legitimate to impose similar covenants in every hiring agreement, licence, lease or transfer to those which the authority imposes on its council tenants and former tenants who purchase their homes. Covenants on tenants and hirers could require them to be responsible for any racial harassment carried out by anyone on the premises and thereby impose a responsibility on them to deal with it. If they did not do so they would risk termination of their right to use the premises. Where premises are being leased or sold to an organisation which itself proposes to license or sublet, a covenant may require the organisation to include a clause on racial harassment in any licence or sublease.

Legal departments of local authorities are familiar with covenants in transfers of properties bought under the "right to buy". If covenants concerning racial harassment are not already imposed in freehold transactions, they are used in leases of flats and can be reproduced in freehold transfers. In addition to "nuisance or annoyance", such clauses could include the words "harassment, whether racial or otherwise" as suggested in the model tenancy clause in Appendix 1.

Consultation

There can be little doubt that authorities may consult as widely as they wish before reaching decisions under their ancillary powers in LGA 1972 s111, and as a matter of good practice many do so. There are two important instances when authorities have a duty to consult. These are:

(a) with tenants on housing management matters (see p96);
(b) with industrial and commercial ratepayers before setting a rate.[55]

Subject to the statutory duties to consult, the process of consultation may be seen as providing a discretionary facility to the individuals and groups consulted. They can therefore withhold such facilities in appropriate circumstances; an authority can always justify withdrawing from a consultation process with any individual or group believed to be unrepresentative.

Unless the groups consulted about particular issues are truly representative of all racial groups the authority itself may not be complying with its duty under RRA s71. Many tenants' associations have few black members. An authority which failed to make arrangements for black tenants in its area to be consulted might risk an action for failing to comply with its duty under RRA 1976 s71. If the consultation process affected allocation of resources, there might also, in practice, be unlawful discrimination. Chambers of commerce may have as members few businesses owned or run by black people. Authorities may be obliged to have some mechanism for involving such businesses in the rate consultation process.

Grants and grant conditions

Authorities have a variety of powers to give grants to organisations, usually voluntary organisations providing similar services to the authority. The powers to give grants under LGA 1972 ss137 and 142 have already been considered see pp35 and 36. Where organisations in receipt of grants are employing staff and/or providing services to the public, RRA 1976 s71 will authorise grant conditions which require equal opportunities employment policies and practices and equal opportunity in service delivery.

If activities are provided at which racial harassment might occur, s71 should authorise requirements that effective policies and practices be operated by the organisation to deal with any people using their facilities who are responsible for racial harassment, usually by withdrawing the facilities.

Organisations may provide facilities which authorities wish to make available to victims. Conditions may therefore be imposed requiring the organisations to provide the facilities to the authority's nominees in certain circumstances. As an incentive for the organisations to do so, some additional funding or exchange facility may be provided by the authority.

In practice, authorities will want to persuade organisations of the importance of certain policies and practices for tackling discrimination and racial harassment. A balance must be struck between interfering to an unacceptable degree in the management of an independent organisation and effective implementation of the authority's racial harassment policy. Nevertheless, conditions may be imposed if necessary, for instance:

(a) Many authorities grant aid housing associations. They may make it a condition of doing so that an association has a policy for dealing with racial harassment by its tenants and providing nomination rights to the authority for rehousing victims.

(b) An authority might wish to use the services of a grant aided community transport service to provide transport for victims to and from school, shops or work. It might agree to provide an extra minibus.

(c) An authority might require a grant aided law centre to act for victims in private prosecutions (subject to the solicitors' practice rules). It could fund an additional staff member.

Works on derelict land

Authorities have power to carry out works on land if it appears to be derelict, neglected or unsightly.[56] Works are authorised for the purpose of reclaiming or improving the land or of enabling it to be brought into use. The power is exercisable by any authority except in a national park where it is restricted to the local planning authority.

The power is exercisable on privately owned land as well as on the authority's land. On land which is not owned by the authority, it is necessary first to obtain the consent of all the persons interested in the land.

The authority itself does not have to do the work on other's land; it can make arrangements for the work to be done by someone else and fix the terms for doing so. In addition, the authority may reach an agreement about management of the land with the persons interested and fix the terms of that agreement.

People interested in the land will include owners, mortgagees (eg building societies and banks), those with leases and tenancies and those who have rights over the land, eg right of way. Where persons interested in the land refuse consent to the authority carrying out works, it may be possible to require them to take action themselves (see p157).

The major use of this section is to remove racist graffiti. Graffiti is certainly "unsightly" and therefore an authority has power to carry out work of removal. This provision allows an authority to set up a procedure for removing graffiti from land in the private sector, eg private rented or owner occupied accommodation, land owned by public utilities or land adjoining the street.

1 Land owned by the local authority

This provision adds nothing to the power which authorities possess in relation to land which they already own.[57] Land owned by the authority includes land that is let to tenants. In the case of secure tenants under the HA 1985, the authority will possess an implied right to enter to carry out repairs.[58] It can also reserve the right to enter to remove graffiti by an express clause in its tenancy agreement if it chooses to do so. Leases of commercial premises owned by the local authority may contain clauses either requiring access to be given to remove graffiti or requiring the lessee to remove graffiti within a specified period.

2 Land previously owned by the authority

Slightly different considerations apply when land has been sold. The authority may reserve rights to itself in the transfer of title as well as imposing covenants on the purchaser. Reservations in such transfers frequently include the authority's right to enter in order to carry out repairs of neighbouring property. Similarly, it might reserve a right of entry for the purposes of removing graffiti on the land that has been sold. Alternatively, a covenant could impose a positive obligation on the purchaser to remove graffiti within a specified time.[59]

Further points on the use of covenants in transfers of land to former tenants under the "right to buy" are in Chapter 6.

3 Other land

Where a person has no legal relationship with the authority, the authority must consider whether it wishes to exercise any of its powers under this provision and, if so, what incentive it can offer to people to utilise its services. It could offer free graffiti removal to owner occupiers and private tenants.

Obtaining consent from all persons interested
Authorities can obtain the names and addresses of the occupier, owner, mortgagee and tenants of land and the person who receives the rent and the extent of their interest by serving a notice on any one of those people under the Local Government (Miscellaneous Provisions) Act 1976 s16 (see p39). Usually the occupier will be the easiest person to identify and serve with the notice.

If an authority is proposing to make widespread use of its powers under this provision it is advisable to seek general permission from all major building societies and banks in the area so that delays do not occur while permission is obtained in individual cases. Since it is in the lenders' interests that the land is kept neat and tidy it should be possible to obtain co-operation.

It would also be advisable to obtain general permission from major landlords in the area. This might include local housing associations, housing trusts and co-operatives. If landlords and building societies are not prepared to give blanket permission they may at least be prepared to give general permission in respect of particular premises on the first occasion this provision is used.

Where owners and occupiers are obstructive, the authority may be able to persuade them to give consent by threatening action under the Town and Country Planning Act 1971 s65 (see p157).

Some landlords, eg local housing associations, may prefer to remove the graffiti themselves under arrangements with the authority, which should also provide for rapid response times. This provision allows such arrangements to be made.

Agreements with owners of land adjoining highways
There are often certain street corners, walls, or bridges within the area that are frequently daubed with graffiti. Authorities can make permanent arrangements with the owners of these walls or bridges regarding graffiti removal. For example, an authority could make arrangements with British Rail that whenever a certain bridge is daubed with racist graffiti this can be removed by the authority. The authority may have the appropriate equipment for removing this type of graffiti, eg lorries usually used for mending street lights. Authorities may consider asking owners, whose walls adjoin the highway, for permission to use particular kinds of paint on their

walls which will not be so susceptible to being daubed or which will allow removal more easily in the future.

Charging for the service
An authority clearly has power to charge for removal of graffiti carried out under this provision, if it wishes to do so. It may charge landlords such as housing associations, co-operatives or large public utilities, eg British Rail, but be less inclined to charge owner occupiers, small shopkeepers or the landlords of private rented premises since the charges may be a disincentive for the person concerned to give the authority permission to carry out the work.

This provision is not specifically limited to graffiti, although this is its most likely use. Any similar form of dumping or damage to property which results in the property being "derelict, neglected or unsightly" entitles an authority to exercise its powers under this provision.

Works on any land: Local Authorities (Land) Act 1963 s2

In addition to the power referred to in the previous section, authorities have power to carry out any works on land "for the benefit or improvement of their area". No express limitation is put on the scope of the power and it would therefore appear to authorise works on land which is not owned by the authority. The only limitation is that if the land is owned by some other person, the authority must have permission from that person to carry out the works, otherwise there will be a trespass. However, there is no need to obtain permission from a mortgagee, eg a building society or bank.

In some ways this provision is similar to that in the previous section, but work under this provision is not restricted in the same way. This provision can be used to justify preventative works which will result in benefit to the area if they prevent future problems with graffiti. Fencing derelict land which is used as a site from which people are racially harassed also results in a benefit to the area.

Licensing

In some circumstances, a local authority is the licensing authority for particular activities.[60] Even if it is not the authority issuing the licence, a local authority may make representations to the licensing authority as to whether the licence should be granted.

There are three important examples where control can be exercised, pub licences, licences for football clubs issued by the magistrates' courts and music and dance licences which are issued by London borough councils and district councils.

1 Pub licences[61]
It is the local magistrates' court which decides whether to grant licences

for public houses. Environmental Health Officers from authorities frequently check pub premises for public health purposes when a licence is being applied for or renewed. However, there is no reason why the authority's involvement should be limited to such narrowly defined public health purposes.

Authorities have other responsibilities and are property owners. They are responsible for the highway and for dealing with nuisances throughout their area. Users of the pub may be racially harassing local tenants or local children attending the authority's schools and may be damaging authority property. In most cases authorities should have little difficulty justifying their appearance before licensing justices to oppose the issuing of pub licences using their powers under LGA 1972 ss111 and 222.

An authority has no power to seek the revocation of a pub licence in the middle of the year but all licences are renewed annually. The rules relating to pub licensing require the local authority to be informed of any application for a licence.[62] Notice of any opposition to the renewal of a pub licence must be given.[63]

It is worth noting that opposition by the local police to the grant of a licence will add considerable force to any opposition by the authority. Decisions about opposition to pub licences by the police are often made at a very junior level. Where there is significant evidence of harassment and illegal conduct by customers of a pub and the police do not intend to oppose the licence application, the authority might decide to make use of press publicity, its local MPs and pressure on more senior police officers. Local people are likely to give their strong support to measures to tackle harassment and nuisances from pub customers.

2 Licences for drinking at football clubs

Special licences are needed for bars to be open at football matches played by the major clubs between two hours before the start of the match and one hour afterwards. Magistrates cannot grant a licence unless satisfied that it is "not likely to be detrimental to the orderly conduct or safety of spectators".[64] Any bar must not be within sight of the match. Where there are problems of racial harassment by football supporters which are exacerbated by alcohol, authorities may wish to oppose the grant of such licences, which, unlike pub licences, can be revoked by magistrates at any time.[65]

3 Music and dance licences

District councils and London borough councils are responsible for the granting of licences for public music and dance.[66] The powers relating to licensing authorise the authority to grant licences on "such terms and conditions and subject to such restrictions as may be specified".[67] This power must be exercised in accordance with the provisions of administrative law (see Chapter 2). Where licences are granted, it is possible for pubs to obtain extensions of drinking hours to cover the period for which the music and dance licence operates.[68] Some pubs obtain extensions in this way until 2am.

The most likely use of these provisions is to refuse the grant of a music and dance licence to an organisation or pub which is used by perpetrators who carry out racial harassment after closing hours.

If a licence is granted, an authority might impose conditions relating to the conduct of customers on the premises. This could include a requirement that anyone committing an act of racial harassment on the premises is removed immediately. RRA 1976 s71 would appear to authorise such a provision.

A licensing authority may also bring into force licensing powers relating to open air music. The extent of the conditions that can then be imposed is restricted.[69] Where conditions are imposed, it is an offence to commit a breach of the conditions or be responsible for a breach. If there is a conviction for breach of condition the authority may revoke the licence.

1 RRA 1976 s32.
2 Ibid s20(1).
3 Ibid sl(1)(a).
4 Ibid sl(1)(b).
5 Ibid s3(1).
6 Ibid s3(2).
7 Ibid s4.
8 Ibid s32.
9 See *Strathclyde RC v Porcelli* [1986] IRLR 134 and *Balgobin and Francis v LB Tower Hamlets* [1987] IRLR 401. See also Palmer and Poulton *Sex and Race Discrimination in Employment* Legal Action Group, 1987.
10 RRA 1976 s5(2)(d). For further details see *Positive Action and Equal Opportunities in Employment* Commission for Racial Equality, 1985.
11 See RRA 1976 s5(4) for the exact requirements.
12 Ibid s35.
13 Ibid s38.
14 Ibid s38(2).
15 *Hughes and Others v LB Hackney* Industrial Tribunal Case 15898/85/LC/B.
16 LGA 1972 s112.
17 Ibid s113.
18 Ibid s142.
19 Ibid s142(2).
20 Ibid s137(1).
21 Ibid s137(2) and (3).
22-23 See, eg, p35 under "Publicity" above; LGA 1972 s142.
24 Police and Criminal Evidence Act 1984 s84(4).
25 Local Government Act 1966 s11.
26 The current Circular is 72/1986 in force from 1 October 1986.
27 See Circular 72/1986 para 21.
28 Local Authorities (Goods and Services) Act 1970 and Local Authorities (Goods and Services) Public Body Order 1972 SI No 852.
29 Local Government (Miscellaneous Provisions) Act 1976 s16.
30 *Hooper v Rogers* [1974] 3 All ER 417, CA.
31 See generally *Halsbury's Laws* 4th ed, Vol 34 para 301 et seq.
32 *Hollywood Silver Fox Farm Ltd v Emmett* [1936] 2 KB 468 and *Christie v Davey* [1893] 1 Ch 316.

33 [1962] CLY 2233.
34 *Esso Petroleum Co Ltd v Southport Corp* [1956] AC 218 and see *Hubbard v Pitt* [1975] 3 All ER 1, CA.
35 *Smeaton v Ilford Corp* [1954] Ch 450 and *Goldman v Hargrave* [1967] 1 AC 645.
36 *Hillen and Pettigrew v ICI (Alakali) Ltd* [1936] AC 65.
37 Highways Act 1980 s263 and see *Tithe Redemption Commission v Runcorn UDC* [1954] Ch 383, CA.
38 See *Halsbury's Laws* 4th edn, Vol 34 para 305.
39 Per Lord Denning in *A-G v PYA Quarries Ltd* [1957] 1 All ER 894 at 902.
40 Highways Act 1980 s130(1).
41 Ibid s130(2).
42 Ibid s130(3).
43 *Jacobs v London CC* [1950] AC 361 at 375 per Lord Simonds.
44 Highways Act 1980 s130(5).
45 See *Hubbard v Pitt* n34. This may also be an offence under the Conspiracy and Protection of Property Act 1875, see p182.
46 A list can be found at the back of *Local Government Encyclopedia* published by Sweet & Maxwell.
47 LGA 1972 s236.
48 *Kruse v Johnson* [1898] 2 QB 91.
49 LGA 1972 s235(3) and see, eg, *Morrissey v Galer* [1955] 1 WLR 110.
50 *Kruse v Johnson* n48.
51 Dogs Act 1871 s2.
52 See pp48 and 50.
53 Representation of the People Act 1983 s95.
54 Local Government (Miscellaneous Provisions) Act 1982 s33.
55 Rates Act 1984 s13.
56 National Parks and Access to the Countryside Act 1949 s89(2) as amended by the Derelict Land Act 1982 s3.
57 By virtue, eg, of LGA 1972 s111.
58 Landlord and Tenant Act 1985 s11(6).
59 Local Government (Miscellaneous Provisions) Act 1982 s33. The covenant must be expressed to be one to which this section refers.
60 For the full list of licensing powers of local authorities see *Local Government Encyclopedia* published by Sweet & Maxwell.
61 See generally the Licensing Act 1964.
62 Licensing Act 1964 Sch 2 para 1.
63 Ibid s7.
64 Sporting Events (Control of Alcohol etc) Act 1985 s3(6); Sports Grounds and Sporting Events (Designation) Order 1985 SI No 1151.
65 Sporting Events (Control of Alcohol etc) Act 1985 s3(5).
66 Local Government (Miscellaneous Provisions) Act 1982 s1 and the London Government Act 1963 Sch 12 as amended by the Local Government Act 1985 Sch 8 para 1.
67 Local Government (Miscellaneous Provisions) Act 1982 s1 and Sch 1.
68 Licensing Act 1964 s77.
69 Local Government (Miscellaneous Provisions) Act 1982 Sch 1 para 4(4).

CHAPTER FIVE
Civil Proceedings

Local authorities have considerable opportunities to combat racial harassment committed by their tenants, through conditions imposed in their tenancy agreements and through taking action in the civil courts. The grounds on which possession orders and injunctions may be sought are discussed. Procedures involved in civil proceedings are explained and suggestions made for tactics to increase the likelihood of success.

All the points made in this chapter apply equally to certain registered housing associations, housing trusts and housing co-operatives.[1]

A. THE TENANCY AGREEMENT

The status of the tenancy agreement

The tenancy agreement is a contract between the housing authority and its tenant and can be enforced like any other contract by a claim for damages and an injunction against the tenant.

The terms of the tenancy agreement

Certain terms are implied into tenancy agreements with which we need not be concerned.[2] It is certainly within the powers of a housing authority to decide what terms and conditions it wishes to include in its tenancy agreements to prevent racial harassment.[3] Breach of any express term of the tenancy agreement may provide a basis for obtaining an order for possession as well as an injunction against the tenant. Specimen clauses covering the most important described below, are in Appendix 1.

Additional clauses to be considered

1 A clause prohibiting nuisance or annoyance (Appendix 1 clauses 1 and 2)
Most local authorities have a clause in their tenancy agreements prohibiting nuisance or annoyance to other tenants. In any event, a possession order can be obtained on the basis of nuisance and/or annoyance to neighbours by the tenant or those residing with the tenant whether or not there is an express clause (see below). The advantage of an express clause is that it can extend the statutory prohibition as follows:

(a) to widen the categories of people for whose conduct the tenant is liable, to include not only members of the family living at the premises but also visitors, other family members, lodgers and sub-tenants;

(b) to cover nuisance or annoyance caused to those visiting or staying temporarily with neighbours;

(c) to define neighbours more clearly, including local owner occupiers and private sector tenants;

(d) to extend the definition of neighbours to include a wider area than might be included in the statutory definition;

(e) expressly to include nuisance or annoyance to neighbours wherever they may be, eg children on their way to school.

It is not clear how far it is possible to extend the definition of neighbours or to regulate conduct away from the premises in question. Tenancy clauses are included under an authority's housing management functions. While it can be argued that it is legitimate to include clauses prohibiting nuisance or annoyance against owner occupiers or private tenants living nearby and against council tenants wherever they may be, it is difficult to justify a clause prohibiting nuisance or annoyance to any resident of the borough wherever s/he may be.

2 A clause prohibiting racial harassment (Appendix 1 clauses 1 and 2)
Almost without exception, acts of racial harassment will fall within the meaning of the phrase "nuisance or annoyance" and will therefore be covered by a clause on nuisance or annoyance. Racial harassment by a tenant or any person living with the tenant can therefore already form the basis for a possession action under the grounds set out in the HA 1985, even if no express clause on racial harassment is included in the tenancy agreement (see p63). Nevertheless, there are advantages in including a clause prohibiting racial harassment and these are considered below.

3 A clause covering nuisance by dogs (Appendix 1 clause 6)
Tenants will usually be held responsible for nuisance committed by dogs. However, it is useful to set out clearly the sort of behaviour by dogs or their owners which the authority will not accept since this will improve the chances of obtaining an order for possession if such behaviour occurs (see p65).
The tenancy agreement can include clauses:
— making the tenant responsible for nuisance caused by dogs owned by the tenant or any family members or visitors;
— prohibiting dogs fouling the common parts or other premises on the estate;
— prohibiting dogs from running loose on the estate or being on the common parts without a lead;

— reserving to the authority the right to require a tenant to get rid of a dog or keep the dog off the estate if it is causing a nuisance or is used to harass other tenants and their visitors;
— specifically prohibiting tenants from allowing their dogs to urinate or defecate except in specified areas;
— requiring the tenant to clean up if the dog urinates or defecates elsewhere or pay the cost of doing so.

It is probably more useful to adopt the procedure suggested in Appendix 1 and prohibit tenants from keeping dogs without the landlord's consent. Consent is then only granted if the tenant agrees to abide by rules relating to the keeping of dogs covering the matters referred to above. Since these rules do not form part of the tenancy agreement they can be altered without following the procedure required for altering tenancy clauses (see p61).

4 A clause making the tenant expressly responsible for acts of others (Appendix 1 clause 5)

Without an express clause the tenant may only be held responsible for nuisance or annoyance committed by members of the family living with him or her. The tenancy agreement can include a clause making the tenant responsible for children whether adult or not, other family members, visitors, lodgers and sub-tenants. Such a clause will make it more reasonable for possession to be granted if there is nuisance or harassment by family members as the tenant has had notice that s/he will be held responsible.

5 A clause covering nuisance or harassment from people attending parties

If the clauses already referred to are used, the tenant will be responsible for guests at any party. This will include those arriving without invitation if they are then admitted.

The tenancy agreement could include clauses:
— requiring parties to finish at a certain time or for music to cease at a particular time;
— making tenants specifically responsible for ensuring that guests leave quietly and without committing racial harassment or other nuisance.

6 A clause covering breach of byelaws (Appendix 1 clause 3)

Breach of byelaws covering a housing estate will be a criminal offence. A clause in the tenancy agreement prohibiting a breach will mean that the authority can seek possession or an injunction in the event of a breach by the tenant. The tenancy agreement could include a clause making the tenant responsible for breaches of byelaws by family members or visitors.

7 A clause prohibiting graffiti or damage to council property (Appendix 1 clause 4)

Damage to council property is a criminal offence. A clause in the tenancy agreement prohibiting graffiti or damage to council property will mean that the authority can seek possession or an injunction in the event of a breach and can hold the tenant responsible for breaches by others.

8 A clause covering the use of the common parts

Conduct on the common parts may be partly covered by byelaws. However, authorities might wish to impose additional restrictions which would not be appropriate for inclusion in byelaws.

The tenancy agreement could include clauses:

— restricting the grant of a right of way over the common parts to pedestrian access direct to the property rented and prohibiting access to other parts except with express permission;

— providing only a licence for tenants to use other common parts and reserving to the authority the right to withdraw permission for use by the tenant or his or her family and visitors.

If the authority grants only the bare minimum rights over the common parts, it can then withhold permission for the tenant or his or her family or visitors to go anywhere else on the estate. If they do so they become trespassers (see below).

The ability to use the law of trespass to take action against perpetrators on housing estates is considered further on p113 and an example of such use is given in Appendix 4 where it is used in conjunction with possession proceedings.

9 Clauses on other rights associated with the tenancy

If authorities wish to be able to withdraw facilities from perpetrators such as garages, parking spaces, laundry facilities etc, they must not grant an absolute right to use these facilities in the tenancy agreement but must reserve the right to withdraw the facilities.

10 Clauses stating what sanctions will be imposed for breach of the agreement

While strictly speaking unnecessary, it is useful to inform tenants what action is likely in the event of a breach of any particular clause of the agreement, as the fact that the tenant has been told the consequences of any breach will affect the reasonableness of making an order for possession (see below). This information should be included in explanatory material if this is provided.

The advantages and disadvantages of clauses on racial harassment

Advantages of a racial harassment clause:

(a) it provides an extra ground for possession if breached;

(b) it gives notice to tenants that racial harassment could lead to eviction which makes it more likely that it is reasonable to order possession;
(c) if publicised, it gives notice to the public that the authority will take all available steps to deal with perpetrators;
(d) it informs victims that the authority will take action against perpetrators and encourages them to report harassment;
(e) it provides the opportunity, where appropriate, for the authority to seek an injunction prohibiting future harassment rather than an order for possession;
(f) it makes tenants expressly responsible for their children, visitors and dogs.

There are no disadvantages in including a clause on racial harassment in a tenancy agreement. Whether or not a clause prohibiting racial harassment is best used as a ground for possession is discussed below (p68).

Variation of tenancy terms

Since most local authorities agreed their standard terms and conditions of tenancy, many have decided to amend their terms to include clauses on racial harassment. The terms can always be varied by agreement with each individual tenant.

In practice, obtaining the consent of every tenant will be impossible and some will not agree to accept clauses relating to racial harassment. The HA 1985 allows authorities to alter the terms of the tenancy without the agreement of each individual tenant provided the following procedure is followed:[4]

(a) The authority decides what variations it wishes to make to the tenancy agreement.
(b) The authority decides on the method of service of the preliminary notice and notice of variation so that service can be proved if necessary.
(c) The local authority delegates authority to officers to sign and serve notices. Authority cannot be delegated to a single councillor.
(d) A preliminary notice is served on each tenant. This notice must:
 • inform the tenant of the authority's intention to serve a notice of variation;
 • specify the proposed variation and its effect;
 • invite the tenant to comment on the proposed variation within a reasonable time specified in the notice;
 • be signed by the properly authorised officer.
 A suggested preliminary notice is contained in Appendix 2.
(e) The authority considers any comments made by the tenants within the specified time. The authority should consider the comments made by each tenant separately and if the tenant presents reasons why the

terms suggested would be inappropriate for his or her tenancy the authority should consider whether to allow that tenant to have different terms and conditions. There will usually be powerful reasons against this but the tenant's comments must be properly considered if the authority's decision is to avoid challenge. The authority should also consider the points made by tenants which are of general application.

(f) If, as a result of the comments received, the authority decides to make amendments to the proposed variation then a further preliminary notice may be necessary.

(g) The authority makes a decision as to the variation it proposes to implement and the date on which it is to take effect.

(h) The authority decides what information is necessary to inform each tenant of the nature and effect of the variation. The authority might decide no information is necessary, or it might include a translation for tenants whose first language is not English or a plain English translation of legal jargon.

(i) A notice of variation is served on each tenant. The notice must:
- specify the variation in the terms of tenancy;
- specify the date on which it takes effect (not less than four weeks or one rental period ahead, whichever is longer);
- be accompanied by any information the authority decided was necessary under stage (h);
- be signed by a properly authorised officer.

A specimen notice is in Appendix 2.

1 Points to watch

Consultation with tenants' associations does not avoid the need to follow this procedure if any variation is to be effective. Thus an attempt to implement a variation made after full consultation with tenants' associations, but without individual consultation with tenants, will be ineffective in law. Local authorities wishing to consult tenants' associations should do so *before* they settle the proposed terms of the variation and serve the preliminary notice on individual tenants.

2 Proof of service

In court proceedings, the authority may be required to prove that the appropriate procedures have been followed if it wishes to rely on a new tenancy clause. Some record must therefore be kept of service of both notices required to complete the procedure. This record should be made by the person actually delivering the notice or putting it in the post or noted by the computer producing individually addressed envelopes or letters. Some officer should still record that all the addressed envelopes or letters produced by the computer were personally delivered or put in the post. Wherever possible, a record should be made on the tenancy file that notices have been served and by whom.

B. POSSESSION PROCEEDINGS

Possession proceedings against perpetrators of racial harassment can be brought on the following grounds:

(a) for breach of an express clause in the tenancy agreement;[5]
(b) for nuisance or annoyance to neighbours;[6]
(c) for committing waste to the common parts.[7]

In each case, in addition to proving the facts required by the ground, it is necessary to prove that it is reasonable for the court to make an order for possession.[8]

Possession proceeedings can be brought by local authorities and housing associations on the grounds of nuisance or annoyance even if there are no express clauses in their tenancy agreements. All authorities and housing associations can therefore use possession proceedings as a sanction to prevent or deter racial harassment.

Details of some of the possession actions so far attempted by local authorities in racial harassment cases are contained in Appendix 5.

Breach of the tenancy agreement

"An obligation of the tenancy has been broken or not performed."[9]

An express clause in the tenancy agreement must have been broken for possession proceedings to be brought under this ground. Where the authority is relying on a new clause, the tenancy agreement must have been properly varied using the procedure referred to above.

Nuisance or annoyance

"The tenant or a person residing in the dwelling-house has been guilty of conduct which is a nuisance or annoyance to neighbours. . .".[10]

This ground can be used even if there is no express clause in the tenancy agreement prohibiting nuisance or annoyance to neighbours.

Key points
- The words nuisance and annoyance have their ordinary meaning.[11]
- All acts of racial harassment will be a nuisance or annoyance within the meaning of this phrase.

- One act may be sufficient to constitute a nuisance or annoyance but is unlikely to be sufficient to justify an order for possession unless it is extremely serious.[12]
- The courts have accepted that obscene language and abuse can amount to nuisance or annoyance.[13]
- The ground exists and an order for possession can be granted even though the nuisance has stopped by the time the matter is heard by the court.[14] (But see below for the effect of the nuisance having stopped on the reasonableness of making an order for possession.)
- "Neighbours" appears to mean those who live near enough to be affected by the conduct of the tenant or a member of his or her family. However, this will be limited to conduct which is connected with their occupation of their home and would not include, for example, acts committed miles away on another council estate.[15] Who is a "neighbour" affected by the conduct will be a question of fact to be decided in each case.
- "Neighbours" is not restricted just to other council tenants. It may include, for example, owner occupiers and private sector tenants living on an estate, in the area of an estate or in the same street.
- The ground includes acts by anyone residing in the property as well as the tenant, but does not include visitors. Therefore tenants are responsible for adult children and partners, sub-tenants and lodgers.

In *LB Camden v Hawkins* (see p301) an order for possession was refused because the judge did not consider that the tenant was reasonably capable of controlling her son of 17.[16] There are two points that can be made to argue that this view is wrong. First, the law clearly intends a tenant to be responsible for the acts of his or her children and other people living with the family, however old or young they may be. A decision that a tenant is not responsible frustrates the purpose of the law. Second, in many homelessness cases authorities have been challenged for holding all family members equally responsible for the acts of one member which led to the family being evicted and regarded as intentionally homeless, and the authorities' decisions have been upheld.[17] It is inconsistent to adopt a completely different approach in possession proceedings.

Waste

"The condition of . . . any of the common parts has deteriorated owing to acts of waste by, or the neglect or default of, the tenant or a person residing in the dwelling-house and in the case of an act of waste by or the neglect or default of a person lodging with the tenant or a sub-tenant of his, the tenant has not taken such steps as he ought reasonably to have taken for the removal of the lodger or sub-tenant."[18]

Key points
- Common parts means parts of the building or estate which the tenant is entitled to use in common with other tenants under the terms of the tenancy.[19]
- Examples of acts of waste are the writing of graffiti and the smashing of windows and lights.
- This ground does not include damage to premises occupied by neighbouring tenants.

Reasonableness

The court cannot make an order for possession under any of the above grounds unless it considers it reasonable to do so.[20] The court must take into account all the relevant circumstances when deciding whether it is reasonable to make an order for possession.[21] There is considerable discretion vested in the judge as to the degree of weight s/he attaches to each relevant factor.

Factors which will make it more likely to be reasonable for an order to be granted, include:
— that the harassment is continuing;
— that there are other victims or potential victims in the area;
— that harassment has occurred on many occasions or over a long period;
— that the acts of harassment are extremely serious;
— that the acts are deliberate and intended to make the victims' lives unbearable and are not merely inconsiderate;
— that the acts are motivated by racial hatred;
— the genuine fears of the victims and other potential victims on the estate even when the harassment has ceased;
— the housing management problems caused by racial harassment both on that estate and borough-wide;
— the extent of racial harassment in the area and the borough;
— that it can be shown that an order for possession in such a case has in the past discouraged and reduced harassment in the area or borough;
— that warnings have been given to the tenant but were ignored;
— that the tenancy agreement or handbook warns that racial harassment will lead to possession proceedings;
— that proceedings have been taken against the same tenant in the past;
— that the perpetrators have been offered alternative accommodation or will be if possession is granted;
— that an injunction will not prevent future harassment;
— that the harassment is being carried out by the tenant him or herself;
— that the harassment is being carried out by members of the tenant's family and the tenant is condoning the behaviour or taking no steps to prevent it although s/he knows of it;

— if the victim has to be rehoused, the financial costs to the victim of setting up a new home and extra fares to work and the inconvenience caused, eg changing children's schools, distance from families and friends;
— the fact that the availability of stock to rehouse victims is diminishing and rehousing does not represent a long-term solution.

Factors which will make it less likely to be reasonable for an order to be granted, include:
— that the tenant has been living there for a considerable time or is elderly;
— that the victim has retaliated or "egged-on" the tenant;
— that the harassment has ceased;
— that considerable time has elapsed since the harassment ceased;
— that the authority is using possession proceedings as a method of punishment rather than for housing management purposes and protection of the victim;
— that the victim has been transferred;
— that the perpetrator has apologised or paid for any damage;
— that the tenant did not commit the acts him or herself and has taken steps to try to prevent a recurrence of nuisance or harassment by people living or staying with him or her;
— that there are young children in the family who are not responsible for harassment.

The fact that the perpetrator has been successfully prosecuted for an offence may be a factor either way. It will be evidence that the criminal offence has been committed and will therefore assist. On the other hand, the judge may consider that eviction will lead to the perpetrator being punished twice for the same act. Nevertheless, the future protection of the victim or potential victims and housing management grounds can still justify an order for possession.

Reasonableness when the nuisance has ceased

Just because a nuisance has ceased does not mean an order for possession cannot be obtained. The continuing fear of the victim even when harassment has ceased is a very relevant factor.[22] However, the longer the period that elapses between the last act of harassment and the hearing, the less likely it is that an order for possession will be reasonable.

Great care must be taken regarding preparation and presentation of the case if it is to succeed. Evidence must be produced to show why it is reasonable for an order for possession to be made, and this must both support the positive points and show why the negative points should be discounted or given less weight. Appeal from a decision of the county court is probably only possible if the judge has specifically chosen to discount a relevant factor.

Choosing the grounds and method of presentation

Authorities should consider the approach they wish to adopt in pursuing possession proceedings against perpetrators. Essentially, possession proceedings may be taken with one or more of the following intentions in mind:

(a) to provide protection for the victim or other potential victims by moving the perpetrator;
(b) to enable the authority properly to manage the housing on the particular estate by avoiding the risk of future racial harassment of other tenants by the same perpetrators;
(c) to enable the authority to manage all its housing with greater ease by making an example of these perpetrators and deterring others;
(d) to punish the individual perpetrator;
(e) to contribute to the authority's fight against racism.

1 Protecting the victim or potential victims

Presentation of the case will concentrate on the fears of the victim, the effect on the victim's family life and the need for a possession order as the only method of ensuring the future safety of the victim. Evidence might be produced of the health effects on the victim and family and of the deterioration in the school work of the victim's children as a result of harassment. Where the victim has been rehoused this argument is diminished, but it may still be possible to show that neighbours have been racially harassed or are living in fear.

2 Housing management grounds

Local housing management difficulties
Evidence will be required of the difficulties in preventing this type of behaviour on the estate except by eviction, and of the fact that black tenants will not accept offers on that estate; this evidence should come from those responsible for interviewing tenants about allocations. Evidence can also be produced of the number of incidents of racial harassment on the estate and the extent of the problem.

General housing management difficulties
If the court is to be persuaded that it is essential that an order for possession be granted because racial harassment is prevalent and is causing fear throughout the black community in the area, then evidence must be produced to this effect. It cannot be assumed that this point will be obvious to a judge who is not an expert in housing management.

Statistical evidence of the extent of harassment will be useful, together with expert opinion evidence from a senior housing officer such as the director as to why it is necessary to make an example of this perpetrator. Consideration might be given to obtaining a witness from the Home Office or Commission for Racial Equality or getting a senior local police officer to give evidence, if the police acknowledge racial harassment as a local problem. If it is frequently the practice of the authority to transfer the victim, evidence should be produced as to why this does not represent a long-term solution to racial harassment problems and of the fact that rehousing is becoming more difficult to achieve. Evidence could also be produced of the cost to the victims of rehousing, both in the disruption to family life, friends, schooling etc and in terms of the financial effect of having to establish a new home.

3 Punishing individual perpetrators

Authorities must be wary of using possession proceeedings solely as a method of punishment. Their primary purpose is as a method of housing management, though that will involve some element of punishment to deter others. There is nothing to stop the need for punishment being taken into account by the court when considering whether it is reasonable to make an order for possession. There will be no element of punishment if a perpetrator is moved to a better estate elsewhere.

Presentation of the case on this basis is likely to be of far more effect where it is the tenant him or herself, rather than some member of their family, who is responsible for the harassment; and it is less likely to succeed if the tenant has already been punished in some other way, eg by a criminal penalty.

4 Acting against racism

The authority may wish to present its case as part of its fight against racism generally. The Wheeler case shows how careful the authority must be when adopting this approach (see p11). Racist views are not illegal. It is only when racism is the basis for illegal acts that action is justified. Authorities cannot therefore use possession proceedings as a method of altering people's views. Adopting this approach on its own is likely to be less successful than the others suggested, because of the probable opposition from judges.

5 Grounds for claiming possession

Having chosen the method of presentation, it is necessary for the authority to choose the grounds upon which it will rely. Many legal authorities have tenancy agreements which specifically prohibit racial harassment. Where this is the case, the important political decision is whether to try and obtain possession on the basis of racial harassment (ie for breach of an express clause) instead of or as well as nuisance or annoyance.

Seeking possession on the ground of breach of an express clause prohibiting racial harassment
(a) **Advantages:** Such an action represents a political stance against racial harassment and makes an example of the perpetrators for publicity purposes. It is hoped that it gradually educates judges about racism.

(b) Disadvantages:

The disadvantages of basing possession proceedings on the breach of an express clause prohibiting racial harassment, include:
— it introduces into the proceedings the need to prove a racial motive which is unnecessary in proceedings for nuisance and annoyance;
— the judge may decide the proceedings are politically motivated and therefore be inclined against the authority;
— the judge is unlikely to understand racism or about racial harassment;
— the judge may become diverted into arguing about racism and ignore serious nuisance and inconvenience to victims, which are the main reasons for bringing the case;
— the judge may consider racial harassment is too vague a term to be relevant;
— racial harassment is a term that is extremely difficult to define legally in a satisfactory way;
— in cases taken to date, where authorities have claimed that harassment has been racial, some judges have been extremely reluctant to accept that racial motives existed or were relevant;
— it cannot be assumed that the judge will understand the reasons for the policy or know about the extent of racial harassment in the area. Evidence from senior council officers will therefore be essential.

Other points that should be considered include the fact that if possession is granted on the ground of nuisance or annoyance and the allegations included racial harassment, the authority can still publicise the case as a successful eviction for racial harassment; any act of racial harassment is included in the phrase "nuisance or annoyance". If an authority decides to proceed on the basis of nuisance or annoyance, it can still argue that the racial motive behind the nuisance is an aggravating factor supporting a possession order.

Practical points on overcoming the disadvantages

The clause suggested in Appendix 1 is drafted in such a way as to overcome some of the disadvantages of a clause which prohibits "racial harassment". In it, the breach of tenancy consists of "harassment" and whether or not this is motivated by racism is a secondary consideration. If a local authority succeeds in proving harassment, it can obtain a possession order even if it fails to prove that the harassment was racial.

In practice, authorities can take possession proceedings on more than one ground. It is therefore advisable to claim possession based on nuisance or annoyance as well as racial harassment (see Appendix 4 for a specimen particulars of claim).

C. INJUNCTIONS

Injunctions are orders of the court which require a person to do or refrain from doing a particular act. A breach of an injunction is a contempt of court and is punishable by imprisonment or a fine.

In the context of racial harassment, injunctions can be used by local authorities in at least six ways:
— permanently to restrain perpetrators from repeating acts of harassment (a perpetual injunction);
— temporarily to prohibit harassment until a possession order is obtained (an interlocutory injunction);
— to restrain proposed harassment of which the authority becomes aware in advance, eg a mass protest outside a tenant's home publicised in advance;
— to restrain criminal offences (see p23);
— to restrain a public nuisance or an unreasonable use of the highway;
— to prevent obstruction of the authority's statutory duty.

Grounds on which courts will grant an injunction

Injunctions of all kinds are a discretionary remedy. This means that it is up to the court whether or not it grants an injunction. Authorities are more likely to succeed in obtaining some kinds of injunctions than others. The grounds for obtaining an injunction to prevent the commission of a criminal offence or a public nuisance or to prevent obstruction of an authority's statutory duty were considered in Chapter 3. For the other three types of injunction the grounds differ according to which type of injunction is being sought.

1 Perpetual injunctions

This kind of injunction will be sought in two instances:
— to stop the tenant breaking the terms of the tenancy agreement; and
— to stop the perpetrator committing a nuisance or a trespass against the authority.

An example of both these uses is contained in Appendix 4.

Injunction to prevent breach of tenancy
Where the only order being sought by the authority is an order restraining a tenant from breaching the tenancy agreement, the court has only a very limited discretion to refuse such an order.[23] The injunction is available almost as of right. The tenancy agreement will have to contain an express clause that has been or is being breached, eg prohibiting nuisance, racial harassment or keeping a dog. The limitation of this type of injunction is that it can only be addressed to the tenant and not to any member of the tenant's family.

Injunction to prevent nuisance or trespass
Where the order being sought is to restrain a perpetrator from committing a nuisance or trespass, the court will consider the following points:
— whether damages are an adequate remedy;[24]
— the motive of the perpetrator;[25]

— the behaviour of the authority;[26]
— the interests of the public;[27]
— whether the act is likely to be repeated.[28]

The motive of the perpetrator will always be malicious in racial harassment cases and the public interest will be in favour of an injunction as there will always be a risk of repetition if an injunction is not granted. Damages will never be an adequate remedy for the authority, since its primary purpose in obtaining an injunction is the protection of the victim.

In practice, therefore, the courts should have limited grounds for refusing an injunction in this type of case.[29]

2 Interlocutory injunctions

An interlocutory injunction may be obtained ex parte or on notice. Obtaining one "ex parte" means that it is obtained without giving any notice to the person against whom it is obtained (the defendant) who has no opportunity to appear at court. This is reserved for very urgent cases, including those where the defendant is likely to react to the service of proceedings by committing further acts of harassment immediately.

The judge granting an ex parte injunction will fix a further hearing date to reconsider the case and will limit the injunction to end on that date. Notice of this further hearing must be served on the defendant who then has an opportunity to attend and argue why the injunction should not be continued. At that hearing the authority can seek an injunction lasting until the final hearing takes place. Examples of an ex parte injunction and notice of application for an injunction are given in Appendix 4.

In theory, an interlocutory injunction is a temporary remedy prohibiting certain acts until the final trial of the case. In the racial harassment context interlocutory injunctions can be obtained in either possession proceedings or in proceedings for a perpetual injunction. In practice, many cases in which interlocutory injunctions are granted never reach final trial.

The following requirements must be satisfied before a court will grant an interlocutory injunction:[30]

(a) there must be a serious question to be tried at the final hearing, ie the claim must have some basis;

(b) the balance of convenience must be in favour of granting an injunction;

(c) damages must be an inadequate remedy for the authority;

(d) the authority may be required to undertake to pay damages to the other party if it is unsuccessful at the trial.

There should be no difficulty satisfying these requirements in most cases of racial harassment. The balance of convenience will always be in the authority's favour when it is merely seeking an order that perpetrators should not breach their contract of tenancy or commit a nuisance or trespass.[31]

3 Obtaining injunctions before harassment occurs

In some circumstances authorities may become aware that some form of harassment is going to occur. For example, they may discover that a demonstration has been arranged on a housing estate outside the house of newly arrived black tenants. In such cases, injunctions can be obtained (known as quia timet injunctions) before any act of harassment has been actually committed. Such injunctions can also be obtained ex parte if the matter is sufficiently urgent.

The same principles apply as in the case of interlocutory injunctions. In addition, the authority has to show:
— that there is a real likelihood of the harassment occurring;
— that there will be grave damage caused by the proposed act.[32]

Provided evidence exists of the likelihood of the harassment occurring, it should be possible to persuade the court to grant an injunction.

The merits of injunctions

1 The advantages

The advantages of injunctions are as follows:

(a) they can be obtained without witnesses having to attend court as they are granted on affidavit evidence (see below);
(b) they are a method of testing the court's attitude to the facts of a particular case;
(c) they transfer the power from the perpetrator to the authority, which is then in control;
(d) the perpetrator knows within days that the local authority means business and that any future harassment will be recorded and reported to the court;
(e) the victim sees results and gets immediate protection;
(f) an application for an injunction forces the perpetrators to obtain speedy legal advice and probably legal aid;
(g) an application for an injunction ensures that the authority has fully prepared its case at an early stage and knows what its witnesses are going to say;
(h) the judge, having heard the facts, may order that the final hearing should be heard more quickly than would otherwise be the case;
(i) if an interlocutory injunction is sought and obtained, this undermines the argument that harassment has ceased so a possession order is unnecessary, because the authority can argue that it has only ceased because of the interlocutory injunction.

2 Disadvantages and limitations of injunctions

(a) An injunction for breach of the tenancy agreement can only be obtained against the tenant and not against those living with the tenant. However, an injunction for trespass may be available and anyone who assists the breach of the injunction by the tenant may be in contempt of court (see below).

(b) Any court proceedings may make the situation worse rather than better. The perpetrators may perceive the victims as the cause of their problems and increase the harassment.

(c) Proceedings for breach of an injunction require proof of a breach after the injunction is granted. Thus a devious and cunning perpetrator may be able to continue harassment after the injunction is granted without being caught.

(d) Proceedings for breach of an injunction involve proof beyond reasonable doubt. The normal degree of proof required in civil proceedings is proof on the balance of probabilities.

(e) Judges are reluctant to imprison for breach of an injunction and may give the perpetrator another chance. However, they can impose a suspended period of imprisonment.

(f) The grant of an injunction may make it less likely that an order for possession is made at the final hearing since it presents the judge with an alternative remedy.

(g) An interlocutory injunction cannot be sought in possession proceedings for at least four weeks after racial harassment has occurred, since possession proceedings cannot be begun until a notice of intention to seek possession has expired. To obtain an immediate injunction it is therefore necessary to start proceedings for a perpetual injunction.

D. PROCEDURE

Legal aid

Legal aid is available to defend possession proceedings. It can be granted to the tenant if s/he is within the financial eligibility limits and has reasonable grounds for defending the proceedings. The Law Society decides whether the tenant should get legal aid. In cases of racial harassment, it is most unlikely that a tenant would be refused legal aid except on financial grounds.

Procedure in possession proceedings

1 Preliminary steps: the notice of intention to seek possession

Before any proceedings for possession can be begun, a notice of intention to seek possession must be served on the tenant. This notice must follow a particular format which is shown in Appendix 4.[33] As with a notice of variation, the notice of intention to seek possession must be signed by a properly authorised officer of the authority, which must be in a position to prove service of the notice if the tenant disputes having received it.

The notice must show the grounds for possession on which the authority intends to rely. The forms prescribed for notices were altered with effect from May 1987. An authority is now required to give "particulars of each ground" on which it is relying and the notes require a "full explanation of why each ground is being relied upon".

Prior to May 1987, authorities had to give their "reasons for taking" the action of serving a notice. The courts interpreted this, in a case on rent arrears, as requiring that the notice must give details of the reasons for using the ground sufficient to allow the tenant to rectify the problem and avoid possession proceedings.[34] The authority therefore had to specify the amount of rent due. Since May 1987, there seems little doubt that authorities must include full particulars of incidents of nuisance, annoyance or racial harassment in their notices of intention to seek possession if these are to be effective. Authorities should therefore include all the information which is to be used in the particulars of claim in possession proceedings. This suggests that the notice should be drafted by the legal department and not by the housing department.

Dealing with defective notices

Defective notices have resulted in local authorities having their claims for possession dismissed without consideration of the evidence. This is inexcusable in cases of racial harassment where victims and witnesses are likely to be taking some personal risk and experiencing considerable personal trauma by agreeing to give evidence.

Defective notices can be dealt with in the following ways.

(a) Reissuing a proper notice as soon as the defect is discovered, before proceedings are begun This remedy might be appropriate if a notice issued by the housing department as a warning to the perpetrator several months ago was defective and it has now been decided to use possession proceedings. There has to be a delay of four weeks before possession proceedings are started.

(b) Reissuing a proper notice as soon as the defect is discovered, even after proceedings have begun Proceedings should not have been begun without detecting a defective notice. The authority could issue a separate notice and then reissue the proceedings once the notice has expired, and hope that the same hearing date already obtained can be used.

Example: If the authority has started proceedings and the trial date has been fixed for eight weeks away, the authority can issue a new notice expiring on the rent day four weeks ahead and re-issue proceedings after this has expired using the same hearing date. It will have to persuade the court staff to keep the same hearing date for a completely different case and to file notice of discontinuance in the old proceedings. It will almost certainly have to pay some of the defendant's costs.

(c) Relying on the particulars stated in the notice and using other incidents of harassment as evidence supporting the reasonableness of an order for possession Provided the facts stated in the notice show that the tenant is in breach of the tenancy agreement or that the tenant or some person living with him or her has been guilty of conduct which is a nuisance or annoyance to neighbours and these facts can be proved, then the notice is valid.

If there are other incidents which were not included in the notice, these can still be referred to in the particulars of claim and proved at the hearing, but only for the purposes of showing that it is reasonable to order possession.

(d) Asking the court to allow the authority to amend its grounds for possession[35] The court can allow the authority to alter or add to its grounds. The extent of this power is unclear. It could have two meanings: either that the court can allow an authority to alter or add to both the grounds and the particulars to support the alteration or addition of those grounds; or that the court can allow an authority to change its grounds but has no power to allow the alteration of particulars.

On either interpretation, there appears to be no power to allow an authority to alter its particulars unless it is also altering the grounds for possession. In racial harassment cases there are two important grounds for possession, grounds 1 and 2 in HA 1985 Sch 2. If only one has been referred to in the notice, another might be added with leave of the court. If the first interpretation were correct, the authority could then also add additional particulars.

The second interpretation appears more logical and does not require the court to imply additional wording into the statute. On this interpretation the power is limited to allowing an authority to rely on additional or altered grounds for possession based on those particulars contained in the original notice. For example, the authority could add a claim for possession based on nuisance or annoyance to a claim based on breach of tenancy agreement where both relied on the same facts. If this interpretation is correct, the power may not assist greatly with defective notices.

2 Starting possession proceedings

In possession proceedings the housing authority is the "plaintiff" and the tenant is the "defendant". Where there are two tenants, they must both be defendants and are then referred to as "the first defendant" etc.

Possession proceedings against secure tenants under the grounds contained in the HA 1985 should be taken in the local county court and it is the county court procedure that is dealt with here. The authority must prove its case on the balance of probabilities. In other words the authority must show that the facts it relies on were more likely than not to have occurred.

The particulars of claim

The authority begins proceedings by preparing the document called the "particulars of claim" which sets out the basis of its claim. This is an important document because the authority will not be able to rely on any additional points unless the court gives it permission to amend its claim.

An example of a particulars of claim for a possession action for racial harassment is in Appendix 4.

The particulars must contain certain information including:[36]
— the ground(s) in the HA 1985 on which possesssion is being sought;
— particulars of the conduct of the tenant or others which is relied on to support each ground;
— the date of service of the notice of intention to seek possession.
In addition, where the authority is seeking to rely on a variation in the tenancy terms, it must give details of the notice of variation served on the tenant and when it took effect.

Before the particulars of claim are prepared, it is essential that the authority is satisfied that it has evidence to support each of the facts it is claiming in support of the grounds for possession. The legal department must therefore have interviewed the necessary witnesses, prepared statements from each of them, ascertained who is able to give direct evidence and obtained their agreement to attend court. Where necessary, appropriate steps must have been taken to ensure the safety and protection of witnesses until the court hearing.

Usually it will be counter-productive to make any allegations in the particulars of claim which cannot be proved. There may be circumstances in which allegations are made which the authority knows it may not be able to prove. For example, a witness may be undecided whether s/he is prepared to attend court.

The first hearing date

The court will send a copy of the particulars of claim to the defendant (the tenant) with details of the first hearing date. If it is intended that the first hearing should be a full trial, the date must be more than 21 days after service of the particulars of claim on the defendant.[37]

In practice, the court usually lists many possession cases by the same authority on certain days of the week, so the total available time for each case is unlikely to exceed five or ten minutes. It is therefore almost impossible for a possession action on the ground of racial harassment to proceed at the first hearing fixed by the court, even if it is undefended. If there is insufficient time at the first hearing, the court will probably adjourn the matter for a further hearing to be fixed.[38] This may result in considerable delay.

The authority, therefore, should inform the court of the time that the case will require even if not defended, and attempt to obtain a first hearing with sufficient time for the case to be heard. The first hearing may thereby be delayed but there may then be enough court time to hear the case and make a final order.

Where directions are considered necessary, these should be sought as soon as possible. If the first hearing provides insufficient time for a full trial, this can be used as a directions hearing or an application can be made for an injunction if appropriate. Notice of application for directions should be given to the defendant. Some courts will allow agreed directions to be made without a hearing.

The defence
The defence is the document lodged by the defendant which sets out which of the allegations made by the authority in the particulars of claim are admitted and which are denied.

As soon as the authority is notified that the defendant intends to defend the proceedings it should contact the defence solicitors and try to agree an estimate for the amount of court time required to hear the case and any directions that are considered necessary. A fully defended case will take much longer than an undefended case. Where interpreters are needed even more time will be necessary. It may be appropriate to agree an adjourment of the first hearing and fix a later hearing with sufficient time for a full trial.

3 Speeding up the process in possession proceedings

One of the factors that may be crucial to the question of whether it is reasonable for an order for possession to be made is the length of time since the last act of harassment. The defendant's legal advisers are likely to advise a perpetrator to refrain from harassing after possession proceedings have been initiated. It will therefore be unlikely that further acts of harassment occur after the proceedings have been begun and they may even stop when the notice of intention to seek possession is served. Legal advisers for the perpetrator will also be aware that the longer they can delay a final hearing, the better the result for the defendant is likely to be.

The authority's legal department, therefore, must take all available steps to ensure an early trial. A failure to do so will severely weaken the case and could result in a strong case being lost.

One dilemma facing local authorities may be whether they should await the results of criminal proceedings. Although a criminal conviction can be relied upon in a possession action, this advantage is almost certainly outweighed by the considerable delay that occurs while a criminal trial takes place. In addition, the perpetrator may eventually be acquitted because of the heavy burden of proof in criminal proceedings, whereas it might be

78 Civil proceedings

possible to prove, on the balance of probabilities, that acts of racial harassment, nuisance or annoyance have occurred to justify a possession order.

Possible tactics to speed up the court process
(a) Applying for an interlocutory injunction Although an ordinary application for legal aid can take a very long time, defendants can apply for emergency legal aid to be represented in urgent proceedings.[39] An application for an interlocutory injunction will provide immediate protection to the victim and will force the perpetrator to apply for emergency legal aid, thus considerably shortening the period before legal aid is granted.

The hearing of an application for an interlocutory injunction on notice can take place at any time after two days following the issue of proceedings. Other advantages of injunctions are listed above.

(b) Asking the judge to order a speedy trial This can be done at any hearing, including that for an application for an interlocutory injunction. It can be stressed that the victim needs urgent protection and a possession order is essential. An application to the court for a trial date can also be made at any time, even if the defendant's solicitors say they are not ready.[40]

(c) Refusing to delay proceedings because of legal aid The authority does not have to agree to wait while the slow, bureaucratic process of dealing with a legal aid application runs its course. If the authority refuses adjournments requested by the defendant, it is up to the court whether or not to allow the proceedings to be delayed. The importance of speed must be emphasised, and it can be pointed out that the defendant can apply for emergency legal aid if necessary.

(d) Fixing the trial date as soon as possible The defendant should be encouraged by the legal department to obtain representation as soon as possible and to make an application for legal aid if one is to be made. Once it is clear that the tenant intends to defend the proceedings, it is advisable to agree an adjournment of the first hearing and attempt to fix a hearing for a full trial as soon as possible. The court is likely to be booked up weeks or months in advance and therefore the sooner the trial date is fixed, the sooner it will be able to take place.

It is important to make an accurate assessment of the length of the trial, taking into account the number of witnesses to be called, otherwise the trial might be adjourned halfway through and the last part delayed several weeks (several months in some courts if the judge changes courts and goes elsewhere).

(e) Making use of procedural applications If it is clear that a hearing will take some time to be fixed and directions are required, an order for directions can be obtained quite quickly. This will impose time limits on the defendant for serving a defence, discovery of documents etc. Where these time limits are not complied with, procedural applications can be made to obtain an order that the defendant be debarred from defending the case.

4 The court's powers in possession proceedings

If the court decides that the grounds in the HA 1985 are satisfied and that it is reasonable to make an order for possession, there are three types of possession order that the court can make.

(a) Immediate outright possession order This order means that the tenancy ceases to exist immediately. The authority can apply for a warrant of possession at once which will be executed by the court bailiff. The bailiff usually takes several days to arrange this; in some courts it may take several weeks. The warrant of possession is the document which authorises the court bailiff to evict anyone on the premises when s/he arrives to enforce it.

(b) Outright possession order in a specified period The tenancy ceases to exist at the end of the specified period, eg in 28 days' time. The court has decided that the tenant should be evicted but should have some time to arrange rehousing or removal. The authority can apply for a warrant as soon as the 28-day period has expired. Again, it may take several extra days or weeks for actual eviction to take place.

(c) Suspended order for possession This order allows the tenant to remain in his or her home provided that s/he complies with any conditions imposed. The suspension can last indefinitely.[41]

In racial harassment cases the condition will usually be that the tenant, or his or her family, does not cause a nuisance or annoyance to neighbours or commit acts of racial harassment against neighbours. If the condition is breached the authority may apply for a warrant of possession immediately. No notice need be given to the tenant.

Speeding up eviction
Several days or even weeks can elapse between the date that a possession order takes effect and the time when the bailiff enforces it. Some authorities have found that judges are prepared to instruct the court bailiff to enforce the order immediately when there are good grounds for doing so. In this way, an order for "possession forthwith" can result in the defendant's being evicted the same day.

Application by the tenant to delay eviction
The tenant can apply to suspend any of the above orders for possession at any time prior to actual eviction. In racial harassment cases, this procedure will, in practice, only be of use to a tenant if an outright possession order is made which is not immediately executed. The court has power to fix a period of suspension which effectively defers eviction but cannot allow the tenant to remain indefinitely.

Thus, a tenant who had been ordered to leave after 28 days might successfully obtain permission from the court to remain for a further 28 days to allow more time to find alternative accommodation. Any application by the tenant must be served on the authority and a hearing will take place. The authority can oppose the grant of further time in the interests of the victim.

Procedure on applications for injunctions

Applications for injunctions may be made to the High Court or the county court. Since, in practice, an application for an injunction may often be combined with a claim for possession, it is the county court procedure that is dealt with here. The High Court procedure is similar in many respects.

1 Interlocutory injunctions

Interlocutory injunctions may be sought:
— in possession proceedings;
— in proceedings claiming damages for a tort (see Chapter 12); and
— in proceedings for a perpetual injunction.
Injunctions relating to the possession, occupation, use or enjoyment of land may be sought independently of any claim for damages in the county court.[42]

(a) The application
To obtain an interlocutory injunction, it is necessary to file the usual documents required to commence proceedings (ie particulars of claim, request for summons and the court fee). In addition, an application for an injunction should include the following documents:
— two copies of the notice of application for an injunction;
— the original affidavits supporting the application (see below); and
— a draft court order.
The application and draft order should contain the exact words of the injunction being sought. An example of such an application is in Appendix 4. The court will fix a hearing date and enter the date in the notice of application.

In ordinary proceedings, court documents may be served by post. Where an interlocutory injunction is being sought the following documents must be served personally on the defendant at least two clear working days (ie excluding Saturday, Sunday or bank holiday) before the hearing:
— the summons issued by the court;
— the particulars of claim sealed by the court;
— a notice of application sealed by the court;
— a copy of the draft court order; and
— copies of all the affidavits submitted to the court by the authority.

The person who serves the papers must prepare an affidavit stating when and where the papers were given to the defendant, and this affidavit is filed at the court.

The defendant may also file affidavits in evidence showing why an injunction should not be granted.

In exceptional circumstances, it may be possible to obtain an injunction ex parte, ie without giving notice to the defendant. An injunction granted ex parte will usually last about a week until the court hears the full application for an interlocutory injunction. The same papers need to be filed at court to apply for an injunction ex parte. If the matter is so urgent that there is insufficient time to prepare all the papers, the court will often grant an injunction provided the authority's solicitor undertakes to file the necessary paperwork within 24 hours.

(b) The hearing
When hearing an application for an interlocutory injunction, the court will usually only consider the affidavits filed by both parties. Exceptionally, if there have been very recent events and insufficient time to file further affidavits, oral evidence will be allowed. Consequently, it is very important that any affidavits contain sufficient information to justify the granting of an injunction, since they usually cannot be supplemented by oral evidence at court.

(c) The powers of the court
The court has a discretion whether to grant an injunction and over the terms of any injunction that is granted. Instead of making an injunction, the judge may decide to accept an undertaking from the defendant.

For our purposes, an undertaking is a promise to the court not to commit certain acts, eg a nuisance or annoyance to neighbours. An undertaking may be in identical terms to a court order and the procedure for breach of an undertaking is identical to that for breach of a court order (see below). The court cannot force a defendant to give an undertaking but can ask whether or not s/he is prepared to do so. However, if asked to give an undertaking, the defendant is in a difficult position. S/he will usually deny any harassment. If all the allegations are denied, there is no hardship in promising not to commit any further harassment. If the defendant refuses to undertake not to harass, s/he gives the impression that there is a risk of breaching the undertaking, which lends support to the authority's argument that harassment has taken place. The defendant is also then shown to be behaving unreasonably.

(d) After the hearing
After the hearing the authority's legal representative waits at the court to collect a copy of the sealed court order or undertaking. The court is obliged to include a notice on the order or undertaking called a "penal notice".[43] This notice informs the defendant that s/he can be sent to prison if the

order or undertaking is breached. An example of such a notice is in the order shown in Appendix 4. The order containing this notice must usually be served personally on the defendant as soon as possible. As explained below, it is also advisable to serve a copy on any other family member or visitor who has been or is likely to be involved in any harassment, together with a letter informing them that they too may be in contempt of court if they aid or abet a breach of the order.

Although the police have no power of arrest for breach of an injunction or undertaking relating to racial harassment (see below) it is probably advisable to provide the police with a copy of any injunction if there is any likelihood of their being called to deal with an incident. This may encourage the police to treat any further incident more seriously and themselves take action against the perpetrator. It may also ensure that the victim is given the necessary support and protection. In case the officers who are called to an incident have no knowledge of the injunction, a copy should be supplied to the victim.

(e) Effect of an order or undertaking

A court order (an injunction) or an undertaking have the same effect. Any breach by the defendant can be punished as a contempt of court, usually by imprisonment. The court will generally have to be satisfied that the injunction has been served on the defendant.[44]

The usual wording of orders and undertakings also makes the defendant responsible for ensuring that his or her "servants or agents" do not breach the order. This will include anyone acting on the defendant's behalf. In racial harassment cases where the defendant is the tenant and there is a possibility that the tenant is encouraging other members of his or her family or visitors to commit acts of racial harassment, this wording can be extended to include the "family and visitors" of the tenant[45] (see the order in Appendix 4).

Injunctions only apply to the person named as the defendant. An injunction against a tenant will therefore not apply to another member of the tenant's family who, *independently*, commits acts of racial harassment. However, anyone who has knowledge of a court order or undertaking and aids or abets the defendant to breach it will also have committed a contempt of court. An application can therefore be made for them to be sent to prison for contempt (see Appendix 4). Because injunctions are essentially limited in effect to the defendant named in them, it is advisable to combine court action against the tenant with court action against individual perpetrators who are family members if it is intended to seek an injunction. The example in Appendix 4 combines an action for an injunction for breach of tenancy agreement against the tenant, with an action for trespass against the perpetrator A, who is the tenant's son. In this way, the authority can be certain of being able to take action to enforce the injunction if further harassment is committed by A.

(f) Breach of the injunction or undertaking

If the defendant breaches an injunction or undertaking or any person aids and abets a breach, the authority can apply for that person's committal to prison. Breach of the injunction or undertaking must be proved beyond reasonable doubt. This is the same degree of proof as is required for a criminal offence. It is usually necessary to prove personal service of the injunction on the defendant before taking proceedings for committal. In exceptional cases, the courts can enforce the injunction even if it was not served, provided the defendant was present when the injunction was made or was informed of its terms, eg by telephone.[46] The court has power to impose a suspended term of imprisonment for a finite length of time.[47]

To enforce an injunction or undertaking when there is a breach, the authority must take the initiative by making a further application to the court. This application is known as a "notice to show cause against committal". It must be served on the defendant at least two days before the hearing and should be supported by an affidavit containing details of the breach complained of. There is no obligation on defendants to attend court but if they do not, an order committing them to prison can be made in their absence.

An application for a defendant's committal to prison for breach of an injunction or undertaking must accurately specify what it is that the defendant has done. If it does not, the court will dismiss the application.[48] An example of an application for committal is shown in Appendix 4. If a committal order is made, the court bailiff will arrest the defendant (usually with police assistance) who will be taken to prison.

(g) Power of arrest for breach of an injunction

There is no power of arrest for breach of an injunction. In practice, some breaches will amount to arrestable criminal offences or breaches of the peace, for which any individual can arrest, in certain circumstances, and hand the person over to the police. More importantly, a police officer can arrest the perpetrator and prosecute. However, the police have no power to bring the perpetrator before the county court judge for punishment for contempt of court.

2 Perpetual injunctions

The procedure for obtaining a perpetual injunction is essentially the same in the county court as for obtaining an order for possession, except that the authority must specify, in its particulars of claim, the terms of the injunction it is seeking (see Appendix 4). As with particulars of claim in possession cases, a claim for an injunction must contain certain specified information.[49] Unlike an application for an interlocutory injunction, evidence on an application for a perpetual injunction will usually be oral and not by affidavit. Points (d) to (g) above apply equally to perpetual injunctions.

1 HA 1985 s80.
2 Eg, Landlord and Tenant Act 1985 s11.
3 HA 1985 s21 and see pp11 and 15.
4 Ibid ss102 and 103, and see *Palmer v Sandwell MBC* (1987) *Times* 12 October.
5 Ibid Sch 2 ground 1.
6 Ibid ground 2.
7 Ibid ground 3.
8 Ibid s84(2).
9 N5.
10 N6.
11 See, eg, *Tod-Heatley v Benham* (1888) 40 ChD 80.
12 This point follows from the fact that the words "nuisance or annoyance" have their ordinary meaning.
13 See *Cobstone Investments Ltd v Maxim* (1983) 15 HLR 113, CA.
14 See, eg, *Florent v Horez* (1983) 12 HLR 1, CA.
15 A statement from Megarry on the Rent Acts approved by the Court of Appeal in *Cobstone Investments Ltd v Maxim* n13 at 121. This case was concerned with the phrase "adjoining occupiers" in the Rent Act 1977 and the remarks were obiter.
16 See Appendix 5.
17 See p90 and for a recent example see *R v East Herts DC ex p Bannon* (1986) 18 HLR 515.
18 N7.
19 HA 1985 s116.
20 N8.
21 *Battlespring Ltd v Gates* (1983) 11 HLR 6, CA and the passages quoted from *Cresswell v Hodgson* [1951] 2 KB 92, CA and *Cumming v Danson* [1942] 2 All ER 653.
22 See *Florent v Horez* n14.
23 *Doherty v Allmann* (1878) 3 App Cas 709 at 720, HL and see generally *Halsburys Laws* 4th edn Vol 24 para 992.
24 *London and Blackwall Railway v Cross* (1886) 31 ChD 354.
25 See, eg, *Hollywood Silver Fox Farm v Emmett* [1936] 1 All ER 825.
26 See, eg, *Hubbard v Vosper* [1972] 2 QB 84, CA.
27 *Miller v Jackson* [1977] QB 966 at 988, CA.
28 *Proctor v Bayley* (1889) 42 ChD 390.
29 *Patel v WH Smith (Eziot) Ltd* [1987] 2 All ER 569, CA.
30 *American Cyanamid Co v Ethicon Ltd* [1975] AC 396, HL.
31 This is illustrated by *Hampstead and Suburban Properties Ltd v Diomedous* [1969] 1 Ch 248 and see n29.
32 *Redland Bricks Ltd v Morris* [1970] AC 652.
33 Housing Act 1985 s82 and Secure Tenancies (Notices) Regulations 1987 SI No 755.
34 *Torridge DC v Jones* (1985) 18 HLR 107.
35 HA 1985 s84(3).
36 CCR Ord 6 r3.
37 Ibid Ord 7 r10(5).
38 HA 1985 s85 and CCR Ord 13 r3.
39 Legal Aid (General) Regulations 1980 SI No 1894 reg 19.
40 CCR Ord 13 r3.

41 *Yates v Morris* [1950] 2 All ER 577.
42 County Courts Act 1984 s22.
43 CCR Ord 29 r1(3).
44 Ibid Ord 29 r1(2).
45 *Acrow (Automation) Ltd v Rex Chainbelt Inc* [1971] 1 WLR 1676, CA and *Seaward v Paterson* [1897] 1 Ch 545.
46 CCR Ord 29 r1(6).
47 *Lee v Walker* [1985] 1 All ER 781, CA.
48 *Chiltern DC v Keane* [1985] 2 All ER 118; *Harmsworth v Harmsworth* [1987] 1 WLR 1676.
49 CCR Ord 6 r4.

CHAPTER SIX

Housing Authorities and Departments

The general management powers of housing authorities give them wide scope to assist and protect their tenants. Their influence can be extended beyond their own tenants by making use of powers relating to allocations, homelessness, grants, loans, control over bed and breakfast accommodation, houses in multiple occupation etc, and by making byelaws and using restrictive covenants in leases and transfers to tenants who buy their homes.

This chapter applies to London borough councils, the Common Council of the City of London, district councils and metropolitan borough councils. (Note: Some of the powers referred to in this chapter may be dealt with by separate works or environmental health departments.)

In the previous chapter, one aspect of the management powers of a housing authority was dealt with in detail — the power to evict perpetrators who are local authority tenants. In this chapter, other powers and duties of housing authorities are examined — powers to deal with harassment in both the public and other sectors of housing.

The application of specific powers will depend on the housing status of the particular victim or perpetrator. At the beginning of each section it is therefore stated to which categories of victims or perpetrators the particular power or duty applies. The phrase "All sectors" means that it applies to those who are council tenants, owner occupiers, private tenants, squatters, housing association tenants and any other kind of occupier.

A. THE DUTIES OF HOUSING AUTHORITIES

Housing authorities are subject to the general duties covered in Chapter 4. However, there are other duties of particular relevance to housing.

Preference in housing allocations

Application: Rehousing of victims from all sectors.
Rehousing of perpetrators who have been evicted for racial harassment from all rented sectors.

Authorities must give "reasonable preference" to "persons living under unsatisfactory living conditions" and to those who are homeless in the allocation of their tenancies.[1] This applies both to transfers and waiting list applicants. Every authority must publish a summary of its rules for allocating housing to those on the waiting and transfer lists.[2] The full rules must be available for inspection at the principal office of the authority at all reasonable hours.[3] Copies must be provided on request at a reasonable fee.[4]

1 Unsatisfactory living conditions

The phrase "unsatisfactory living conditions" is not defined. At its narrowest interpretation it could refer just to the physical state of the premises and their surroundings. A wider interpretation would require an authority to consider all aspects of the living conditions including the existence of any racial harassment. The phrase "living conditions" also appears in the power to make control orders on houses in multiple occupation.[5] The Code of Guidance issued by the DoE in its reference to control orders states that "noise, rowdyism or anti-social behaviour" should be taken into account when considering living conditions.[6] An interpretation including these factors which would take account of racial harassment appears preferable and would mean that all authorities are obliged to give reasonable preference in their allocation policy to victims who wish to be rehoused both from other council homes and from any other form of housing, eg private rented or owner-occupied housing.

2 Homeless

Perpetrators who are evicted for racial harassment are homeless. It would therefore appear that authorities are obliged to give "reasonable preference" in their waiting lists to perpetrators seeking rehousing after eviction. The waiting list priority is separate from the obligation to go through the usual homelessness procedure, so reasonable preference must be given even to those who are intentionally homeless (see below).[7]

3 Reasonable preference

Giving particular categories "reasonable preference" in an allocations policy does not mean that there is an obligation to rehouse those categories in every case. There are other categories to whom an authority is also obliged to give reasonable preference.[8] The extent of the preference given is a discretionary matter for an authority provided that its decision is made within the general principles of administrative law (see p6). With current pressure on housing resources some categories that are given "reasonable preference" may, in practice, never be rehoused at all. A failure by an authority to give any preference to the victims of racial harassment or to perpetrators who have been evicted might be unlawful.

Examples
The wide discretion given to authorities allows very high priority to be given to racial harassment victims and very low priority to be given to perpetrators who are homeless having been evicted for racial harassment. Perpetrators

The duty towards the homeless

Application: To victims from all sectors who have given up their homes. Perpetrators from all rented sectors who have been evicted for racial harassment.

Authorities are under a duty to ensure that accommodation is made available to those who are homeless, in priority need and who did not become homeless intentionally.[9] In addition, they must ensure that temporary accommodation is available to those whom they have reason to believe may be homeless and in priority need while enquiries are made to establish whether they are homeless, in priority need or became homeless intentionally.[10]

1 Racial harassment victims

Homeless
Until recently, a victim who had a legal right to live in accommodation could not usually be homeless even if s/he could not return there because of serious racial harassment. To become homeless, victims had to give up the right to the home voluntarily, eg by surrendering their tenancy or selling their home.

The position in domestic violence cases was different. A person was homeless if s/he had a right to use accommodation but it was probable that occupation would lead to violence from some other person residing there. This did not extend to violence which was part of a campaign of racial harassment by persons from outside the home. The definition of homeless was changed in January 1987. It now includes a clause which states: "a person shall not be treated as having accommodation unless it is accommodation which it would be reasonable for him to occupy".[11]
Victims can therefore now become homeless in two ways:
— by voluntarily giving up the right to their home as before;
— where victims still have the right to live in their home but it is not reasonable for them to occupy the home because of racial harassment.

Priority need
The following categories of people or anyone who might reasonably be expected to live with them fall within the category of people in "priority need":[12]
— pregnant women;
— people with dependent children;
— people who are vulnerable as a result of old age, mental illness or handicap or physical disability or other special reason;
— people who are homeless as a result of an emergency such as flood, fire or other disaster.

The Code of Guidance issued on homelessness advises authorities that they should consider the victims of domestic violence as vulnerable due to "any other special reason". For similar reasons, as a matter of good practice, authorities should also consider victims of racial harassment to be vulnerable. Victims who have lost their home through arson attack will be in priority need by reason of emergency.

Intentionally homeless
A person becomes homeless intentionally if "he deliberately does or fails to do anything in consequence of which he ceases to occupy accommodation which is available for his occupation and which it would have been reasonable for him to continue to occupy".[13] Giving up the right to a home or moving out of a home are deliberate acts. The question therefore is whether it would have been reasonable for the victim to remain living there.

To reach a decision as to whether it was reasonable for a victim to continue to suffer harassment in the home rather than leave, the authority must take full details of the extent of the harassment, its effect on the family and the likelihood of its continuing. In many cases, there are good reasons why victims justifiably feel unable to remain in their home.

Where a victim has left home but still retains the right to return, authorities may no longer fail to treat the victim as homeless because s/he has the legal right to return. Authorities must now treat any applicant as homeless and make the enquiries required by the HA 1985. In the meantime the duties regarding temporary accommodation will apply.

Authorities have considerable leeway in the decisions they reach on these points provided they follow the general principles of administrative law (see p6). They are entitled to take account of local pressure on housing resources.[14]

The duty
As soon as victims have given up the right to their home or inform the authority that they cannot return home because it is unsafe to do so, an authority has an immediate duty to ensure that they have temporary accommodation while enquiries are made, provided that there is reason to believe that the family is in priority need.

In addition to the obligation to provide temporary and permanent rehousing, an authority has a duty to take reasonable steps to protect the victim's property if there is a danger of its being lost or damaged.[15] Protection measures can include storage or arranging storage and an authority can enter the previous home of the victim at reasonable times to remove the belongings. This is a particularly useful power where victims may have left their homes very hurriedly without having had time to pack their personal property. The authority can charge for this service.

In some areas, many flats on council estates are broken into and vandalised as soon as they are vacated. Landlords of private tenants who have left often enter the flat and remove the tenant's belongings if they think the tenant is not returning. An authority has to move fast to take adequate steps to protect victims' belongings. The job will probably require skilled removers; an attempt to use council staff who are used to disposing of everything left in flats by departing tenants may lead to the victims suffering additional distress because their belongings have been damaged or lost.

2 Perpetrators of racial harassment

Perpetrators who have been evicted because they have committed racial harassment will be homeless. Perpetrators may be evicted either by the authority itself or by a housing association or even a private sector landlord. Perpetrators may be in priority need under the definition given above. Those who are not do not have to be rehoused under the homelessness procedure though they must still be dealt with under the normal allocation procedure.

If perpetrators are in priority need, an authority may be obliged to rehouse them unless the authority can find them to be intentionally homeless. The definition of intentionally homeless has been given above.

Intentionally homeless
There is no difficulty finding a person intentionally homeless if it is s/he who committed the acts of racial harassment which led or contributed to the eviction. Where it was conduct by one family member which led or contributed to an eviction, an authority can look at the family as a whole and assume, unless there is evidence to the contrary, that all the other family members were party to that conduct.[16] However, it must still consider each family member separately and decide whether evidence to the contrary exists. In practice, this means that there will be no difficulty in finding a parent intentionally homeless if it is acts of racial harassment committed by his or her children which led or contributed to eviction.[17] Similarly there should be no difficulty finding a former tenant intentionally homeless if s/he was evicted because of racial harassment by other family members who lived in the property with him or her. Tenants can also be found responsible for the acts of lodgers if those led to or contributed to the eviction and the tenant took no steps to stop the harassment or get the lodger to leave.[18]

Applying the principles above it should be possible to hold tenants responsible for visitors. However it should be noted that council tenants cannot be evicted because of the conduct of their visitors unless the tenancy agreement contains an express clause stating this (see Chapter 5).

To hold a perpetrator intentionally homeless on the basis of racial harassment, the harassment must be the ground on which the court ordered possession. For example, possession proceedings might be taken for both racial harassment and arrears of rent. The judge might indicate that s/he would be prepared to evict on the grounds of arrears and might try to persuade the authority not to proceed on the ground of harassment. If the authority does not pursue allegations of harassment and a possession order is made solely on the basis of arrears, the authority cannot hold the family intentionally homeless on the ground of racial harassment. The authority could still hold the perpetrators intentionally homeless on the ground of rent arrears. If possession is given on a number of grounds then the perpetrator can be found intentionally homeless provided that the harassment formed at least part of the basis for the decision to make a possession order. The authority cannot rely on the decision of the court in the possession proceedings but must itself consider whether the perpetrator is intentionally homeless under the homelessness provisions of the HA 1985.

The duty
Unless authorities set up efficient mechanisms for dealing with applications by perpetrators they may be obliged to provide temporary accommodation for a considerable time while enquiries are made. Even if perpetrators are then found intentionally homeless an authority must ensure that accommodation is available for a short period to give the perpetrator a reasonable opportunity to find alternative accommodation.[19]

Homelessness policy
When operating a policy on intentional homelessness following eviction for racial harassment, authorities must be careful to follow the general principles of administrative law outlined in Chapter 2. In particular, authorities must consider each case individually and must not have a blanket policy applying to every case, ie they must not fetter their discretion.

In practice this will not prevent authorities finding perpetrators intentionally homeless. A proper procedure should be established to ensure that each case is considered on its merits as rapidly as possible.

Examples
A procedure along the following lines could be adopted. Most of the steps are completed between the time when the court makes an order for possession and the date of eviction so that an authority can avoid having to provide any form of temporary accommodation to the perpetrator following eviction for more than a short period.

(a) As soon as the possession order is made the authority considers the position of each member of the perpetrator's family as potentially homeless. If the family is not in priority need it is informed accordingly and given advice and assistance to find alternative accommodation.[20]
(b) If the family is in priority need, the authority indicates it may be found intentionally homeless and invites each family member to attend an interview to give reasons why s/he should not be considered intentionally homeless or to give the reasons in writing.
(c) Interviews are held at which family members are invited to explain their case.
(d) The authority makes an initial decision on the question of intentional homelessness.
(e) The authority immediately notifies the family members of the decision and gives advice and assistance to find alternative accommodation.

(f) The perpetrators are evicted.

(g) If the perpetrators are in priority need the authority provides temporary accommodation and gives the perpetrators the opportunity to give reasons why its original decision in (d) should not be confirmed. A strict time limit should be imposed of a few days since the authority has carried out all the enquiries necessary already.

(h) The authority considers any reasons provided by the perpetrators and reaches a final decision on intentional homelessness and on a reasonable period to allow them to find alternative accommodation. The period allowed takes account of the fact that advice was provided to the perpetrators at step (e) and they were warned they were likely to be considered intentionally homeless.

(i) The authority ceases providing temporary accommodation when the period in step (h) expires.

Duty not to discriminate in housing allocation: Race Relations Act 1976 s21

Application: To victims in all sectors who seek rehousing from an authority.

An authority must not discriminate in the allocation of its housing on racial grounds. Discrimination by authorities was covered fully in Chapter 4 and the points considered there are equally applicable to discrimination in housing allocation (see p31).

Rehousing families in housing vacated by victims

When a victim of racial harassment is rehoused this often achieves the object of the perpetrators of the harassment. It is nevertheless justified as being in the long-term interests of the victim. A difficult dilemma for local authorities arises in the allocation of the vacated dwelling. There may be a likelihood of further racial harassment if a black family moves in.

Several points should be made:

(a) the authority cannot omit to offer these dwellings to black families since this is likely to amount to unlawful discrimination;

(b) as a matter of good practice, an authority should not offer such a dwelling to a black family without explaining the circumstances in which the previous tenant vacated;

(c) as a matter of good practice, the authority should offer protection measures to new families being offered the accommodation. Examples of such measures occur later in this chapter;

(d) the authority should monitor the level of refusals by black families in such dwellings to ensure that they are not, in practice, excluding black families from desirable housing and so that statistical evidence might be available in proceedings against perpetrators in future to show the effect of their harassment, even if the individual victim is transferred.

Racial harassment victims receiving high priority
Priority housing for racial harassment victims will only be lawful if one of the following three options is adopted:
— the victims of all types of harassment, whether racial or not, receive equal priority; or
— racial harassment is not defined or operated in such a way that victims must be from ethnic minorities; or
— an authority uses the exception allowed by RRA 1976 s35 to provide priority housing to particular specified racial groups to meet their special needs in regard to their welfare.

Racial harassment victims receiving low priority
If racial harassment victims are given lower priority than other victims of nuisance, annoyance or harassment then this will probably amount to unlawful discrimination.

If victims of nuisance or harassment must comply with certain conditions before they can be rehoused and victims of racial harassment find it harder to comply with these conditions than others, this may amount to discrimination too.[21] For example, an authority which rehouses harassment victims but only if they have lived in their accommodation for five years may be unlawfully discriminating. Those who suffer racial harassment may be likely to have lived less than five years in their present home and will find it more difficult to comply with the condition than others.

Contractual duty to repair

Application: Victims who are council tenants.

Like other landlords, authorities have a contractual duty to repair the structure and exterior of any dwelling-house and to keep installations in repair and proper working order when they have notice of the need for repair.[22] In addition, authorities have a duty to take reasonable care to keep the common parts, which are necessary for the reasonable enjoyment of a dwelling, in reasonable repair.[23]

Structure and exterior
The duty is to repair within a reasonable time. How much time is reasonable will depend upon all the circumstances. Where repairs are needed to make the premises secure and there is risk of racial harassment, a reasonable time may be very short indeed. Graffiti will not constitute disrepair under this provision.

94 Housing authorities and departments

Common parts
The duty to repair the common parts is less extensive. It is a duty to act reasonably. Where items of disrepair on the common parts make them dangerous an authority must to take steps to carry out repairs as soon as possible. This may include a situation where lighting is damaged and it is probable that victims of racial harassment will be attacked on dark and unlit stairs.

An authority in breach of either of these duties risks a claim by the victim for a court order requiring it to carry out the repairs and possibly a claim for damages for any loss suffered as a result of the failure to repair.[24] An authority must therefore have a system for ensuring that disrepair caused by vandalism, as part of a campaign of racial harassment, is rectified as quickly as possible, particularly where the security of the victim's home or of the victim using the common parts is jeopardised.

Examples
The most likely repairs to be necessary are to:
— windows and doors of the victim's home to make them secure;
— smashed lighting of common parts;
— broken entry-phones or doors to common parts of the building.
As a matter of good practice authorities should remove graffiti and consider carrying out improvements to increase future security rather than simply carrying out repairs.

Duty to take action against perpetrators

Where harassment occurs on a housing estate, often both perpetrator and victim may be tenants of the same authority. Each will have a separate tenancy agreement with the authority. The perpetrator's tenancy agreement may prohibit racial harassment or nuisance. There is no express duty on the authority to take action against perpetrators under the tenancy agreement. However, circumstances may arise where, in practice, a duty to take some steps against perpetrators may arise or the victim may be able to go some way towards forcing the authority to take action against the perpetrator provided s/he can be identified.

1 Circumstances in which a duty may arise

In Chapter 4, the extent to which authorities might be under a duty to have a policy of dealing with racial harassment by virtue of the RRA 1976 s71 was considered. The same points can be made in respect of the question whether an authority has a duty to take action against individual perpetrators. It is impossible to say, but just as a complete failure to develop any policy may amount to breach of RRA 1976 s71, so may a complete failure to act against identified perpetrators.

Furthermore, a blanket refusal to consider any action against perpetrators may in effect amount to a refusal to exercise the management powers which an authority possesses (see p104) and therefore be an unlawful fettering of an authority's discretion. In both cases, legal action would be extremely difficult.

2 Action by a victim against the authority for nuisance

It is possible that an authority might be held liable to compensate victims for nuisance caused by perpetrators who are tenants or tenants' family members or visitors. Consequently the authority could only avoid liability by taking steps to stop racial harassment occurring.

Consideration of this point requires a distinction to be drawn between racial harassment committed from other dwellings (eg throwing stones or other objects from windows, noise, throwing rubbish etc) and acts of harassment committed on the common parts of an estate.

Racial harassment committed from other dwellings
The general rule is that a landlord is not liable for acts of nuisance committed from dwellings which are let out to tenants unless s/he has authorised the nuisance. The tenant will be liable for his or her own acts and the acts of visitors and resident family members.

There have been several cases in which tenants have sought to force their landlords to take action against neighbours who are causing a nuisance. These cases establish the following principles:

(a) An authority cannot be liable in negligence for failing to take action against perpetrators or for allocating a flat to a tenant who is likely to cause a nuisance or harassment.[25]

(b) An authority cannot be liable in nuisance on the ground that it has authorised a nuisance by allocating a flat to a family it knows will cause a problem.[26]

(c) It has never been clearly established whether a landlord can be said to have authorised a nuisance and be liable for a nuisance committed by a tenant if s/he has power to take steps to abate the nuisance but, after becoming aware of it, failed to take reasonable steps to remove the cause of the nuisance within a reasonable time.[27]

It is therefore still possible that a victim may be able to take action directly against the landlord for nuisance caused by neighbouring tenants if the landlord fails to act within a reasonable time.

Racial harassment committed on the common parts
The common parts of a housing estate are the responsibility of the authority which owns them. It is the occupier for the purposes of the law of nuisance and is therefore legally liable for any nuisance caused by people who use the common parts who are under its control.

Consequently a victim should be able to take proceedings against an authority to obtain damages for nuisance caused by people using the common parts who are given permission to do so by the authority. This would include members of the public allowed onto a housing estate. Where harassment is committed from the common parts by tenants or their families with a right of access, they will be trespassing if they are exceeding the extent of the rights that have been granted, which will usually be a right of way only (see p113). The authority may therefore be liable if it fails to take reasonable steps to abate the nuisance within a reasonable time after it becomes aware of it.[28]

3 Action by a victim enforcing the tenancy agreement

The victim's tenancy agreement can make the landlord authority responsible for enforcing the racial harassment clause in the perpetrator's tenancy agreement. For responsibility to arise in this way an authority must voluntarily have put itself under an obligation to its tenants to enforce clauses in the tenancy agreement against neighbouring tenants.

Because landlords are not generally under any obligation to enforce clauses against neighbours, it is extremely common for long leases of flats in the private sector (eg for 99 years) to contain clauses which provide that the landlord will ensure that identical clauses are included in any other leases granted in the building and that the landlord will enforce the clauses in the other leases against the tenants if asked to do so. It is usual for the tenant requiring the clause to be enforced to have to pay the landlord's costs.

A clause of this nature would mean that the victim could require an authority to take action under the perpetrator's tenancy agreement. The clause about payment of costs is not appropriate for a local authority landlord; it would effectively destroy the usefulness of the clause since no legal aid would be available to the victim for paying the costs of the authority, which could reach several thousand pounds. An authority might consider including certain conditions to be fulfilled before action must be taken against perpetrators.

Authorities which have an effective system for dealing with perpetrators should not need to put themselves under any contractual obligations to victims.

An example of a contractual clause is shown in Appendix 1.

The duty to consult tenants on housing management issues: HA 1985 s105

Application: All council, housing association and housing trust tenants.

Authorities must have arrangements to inform tenants about certain housing management matters and for tenants to give their views. The views expressed must be considered by authorities before they reach a decision.[29]

Housing management matters
A housing management matter is one that, in the opinion of the authority,

applies to the dwellings it lets out to its tenants in relation to one of the following:

— management;
— maintenance;
— improvement;
— demolition;
— provision of services or amenities.[30]

Rents and charges for services are specifically excluded from the definition of housing management matters.

Consultation is required on new programmes of maintenance, improvement or demolition or changes in policy and practice which "are likely substantially to affect" all tenants or particular groups of tenants (eg on a particular estate). An authority must publish its arrangements for consultation. Details must be available for inspection at its principal office at reasonable hours and a copy must be made available at a reasonable fee to any member of the public.[31]

Housing associations and housing trusts must lodge a copy of their arrangements with the local authority for any area in which it has dwellings.[32] Co-operative housing associations do not need to comply with this requirement.[33]

The arrangements made for consultation must take into account RRA 1976 s71. The duty under s71 is particularly important in respect of consultation. Unless an authority adopts a consultation procedure which has some mechanism for consulting representatives of all racial groups it is difficult to see how the authority can argue that it is properly considering the need to eliminate unlawful discrimination. If, in practice, the groups that are consulted tend to achieve better services from an authority as a result of the consultation, then the authority may be unlawfully discriminating against those racial groups which are unrepresented in the consultative process.

Examples
An authority retains a substantial degree of discretion as to the form of any consultation. Clearly, it must have considered the need to ensure that all racial groups are involved or represented in the consultative process. An authority might set up an organisation of black tenants to consult as part of its arrangements. Alternatively, it might use local black organisations that have a significant number of tenants amongst their membership.

Authorities should not assume that tenants' associations represent their estates unless they can show that they have made efforts to involve and interest people from all racial groups. As part of the arrangements required under the HA 1985, authorities would be free to draw up guidelines with which tenants' associations must comply in order to qualify as sufficiently representative to be consulted on housing management issues. Alternative methods of consultation should be considered both on estates where a tenants' association is insufficiently representative and for tenants who do not live on estates but in individual houses, maisonettes or small blocks of flats.

Tenants' associations are given considerable status by being consulted. Making consultation dependent upon the tenants' association's success in involving tenants may considerably improve the representative nature of associations. It may also provide the necessary stimulus for them to take active steps to discourage racial harassment on their estates and provide support to victims when it occurs. Authorities should be wary of taking action which could be seen to be punishing an association because it refuses to adopt the views of the authority rather than because it is unrepresentative of its tenants (see p13).

B. POWERS TO ASSIST VICTIMS WITH REHOUSING

Information on possible sources of housing

Information provided under the LGA 1972 s142 can include the availability of housing from other authorities under mobility and exchange schemes. Under the HA 1985 s65 authorities have a duty to provide "advice and such assistance as they consider appropriate" to people who are homeless or threatened with homelessness to help them obtain alternative accommodation when the authority itself has no duty to make accommodation available (eg to single childless people who are not in priority need).

Advice has a wider meaning than information. Merely to provide a list of accommodation agencies or of housing associations is probably insufficient; an authority should be able to advise on all possible methods of rehousing available to victims. The advice should include the advantages and disadvantages of each method and the likely time within which rehousing can be achieved.

Examples
An authority ought to be able to provide information on the policies and practices of building societies and banks in the area for those who might be able to purchase, in addition to the allocation practices of local housing associations. Details of shared or part-ownership schemes run by local housing associations should also be available.

Rehousing by an authority in its own accommodation

Application: Victims in all sectors.

Subject to their duties to give reasonable preference to certain categories of applicant on the waiting and transfer lists, and to their duties to rehouse homeless people in priority need, authorities have total discretion in the degree of priority given to particular categories of people requiring housing (see pp86 and 88). The power to rehouse victims applies not only to victims who are already council tenants but also to those living in owner occupied, bed and breakfast, private rented or housing association accommodation.

Payment of removal costs

Application: Victims who are local authority tenants who are being rehoused to alternative accommodation in any sector.

Where a tenant moves from local authority accommodation to another home the authority may pay the expenses of the removal.[34] The power only applies where the person to be moved is a tenant of the authority. It does not apply to those moving from the private sector into council accommodation.

The power is limited to "the expenses of the removal". This could include expenses such as the disconnection and reconnection of cookers and washing machines, or a narrower definition could limit expenses to the fees paid to removers. On either interpretation, it does not seem possible to pay the sorts of expenses covered by disturbance payments, eg telephone reconnection, redirection of mail, adaptations to carpets and curtains etc. The courts have never decided which of the two meanings is correct, so authorities are entitled to adopt the wider interpretation.

Additional payments may be possible under housing management powers (see below).

Other financial assistance to victims being transferred to other council accommodation

The express power to make payments to tenants obtaining transfers to alternative council accommodation is limited to "expenses of removal" referred to above. However, authorities also have statutory powers to manage, regulate and control their housing stock[35] and the ancillary powers provided by the LGA 1972 s111. These two powers combined can be used to provide a legal basis for making additional payments to victims who are transferred because of racial harassment. Any payments made must be considered to be in the interests of the general management, regulation or control of the housing stock.

The social services department may also have powers to make payments where there are children in the family being transferred (see Chapter 7).

Local Government Act 1972 s111
The power under the LGA 1972 s111 includes the power to spend money and to lend money. It should be possible to justify the need to compensate victims of racial harassment on housing management grounds for the following reasons:

(a) Part of the management function is to ensure that tenants occupy dwellings that are appropriate to their needs. The extent to which victims of racial harassment might be considered to be living in "unsatisfactory living conditions" has been discussed above (see p87). The HA 1985 clearly intends that those living in unsatisfactory conditions should be rehoused. Measures to encourage victims of racial harassment to move to more appropriate accommodation, where living conditions will be satisfactory because the family will be safe, can be considered as part of good management practice and in accord with the purpose and intention of the HA 1985.

(b) The rehousing of a victim may save an authority money because there may be less need for repairs, graffiti removal, extra caretaking patrols etc.

(c) An authority cannot force a victim to move, but payments or loans to victims may encourage them to move and can be justified on housing management grounds.

(d) It might be possible to go one step further and justify a payment when a victim is being nominated by the authority to a housing association.

Any use of this power must be considered experimental. There has been no guidance from the courts on the use of these powers to compensate victims. The courts are more likely to uphold a payment to a victim which directly compensates him or her for expenses incurred in moving and settling in the new home than they are to uphold an authority's policy to pay a set amount compensating hurt feelings and distress, though both may be acceptable. Hurt feelings and distress are barely recognised by the courts as a basis for any compensation and the courts appear more likely to disapprove of a direct cash incentive to move than they would a payment which removes some of the disincentive of moving because of the cost of doing so.

Examples
Authorities are not limited to making outright payments. As an alternative, loans could be made allowing victims to buy the things they need for their new home and repay the authority over a set period. Where moving home occurs as an emergency there are often substantial payments to be made in a very short period which few families can meet from their normal income. Instead of leaving the victim to borrow from friends or finance companies charging excessive interest, an authority could set up a loan scheme to spread the cost over a more manageable period, depending on the victim's income.

Loans or payments could be considered for the following:
— removal contractors' fees;
— mail redirection;
— reconnection of phone at new home;
— reconnection charges for gas and electricity;
— disconnection and reconnection of cooker and washing machine;
— security devices at the new home;
— shelving, carpets and curtains at the new home which cannot be re-used or adapted from the old home;

— the cost of decoration if not carried out by the authority;
— new school uniforms for the children;
— the cost of items of furniture that have to be replaced because of different sizes or shapes of rooms in a new home or because it is smaller;
— loans to buy extra furniture required for a new home.

Provision of furniture and fittings in housing

Authorities have power to fit out, furnish and supply accommodation provided by them with all requisite furnishings, fittings and conveniences.[36] This provision appears to allow authorities to provide furniture for their dwellings as well as to install fixtures and fittings, eg shelving, cabinets, kitchen units. Any furniture provided would remain the property of the local authority and it would probably be unlawful to fail to take account of the provision of furniture when fixing an appropriate rent.

The authority has power to sell the furniture to the tenant or to provide it on hire purchase or conditional sale.

Rehousing in accommodation managed by other organisations

Application: Victims in all sectors.

Authorities often provide land, buildings and grants to housing associations in their areas. In return, they are able to negotiate nomination rights either to the association's property in their borough or elsewhere. The right to make nominations may be made a condition of the financial grant or of the granting of a lease or licence of property.[37]

Authorities may delegate to management co-operatives the management of some of their estates including the allocation of tenancies, but in any agreement with a management co-operative an authority can retain the right to nominate prospective tenants either generally or in certain circumstances.[38]

Voluntary organisations providing housing to the homeless may be grant-aided or have premises supplied by the local authority. Rights to nominate people for emergency temporary rehousing if they are the victims of racial harassment can be negotiated by the authority as a condition of any grant.[39]

Housing associations may have property in other areas which is nearer to friends and relatives of the victim household and an authority may be able to negotiate nomination rights to those properties, as well as to those in its area in exchange for grants or leases of additional premises for homes. Authorities may wish to offer a mechanism whereby they rehouse housing association tenants who are victims of racial harassment.

Special procedures may be necessary for racial harassment cases to ensure that the victim is rehoused rapidly. There may be a need to improve communication between the authority and other organisations, and the allocation procedure of the housing association or co-operative concerned may need adaptation so that decisions can be made sufficiently quickly.

Rehousing by other authorities

London borough councils are given specific power to make arrangements for rehousing their tenants with other London boroughs. The London Area Mobility Scheme has been set up under this power.[40] In addition there is a National Mobility Scheme which enables authorities to nominate people to housing elsewhere in the country.

Outside London, it appears that authorities should be able to justify making reciprocal arrangements with neighbouring authorities for the rehousing of victims of racial harassment on the ground of good housing management.

Example
Victims may wish to be rehoused by another authority where they have friends or relations in that area. The availability of different types of accommodation varies among authorities and some arrangements for rehousing may result in allocations to victims occurring more quickly. For instance, a neighbouring authority may have a greater number of larger properties but an acute shortage of smaller ones. It may be willing to allow nominations for its larger properties in return for being able to nominate prospective tenants for smaller ones.

Assisting victims to buy their own homes

1   Loans for the purchase of homes

Application: Victims in all sectors.

Authorities may lend money to any person to acquire a house or flat or to help them pay off a previous loan used for that purpose.[41] The house or flat need not be in the authority's area.[42] The loan must be secured by a mortgage and cannot exceed the value of the house or flat on which it is secured. Similar terms must be imposed to those with building society mortgages save that part of any loan to first-time buyers may be made interest-free for up to five years (see below).

Examples
This power can be used to assist victims to obtain their own rehousing. It applies to victims whatever their previous tenure, eg bed and breakfast, private tenants or owner occupiers who are prepared and able to buy alternative accommodation.

It will be of most use in the following circumstances:

(a)   To give 100% mortgages so that victims need no deposit.

(b) To give mortgages in excess of the amount that a building society or bank would provide based on the victim's income (though it is always in the victim's interest to make sure s/he is able to make the repayments).

(c) To provide mortgages more quickly than could be provided by banks or building societies, to assist rapid rehousing.

(d) To provide mortgages on properties in need of improvement or of a type on which building societies and banks are reluctant to lend.

2 Guaranteeing mortgages

Application: Victims in all sectors.

Authorities have power to guarantee repayment of mortgages provided by banks and building societies.[43] As an alternative to providing the mortgage themselves, authorities can encourage banks and building societies to provide mortgages by offering to guarantee repayment.

This power will be of use in the same circumstances as the power to provide mortgages, ie to allow a victim to obtain a loan to buy a home when s/he would not usually qualify to do so or where the home would not usually be acceptable to the lender. The major difference for an authority between this power and the power to provide a mortgage is that it does not have to find any money from its budget unless the borrower defaults. In order to consider making full use of this power, authorities can obtain details of the policies and practices of local lenders such as building societies and banks to see what types of assistance can best be provided.

3 Assistance for council tenants with legal costs of purchase

Application: Victims moving from council sector to owner-occupied housing.

Where a victim is moving from council accommodation to buy a home, an authority can pay any expenses incurred in connection with the purchase other than the purchase price.[44] There is no fixed cash limit, and payments can cover legal fees, stamp duty, land registry and search fees.

4 Assistance with legal costs of obtaining a mortgage

Application: Victims in all sectors.

An authority may assist with costs incurred in connection with a mortgage provided by a building society or bank.[45] The maximum amount of assistance is currently £200,[46-49] and this may be paid as an outright grant to cover matters such as legal fees, stamp duty or survey fees.

No assistance can be given where the authority itself is providing the mortgage but the authority may use its own surveyors and lawyers and make no charge for their services to the borrower.

C. POWERS TO PROTECT AND ASSIST VICTIMS IN THEIR HOMES

Some victims do not wish to be rehoused, or rehousing will not be available. Victims who are rehoused may be potential targets of racial harassment in their new homes. This section deals with the powers of local authorities to provide protection for victims or help them provide their own protection. These powers are in addition to the powers of every authority to set up self-help or security schemes using grant aid under LGA 1972 s137.

Some measures under this heading may be more appropriately dealt with by another authority, eg setting up playgroups or youth clubs so that children who are the victims of racial harassment have somewhere to play other than the common parts of the estate where harassment is occurring.

General powers to manage the housing stock[50]

Application: Protection of victims who are council tenants.

A housing authority has general powers to manage, regulate and control its housing stock. It also has powers to appoint any staff necessary to do so.[51] These general powers are supplemented by the ancillary powers in LGA 1972 s111 (see Chapter 2). There is no limit to what a housing authority can do under these powers provided it can justify the decision under the general principles of administrative law as being part of the management, regulation or control of its housing. All decisions on the exercise of the power must be made subject to the duties imposed on all authorities referred to in Chapter 4 and the duties which specifically apply to housing authorities dealt with at the beginning of this chapter. In particular the needs referred to in RRA 1976 s71 must always be considered.

Management and regulation of the housing stock includes power to do repairs and improvements. Repairs or improvements that involve the use of capital money must be considered as part of the Housing Investment Programme and Project Control Approval may be required. Minor repairs and improvements to individual dwellings can be carried out using revenue resources. Minor improvements will be completely within the authority's discretion. A council usually owes a contractual duty to its tenant to carry out repairs (see p93).

1 Power to provide security devices and improvements to security

These could include:
— replacement windows with safety glass;
— window locks;
— fireproof containers with lids behind letter-boxes to catch burning material;
— strengthened front doors;
— installation of telephones for victims;

— spy-holes;
— additional or better locks;
— more, better or higher fencing around garden or common parts to prevent or deter access, or items being thrown into the garden or at a dwelling;
— entry-phones to the block;
— installation of a locked door to the particular landing on which the victim lives with ordinary door bells for all those who live there (this helps to overcome the problem if a perpetrator lives in the same block, and avoids the risks of vandalism to an entry-phone system);
— additional or better lighting to common parts outside victims' homes;
— the use of materials which are vandal proof or more difficult to damage.

2 Power to provide communication equipment for victims to raise the alarm

These could include:
— telephones for victims (these might also be considered by the social services department using their powers under the Child Care Act 1980 s1; see Chapter 7);
— walkie-talkies, particularly if telephone wires have been cut as part of harassment;
— installation of burglar alarms or alarms operated by the victim if attacked.

3 Power to provide staff to increase security on an estate

These could include:
— extra caretaking patrols;
— security guards with dogs;
— investigators responsible for identifying those responsible for breaches of the tenancy agreement or acts of nuisance on the estate.

4 Power to give loans or grants to tenants to allow them to install security devices and to carry out improvements

Housing Act 1985 s21 gives the authority power to manage, regulate and control its housing. LGA 1972 s111 gives the authority power to do anything conducive or incidental to that management which may or may not involve expenditure. These combined powers should allow the authority to make payments to tenants if this furthers the management of its housing.

If an authority can carry out work itself, it should also have the power to pay a tenant to carry out the same work. This power must be implied by LGA 1972 s111 (see p15). Payment may be in full or by way of a contribution to the cost. The contribution may be made outright or by way of a loan repayable over a specified period. This power is in addition to any power to award an improvement grant to a tenant (see below).

Power to give victims permission to carry out their own improvements and security measures and to reimburse the tenant when they move

Council tenants cannot carry out improvements without the consent of their landlord.[52] Where a tenant has carried out improvements at his or her own expense, an authority may reimburse the cost in some circumstances.[53] An authority may also be able to give an improvement grant.

Written consent is required for tenants to be able to carry out improvements. Reimbursement of the cost of improvements is expressly authorised by the HA 1985 provided the improvement materially adds to the value of the dwelling on the open market or its market rent.[54] It can be argued that major security improvements add to the market rent or value of a dwelling.

Where minor improvements are contemplated, the general power of management may allow an authority to reach an agreement with tenants to reimburse the cost if they move.

Examples

Some authorities take many months to respond to requests by tenants to carry out improvements. Requests for permission to carry out improvements to the security of a dwelling should be dealt with immediately. A special procedure may be necessary.

Tenants may seek permission to carry out works to the common parts for their own security, eg the erection of a locked door to the landing. An authority can give permission for this work provided all the tenants on the landing agree with the suggestion.

Improvement grants

Application: To victims who are owner occupiers including long leaseholders, council or housing association tenants or protected tenants under the Rent Act 1977.[55]

An authority can give a grant for the improvement of a dwelling.[56] The word "improvement" is not defined in the HA 1985 but additional security measures to a dwelling would certainly be considered improvements within the ordinary meaning of the word.[57] The word "dwelling" is defined to include gardens, so improvements could include new or better fencing.[58]

Improvement grants are discretionary. There is no obligation on an authority to award a grant.[59] Grants may generally be paid only for the improvement of dwellings built before 2 October 1961.[60] Tenants will need their landlord's permission before carrying out improvements.

The maximum proportion of the cost of the works that can be met by a grant is 50 per cent. Where an authority believes that an applicant cannot pay the other 50 per cent without undue hardship it may increase the grant to 65 per cent.[61] However, an authority could consider paying or lending the balance of the cost of the works under its general management powers if the applicant is a tenant of the authority. Alternatively, the social services authority might consider paying for the balance of the cost under its powers under the Child Care Act 1980 s1 if there are children in the victim's family.

An authority cannot award a grant to an owner unless the owner certifies that the house will be used for future occupation as the owner's residence or that of his or her family for up to five years or will be available for letting for this period.[62] Where a tenant applies for a grant an authority can require the landlord to provide a certificate stating that the dwelling will be available for letting. This requirement is not obligatory.[63] Where the applicant for a grant is an owner occupier the rateable value of the dwelling must not exceed £400 in Greater London and £225 elsewhere.[64]

When the works are completed the dwelling must conform to specified standards relating to repair, amenities and condition.[65] An authority can dispense with these requirements if it is satisfied that the applicant cannot finance the works except by a grant without undue hardship.[66]

Examples
Improvement grants are not usually given for security measures but there appears no reason why they should not be. A relatively small amount of grant to victims could result in considerable improvements in security in the home. Most of the measures referred to on pp104-5 above can be considered for grant aid and assistance can therefore be provided to allow owner occupiers and private sector tenants to obtain these security devices.

The restriction on the age of the property may mean that tenants on some council estates cannot be assisted by improvement grants. It may still be possible to assist under general management powers.

Loans for improvements in owner-occupied housing

On p102 the power to provide loans to purchase homes was discussed. The power extends to allow authorities to lend money to owner occupiers to carry out improvements to their homes.[67] Any loan must be secured by a mortgage, but the HA 1985 does not specify that the authority must have a first mortgage.[68] An authority can therefore lend money for improvements on a second mortgage where, for example, the first mortgage is with a building society. Alternatively, an authority can take over and extend the first mortgage.

Before lending money an authority must be satisfied either that the dwelling will be fit for human habitation following the improvements or that the effect of the advance will be to meet the housing needs of the applicant by allowing him or her to carry out improvements. In most cases this should present no difficulty.[69]

Example
Suppose Mr and Mrs A own a house worth £50,000. They have a building society mortgage on which they owe £20,000. They wish to spend £2,000 on security improvements. The authority can either take a second mortgage for £2,000 or pay off the building society and let Mr and Mrs A have a single mortgage for £22,000.

Loans and improvements grants can be used in tandem. Mr and Mrs A could be given an improvement grant of £1,000 (50 per cent of the cost) and they would then only have to borrow £1,000.

Allocation of flats to tenants who will provide support and back-up to victims

Authorities have substantial discretion in the allocation of their dwellings. It is within their powers to allocate dwellings to tenants who will provide support or back-up to victims on particular estates. Where the prospective tenants concerned are homeless they may be offered the dwelling on a tenancy which is not a secure tenancy for up to 12 months.[70] This power can be used to allocate flats as dwellings to prospective tenants who, in return, undertake to assist the authority and the victim.

Since authorities are obliged to publish their allocation rules some residual category of management allocations or transfers will be necessary within those rules to allow the use of this power.

The primary object of housing allocation powers is to meet housing need. Thus prospective tenants must be in housing need if an authority is to be able to justify the provision of accommodation to them. See below for allocation of premises to a support group.

Before considering the use of this power it is important for an authority to be clear as to what is expected of the tenants concerned. There are differing degrees of involvement which tenants may be prepared to accept. These might, for example, include:
— emotional support to victims from family and/or friends housed nearby;
— escort to school for the victim's children by parents of other children who attend the same school;
— going to the shops with the victim to deter attacks;
— shopping for the victim so the home need never be empty;
— agreeing to be alert to possible attacks on victims and to make a note of observations;
— allowing the police or council officers to use their flat for observation purposes;
— agreeing to be available to go to the support of a victim immediately an attack occurs;
— agreeing to call the police whenever an attack occurs;
— agreeing to provide a presence in the flat by tenants or friends or members of a support group for 24 hours a day to observe attacks and go to the support of victims and identify perpetrators.

Some of these commitments may expose the tenants concerned to some risk themselves which they must be made aware of before undertaking the task. Some authorities are considering seeding their estates with tenants who agree to provide support to victims of harassment or who will record any instances and provide a detective element on the estate.

If a tenant is given accommodation near a victim from which s/he is expected to go to the victim's assistance when an attack occurs, it is probably sensible to establish some kind of link by telephone or radio between them so that they can be called on at short notice. This will provide a considerably quicker response than that of the police.

The power to temporarily rehouse homeless people can be used to allocate flats to tenants who will provide support to victims on a temporary basis for up to a year before being moved to permanent accommodation.

Allocation of grants, facilities and premises to a support group

Support groups sometimes develop spontaneously in response to particular acts of racial harassment or may be formed by a community, perhaps with support from the authority, to tackle racial harassment that is prevalent in a particular area. Authorities can encourage and promote support groups by providing grants, facilities and premises for them to carry out their activities.

1 Grants and facilities

The main power to provide grants under LGA 1972 s137 is discussed on p36 above. Housing authorities already justify grants to some tenants' associations using their general management powers. Grants to groups which will take steps to tackle racial harassment on housing estates could also be justified under general management powers.

The Local Authority (Goods and Services) Act 1970 enables authorities to provide administrative and technical facilities to support groups (see p38).

Examples
Support groups may need to produce publicity material both to recruit members and to warn perpetrators that they risk being identified. They may wish to use educational propaganda to attempt to dissuade perpetrators from racially harassing tenants. Equally important, they may wish to distribute publicity to try to get the support of the majority of white tenants for the victims of racial harassment and encourage peer group pressure on the perpetrators to stop their harassment. Grants can cover such things as the salaries of organisers for volunteers, practical security devices, apparatus for assisting identification of perpetrators, printing, stationery and telephones. An authority can allow its own printing facilities to be used free of charge.

2 Premises

A support group providing day-to-day support for victims will wish to be as close as possible to those it is assisting. If possible, it will want to use a dwelling near the victim's home. At the very least, it may want premises on the same estate.

Dwellings
Authorities cannot rent dwellings to support groups without the consent of the Secretary of State.[71] If it is desired to rent premises in this way special permission must be obtained. Authorities may, however, provide dwellings on a temporary basis, on licence, to support groups since that would not amount to a "disposal" requiring ministerial consent. Where one member of the support group is in housing need and happy to accept a permanent or temporary council tenancy of neighbouring property, it may be easier to allocate a flat to that member, who can then allow other members of the group to use the flat while the harassment continues.

Examples
As with the allocation of flats to individual tenants who will assist victims, an authority needs to establish with a support group exactly what its role will be in a particular situation before deciding whether to provide premises. Where a group intends to try and identify perpetrators it may need a flat with a direct view of the victim's home for visual observations or for using a video or still camera. Obviously, it will not always be possible to provide the premises required.

Other premises
An authority may have other premises on the estate which are not dwellings, eg estate offices which are only used once a week, rent collection offices, community halls or other facilities. Consent to use these premises will not be required from the Secretary of State if the main purpose for which they were designed remains unchanged. If a housing office were to be taken over completely by a support group and cease to be a housing office, it appears that ministerial consent may be required.[72]

D. POWERS TO DETER AND PUNISH PERPETRATORS ON COUNCIL ESTATES

Various methods of acting against perpetrators have been considered in previous chapters, eg legal action to protect council property or sanctions against individuals or organisations by the withdrawal of services. Criminal prosecutions against perpetrators are considered in Chapter 10. In Chapter 5, the most important methods of dealing with perpetrators who are tenants of council accommodation — the use of possession proceedings and injunctions — were examined.

Earlier in this chapter the extent of any duty imposed on an authority to take action against perpetrators and the ability to find perpetrators intentionally homeless were discussed. Here, other measures to deter and punish perpetrators in tenanted council property are considered. The last section in this chapter will look at powers of authorities in other sectors of housing, including bed and breakfast.

General powers to manage, regulate and control the housing stock[73]

The general power to manage the housing stock gives authorities discretion to take steps against perpetrators of racial harassment as well as steps to protect victims. Many examples are given in Chapters 2 and 4, see particularly devoting resources to identifying perpetrators (p39) and taking steps to protect council property (p40).

Tenants' associations

Tenants' associations can to be a useful ally in the fight against racial harassment. The most successful way of getting them to support the authority's campaign against racial harassment is by persuasion rather than threats. This section considers particular ways in which an authority can exert influence over a tenants' association and, if necessary, refuse to recognise one that is overtly racist. Readers are referred to Chapter 2 for a list of the circumstances in which measures against organisations may be justified by the RRA 1976. Chapter 4 deals with this point in the context of consultation with community groups and the points made there will apply to tenants' associations.

1 Conditions on the use of land (p48)

Tenants' associations are frequently given the right to use council premises on housing estates. Conditions in licences or leases of premises can make the association responsible for any racial harassment occurring on the premises and give an authority the right to terminate its use of the premises if harassment occurs and no action is taken to prevent it.

An authority should set out what action it expects to be taken against those who racially harass on the premises, eg their removal and permanent ban. Authorities may wish to reserve the right to ban particular individuals from the use of the premises when granting a licence to a tenants' association.

2 Discretionary facilities (p46)

Discretionary facilities such as the use of premises or council equipment by tenants' associations might be withdrawn or withheld in the circumstances suggested in Chapter 2. Authorities can draw up good practice guidelines with which they require tenants' associations to comply before they are provided with any discretionary facilities. This could include a requirement to have a constitution conforming to a certain model.

> **Example:** *A model tenants' association constitution could provide for representation from different groups on an estate to ensure a satisfactory balance of interests, or for other local community groups to make nominations of tenants on to the committee. For example, a local black community group might be given the right to nominate one tenant as a member of the tenants' association committee.*

A model constitution might include the elimination of discrimination and racial harassment as one of its objects, a requirement that the association has an equal opportunities policy, and that those responsible for racial harassment be excluded from the association and its functions.

Where tenants' associations support an authority's stance, the authority might discuss the practical steps that can be taken on a particular estate to prevent or eliminate racial harassment.

3 Consultation (p49)

The duty to consult was discussed on p96. As part of its consultation arrangements, it is certainly legitimate for an authority to lay down guidelines of the sort suggested in the preceding paragraph with which tenants' associations must comply before they are entitled to be consulted.

4 Grants and grant conditions (p50)

Some tenants' associations receive grant aid which can be withdrawn or withheld in the circumstances described in Chapter 2. Groups receiving grant aid can be required to abide by grant conditions which require certain action on their part in exchange for the grant. This could include the use of money for specific purposes, eg publicity against racial harassment, or the showing of an authority video at a meeting of the association.

Other community groups on housing estates

Other community groups such as playgroups, parent-and-toddler groups, youth clubs and similar organisations use facilities and premises on housing estates and receive local authority grants. The points made above in relation to tenants' associations apply equally to these other community groups.

Byelaws on council estates

Application: All perpetrators who are on council estates wherever they live.

In addition to its powers to make general byelaws (see p45), housing authorities may make byelaws for "the management use and regulation of their houses" and with respect to the use of other land held by them for housing purposes.[74] There are two separate powers. The first is the power to make byelaws affecting individual dwellings. The second relates to the use of the common parts of a housing estate. The general administrative law principles applying to byelaws generally (see p45 above) apply to byelaws made by housing authorities.

Byelaws covering dwellings apply to individual flats as well as houses.[75] The power to make byelaws affecting the use of the common parts excludes the common parts of blocks of flats inside the building.[76] It is not entirely clear whether the power to make byelaws for "flats" allows byelaws to be made for blocks of flats as well as individual flats.[77] It would seem absurd if the HA 1985 allows byelaws for individual flats and common parts of an estate but excludes the stairs and landings of blocks of flats. For this reason, the ambiguity in the Act should be interpreted as allowing byelaws for staircases and landings of blocks, in addition to areas clearly covered by the provision such as common courtyards, roadways, play areas and open spaces.

Byelaws can extend to facilities such as shops, recreation grounds and halls which are provided by a housing authority for its tenants on an estate.[78]

The procedure set out in the LGA 1972 s236 must be followed before byelaws on housing estates can be brought into force.

Examples
Byelaws might be used for the following purposes:

(a) to ensure that acts of racial harassment by anyone on an estate are punishable as criminal offences by the authority. This will include visitors or members of the public;

(b) in exceptional circumstances, to enable an authority to seek an injunction to prevent the commission of further criminal offences;

(c) to regulate the control of dogs on the estate;

(d) to regulate the dumping of rubbish on the estate;

(e) to control other behaviour such as spitting, throwing stones, letting off fireworks, possessing catapults or air pistols or setting fire to paper;

(f) to enable an authority's officers to require people who are not tenants to leave the estate at any time, eg young people hanging around staircases and landings waiting for victims.

Permission to enter housing estates can be given to the public generally on condition that they do not commit acts of racial harassment on the estate. If they do so, they become trespassers and the authority has a right to take direct legal action against them. In order to limit permission in this way, notices would probably have to be erected at the entrances to estates.

Trespass

It is a trespass to damage property, enter without authority or exceed the authority to enter (see p42). The grounds for obtaining an injunction to restrain a trespass were considered on p70 above. In addition to its use against members of the public who are racially harassing others, the law of trespass represents the most useful legal remedy against perpetrators who live on council estates but are not tenants. An illustration of the use in this context is provided in Appendix 4.

Trespass on housing estates falls into two categories: entering part of the estate which a person has no permission to enter, and using the estate for a purpose which is prohibited or for which no permission has been granted, eg racial harassment. In both cases, the person concerned should have been informed of the limits on their permission. In cases of perpetrators already identified, this should be done by letter. In any event notices can be erected around estates.

Tenants, their resident family members and visitors
The extent to which the law of trespass can be used against tenants and their families depends on the rights granted in the tenancy agreement. Consequently it will depend on the precise legal effect of the wording of the agreement.

No mention of access or use of common parts in the tenancy agreement
If no right of access to premises is mentioned in the tenancy agreement, the law implies a right for a tenant and the family living with the tenant to walk from the front door of the dwelling they rent to the public highway by the shortest possible route. Without this right the tenancy of a dwelling would be useless as it would be impossible to gain access to it. No other right to use the common parts would be implied into the tenancy agreement. Tenants and their families would, in addition, have the same implied licence to enter and use the common parts that was given to other members of the public but this licence could be terminated at any time.

Right to use the common parts referred to
In some cases authorities may expressly or by implication confer greater rights on their tenants when they grant tenancies, allowing them to make use of the common parts on the entire estate. Even if greater rights are provided or implied, the purposes for which these rights are granted may be stated or there may be an implication that the right to make use of the common parts is for normal use and not for unlawful purposes such as acts of racial harassment.

Normal use of the common parts will include:
— entering and leaving the premises let, from and to the highway;
— using communal facilities for the purpose for which they were intended, eg drying clothes, rubbish disposal etc.
— parking cars in spaces or areas provided;
— allowing children to play in the courtyard or playground.

Any right that is neither expressly stated in nor implied into the tenancy agreement can be withdrawn or limited. The use of the common parts by a tenant or a resident family member in excess of the rights granted by the tenancy agreement will amount to a trespass and action can be taken for an injunction (see Appendix 4).

The public
Members of the public who are not visiting tenants can always be prohibited from entering an estate by terminating any implied permission they may

have to enter, either by notice addressed to them individually or a general notice at the entrance to the estate.

The usefulness of the law of trespass is amply illustrated by the example given in Appendix 4.

The law on trespass can be used to prevent a perpetrator even getting within striking distance of a victim's home. Mere presence in an area of the estate without permission is a trespass. If an injunction has been granted restraining trespass, it will be comparatively easy to obtain evidence of breach. Housing officers, tenants' association committee members or caretakers are more likely to see a perpetrator in an area of the estate from which s/he has been banned than they are to happen to see an act of racial harassment that may be committed very quickly.

To enforce racial harassment or nuisance clauses requires evidence that the perpetrator committed particular acts which must have been witnessed. A perpetrator may stand on a landing for hours and throw a stone as soon as no one is watching.

Action to prevent pressure on an authority to discriminate

Under the RRA 1976 it is unlawful to induce or attempt to induce a housing authority to discriminate in its housing allocation.[79] Action against those responsible for such conduct can only be taken by the Commission for Racial Equality under the RRA 1976.[80]

However, authorities have a statutory duty under the Act not to discriminate in housing allocation and to consider the needs to eliminate unlawful discrimination and to promote equality of opportunity and good relations between different racial groups (see p11). This may justify action by an authority for an injunction to restrain a perpetrator from preventing it from carrying out its statutory duty (see Chapter 3). Intimidation of black tenants or prospective tenants on a housing estate by white tenants who wish to preserve the estate's all-white composition may effectively force an authority to operate a discriminatory housing allocation system whereby black families cannot be housed on the best estates or will not accept housing on those estates.

It is by no means certain that a power such as this exists, and the Commission for Racial Equality should be encouraged to act. Action by an authority may be necessary to provide a rapid response in urgent cases.

Example
On some estates, "reception committees" appear when prospective tenants are shown round empty flats. Where the prevalence of such "committees" in particular areas and on better estates affects the allocation of housing by an authority, court action to obtain an injunction against the participants might be justified.

E. POWERS TO ACT AGAINST PERPETRATORS IN THE PRIVATE SECTOR

It is only when considering the powers of a housing authority that it is necessary to consider the private sector separately from other sectors of housing. Other departments will have powers against perpetrators regardless of the sector of housing in which they live. The general powers to act against perpetrators discussed in Chapter 4 are available to housing authorities in addition to the power to prosecute for certain offences considered in Chapter 10.

Former council tenants who have bought their homes

1 Restrictive covenants in leases and transfers

When authorities sell houses or flats to their tenants, either voluntarily or under the "right to buy" provisions of the HA 1985, they are entitled to impose some restrictions on activities that can be carried on within the dwellings.[81] These are called "restrictive covenants" in freehold houses and "covenants" in leases of flats or houses. Both types of covenant remain valid and can be enforced against future owners of the same dwelling.

Covenants restricting nuisance or annoyance to neighbours are included in almost every lease in the private sector and many transfers of freehold houses on private estates. Local authorities can also adopt this practice and extend it to clauses prohibiting racial or other forms of harassment. Some authorities already include clauses on nuisance or annoyance in their transfers of freeholds and probably every authority does so in its leases.

Enforcement of restrictive covenants in transfers of freehold houses can only be by way of injunction and only against the owner. There is no possibility of eviction. If a perpetrator is prosecuted by the police, bail conditions may be imposed requiring the perpetrator to live elsewhere for a limited period (see p170).

Enforcement of covenants in leases requires a special procedure and can eventually lead to eviction. The procedure is begun in a similar manner to possession proceedings, with the service of a notice informing the lessee what s/he has done in breach of the lease. After the notice has been served, it is not possible to apply to the court to bring the lease to an end unless racial harassment is repeated.[82] If harassment is repeated, following service of the notice, proceedings can be brought against the leaseholder to forfeit the lease. The lessee can ask the court to exercise its discretion not to forfeit the lease and the court can impose the equivalent of a suspended possession order or an injunction restraining future breach.[83]

This power will be most useful on estates where a few houses or flats are sold off. By imposing restrictive covenants in transfers and leases, an authority retains a direct legal relationship with the purchaser of every house or flat and any subsequent owners, which can be enforced against both freeholders and leaseholders, by proceedings for an injunction, and, in the case of leaseholders, by an action for forfeiture of the lease.

2 Restrictions on the right to use the common parts

The HA 1985 obliges authorities to grant purchasers of their own homes under the "right to buy", the same rights as they enjoyed as tenants and any rights of way necessary for the reasonable enjoyment of the dwelling.[84]

A right of way is implied into a tenancy if there is no express mention of any such rights (see p114 above). If an authority gave only limited rights under its tenancy agreement it can similarly limit the rights granted in a transfer or a lease. To satisfy the provisions of the HA 1985 the rights of way must include:
— those rights of way enjoyed by the purchasers before they bought; and
— those rights of way which are "necessary for the reasonable enjoyment" of the dwelling.

"Rights of way necessary for reasonable enjoyment" may mean, at its narrowest, only the minimum right of way implied by law, ie a passage on foot to the road. However, the element of reasonableness may introduce a wider right. The owner might, for example, argue that s/he needs access to various different routes off the estate and needs to bring his or her car onto the estate.

It is certainly possible to impose some restrictions on the rights of way of owner occupiers over the common parts of an estate. If they live in a flat, they will not need access to any block other than their own, nor do purchasers need access to parts of the estate far away from their home. Any access they may want should be as visitors of other tenants.

Housing associations

The term "housing associations" for these purposes includes housing trusts, co-operative housing associations and other housing co-operatives but does not include management co-operatives set up to manage local authority housing; these are covered in the next section.[85]

Most housing association tenants are secure tenants under the HA 1985 and the same points about the terms of tenancies can be made with respect to housing association tenancy agreements as are made for local authority tenancy agreements. The exceptions are tenants of registered co-operative housing associations who are neither secure tenants under the HA 1985 nor protected tenants under the Rent Act 1977. Their only security lies in the fact that they can take part in the management decisions.[86]

Housing associations are able to adopt the same policies for dealing with racial harassment by their tenants under their tenancy agreements as are adopted by housing authorities. The influence that a housing authority can exert in the housing association sector lies in its ability to influence the management practices of housing associations. Housing authorities frequently provide buildings and grants to housing associations. As a condition of providing buildings they can make it a requirement that an association has a satisfactory policy and procedure for dealing with racial harassment by its tenants. Authorities also frequently make grants or loans to registered housing associations or provide a guarantee for any money borrowed by a housing association. Such grants, loans and guarantees can be made on such terms and conditions as the authority thinks fit.[87]

The justification for imposing grant conditions has been discussed above (see p112). The points made there apply to grants to housing associations. It is possible to draw up written grant conditions requiring certain action by an association in exchange for the grant. A failure to comply can result in withdrawal of future funding.

There is one restriction on the use of this power. The Secretary of State has a residual power to alter the terms of any agreement between a local authority and a housing association at the request of the latter.[88] It is therefore important to seek the agreement of the association to the proposed conditions, and it is necessary to be able to justify the need for such clauses if the Secretary of State is asked to intervene.

Examples
The following are the sort of requirements an authority might impose on a housing association:
— to insert specific clauses in its tenancy agreements relating to racial harassment;
— to make available housing for victims of harassment;
— to have a policy similar to that of the authority regarding action against perpetrators;
— to introduce records of reported incidents of racial harassment and provide statistical evidence to the authority;
— to publicise the policy to all association tenants.

Management co-operatives and other managers of local authority housing

Authorities have power to enter into agreements with co-operatives, formed by tenants on an estate or in a particular area, allowing the tenants to exercise some or all of the authority's management functions.[89] Since early 1987, this power has been extended to allow authorities to enter into management agreements with any person or organisation and is clearly intended to allow private sector management of local authority housing estates. Both forms of management agreement now have to be approved by the Secretary of State.

Authorities may exert the same kind of influence over managers of their housing as they exert over housing associations, with regard to policies and procedures for dealing with racial harassment. Any management agreement can contain details of the terms and conditions on which the authority's functions are to be exercisable by the manager. This might include requirements for dealing with racial harassment, recording incidents and passing information to the authority. However, any such clauses require the consent of the Secretary of State.

Under the pre-1987 rules, the housing authority retained control over the finances and could therefore exert considerable control over a co-operative.[90] This provision is now repealed and the Secretary of State can give financial asssistance directly to those managing local authority housing, thereby considerably reducing the element of control exercised by the housing authority.[91]

The sort of conditions that an authority might include in a management agreement, either with a co-operative or a private sector manager, would be similar to those examples given in the case of housing associations above.

Bed and breakfast accommodation

1 The management practice of the owner

Authorities are major customers of the proprietors of bed and breakfast accommodation in some areas and provide the proprietors with a significant income. This may give an authority considerable financial influence over the way in which premises are managed. Where two or more authorities, using the same bed and breakfast accommodation, adopt a joint approach, the pressure they can bring to bear is substantially increased.

The discretion to choose the suppliers of services is subject to the duty under RRA 1976 s71. An authority that continued to use a bed and breakfast establishment, when the people it placed there were being harassed, might be in breach of its duty under the RRA 1976 if it failed to consider placing families elsewhere (see p30). The freedom of choice of an authority must depend on the availability of reasonable alternatives.

Some of the provisions relating to houses in multiple occupation may also apply to bed and breakfast accommodation such as hostels and hotels used for homeless families (see below).

Although it is not usual practice, there is no reason why authorities should not negotiate general agreements with owners of bed and breakfast accommodation covering management practices including the steps the management must take to deter or prevent racial harassment and the steps to be taken when racial harassment occurs on the premises.

Examples
An agreement with the owner of bed and breakfast accommodation might include obligations:
— to require any perpetrator to leave immediately;
— to notify specified authorities of any complaints of racial harassment on the premises;
— to allow officers of placing authorities access at all times;

— to put the names and phone numbers or addresses of contact officers from placing authorities on a prominent noticeboard for occupants to see;
— to require perpetrators or suspected perpetrators to use only specified shared facilities to try to keep them apart from victims who have complained of racial harassment, eg shared kitchen or sitting room.

The agreement could cover other matters, such as the state of repair, management code, fire escapes, facilities, heating etc.

Authorities might jointly agree to use only bed and breakfast premises on an approved list. To qualify for inclusion on an approved list owners would have to enter into general management agreements with the authority in whose area they were situated. The London boroughs have adopted a joint code of practice in relation to bed and breakfast accommodation but it does not, at present, include most of the matters suggested above, though it is in the process of being revised.

2 Other measures to deal with racial harassment

A situation occurring frequently is that several different authorities place families in the same bed and breakfast accommodation, often well outside their own areas. To assess what measures can be taken to deal with racial harassment a typical example will be considered.

> **Example:** *Local authority A places a victim in bed and breakfast accommodation (a hotel) situated in the area of local authority B; local authority C places a perpetrator in the same hotel.*

Local authority A will be called "the victim's authority", local authority B "the owner's authority" and local authority C "the perpetrator's authority". Obviously, in some cases two or all three of these authorities may be the same, in which case the authority concerned has the cumulative powers referred to under each type of authority.

The victim's authority
(a) *Action to protect victim* The only steps the victim's housing authority can take to provide direct protection for the victim is to move him or her to alternative accommodation. The victim's social services authority has all the powers considered in Chapter 7.

Security measures will be inappropriate since the hotel is private property, although it may be possible to persuade the owner to introduce extra security to prevent harassment under threat of removal from the approved list of accommodation and consequent loss of income.

(b) *Action against perpetrators* As the victim's authority there will be no housing powers available to take any action against a perpetrator. There may, however, be powers to prosecute under the Protection from Eviction Act 1977. This power is not limited to offences within the area of the authority and could be used where a victim housed by the authority is harassed in another area. The victim's authority is probably best placed to prosecute since it will be in close contact with the primary witness. In addition, the victim's social services authority may have powers to use the wardship jurisdiction in exceptional circumstances where there are children in the victim's family (see Chapter 7).

Again it may be possible to persuade the owner of the premises to take direct action against the perpetrator by threatening to remove the premises from an approved list.

The perpetrator's authority
(a) *Action against the perpetrator* Perpetrators of racial harassment can be moved to other accommodation immediately if the perpetrators' authority is paying for their accommodation. If there is no duty to house the perpetrators under the homelessness provisions then the authority can decide to take no further responsibility for their housing costs and offer no alternatives. It must then offer advice and assistance with finding alternative accommodation from some other source (see p88).

(b) *Finding the perpetrator intentionally homeless* The fact that a perpetrator may have committed acts of racial harassment in bed and breakfast accommodation will not render him or her intentionally homeless. The definition of "intentionally homeless" is doing anything "in consequence of which he ceases to occupy accommodation...".[92] Thus the racial harassment must lead to the loss of accommodation. Those placed in bed and breakfast accommodation by a local authority will, almost without exception, have been placed there because they have already lost their previous accommodation. They may therefore have already become homeless unintentionally. Acts committed after their arrival at the bed and breakfast accommodation cannot change the reason why they lost their original home.

Although the perpetrator's authority cannot find the perpetrator intentionally homeless, racial harassment committed in temporary accommodation may affect the policy of that authority when offering permanent accommodation to the perpetrator. Authorities generally offer their own housing accommodation when complying with their duties, and in this case, points that authorities could consider include:
— reducing the number of offers made to perpetrators to one;
— making offers of less desirable property in areas where there will be no risk to other potential victims;
— giving special consideration to the terms of the perpetrator's tenancy to ensure that any further racial harassment can be restrained.

Records of incidents of racial harassment reported against perpetrators while living in bed and breakfast accommodation can be attached to their tenancy or rehousing records. A clear written warning should be given to the perpetrator at the beginning of any new tenancy that future racial harassment of any nature will lead to eviction. A previous incident together with a subsequent clear warning will increase the likelihood of a possession order being made in any proceedings arising from further incidents of racial harassment as it will be a factor which affects the reasonableness of making a possession order.

There would be little point in adopting this procedure unless all homeless families were informed of the policy before being rehoused in bed and breakfast accommodation, since the major objective is to deter racial harassment from occurring at all.

(c) *Action to protect the victim* The perpetrator's authority could itself rehouse the victim if the victim wished. Otherwise, there is no action the perpetrator's authority can take to protect the victim.

The owner's authority
The owner's authority is the authority primarily responsible for education, social services, public health laws and fire protection and is the authority responsible for the highway and local byelaws.

(a) *Action to protect the victim* The owner's authority can exercise any of the powers for authorities other than housing authorities described elsewhere in this book for the protection of victims, where these can be applied to bed and breakfast accommodation. As a housing authority it can itself rehouse the victim. It is also the authority responsible for exercising the powers relating to houses in multiple occupation (see below).

The powers to protect victims against racial harassment by other occupiers of bed and breakfast accommodation by practical prevention measures are limited.

(b) *Action against perpetrators* The owner's authority has all the general powers referred to in other chapters for dealing with perpetrators that might be exercisable by social services, education or highway authorities. It has power to prosecute for an offence under the Protection from Eviction Act 1977. In view of the limited civil action available to protect victims in bed and breakfast accommodation, the use of criminal proceedings presents the only real possibility of obtaining protection for the victim through the courts (see Chapter 10).

3 Procedures for dealing with racial harassment in bed and breakfast accommodation

It will have become apparent from the points made above, that an effective strategy to deal with racial harassment can only be developed in bed and breakfast accommodation used by a number of different authorities if the authorities adopt a joint approach to tackling the problem.

It would be sensible for associations of local authorities to adopt a standard form of notification of racial harassment in bed and breakfast. Complaints of racial harassment might be received by:
— a health visitor employed by the health authority;
— the teacher of a child living at the bed and breakfast accommodation;
— a local voluntary organisation;
— a housing welfare or homelessness officer employed by the victim's authority;

— a social worker from the owner's authority or the victim's authority;
— the police;
— some other officer such as an environmental health officer employed by the owner's authority.

It is particularly important that the placing authorities of both victim and perpetrator are informed immediately any incident occurs. To establish a mechanism by which a joint approach can be achieved, each authority should appoint one officer responsible for liaison with other authorities and for receiving all reports of racial harassment. The owner's authority can use records for monitoring the management practices of each owner of bed and breakfast accommodation in its area.

So that information concerning victims and perpetrators can be correlated, it would be sensible to appoint the same officer to receive information about both victims and perpetrators living in bed and breakfast accommodation. All those placed in hostels should be given information on whom they should complain to about any instances of racial harassment. This officer should be the person responsible for receiving reports of harassment for the victim's authority.

If victims and witnesses are to be interviewed, it may be sensible for all three authorities to do so jointly if legal action is being considered and for one authority to play a lead role. The victim will have most dealings with his or her own authority and so it may be the victim's authority which should take a lead role. In any event, agreed procedures should be adopted which avoid the victim having to repeat the same story three times.

Houses in multiple occupation (HMOs)

Where racial harassment is being committed by one occupier of a multi-occupied dwelling against another, it is sometimes by the use of an authority's powers in relation to HMOs that the most effective action can be taken against racial harassment.

In addition to their powers to obtain information under the HA 1985, authorities have a general power to obtain information from the occupiers or owners of premises as to the names and addresses of all those interested in or occupying the premises if that information is required to carry out their functions.[93]

1 What is a house in multiple occupation?

A house in multiple occupation is a house which is occupied by persons who do not form a single household.[94] It will be apparent from what is said below that much private sector rented and bed and breakfast accommodation may fall within the definition.

House
Whether a particular building constitutes a house is often a difficult legal

question to answer and cannot be dealt with in detail here. It is a mixed question of law and fact. The word "house" has been interpreted to include a large purpose-built hostel or lodging house[95] and a house converted into self-contained flats.[96] The fact that a building has previously been used as a single dwelling may be a relevant factor when deciding whether it is now a house.[97] The definition might also include a women's refuge,[98] a hostel providing temporary accommodation for alcoholics or the mentally ill[99] or many smaller lodging houses or hotels[100] where these are based in a building that can be described as a house. Certainly the interpretation appears to include any normal meaning of the word "house" in common usage.

Occupied
The word occupied appears to mean "lived in". It may therefore not include bona fide hotels where guests stay only for a few nights but can include hotels used for homeless families who stay for many months and use the premises as their home.[101]

2 Registration

Authorities have power to adopt a scheme for their area or a part of their area requiring the registration of all HMOs or certain types of HMOs.[102] The purpose of registration is to alert the authority to the existence of an HMO so that the authority can consider whether it needs to exercise any of its powers. Such a scheme must be confirmed by the Secretary of State.

Failure to supply information required is a criminal offence punishable by a fine.[103] Any scheme can contain control provisions preventing multi-occupation of any house within the scheme's area unless it is registered. A failure to comply is punishable by a larger fine.[104] An authority may refuse to register an HMO on the ground that the person having control of it or the person intended to manage it is not a fit and proper person to do so. The authority must give written reasons for the decision and the person who applied for registration can appeal to the county court.[105]

Having established a scheme, an authority can require information from any person who has an interest in an HMO or who lives in it which it reasonably requires in order to decide whether it is registerable.[106] Clearly, a registration scheme can be used to obtain a fuller picture of the private rented sector or bed and breakfast accommodation. The powers might also be used to prevent particular owners or managers from being involved in HMOs. Where there have been numerous complaints in the past of racial harassment in houses managed by particular individuals an authority might refuse to register any further applications.

Once registered, there appears to be no mechanism for removing an HMO from the register. The authority will have to use other powers listed below to tackle racial harassment.

3 Control orders

Authorities have powers to serve notices in respect of HMOs:
— requiring works to make the house reasonably suitable for the number of individuals or households living there;[106A]
— requiring works to make good neglect to a house caused by a failure to comply with the prescribed management code;[107]
— limiting the number of occupants;[108]
— applying the prescribed management code.[109]

If any one of these notices has been served, or the authority considers that the state or condition of the house requires it to take action by serving any such notice, it may make a control order if the following condition is satisfied:

> "it appears to the authority that the living conditions in the house are such that it is necessary to make the order in order to protect the safety, welfare or health of persons living in the house."[110]

This condition must be satisfied at the time of making the control order and the decision must be made in accordance with the general administrative law principles discussed in Chapter 2.

The preconditions justifying the service of a notice require some defect in the physical condition of the premises. However, once the preconditions are satisfied the protection of the safety, welfare and health of the persons living in the house appear to allow consideration to be given to the presence of racial harassment within the house when deciding whether to make a control order. The Code of Guidance issued by the DoE covering the powers of local authorities under these provisions states: "in forming a picture of the living conditions, the local housing authority would appear to be entitled to add such evidence of the environment in which the residents live (eg noise, bad smell, rowdyism, or other anti-social behaviour within the house)".[111] Racial harassment will most probably affect the health, safety and welfare of those who are its victims within the house.

The landlord can appeal against the making of a control order to the county court and almost certainly will do so. If the justification for making the order is that acts of racial harassment are being committed without any steps being taken by the owner, the authority will require some direct evidence to support the allegations. The authority can rely on hearsay but they will need to be able to show that it was reasonable of the authority to do so, for example many complaints from different occupiers or some other corroborating evidence, eg physical damage to a door or bruising on a victim.

Once a control order is made the authority immediately becomes responsible for the management of the HMO.[112] The authority stands in the landlord's position, in relation to the tenants or licensees at the premises, so that the private sector security of tenure provisions apply.[113] The authority therefore cannot impose the terms of its own tenancies on existing occupiers. It can, however, seek possession against the perpetrators of racial harassment on the ground of nuisance or annoyance to adjoining occupiers.[114] The same points about presentation and tactics and the reasonableness of making an order for possession will apply to such proceedings as apply under the HA 1985.

A control order lasts for five years. The local authority is entitled to be reimbursed for all its expenses in connection with carrying out the order and any works that are required.[115]

Procedure for control orders
Where the landlord is responsible for racial harassment, control orders should be made without warning. It is not necessary to serve notices before making a control order. Where harassment is from other tenants, attempts might first be made to try to persuade the landlord to act against those responsible.

One of the problems with many notices served by environmental health officers is that their effect is suspended if the landlord appeals against the notice. Control orders are not subject to the same rule and this works to the advantage of the authority. Once a control order is made, it remains in force until overturned by a court, on appeal. The appeal may take many months or even years. The main purpose of a control order is to provide immediate protection for victims. Even if the authority eventually loses the appeal, the victims will have been given immediate protection and the authority will have had some time to rehouse them.

Compulsory purchase of rented housing

Authorities have power to compulsorily purchase houses, flats, lodging houses and hostels for housing accommodation with the consent of the Secretary of State.[116] These powers include the ability to compulsorily purchase an HMO following a control order.[117]

Compulsory purchase is only justified if it is used as a means of providing housing accommodation. It follows that where the premises concerned are already providing housing accommodation, it will be extremely difficult and in most cases impossible to justify compulsory purchase of the premises. However, in *R v Secretary of State for the Environment ex parte RB Kensington and Chelsea*,[118] the court held that "housing accommodation" meant proper housing accommodation. Harassment, intimidation or other grave conduct by the landlord could prevent accommodation being proper, by depriving it of the essential ingredient of quiet enjoyment.

The case cited above suggests that racial harassment by a landlord might justify the making of a compulsory purchase order. It will not justify a compulsory purchase order against a perpetrator where s/he lives in separate premises to the victim and is an owner occupier.

If harassment by a landlord prevents accommodation from being proper housing accommodation, it could be argued that racial harassment by another tenant could have a similar effect. The effect on the life of the victim is identical whoever the perpetrator is. In the case of HMOs, a control order can be made immediately and followed by a compulsory purchase order shortly afterwards.

Voluntary organisations providing temporary accommodation for the homeless

An authority has power to provide premises or give grants or loans to voluntary organisations providing accommodation for the homeless. The authority can impose terms and conditions[119] in the same way as it can for housing associations, save that voluntary organisations cannot ask the Secretary of State to alter the conditions of grant.

Squatters

1 Action against perpetrators who are squatters

Squatters in local authority premises can be evicted very rapidly. In practice, local authorities often take weeks to evict squatters but the procedure allows an order for possession to be obtained within one or two days in cases of emergency.[120] This could include the situation where the squatters were responsible for racial harassment.

The only powers available against squatters in other premises will be the general powers to prosecute for criminal offences and the powers of social services, environmental health, highways and education departments.

2 Action to protect victims who are squatting

Squatters are homeless and can always be rehoused by an authority. If the council owns the premises where the victim is squatting, it can carry out security works to them. It may also have a right to take direct legal action against the perpetrators for trespass, nuisance or damage to council property (see Chapter 4).

Where victims are squatting in privately owned premises, no protection measures can be taken by the authorities. The only assistance that can be offered is rehousing.

Local authority hostels

People living in local authority hostels will usually be homeless families who have licences and are sharing facilities with other families in the building. For the purpose of this paragraph a hostel is a building where the occupants are provided with a separate bedroom for their families but share living rooms, kitchens or dining rooms. Bathrooms and toilets will probably also be shared. In some hostels, food may be provided.

Licences issued to people living in local authority hostels should contain similar clauses to those in tenancy agreements prohibiting racial harassment and allowing the authority to terminate the licence immediately if harassment occurs and in any event after a specified amount of notice.

1 Action against perpetrators

Licences can be terminated so that the perpetrator has no right to remain in the hostel. If the licence contains a clause allowing it to be terminated immediately if racial harassment occurs, then the authority can take steps straight away to move the perpetrator elsewhere. If the licence contains no such clause, it must be terminated by reasonable notice. Notice may have to be a few days or even several weeks if the person concerned has been living at the hostel some time. For the reasons explained on p121, the perpetrator will usually have to be provided with alternative accommodation is s/he has been accepted as not intentionally homeless and is evicted from the hostel.

2 Action to protect the victim

A housing authority has power to manage its hostels and, as such, has ancillary powers to take steps to protect victims. Since the accommodation is intended to be only temporary, an authority may decide that measures to protect the victim involving appointment of additional staff or security measures cannot be justified and it is more sensible to rehouse the victim. In most cases, that is what the victim will be seeking.

Byelaws for lodging houses

Authorities have power to make byelaws for their lodging houses,[121] which are houses where the occupants share kitchens, living rooms or bedrooms. A lodging house may also be an HMO. Hostels under the definition on p127 may also be lodging houses.

Byelaws can be made "for preventing damage, disturbance, interruption and indecent and offensive language and behaviour and nuisances".[121] Few acts of racial harassment would not fall within this provision. The byelaws can therefore effectively outlaw racial harassment within lodging houses. The general administrative law principles applying to byelaws, referred to in Chapter 4, will apply under this provision. Breach of the byelaws will be a criminal offence which can be prosecuted by a local authority.

Common lodging houses

A common lodging house is a house used for "accommodating poor persons" who occupy the same room and are not members of the same family, ie dormitory accommodation.[122]

1 Registration

Common lodging houses must be registered with the local authority.[123] Registration can be refused in certain limited circumstances. The relevant one for present purposes is if the applicant or a person proposed to be employed is not a fit person to keep or be employed at a common lodging house.[124] If complaints are received from the occupants of a lodging house of racial harassment by members of staff, and these complaints can be substantiated by corroborating evidence or by the victim giving evidence, then an authority may be justified in refusing to renew the registration when it expires (registration is for a period of up to 13 months) unless the owner dismisses the employee concerned. Two major problems are that the occupants of lodging houses are unlikely to be available as witnesses, and would be evicted if the lodging house were to close.

An authority must give written reasons why registration is being refused.[125] Appeals against refusal of registration are to the magistrates' court.[126]

2 Byelaws

Authorities may make byelaws for common lodging houses "for the well-ordering of such lodging houses" as well as for other matters.[127] Byelaws could include provisions prohibiting racial harassment of other occupiers.

Breach of byelaws is an offence. The byelaws themselves could require the owner to refuse entry to any person in breach of the byelaws and to be responsible for removing from the premises immediately anyone committing racial harassment or a nuisance. The owner would then be committing an offence by failing to do so.

1 Housing Act (HA) 1985 s22.
2 Ibid s106(1).
3 Ibid s106(2).
4 Ibid s106(4).
5 Ibid s379.
6 DoE Circular 12/86 para 3.9.2.
7 See p88; s22 imposes a duty to give reasonable preference to all those to whom a local authority owes a duty under ss65 or 68. This includes any homeless applicant whether or not in priority need and whether or not intentionally homeless.
8 HA 1985 s22.
9 Ibid s65.
10 Ibid s63.
11 Ibid s58 as amended by Housing and Planning Act 1986 s14.
12 HA 1985 s59.
13 Ibid s60.
14 Ibid ss60(4) and 69(4).
15 Ibid s70.
16 See *R v North Devon DC ex p Lewis* [1981] 1 WLR 328; *R v Swansea CC ex p Thomas* (1983) 9 HLR 64 and *R v East Herts DC ex p Bannon* (1986) 18 HLR 515.
17 See, eg, *Devenport v Salford Corp* (1983) 8 HLR 54.
18 *Smith v Bristol CC* (1981) *LAG Bulletin* 287 and *R v Swansea CC ex parte John* (1982) 9 HLR 56.
19 HA 1985 s65(3).

20 This is obligatory under HA 1985 s65(3)(b).
21 This will be indirect discrimination under RRA 1976 sl(1)(b).
22 Landlord and Tenant Act 1985 s11 and see *O'Brien v Robinson* [1973] 1 All ER 583.
23 *Liverpool CC v Irwin* [1977] AC 239, HL.
24 See, eg, *McGreal v Wake* (1984) 13 HLR 107, CA and Landlord and Tenant Act 1985 s17.
25 *Smith v Scott* [1972] 3 All ER 645 and *O'Leary v LB Islington* (1983) 9 HLR 83.
26 *Smith v Scott* n25.
27 This point was made by Ackner LJ in *Page Motors v Epsom and Ewell BC* (1982) 80 LGR 337, CA at 347-348. He points out that the case of *Sedleigh Denfield v O'Callaghan* [1940] AC 880, HL was not cited in *Smith v Scott* (n25) and the issue of whether a landlord could authorise a nuisance by failing to act against a tenant was not raised. The point was also not raised in the more recent case of *O'Leary v LB Islington* (n25) and can therefore be considered to be open.
28 See n27.
29 HA 1985 s105.
30 Ibid s105(2).
31 Ibid s105(5).
32 Ibid s105(6).
33 Ibid s109.
34 Ibid s26(1)(a).
35 Ibid s21.
36 Ibid s10.
37 Housing Associations Act 1985 s58.
38 HA 1985 s27(1)(a).
39 Ibid s73.
40 Ibid s15.
41 Ibid ss435 and 437.
42 Ibid s435(3).
43 Ibid s442.
44 Ibid s26(1)(b).
45 Ibid s443.
46-49 1984 SI No 117.
50 HA 1985 s21.
51 LGA 1972 s112.
52 HA 1985 s97.
53 Ibid s100.
54 N53.
55 Ibid s463.
56 Ibid s467.
57 The Circular 21/80 issued by the DoE makes no mention of this use of improvement grants but is guidance only. The statute takes precedence.
58 HA 1985 s525.
59 Ibid s470.
60 Ibid s462(1)(b).
61 Ibid s473 and Grants by Local Housing Authorities (Appropriate Percentage and Exchequer Contributions) Order 1987 SI No 1379.

Housing authorities and departments 131

62 HA 1985 s464.
63 Ibid s464(4).
64 HA 1985 s469 and Improvement Grant (Rateable Value Limits) Order 1977 SI No 1213.
65 HA 1985 s468.
66 Ibid s468(4).
67 Ibid s435(1)(d).
68 Ibid s436 which does not use the word "unencumbered".
69 Ibid s439.
70 Ibid Sch 1 para 4.
71 Ibid s32.
72 Ibid s12(1)(c).
73 Ibid s21.
74 Ibid s23.
75 Ibid s56.
76 Ibid s23(2).
77 This follows from the ambiguous reference to "housing accommodation" in s56.
78 Provided under the powers of HA 1985 s12.
79 RRA 1976 s31.
80 Ibid s53.
81 HA 1985 s139 and Sch 6 para 5.
82 Law of Property Act 1925 s146.
83 Ibid s146(2).
84 HA 1985 Sch 6 paras 2 and 3.
85 Housing Associations Act 1985 s1.
86 HA 1985 s80 and Rent Act 1977 s15.
87 Housing Associations Act 1985 s58.
88 Ibid s69.
89 HA 1985 s27 as amended by the Housing and Planning Act 1986 s10.
90 HA 1985 s27(4).
91 Housing and Planning Act 1986 s16 inserting a new section 429A in the HA 1985.
92 HA 1985 s60(1).
93 Local Government (Miscellaneous Provisions) Act 1976 s16.
94 HA 1985 s345.
95 *R v LB Camden ex p Rowton (Camden Town) Ltd* (1983) 10 HLR 30.
96 *Okereke v LB Brent* [1967] 1 QB 42, CA.
97 *Reed v Hastings Corp* (1964) 62 LGR 588 per Harman LJ.
98 *Simmons v Pizzey* [1979] AC 37 and see n99 below.
99 *Silbers v LB Southwark* (1977) 76 LGR 421 which, together with the case referred to in n98, concerned the issue of multi-occupation, but the fact that the premises were "houses" was assumed.
100 See *R v LB Camden ex p Rowton* n95 at 42 per McCullough J.
101 *Thrasyvoulou v LB Hackney* (1986) 18 HLR 370.
102 HA 1985 s346.
103 Ibid s346(6).
104 Ibid s347.
105 Ibid s348(1)(b).
106 Ibid s350.

106A Ibid s352.
107 Ibid s372.
108 Ibid s354.
109 Ibid s370.
110 Ibid s379.
111 DoE Circular 12/86 para 3.9.2.
112 HA 1985 s381.
113 Ibid s382.
114 Rent Act 1977 Sch 15 ground 2.
115 Ibid s390 and Sch 13.
116 HA 1985 ss8, 9, 17 and 56.
117 There are special provisions in HA 1985 Sch 13.
118 *R v Sec of State for Environment ex p RB Kensington and Chelsea* (1987) 19 HLR 161.
119 HA 1985 s73.
120 CCR Ord 24 and RSC Ord 113.
121 HA 1985 ss23(3) and 56.
122 Ibid s401.
123 Ibid s402.
124 Ibid s404.
125 Ibid s404(5).
126 Ibid s405.
127 Ibid s406.

CHAPTER SEVEN
Social Services Authorities and Departments

Social services authorities have a statutory duty to promote the welfare of children, including taking care proceedings if necessary; they also have statutory powers to provide facilities for young, elderly, sick and disabled people. In both areas there is clearly scope to assist victims and their families, and, by the use of wardship proceedings, supervision orders and withholding certain facilities, action can be taken against perpetrators.

This chapter applies to London borough councils, the Common Council of the City of London and county councils.

The powers of authorities, both to deal with the perpetrators of racial harassment and to assist the victims, are not limited to housing authorities or housing departments within authorities. Social services authorities or departments (SSAs) have considerable powers and some duties which are relevant to any policy for tackling racial harassment. One big advantage the SSA has over the housing authority is that all its powers apply whatever the type of housing in which the victim or perpetrator live. They are as applicable to harassment by an owner occupier against a private tenant as they are to racial harassment occurring between tenants on a housing estate.

To achieve maximum effect, authorities should ensure close liaison between departments so that policies for prevention, assistance and support for victims and action against perpetrators can be developed using the most appropriate powers from all relevant departments. Like all other authorities and departments, SSAs must carry out all their functions taking account of the obligation imposed by RRA 1976 s71.

The functions of SSAs relate primarily to children, the sick and elderly and people with disabilities whether mental or physical. It is outside the scope of this book to go into social services powers in detail and only those which are most likely to be particularly relevant for developing a strategy for preventing or dealing with racial harassment will be examined here.

A. THE DUTIES OF SOCIAL SERVICES AUTHORITIES

SSAs are subject to all the duties referred to in Chapter 4. However, they have additional duties which are relevant, and are discussed here.

Duty to promote the welfare of children

It is the duty of every SSA:

> "to make available such advice, guidance and assistance as may promote the welfare of children by diminishing the need to receive children into or keep them in care, and any provisions made by a local authority under this subsection may, if the local authority think fit, include provision for giving assistance in kind or, in exceptional circumstances, in cash".[1]

When considering measures to diminish the need to receive a child into care a "child" for these purposes is a person under 17.[2] The duty is therefore limited to measures to protect a family which includes children under 17.

This is a duty not a power. Every authority must therefore consider what advice, guidance and assistance is required to diminish the need to receive children into care. If it refuses to consider the needs for assistance in a particular case, or has adopted a rigid policy as to the circumstances in which assistance is to be withheld, the authority is likely to be in breach of its statutory duty.

This point is illustrated, to some extent, by a case in 1981. Wandsworth council had a policy that the social services department would not pay for accommodation for families held intentionally homeless by the housing department. This decision was overturned by the courts. The authority could not have a policy that it would not provide assistance which it was under a duty to provide.[3] In a more recent decision, however, in *R v LB Tower Hamlets ex parte Monaf and Others* the Divisional Court considered that the SSA was entitled to refuse assistance because it was under no duty to take children into care whose parents were intentionally homeless.[4] This decision is currently the subject of an appeal, but, whatever the outcome, what is clear is that, regardless of the position adopted by the housing authority in a particular case, the SSA must separately determine what action it should take under its own legal duties.

There is no limit to the extent of the assistance that can be given under this provision provided it diminishes the need to receive a child into care and the Wandsworth case mentioned above decided that the duty to provide "assistance" could include a duty to provide accommodation for a child and its parents.

The need to take a child into care can arise in two ways. First, when the child's parent puts the child into care voluntarily. The SSA has a duty to receive a child into care if it is necessary in the interests of the welfare of the child and "the parents are for the time being prevented from providing for his proper accommodation . . . or upbringing".[5] This could certainly be considered to be the case when serious racial harassment is occurring. Second, there may be a ground for taking care proceedings if:
— a child's proper development is being avoidably impaired;
— a child's health is being avoidably impaired;
— a child is being ill-treated.[6]

Almost every child who is a member of a victim's family will satisfy all three requirements. Of course, it is not in any way the fault of the parents. They are experiencing the same effect; the effect on the child does not need to be caused by the parents to justify care proceedings. Thus, it can be argued that most assistance to families with children which protects them from racial harassment or prevents further harassment, is justifiable under this provision.

The arrangements an authority makes to carry out its duty under this provision can include the use of voluntary organisations. It is important to remember that the duty also applies to perpetrators where there are children in the family.

1 Assistance to the victim

An SSA is not limited by departmental boundaries in the steps it can take. Measures may involve steps usually within housing or education departmental responsibility. Using this provision authorities might be obliged to consider providing the followings sorts of assistance:

(a) Providing or paying for temporary rehousing regardless of the attitude of the housing department until such time as steps have been taken to obtain permanent alternative accommodation. Temporary accommodation will be appropriate for victims living in all sectors of housing including owner occupied, perhaps while they go through the lengthy process of selling their house and purchasing an alternative. Where a family is receiving benefits, assistance might include making good any loss incurred whilst living in temporary accommodation because of difficulties over housing benefit or supplementary benefit for mortgage instalments on the old home.

(b) Paying for a transport service to and from school for children who are being racially harassed during the journey.

(c) Paying playgroup fees so that very young children in the family do not have to play on the estate where they are subjected to racial harassment.

(d) Taking steps to make the home more secure, similar to the examples given on p104 only not limited to local authority housing, and possibly other payments to assist with rehousing.

Measures such as those suggested on p104 could be paid for in relation to other types of housing.

2 Assistance to the perpetrator

The duty to provide assistance applies to perpetrators as well as victims. Discharging this responsibility may involve providing assistance with rehousing to perpetrators who are found intentionally homeless by the housing department although the exact nature of this duty must await the result of the appeal in the Tower Hamlets case referred to above. There is a clear potential conflict of interest between the housing and social services departments which will inevitably arise where a perpetrator has children. It is irrelevant that the children may be those responsible for the racial harassment which led to the eviction.

If authorities are to avoid antagonism between staff in different departments and the possibility of the perpetrators taking advantage of a communication breakdown between departments, discussions as to the correct approach to be adopted where conflicts of interest arise should begin as soon as possible. This issue is discussed further in Chapter 13.

Duty to co-operate with housing authorities

SSAs are under a duty to co-operate with their local housing authority or the housing department in their own authority when the housing authority requests assistance in carrying out its duties towards the homeless or those threatened with homelessness. When a request is made, social services must co-operate in rendering such assistance in the discharge of the housing authority's functions as is reasonable in the circumstances.[7]

It is for the housing authority to decide what assistance it requires from the SSA, which must be within the scope of the authority's function. It is then for the SSA to make the decision as to what assistance is reasonable in the circumstances. There is substantial discretion vested in the SSA and provided it considers the matter correctly, any decision it makes is likely to be difficult to challenge.

Examples of the application of this provision in the context of racial harassment might include:

(a) an emergency service for rehousing, out of hours, in hotels or bed and breakfast;
(b) joint interviews with housing to assess the needs of a victim's family for additional facilities such as child minder, playgroup, youth club, women's group etc immediately or at their new home to try to reduce the feelings of isolation and ensure that all family members can spend some period out of the home if they wish to;
(c) any of the assistance referred to on p135.

Duty to make enquiries and take care proceedings

An SSA may bring a child or young person before a juvenile court if it reasonably believes that there are grounds for making:
— a care order;
— a supervision order; or

— an order requiring the child's parent to enter into a recognisance to exercise proper control or take proper care of the child.[8]

When an authority receives information suggesting that there are grounds for bringing care proceedings, it has a duty to make enquiries unless it is satisfied that such enquiries are unnecessary.[9] If the authority considers there are grounds for bringing care proceedings it has a duty to institute proceedings unless it is satisfied that it is neither in the child's interest nor the public interest, or that the police are about to bring care proceedings or are going to charge the child with a criminal offence.[10]

It is important to stress that the decision of the SSA whether to take care proceedings is not solely based on the interests of the individual child. It must also be based on the public interest. This means the SSA must consider the interests of those who may be suffering as a result of the child's behaviour.

1 The grounds for care proceedings

A child or young person includes any person under 17 unless s/he is married and below that age.[11] A juvenile court can make one of the three orders referred to above if it is of the opinion that one of several possible conditions is satisfied. The court must also be satisfied in all cases that the child is in need of care and control which s/he is unlikely to receive unless the court makes the order. "Care" includes guidance and "control" includes discipline.

The relevant conditions for a child who is perpetrating racial harassment are:
— his or her proper development is being avoidably prevented or neglected;
— s/he is exposed to moral danger;
— s/he is beyond the control of his or her parent or guardian;
— s/he is guilty of an offence excluding homicide.[12]

The most likely grounds on which this power will be relevant in the racial harassment context are in respect of a child who is beyond the control of his or her parents or who is guilty of an offence. However, no child under the age of 10 can be guilty of a criminal offence. When care proceedings are brought on the ground of an offence having been committed, the burden of proof is the same as in criminal proceedings, ie proof beyond reasonable doubt.[13]

2 When does the duty to make enquiries arise?

The duty to make enquiries will arise when the social services receive a complaint about the behaviour of a particular child. It will usually be the housing authority which receives complaints of racial harassment and these should be passed on to the SSA when a child is the perpetrator. The victim or a neighbour may make a direct complaint or one can be made on his or her behalf.

It is difficult to see that an SSA can ever say that it is unnecessary to make enquiries, particularly where there are children in the victim's family unless they are already aware of the facts.

3 When does the duty to take care proceedings arise?

Proof of the grounds
Before the duty to take proceedings arises the authority needs to have evidence which shows there are grounds for bringing care proceedings. This evidence may be obtained and presented to them by other sources such as the housing department or other organisations on behalf of the victim.

The emphasis, in terms of evidence, will usually concentrate on showing that the child needs control that s/he will not receive unless an order is made.

Policy decision
The onus is on an authority to take care proceedings unless it is satisfied of certain matters. It must therefore take a definite decision not to act. It may consider that it is not in the child's interest to take proceedings but, unless it is also not in the public interest, it must take proceedings. It will rarely be in the public interest not to take proceedings when acts of racial harassment are being committed, so it is difficult to see how an SSA can avoid taking care proceedings as a matter of policy.

Action by the police
The authority is relieved of its duty to take proceedings on the ground of a criminal offence if the police are prosecuting.

The court's powers
The court has the power to make five orders:

(a) *Care order* A care order removes the rights of the parent and makes the authority into the child's guardian, responsible for decisions about its life and, in particular, where it should live. Among the options, the SSA might decide to allow the child to remain with his or her parents on the basis that this is in the child's best interest. Again, this decision is likely to lead to a conflict of interest with the housing department and this should be resolved by close liaison.

(b) *Supervision order* A supervision order leaves custody in the hands of the parents, vesting some powers in the supervising authority. Those powers are dealt with below (p167).

(c) *Recognisance by parent* An order requiring a parent to enter into a recognisance to keep his or her child under proper control cannot be made without the parent's consent. That consent will usually be forthcoming if the alternative is a full care or supervision order. A recognisance is almost identical to a bind over to keep the peace. Parents who fail to comply with their promise to keep their children under control can be brought before the court on a complaint by any person, and all or some of the recognisance can be forfeited. A recognisance can be for up to £1,000 and for up to three years.

(d) *Compensation order* Where the court in care proceedings finds that the child has committed an offence, it may make a compensation order (see p166). If it does, it must order the child's parent to pay in the same circumstances as in criminal proceedings (see p168).

(e) *Bind over* Where the court in care proceedings finds that a child between 14 and 17 has committed an offence, it may order the child to be bound over in a sum up to £50 to be of good behaviour and keep the peace for up to one year. This order requires the child's consent (see p168).

Care proceedings may be extremely effective in ensuring that a parent prevents his or her child from committing racial harassment.

Most acts of racial harassment will be criminal offences. Many will show that the child is beyond parental control. The grounds entailing proper development being avoidably prevented or the child being in moral danger are only likely to apply when the parent allows the child to be indoctrinated with racist beliefs.

Just the threat of care proceedings may be sufficient to prevent future racial harassment. The threat of proceedings may be used to negotiate with the parent over housing, alternative schooling or attendance at other facilities which may assist to keep the child perpetrator away from the victim and better occupied. Indeed, it may be the SSA's duty to provide such facilities to the perpetrator in order to reduce the need to take the child into care.

Duty to provide court reports

SSAs are under a duty to provide court reports on persons under 17 appearing before the courts on criminal charges.[14]

SSAs must make investigations and provide the court with such information relating to the home surroundings, school record, health and character of a child as appear likely to assist the court unless it is of the opinion that such information is unnecessary. In some areas, the probation service provides such reports for children over 13 instead of the SSA.

Court reports usually make recommendations as to an appropriate sentence. Where a child who has been involved in racial harassment appears on a criminal charge, the SSA has considerable influence over the manner in which s/he is dealt with by the court.

A court report should consider measures that are necessary to protect victims or will reduce the likelihood of further offences. These might include:
— measures to remove a child from an estate during particular hours;
— conditions on supervision orders (see p167 below);
— custodial sentences.

The court's powers are considered further in Chapter 10.

B. THE POWERS OF SOCIAL SERVICES AUTHORITIES

Powers to assist victims

One important power derives from the duty referred to above on p134. The general powers dealt with in Chapter 4 apply to SSAs. For example, a social worker appointed to work with families who are victims of racial harassment could be seconded to a voluntary organisation such as a support group.

1 The provision of facilities

In section A above, some of the considerable powers an authority has to promote the welfare of children were discussed. SSAs have powers to provide a variety of discretionary facilities for children, the sick and elderly and people with disabilities. The welfare of children is usually dependent on their parents, so promoting the children's welfare will generally justify work with the entire family.

It is not proposed to go into details of the discretionary facilities provided by SSAs. Some examples will be given of the way in which some of those facilities might be used to break down any feeling of isolation that victims may feel, allow victims some period when they are free from the fear of harassment and away from the home, and assist victims to regain their confidence. The fact that examples are restricted to elderly, sick or disabled people when victims have no children is not intended to suggest that victims always fall into these categories. It is merely that the powers of SSAs are almost exclusively restricted to meeting the needs of those categories of people.

2 Provision for parents and children

— Places in local playgroups or youth clubs;
— places in day nurseries or parent-and-toddler groups;
— places in after-school activities;
— forms of counselling to assist a child or parent to overcome the psychological effects of racial harassment;
— places for parents in support groups, eg a women's group for mothers.

3 Provision for elderly people and sick people

— Places in lunch clubs;
— home helps and meals on wheels, increasing visits to the home by local authority officers;
— provision of transport to other services.

4 People with disabilities

— Provision of transport to allow journeys from the home;
— places in a day-care centre.

Powers to act against perpetrators

The duty of an authority to take care proceedings has already been considered above (p136).

1 The power to take wardship proceedings

An SSA has the power to take wardship proceedings in the High Court to protect any child.[15] When a child is made a ward of court the Court becomes the child's guardian and must be involved in all decisions about his or her welfare. The Court has considerable powers at its disposal to protect the child by making orders as to what must or must not be done. In particular, the Court can make injunctions, including ones prohibiting any form of racial harassment. There are few specific limits to what the Court can order to be done to protect a ward of court. Injunctions in wardship proceedings might therefore cover matters which other proceedings could not. Usually, wardship is used as a long-term method of protecting a child's welfare and deciding the custody of the child. In the context of racial harassment, wardship would be used only for the purposes of seeking an injunction. The effect of an application for wardship and an injunction is that the custody of the child who is the victim of racial harassment would be removed from the parents and become vested in the Court. Once this has occurred, the Court has total discretion about the care and control of the child until the wardship is discharged. For this reason, it would be essential that the parents of the child agreed to the use of wardship after obtaining their own independent legal advice and were parties to the proceedings as applicants as well as the authority. Because the effect of wardship is a loss of control over their child by the parents of the victim, it should only be used as a last resort where no other remedy exists.

In practice, at the first hearing for an injunction, the Court will make an order granting care and control of the child to the parents but all major decisions will still require the Court's consent, eg whether the child should have an operation. Unless general consent is given, the Court's permission would also be needed before the child could leave England and Wales for a holiday.

A wardship judge is likely to be far less reluctant to imprison a perpetrator who has defied a court order protecting a ward of court than a county court judge would be for a breach of tenancy agreement.

The use of wardship proceedings in this context would be experimental and would only be as a last resort. An injunction should be seen as a temporary measure pending a permanent solution to the problem, either by the eviction of the perpetrator or by the rehousing of the victim, at which point the wardship could be discharged.

Using wardship proceedings, it might be possible to get an injunction prohibiting a perpetrator from continuing to live in his or her flat nearby and ordering the perpetrator to keep a certain distance from the victim's flat and the child's school. Such an order would not be available in any other civil proceedings though it could be imposed as a bail condition in criminal proceedings (see Chapter 10).

2 Powers under supervision orders

A supervision order is a court order placing a child under the supervision of a local authority.[16] Supervision orders may be made in care proceedings or after a criminal conviction. A number of conditions may be imposed in supervision orders which restrict the freedom of the child concerned.[17]

A supervision order can require the child to live with a named individual who agrees to the requirement. This need not necessarily be the child's parent. A supervision order can also require the child to comply with any directions given from time to time by the supervisor (who is a local authority social worker) which requires him or her to do any of the following things:
— to live at a specified place for a specified period;
— to attend at particular activities or places at specified times and take part in the activities.[18]

It is up to the supervisor to decide whether and to what extent s/he exercises any power to give directions. These requirements can be imposed for a maximum of 90 days. The court has additional powers that will be considered on p167.

Provided it is given the power to do so by the court, the local authority may require a child who is subject to a supervision order to live away from home for up to 90 days or to attend particular activities or at a particular place. The supervisor can use these powers to reduce the possibility of further offences being committed. Thus, a child who has racially harassed others might be instructed to live with grandparents for three months while the victims are rehoused. Alternatively, if a child is responsible for racial harassment on the way home from school, the supervisor might require the child to attend some after-school activity for a term.

Alternatively, the power to require attendance at particular activities might be used to try and break down the racism with which the child has been indoctrinated, if such facilities exist.

3 The power to withhold discretionary facilities from perpetrators

The circumstances in which discretionary facilities might be withheld from individual perpetrators were dealt with on p47. Withholding facilities probably cannot be used by SSAs as a form of punishment since to do so would frustrate the policy and object of the Act under which the facilities are provided. This principle does not prevent facilities being withheld in the interests of good management of the service being provided.

Examples of situations where the management of the service requires facilities to be withheld from perpetrators were given on p47. In the social services context these might include:
— facilities such as playgroups, day centres or residential accommodation where withholding may be in the interests of other users;

— facilities where black staff may be subjected to racial harassment, eg home helps, meals on wheels.

4 Powers to manage residential accommodation

It is not only a housing authority which provides residential accommodation. SSAs provide residential accommodation in the form of children's homes, accommodation for elderly people and people with disabilities, resettlement units and accommodation for the mentally ill. In most cases, occupants of housing accommodation provided by an SSA will be licensees and the points made with respect to local authority hostels on p127 and the power to act against a perpetrator or to protect a victim will apply to social services accommodation. Therefore, where residents of such accommodation are responsible for racial harassment of other residents, the SSA can terminate their permission to remain there. In many cases, the authority will be under a duty to provide some alternative residential facilities.

SSAs should consider developing policies to deal with racial harassment in their residential accommodation. Hopefully, the extra level of supervision in such accommodation will make the instances of racial harassment considerably fewer than might otherwise be the case.

Intervention in the private sector

1 Private residential homes

Homes providing both board and personal care because of age, disability, dependence on drugs or alcohol or mental illness must be registered with the SSA.[19] Authorities are entitled to refuse to register a residential care home if the applicant or any person concerned with the running of the home is not a fit person to do so.[20] They may also refuse to register the home if staffing levels are inadequate.[21]

Registration can be cancelled on either of these grounds.[22] In urgent cases a magistrate can make an order cancelling registration if there is serious risk to life, health or well-being of the residents.[23]

If a person who had racially harassed residents of a private residential care home applied to register a home, that application could be refused; if the same person joined the staff of a home that was already registered, the authority could cancel the registration. The mere threat of cancellation of registration might persuade the owner not to employ the person concerned.

2 Grants, facilities and premises for voluntary organisations

SSAs, like other authorities, provide grants, facilities and premises for voluntary organisations. When doing so they can influence the activities of those organisations and encourage them to take action against racial harassment and introduce preventative measures (see p38, 48 and 50).

Organisations which might be funded or assisted by social services authorities include:

144 Social services authorities and departments

— playgroups;
— day nurseries;
— after-school groups;
— parent-and-toddler groups;
— luncheon clubs;
— other clubs for people with disabilities or elderly people;
— voluntary organisations providing residential accommodation for people with disabilities, elderly people or people who are mentally ill.

3 Private nurseries and child minders

Private nurseries and child minders must register with the SSA if they look after children for more than two hours per day.[24] Registration can be refused if the SSA is satisfied that any child minder or person employed or to be employed at the nursery is not a fit person to look after children. The SSA has a right to enter and inspect the nursery or child minder's home at all reasonable times.

The SSA may not impose any conditions relating to racial harassment. Anyone refused registration may appeal to the magistrates' court.

1 Child Care Act 1980 s1.
2 Child Care Act 1980 s1(4) which gives the age as 18 but the power to take care proceedings and the duty to take into care only apply to children up to the age of 17. The relevance of this section to children who are already 17 appears to arise only when considering measures to diminish the need to keep such children in care above that age.
3 *A-G ex rel Tilley v LB Wandsworth* [1981] 1 All ER 1162, CA.
4 (1987) *Times* 6 August. This conclusion followed from the wording of the Child Care Act 1980 s2(1)(b), "the parents for the time being are prevented . . . from providing accommodation". The Divisional Court interpreted this as excluding homelessness which was the result of a voluntary act and therefore families who were intentionally homeless could be excluded.
5 Child Care Act 1980 s2(1)(b).
6 Children and Young Persons Act 1969 s1.
7 HA 1985 s72(b).
8 N6.
9 Children and Young Persons Act 1969 s2(1).
10 Ibid s2(2).
11 Ibid ss1(5) and 70(1).
12 Ibid s1(2).
13 Ibid s3.
14 Ibid s9.
15 RSC Ord 90.
16 Children and Young Persons Act 1969 s11.
17 Ibid s12.
18 Ibid s12(2).
19 Registered Homes Act 1984 s1.
20 Ibid s9(a).
21 Ibid s9(b).

22 Ibid s10(a).
23 Ibid s11.
24 Nurseries and Child Minders Regulation Act 1948 s1.

CHAPTER EIGHT

Education Authorities and Departments

Education authorities can protect children while at school from harassment by other pupils, parents or outsiders. Their powers extend to protection of pupils travelling to and from school.

This chapter applies to London borough councils except in inner London, the Inner London Education Authority and county councils.

Local education authorities (LEAs) are uniquely placed to take steps to prevent racial harassment by challenging and overcoming the ignorance and prejudices that form the basis of racism. It is within education authorities that long-term policies to prevent racial harassment must be developed.

Both the victims and the perpetrators of racial harassment are often children. Racial harassment committed by children in a locality is quite likely to be mirrored by similar behaviour within school. The same children may be the victims of harassment both inside and outside school.

The legal responsibility of teachers usually ends when a child leaves school at the end of the day and the LEA ceases to be responsible for the welfare of a child unless it provides transport to and from school. However, LEAs can intervene and take action to protect children from racial harassment on their way to and from school.

A. DUTIES OF EDUCATION AUTHORITIES AND DEPARTMENTS

The duty under RRA 1976 s71

Like other authorities, LEAs must carry out all their functions taking into account the need specified in the RRA 1976 s71. The effect of this duty on LEAs is particularly important. An LEA is obliged to make arrangements to ensure that those responsible for the development of the curriculum, of syllabuses and for the preparation of individual lessons consider the need to eliminate unlawful discrimination and promote equality of opportunity and good relations between different racial groups. An LEA or school which completely failed to consider these needs when developing its curriculum would be in breach of the duty imposed by the RRA 1976.

A policy on discrimination and harassment occurring within schools is not enough. Syllabuses and methods of teaching should be closely examined to ensure that they are anti-racist in nature and teachers require clear guidelines as to what action they should take to challenge racially motivated remarks or acts. Syllabuses should be designed to break down stereotypes and prejudices.

Duty to provide transport to and from school and further education

Transport must be provided for pupils under eight years old whose nearest available route is over two miles to school and for other pupils whose route is over three miles.[1] This transport must be free of charge and be provided all the way to the school.[2] An LEA also has power to pay the travel expenses of pupils for whom it has no obligation to provide transport.[3]

An "available route" is a route which a child can walk, using roads and public footpaths. It must be reasonably safe for the child to walk along the route when accompanied by an adult.[4] The dangers inherent in a particular route are a factor that an authority should take into account when considering what transport it ought to provide.[5]

An LEA should consider factors other than distance and public transport when deciding what transport should be provided. Although the cases cited on the interpretation of this provision concern dangerous roads, it is possible that racial harassment on the way to and from school may prevent a route from being reasonably safe. Some routes may be dangerous to children subjected to racial harassment even if they are accompanied by a parent or other adult. In those circumstances, the nearest available route which avoids racial harassment may be greater than the two- or three-mile limit and an authority may have an obligation to provide transport.

A school bus, payment of taxi fares or the hire of a local community minibus might be considered for children who are regularly harassed on their way to and from school and could be funded under this provision.

B. POWERS OF EDUCATION AUTHORITIES AND DEPARTMENTS

Powers to assist victims

1 Powers under the LGA 1972 s111

The scope of LGA 1972 s111 was discussed in Chapter 2. In the education context, s111 allows LEAs to extend their influence to matters outside the school environment if these are affecting the education of children. These powers could be used to assist victims, for instance, by the provision of a staff escort for children who are racially harassed on the way to or from school.

2 Appointment of special staff

LEAs must not discriminate when carrying out their functions but special facilities can be provided for particular racial groups to meet the special needs of those groups in regard to their education, training or welfare, or any ancillary benefits.[6]

LEAs can assist victims of racial harassment to build their own support networks using the exemption from the RRA 1976. Some possible ways include:
— appointing education welfare officers from particular racial groups to provide links with the community and bring isolated families together;
— providing special courses for particular racial groups as a way of bringing people together and encouraging them to set up their own support groups;
— appointing staff to assist communities to establish their own additional education programme.

Extra staff might be funded using the Local Government Act 1966 s11, see p37.

Powers to act against perpetrators

1 Power to suspend or to expel children

LEAs are obliged to adopt Articles of Government for their schools which set out the powers and responsibilities of the authority, governors and head relating to the suspension or expulsion of children from a particular school. Powers of suspension for a short period usually lie with the headteacher; where longer periods are concerned the school governors generally have to be involved. Decisions to expel in LEA-maintained schools can only be made by the governors or the LEA and there must be reasonable grounds.[7] Serious racial harassment of another child will constitute reasonable grounds for expulsion.

Any child expelled from school must be provided with alternative education provision if of compulsory school age.

The power to suspend and expel can be used to prevent racial harassment within school, and also to make a child perpetrator move to another school when racial harassment occurs between pupils outside school. The education of a victim is likely to be affected detrimentally if s/he shares a class with a perpetrator who is consistently terrorising him or her outside school.

2 Protecting school and other educational premises

As the owners and occupiers of school and other educational premises, LEAs have power to take action for any nuisance or trespass which affects their property, see p40.

Trespass on school premises

An LEA can require any person to leave school premises at any time or prohibit them from entering. In cases of persistent trespass an injunction can be obtained against a named individual restraining him or her from trespassing. Where there is any footpath or driveway leading to a school or playing fields or playgrounds which are owned by the authority and over which there is no public right of way, an action for trespass can extend to this property as well.

Trespass on the highway
An unreasonable use of the highway adjacent to school premises may amount to a trespass against the highway authority. In many cases, the LEA will also be the highway authority. An action in trespass can be taken against a person who persistently hangs around just outside school premises and harasses or intimidates school children as they enter and leave or who distributes racist literature. "Highway" includes any footpath over which there is a public right of way.

Nuisance
Groups of people loitering outside schools, harassing or intimidating children or handing out racist literature may also be committing an act of nuisance against the LEA. An action in nuisance can be maintained whether or not the persons responsible are on other private property or on the highway.

Damage to school premises
Graffiti and broken windows are two examples of damage to school property for which an LEA can take action for compensation either through the civil courts or by seeking a compensation order when the offender is prosecuted. Where damage is recurring an LEA may be able to seek an injunction against those responsible.

3 Public nuisance

Public nuisances were defined on p43. Like other local authorities, most LEAs can take action for an injunction to prevent a public nuisance or can prosecute. ILEA cannot take action for public nuisance but can for trespass or private nuisance relating to school premises.

An LEA is justified in taking action for public nuisance within the sphere of its responsibility. This will extend to public nuisances affecting school premises and those affecting pupils on their way to and from school. Widespread intimidation of black children on their way to or from school may amount to a public nuisance and an LEA could seek an injunction or prosecute those responsible if they can be identified.

4 Prosecutions for causing or permitting a nuisance or disturbance on school premises

It is a criminal offence to be present on school premises without authority and to cause or permit a nuisance or disturbance to the annoyance of persons who use the premises.[8] An LEA may authorise any person to remove offenders from school premises.[9] This provision extends to premises used for further education which are provided by an LEA and to playgrounds, playing fields and outdoor recreation facilities.[10]

Almost without exception, acts of racial harassment will be acts of nuisance or annoyance. An offence is only committed where the nuisance or disturbance is committed by a person who is on school premises. In addition, that person must be on the premises without permission.

The provision gives an LEA specific power to nominate individuals who have power to remove people from school premises whom they have reasonable cause to suspect are committing an offence.[11] This is in addition to the common law power to remove trespassers using reasonable force. Police officers also have specific power to remove those responsible for a nuisance or disturbance.[12] This extends their normal powers which do not allow them to remove people from private premises unless they are arresting them or there is a breach of the peace. Most police officers are probably unaware of these powers and LEAs should remind them in appropriate circumstances.

This provision clearly covers racial harassment occurring within school committed by outsiders. It does not cover racial harassment committed by pupils, teachers or parents, unless they have first been instructed to leave the premises and have continued to cause a nuisance or disturbance. It will therefore apply to a pupil who has been suspended or expelled and who returns to repeat acts of racial harassment. LEAs should consider giving authority to senior staff both to withdraw permission from pupils or parents to be present on the premises and also to remove any person committing a nuisance or disturbance. Alternatively, LEAs should make arrangements with the local police to ensure that police officers are aware of their powers and will attend when requested by school staff.

Where outsiders are regularly attacking children inside the grounds of a particular school, an authority might employ a security firm to keep trespassers off the premises and authorise employees of the firm to remove people.

Intervention in the private sector

1 Protection of pupils at schools not owned or managed by the authority

Many schools are not managed by LEAs. These include private fee-paying and church schools. In this section they will be called private schools.

The powers of LEAs are considerably more limited for dealing with racial harassment affecting pupils in private schools than in LEA-maintained schools. Those powers that an authority possesses mainly derive from the general ancillary power in LGA 1972 s111. This allows some limited action to protect children if it is in the interests of their education, even though they may be attending a private school.

Public nuisance
An action for public nuisance should be possible to protect children travelling to and from school if harassment or intimidation is aimed at a number of children.

Action as the highway authority
An LEA may be able to take action as the highway authority against perpetrators who racially harass children on their way to and from private schools or immediately outside their schools.

Prosecution for nuisance or disturbance on school premises
An offence is committed under the provision referred to above (see p149) where the nuisance or disturbance occurs on the premises of a private school. The school governors of a private school have the same powers as the LEA has for its own schools.[13] In addition, school governors can give their consent to the LEA to authorise persons to remove offenders from private school premises or to prosecute offenders.[14]

2 Other powers in the private sector

It is not proposed to repeat the general points made in Chapter 4 about the powers of local authorities in the private sector. Like other authorities, LEAs are major customers for goods and services and major employers of staff, and so have scope for influencing suppliers and employment in their area.

LEAs provide discretionary facilities to groups and individuals which can be withdrawn on the grounds discussed in Chapter 2. LEAs provide grants to many voluntary sector organisations and can influence the manner in which those organisations carry out their activities and use their powers to give victims opportunities to develop their own support groups.

Where school premises and other premises owned or managed by the LEA, such as adult education institutes, are used by other groups during the evenings or holidays, an LEA can ensure that such groups are genuinely open to people from all racial groups and that those responsible for the function ensure that racial harassment does not occur against those participating.

---

1 Education Act 1944 s39(5).
2 Ibid ss39(2)(c) and 55 and see *Surrey CC v Ministry of Education* [1953] 1 All ER 705.
3 Education Act 1944 s55(2).
4 *Rogers v Essex CC* [1986] 3 All ER 321.
5 N4.
6 RRA 1976 ss18 and 35.
7 Pupils Registration Regs 1956 SI No 357 reg 4.

8 Local Government (Miscellaneous Provisions) Act 1982 s40.
9 Ibid s40(3).
10 Ibid s40(2).
11 N9.
12 N9.
13 Local Government (Miscellaneous Provisions) Act 1982 s40(4).
14 Ibid s40(5) and (8).

CHAPTER NINE
Other Powers and Duties of Local Authorities

Local authorities' powers to deal with statutory and noise nuisances and rubbish disposal give them opportunities to tackle some forms of racial harassment. As well as allowing authorities to act against perpetrators, they enable them to assist victims and to require the removal of graffiti from private property.

In addition to the duties and powers applicable to all departments and local authorities dealt with in Chapter 4 and those of housing, social services and education authorities dealt with in subsequent chapters, there are several other areas in which authorities have scope for tackling racial harassment. Several of the powers described below involve criminal sanctions. They are included in this chapter since authorities can also use injunctions as an alternative remedy.

A. DUTIES OF LOCAL AUTHORITIES

Duty to inspect the area for nuisances

District councils and London boroughs have a duty to arrange for the inspection of their districts from time to time in order to detect the existence of statutory nuisances.[1] A wide variety of matters fall within the definition of statutory nuisance. The following are relevant to racial harassment:
— any premises in such a state as to be a nuisance;
— any animal kept in such a place or manner as to be prejudicial to health or a nuisance;
— any accumulation or deposit which is prejudicial to health or a nuisance.[2]

The extent of this duty to inspect is unclear and, unless an authority clearly made no attempt to inspect its district at any time, it would be difficult to enforce. However, it is clearly intended that authorities should be active in seeking out statutory nuisances rather than simply reacting to complaints. When a complaint is made, the authority has a duty to investigate its validity in order to decide whether any action is necessary.

Duty to act to abate statutory nuisances

When an authority is satisfied that a statutory nuisance exists it must serve a notice on the person responsible for the nuisance requiring it to be abated, ie stopped.³ The usual enforcement procedure is criminal but the use of injunctions in the High Court should be seriously considered when statutory nuisances are being created deliberately as a form of racial harassment.⁴

1 Procedure

Service of the notice

Action by an authority under this provision begins by the service of a notice. This must be served on the person "by whose act, default or sufferance the nuisance arises or continues". If s/he cannot be found then either a notice must be served on the owner or occupier of premises or if it is clear that the owner or occupier is not responsible for the nuisance, the authority may itself do whatever is necessary to abate the nuisance and prevent its recurrence.⁵ Any notice served must require the person served with it to abate the nuisance, and should state a reasonable time for compliance.

Enforcement

If a notice is not complied with and the statutory nuisance still exists, an authority must apply to the magistrates' court for a summons requiring the person on whom the notice was served to appear at court. Failure to comply with a notice under this provision is a criminal offence and it is therefore necessary to prove beyond reasonable doubt that the person summonsed is responsible for the statutory nuisance in order to obtain a conviction.⁶

The court has power to do four things:

(a) make a nuisance order requiring the person named in the notice to abate the nuisance within a specified time; and
(b) prohibit a recurrence of the nuisance; and
(c) fine the person named in the notice up to £1,000; or
(d) authorise the authority to carry out the terms of the nuisance order where the person responsible for the nuisance or the owner or occupier of the premises cannot be found.⁷

A failure to comply with a nuisance order is a continuing criminal offence which can lead to a fine of £2,000 and a daily fine of up to £50.⁸ Where a nuisance order has not been complied with, the authority may abate the nuisance and do whatever may be necessary to execute a nuisance order and recover the costs from the person responsible.⁹

2 Injunctions

Where an authority considers that a notice and criminal prosecution will be an inadequate remedy it may apply for an injunction in the High Court.¹⁰

3 Recurring nuisances

A notice can also be served where a statutory nuisance has occurred and an authority is satisfied that it is likely to recur.¹¹ Slightly different procedures

Other powers and duties 155

apply. In particular, no conviction or order from the magistrates' court can be obtained unless the nuisance has recurred following the service of the notice and an authority can prove that the perpetrator is likely to repeat the nuisance.[12]

Powers of entry
Properly authorised council officers with proof of authorisation have powers of entry to premises at reasonable hours to investigate whether there has been a breach of the above provisions. Where access is refused a warrant to enter may be obtained from a magistrate.[13]

4 Racial harassment amounting to statutory nuisance
Several forms of racial harassment may constitute statutory nuisance. Those responsible for any nuisance need not be neighbouring occupiers. Provided it is possible to identify those responsible, perpetrators living anywhere may be served with a notice if they have deliberately created a nuisance, eg by dumping rubbish outside a victim's home.

Racial harassment might take the form of deliberately creating a nuisance on neighbouring premises or the common parts of a housing estate, eg dumping rotting rubbish or excreta in premises adjoining the victim's home or on the common parts or allowing a dog to urinate outside a victim's home. A dog may be used to cause a nuisance,[14] eg constant barking or intimidation of children on the common parts by a vicious dog.

Where it is known who caused the nuisance, the abatement notice should be served on the perpetrator. The notice could require the following:
— the removal by the perpetrator of rubbish or excreta that has been dumped in the common parts or on neighbouring land;
— steps to be taken to prevent a dog causing a nuisance.
Where rubbish has been dumped on land owned by the victim, an authority can exercise its power to remove the rubbish itself.

The use of an injunction is likely to be appropriate and most effective where offences are being committed on a regular basis, particularly where they are part of a campaign of racial harassment, or where immediate action is needed and the procedure in the magistrates' court will take too long.

Duty to inspect the district to detect noise nuisance

District councils and London boroughs have a duty to arrange for the inspection of their districts from time to time in order to detect noise nuisances.[15] The same points can be made about the effect of this duty as were made above (see p153).

Duty to act to abate noise nuisances

Where an authority is satisfied that a noise amounting to a nuisance is occurring or is likely to occur or recur it must serve a notice requiring the abatement of the nuisance or prohibiting or restricting its occurrence or recurrence.[16] The notice must give a time for compliance.

It appears that a notice may only be served when noise originates from premises, although the provision makes no reference to such a restriction.[17] It will be a question of fact whether a particular form of noise amounts to a nuisance. The fact that the noise is deliberate and intended as harassment should reduce the level of noise necessary to amount to a nuisance.

1 Procedure

Service of the notice
The notice must usually be served on the person responsible for the nuisance. If that person cannot be found it must be served on the owner or occupier of the premises from which the noise has emanated.[18] The person served with the notice can appeal to the magistrates' court against the notice. The notice is usually suspended while an appeal is in progress but an authority may include a certificate in the notice which makes it continue in force even while an appeal is pending.[19]

Enforcement
Any person who contravenes a notice without reasonable excuse commits a criminal offence punishable by a fine of up to £2,000 for the first offence and a further fine of up to £2,000 and a daily fine of up to £50 for further offences.[20] Because it is a criminal matter, the act of contravention must be proved beyond reasonable doubt.

2 Injunctions

As in the case of statutory nuisances, an authority can seek an injunction in the High Court to prevent a noise nuisance if it considers that the normal procedure provides an inadequate remedy.[21] An injunction will be appropriate in similar circumstances to those relating to statutory nuisances (see p154 above).

3 Powers relating to noise nuisances

Powers of entry
Authorised council officers with proof of authorisation have power to enter premises at reasonable times to carry out any functions under these powers or to measure noise levels.[22] Where entry is refused a warrant can be obtained from a magistrate.[23]

Notice requiring information
An authority has power to serve a notice requiring any person to give information which the authority needs to carry out its functions under these provisions, for example, the names of owners or occupiers.[24] Failure to provide information requested is a criminal offence punishable by a fine of up to £2,000.

4 Racial harassment constituting noise nuisance

Perpetual noise from neighbours can have an extremely detrimental effect on family life, particularly if it results in serious sleep deprivation. Most noise nuisances occur after normal working hours and many authorities operate a special noise patrol team in order to carry out their statutory duty to inspect for noise nuisance.

It is not essential for an authority's environmental health officers either to measure or to hear a noise nuisance in order to serve a notice. It is the effect the noise has on the victim which makes it an actionable nuisance, provided that the victim is not abnormally sensitive.[25] A slight degree of noise over a long period may be just as much a nuisance as a loud noise for a short period. Noise at 3am every night is more likely to be a nuisance than noise at 3pm.

An authority might not wish to proceed solely on the evidence of one family, but other supporting evidence might be available from other families, the police, housing officers, health visitors, or social workers who have themselves heard the noise. Tape recordings may have been made, volunteers from community groups might be prepared to sleep in for several nights and experience the effect of the noise and be available to give evidence.

Where noise is a form of harassment as opposed to merely inconsiderate behaviour, it is more likely to be regular and frequent and should be easier to detect, provided that an authority sets up procedures for doing so. It might consider lending measuring equipment to victims or local community groups.

B. POWERS OF LOCAL AUTHORITIES

Powers to protect and assist victims

1 Land adversely affecting the amenity of the neighbourhood

If London boroughs or district councils consider that the amenity of a neighbourhood is "adversely affected by the condition of land in their area" they can serve a notice on the owner and occupier of the land requiring steps to be taken to remedy the condition of the land.[26] "Amenity" is not defined and is therefore likely to have its dictionary meaning. "Land" includes buildings.[27] This provision came into force only in 1987 replacing a far more restricted power.

Any notice must specify a time within which work must be done. If any work required by a notice is not carried out, an authority has power to do the work itself and recover the cost.[28] The person served with the notice who fails to comply commits a criminal offence for which the maximum fine is £400 with a further daily fine of up to £40.[29]

Owners and occupiers may appeal to the magistrates' court against the notice. Pending such an appeal, the notice is suspended and no action can be taken by the authority.[30] There is no express power to seek an injunction under this provision.

This power will probably be most useful in respect of land that has been vandalised, eg by the dumping of rubbish or by racist graffiti. Authorities may require graffiti to be removed from railway bridges, walls or hoardings in their area which are constantly covered by racist graffiti. The threat of future notices being served for graffiti removal may be used to persuade the owners to take better precautions against future graffiti writing, eg better fencing, anti-climb paint etc.

2 Street lighting

Highway authorities (London borough councils, metropolitan district councils and county councils) have powers to provide street lighting for highways for which they are responsible.[31] The definition of "highway" includes not only roads but footpaths where there is a public right of way.[32]

Where records of instances of racial harassment or reports from local groups or schools show that particular streets or footpaths are poorly lit and attacks are being made along them, an authority should consider providing improved lighting which may deter some of the attackers.

3 Removal of waste

Where waste has been dumped on land and the occupier is not responsible for dumping the waste, London borough councils and district councils may remove it.[33] This provision covers household, industrial or commercial waste.[34] Where the occupier was not responsible for dumping the waste, the authority may recover the cost of removal and disposal of the waste from the person who dumped it.[35]

If rubbish is dumped on a victim's land as a form of racial harassment, an authority may remove the rubbish itself, at no cost to the victim, and charge the perpetrator for the cost of removal.

See below for remedies where rubbish is dumped by a perpetrator on his or her own land.

Powers to act against perpetrators

1 Powers in relation to collection of rubbish

London borough councils and district councils have a duty to collect household waste free of charge,[36] and may serve a notice on any premises requiring the occupier to comply with certain requirements relating to rubbish.[37]

Notice served under this provision can specify:
— that the occupier must place household waste in dustbins provided by the occupier or by the authority;
— that s/he must keep the dustbins in a certain place;
— the type of bins and the number required;
— the substances which may or may not be put into the bins.[38]

The occupier may appeal to the magistrates' court on the ground that a requirement in the notice is unreasonable or that existing bins are adequate. Pending the outcome of the appeal the notice is suspended and no action by the council is possible.[39] Once the notice is in force, it is an offence to fail to comply with it punishable with a fine of up to £400.

Authorities could serve notices under this provision on perpetrators who dump rubbish outside victims' homes as a form of racial harassment.

2 Powers in relation to rubbish dumping

London borough councils and district councils may require an occupier to remove waste which has been dumped on land.[40] The notice must specify a period exceeding 21 days for removal of the waste.

The occupier may appeal to the magistrates' court, which can quash the notice if satisfied that the occupier did not dump the rubbish or there is some defect in the notice. During any appeal, the notice is suspended and no action can be taken by the council.[41] Once the notice is effective, failure to comply is an offence punishable by a fine of up to £2,000 and £50 per day.[42]

Where an authority considers that there is a danger to public health caused by the waste, it need not serve any notice but may itself immediately remove any waste and charge the occupier of the land for doing so.[43]

3 Byelaws for the prevention of nuisances

London borough councils and district councils have power to make byelaws preventing the occurrence of nuisances from filth, dust, rubbish and the keeping of animals so as to be prejudicial to health.[44] Breach of byelaws is a criminal offence (see p177).

1 Public Health Act 1936 ss1 and 91.
2 Ibid s92.
3 Ibid s93.
4 Ibid s100.
5 N3.
6 Public Health Act 1936 s94.
7 Ibid s94(2) and (6).
8 Ibid s95(1).
9 Ibid s95(2).
10 N4.
11 Public Health (Recurring Nuisances) Act 1969 s1.
12 Ibid s2.
13 Public Health Act 1936 s287.
14 Ibid s92(1)(b) but cf *Morrissey v Galer* [1955] 1 WLR 110 doubted in *Coventry CC v Cartwright* [1975] 1 WLR 845.
15 Control of Pollution Act 1974 ss57 and 73(1).
16 Ibid s58(1).

160 *Other powers and duties*

17 *Tower Hamlets LBC v Manzoni and Walder* [1984] JPL 436.
18 Control of Pollution Act 1974 s59(2).
19 Ibid s70 and Control of Noise (Appeal) Regulations 1975 SI No 2116.
20 Control of Pollution Act 1974 s74.
21 Ibid s58(8) and see *LB Hammersmith v Magnum Automated Forecourts Ltd* [1978] 1 All ER 401, CA.
22 Control of Pollution Act 1974 s91.
23 Ibid s91(2).
24 Ibid s93.
25 See Knight Bruce VC in *Walter v Selfe* (1851) 4 De G & S 315 at 322.
26 Town and Country Planning Act 1971 s65 as amended by the Housing and Planning Act 1986 s46 and see Town and Country Planning Act 1971 s1(1).
27 Ibid s290.
28 Ibid s107.
29 Ibid s104.
30 Ibid s105.
31 Highways Act 1980 s97.
32 Ibid s328.
33 Control of Pollution Act 1974 s16(5).
34 Ibid ss16(1) and 30.
35 Ibid s16(6).
36 Ibid s12.
37 Ibid s13.
38 Ibid s13(7).
39 Ibid s13(3).
40 Ibid s16(1).
41 Ibid s16(2) and (3).
42 Ibid s16(4).
43 Ibid s16(5).
44 Public Health Act 1936 s81.

CHAPTER TEN

Criminal Proceedings

Local authorities have the power to take criminal proceedings in various circumstances. These are discussed and the procedure in criminal courts described. The requirements for some more important criminal offences are considered in detail.

Most acts of racial harassment are criminal offences. Some are offences the law considers to be minor where the maximum penalty is a small fine. Others are far more serious where penalties can include long periods of imprisonment.

Children under 10, in law, cannot commit criminal offences, so criminal proceedings are unavailable against a child under this age. However, care proceedings may be possible on the basis that the child is beyond his or her parents' control (see Chapter 7).

As described in Chapter 3, local authorities are given legal powers to take criminal proceedings in three ways. In this chapter, for convenience, we shall divide criminal offences into those in respect of which an authority is given express statutory power to prosecute or where the power is clearly implied by LGA 1972 s111 and those where the power to prosecute is inferred from LGA 1972 s222. Only brief mention of the latter type of offence is made. The limitations on the power to prosecute provided by s222 are discussed in Chapter 3. They must be read in conjunction with part C of this chapter.

Although many of the offences for which local authorities are given express power to prosecute give rise to only minor penalties, the use of these powers should still be considered. A conviction can be used in subsequent civil proceedings as conclusive evidence that the offence has been committed (see Chapter 14).

A. AN OUTLINE OF CRIMINAL PROCEDURE

Powers of arrest for criminal offences

In respect of each of the offences listed in this chapter it is stated whether the offence is arrestable. Both private citizens and police officers have powers to arrest those responsible for arrestable offences. There is also a power of arrest for breach of the peace which is discussed in Chapter 11.

Arrestable offences

Arrest at the time the offence is being committed
Where an offence is arrestable, anyone can arrest a person:

— who is in the act of committing the offence; or
— whom s/he has reasonable grounds for suspecting to be committing the offence.[1]

The arrest must be made at the time the offence is being committed.

Arrest after the offence has been committed
Where an arrestable offence has been committed anyone can arrest a person:
— who is guilty of the offence; or
— whom s/he has reasonable grounds for suspecting to be guilty of the offence.[2]

If, in fact, it turns out that no offence has been committed, an arrest by a private individual will have been unlawful and the person arrested may be able to claim damages from the person who made the arrest.[3] For this reason "citizens' arrests" after the event involve a degree of risk.

Police officers have additional powers (dealt with in Chapter 11) which give them considerable protection against claims for wrongful arrest. The police also have limited powers in relation to offences which are not arrestable.

The criminal courts

1 The adult courts

Criminal offences by adults (17 or over) are tried either in the magistrates' court or the Crown Court. Magistrates' courts consist either of a legally qualified stipendiary magistrate sitting alone, or three lay magistrates. The clerk is legally qualified and advises the magistrates on the interpretation of the law. The Crown Court consists of a judge and a jury of twelve people.

Offences are one of three kinds, summary, triable only on indictment or triable either way.

Summary offences
Minor offences can only be tried in the magistrates' court and are known as summary offences. Neither the defence nor the prosecution has any choice about where the offence is tried.

The full trial will take place in the magistrates' court with witnesses giving evidence. If the defendant pleads guilty or is found guilty, the magistrates' court will impose sentence. It can impose no more than the maximum sentence laid down for the offence, which is usually a fine and possibly a short period of imprisonment.

Offences triable only on indictment
Very serious offences can only be tried in the Crown Court. This is known as trial on indictment. Again neither the defence nor the prosecution has any choice about where the offence is tried.

Proceedings for the offence will start in the magistrates' court with committal proceedings. These involve a preliminary consideration of the prosecution case to ascertain whether there is enough evidence against the defendant to justify a committal to the Crown Court for a full trial. It is usually only the prosecution evidence that is considered at committal proceedings. If the defence agrees, committal often takes place on the basis of written statements from the prosecution witnesses.[4]

Offences triable either way
Many offences may be tried either in the magistrates' or Crown Court and are known as offences triable either way.[5] The proceedings always begin in the magistrates' court which determines whether the offence is to be tried by the magistrates or Crown Court. This is known as the "mode of trial" procedure.[6]

The choice of court for the trial is decided in the following way:

(a) The magistrates hear the views of the prosecution and defence on whether the case is more suitable for trial in the magistrates' or Crown Court.[7]

(b) The magistrates decide where they think the trial should take place.

(c) If the magistrates think the matter should be heard by the Crown Court then neither defence nor prosecution has any choice.[8]

(d) If the magistrates think the matter should be tried in the magistrates' court, the defendant has a right to insist on jury trial. The prosecution cannot insist on a Crown Court trial.[9]

(e) If the matter is to be tried in the magistrates' court the procedure is then identical to summary proceedings except that if the defendant pleads guilty or is found guilty the magistrates can commit the defendant to the Crown Court for sentence if they think their powers are insufficient.[10]

(f) If the matter is to be tried in the Crown Court, committal proceedings take place in the same way as for indictable offences.

The magistrates' court cannot impose a fine exceeding £2,000 or imprison anyone for a period exceeding six months.[11] Heavier sentences for an offence triable either way can only be imposed by the Crown Court.

2 The juvenile court

Offences committed by juveniles (under 17) are all tried in the juvenile court unless the juvenile is jointly charged with an adult or the offence is very serious. Juveniles charged jointly with an adult are treated in the same way as the adult charged, so they can be tried in the magistrates' or Crown Court. Very serious offences by juveniles are tried in the Crown Court.

The maximum fine that a juvenile court can impose is £100 on a child aged 10-13 and £400 on a child aged 14-16. Other sentences which can be imposed by the juvenile courts are considered below on p166.

Juvenile courts consist of three magistrates, one of whom may be a legally qualified stipendiary magistrate.

3 Starting criminal proceedings

Criminal proceedings may be begun in one of two ways, either by a charge, or by laying an information.[12] In the context of racial harassment only the police can lay charges. Officers or solicitors representing local authorities or private individuals must lay an information before a magistrates' court and ask for a summons or warrant to be issued.

Charges

Most prosecutions for serious offences are begun by the police arresting and then charging a suspect. The police then produce the person charged (the defendant) in court on the next available day or grant the defendant bail to appear at some later date.[13] Police powers to grant bail in these circumstances are considered in Chapter 11.

Laying an information

Authorities usually lay an information and ask for a summons to be issued. The summons merely notifies the defendant of the charge and the date of hearing and instructs him or her to attend. If the defendant fails to attend, the case can proceed in his or her absence provided service of the summons can be proved. Alternatively, the court may at this stage issue a warrant if the offence is punishable by imprisonment. The defendant is then arrested by the police and brought to court.

An information can be laid by an officer of the local authority who has responsibility for the matter or by the authority's solicitors.[14]

For more serious offences, and to ensure that the defendant is kept in custody or only released on certain bail conditions (see below), authorities can ask the magistrates' court to issue a warrant instead of a summons, if the offence is punishable by imprisonment.[15] In practice, this includes any offence which is triable either way. To obtain a warrant, an officer of the authority must give information on oath of the circumstances of the offence. This information is not limited to evidence which is admissible in court but can include information obtained from statements made to the authority by witnesses. A warrant is an authority to the police to arrest the defendant and bring him or her to court.

Warrants may require the police to grant bail to the defendant once s/he has been arrested. If no such requirement is included in the warrant, the police have a discretion whether to grant bail following arrest.

4 Adjournments and remands

If the defendant denies the offence it is extremely unusual for criminal proceedings before magistrates to be dealt with at the first hearing. Where the court fixes a later date for the matter to be heard, the proceedings are adjourned. The defendant may be remanded either in custody or on bail.

Adjournments

Adjournments with neither remand in custody nor on bail are appropriate where a summons has been issued, but not where a defendant has been charged by the police or arrested under a warrant applied for by a local authority or private individual. If the defendant does not appear at the adjourned hearing, the court can proceed in his or her absence or issue a warrant for his or her arrest if the offence is punishable by imprisonment.[16] The defendant commits no offence by failing to appear at the hearing.

Remands in custody

Defendants have a general right to be released on bail but the court can refuse bail on certain grounds. Where the offence is punishable by imprisonment these include:

(a) that there are substantial grounds for believing s/he would commit an offence while on bail;
(b) that there are substantial grounds for believing s/he would interfere with witnesses while on bail;
(c) if s/he is under 17, that s/he ought to be kept in custody for his or her own welfare.[17]

A defendant remanded in custody will spend the time until the trial in prison.

Remands on bail

Bail is very important in the context of racial harassment. If defendants are released until the trial, which in most cases they are, bail gives the criminal courts power to protect victims and other witnesses from the time the criminal proceedings are started to the time they are completed.

The granting of bail is a process whereby either the police or a court release the suspect or defendant on condition that s/he surrenders to custody at a particular place, time and date. Failure to do so is a separate criminal offence.[18]

In the case of a suspect who has not been charged, the police will bail a person to return to a police station while they carry out more enquiries and decide whether they have enough evidence to prosecute. This is often known as "police bail" and is considered further in Chapter 11. Once a person is charged, or after they have been arrested under a warrant, the police can bail a defendant to appear in court on a particular date.

The court can bail defendants to appear at the next hearing. When a case is to be remanded to a later date the court *must* consider whether to grant bail to the defendant.

Bail conditions

The ability of courts to impose bail conditions provides protection for witnesses and victims. They can be imposed to ensure that the defendant does not:

166 Criminal proceedings

— commit any further offences while on bail; nor
— interfere with witnesses or obstruct the course of justice.[19]

Breach of a bail condition is not an offence, but the person on bail can be arrested for breach of conditions and is likely to be refused bail when taken before the court.[20]

Where the defendant is a juvenile, his or her parent may be required to enter into a recognisance to ensure that the child complies with bail conditions. This can be for an amount up to £50.[21]

Procedure for bail

If the prosecution asks that a defendant should be kept in custody until the trial or asks for special conditions to be imposed on any bail that is granted, the court will probably have to consider a bail application by the defendant's legal representative. The prosecution may call a witness to give evidence of the reasons why a remand in custody or bail conditions are appropriate. The witness will be questioned by the court and by the defendant's representative. The procedure is similar to a short trial but is dealing only with bail. Unlike a trial, the strict rules of evidence do not apply (see Chapter 14). This allows the prosecution witness to give evidence that s/he believes the defendant has committed other offences and to report hearsay evidence.

5 Relevant court sentencing powers

It is not proposed to deal with the sentencing powers in detail. However, it is useful to have some idea of how these powers might be used to protect victims.[22] The power of the courts to make orders against parents when their children are found to have committed offences is dealt with separately on p168.

Immediate custodial sentences

The defendant is kept in custody and thus cannot commit further acts of racial harassment until released. These sentences include:
— imprisonment (21 and over);
— youth custody (15 and over but under 21);
— detention centre (14 and over but under 21).

Immediate financial penalties

These provide no protection for the victim. The available sentences are fines and compensation orders. A compensation order requires the defendant to recompense the victim. The money is paid through the court which has the responsibility for recovering the compensation if it is unpaid. The amount of compensation that can be awarded by the magistrates' court is limited to £2,000. Compensation orders are not limited to damage to property. They can be paid to compensate for injuries and also for terror or distress caused by the offence.[23]

Deterrent sentences
These sentences will provide some protection for the victim. If the defendant is found guilty of another crime within a set period, s/he can be resentenced for the first offence. Sentences within this category are:
— suspended sentence of imprisonment;
— conditional discharge;
— community service order (see below);
— probation order (see below).

Sentences falling short of detention
Several sentences are available which allow restrictions to be imposed on the defendant's conduct. These are:
— probation order (17 and over);
— community service order (16 and over);
— attendance centre order (10 and over but under 21);
— care order (under 17);
— supervision order (under 17).

(a) *Probation orders* Probation orders place the defendant under the supervision of a probation officer. They will not be imposed without a report from the probation service being produced to the court. Orders allow the conduct of the defendant to be controlled since conditions can be imposed. These conditions can require the defendant to:
— reside at a particular address;
— refrain from certain activities, eg attending a particular pub, school or housing estate;
— take part in certain activities, eg possibly an evening activity.
A probation order can last for six months to three years. There are penalties for breach of conditions or the court can resentence the offender.

(b) *Community service order* As the name implies, the defendant is required to perform some service of benefit to the community. The types of project available vary with the locality. A report from the probation service or social services authority has to be presented to the court. The supervisor gives instructions as to the work to be carried out and the times. The total period must be between 40 and 240 hours.

(c) *Attendance centre order* The offender is required to attend the centre at specified days and times for between 12 and 36 hours.

(d) *Care order* A care order puts the local social services authority in the position of the child's guardian. The authority can then decide where the child should live, what school s/he should attend etc.

(e) *Supervision order* A supervision order places a child under the supervision either of the local social services authority or the probation service. The supervisor can be given the power to impose similar conditions to those in probation orders for a period of up to 90 days (see above). In addition, a night curfew can be imposed by the court for a limited period, requiring the child to remain at home for any 10 hours between 6pm and 6am. However, the child can leave the home if accompanied by his or her parent.

6 Bind overs[24]

The magistrates' court has power to require any person appearing before it, including a witness, to enter into a recognisance to keep the peace and be of good behaviour. An order is justified only if there is likely to be a breach of the peace in the future or some other criminal conduct. Any potential violence or threats of violence will justify a bind over, as may arguments between parties in court. No conviction is necessary for a bind over. The person bound over enters into a promise to pay a specified sum if s/he breaches the peace or is not of good behaviour within the period of the bind over.

Where victims prosecute for common assault, it is extremely likely that the court will seek to bind over both parties. This does not prevent the victim from proceeding with the prosecution which the court is obliged to hear.

7 Action against parents for their children's criminal activities

Apart from the imposition of care or supervision orders there are two ways in which the courts can hold parents responsible for their children's acts.

Recognisance to exercise proper care and control

When a child under 17 is found guilty of an offence, the magistrates' or juvenile court may order the child's parent to enter into a recognisance to take proper care and exercise proper control over his or her child. The order requires the parent's consent which is likely to be forthcoming if the parent believes that a more severe sentence is the alternative. The order can last for up to three years or until the child is 18, whichever is shorter and can be for an amount up to £1,000.

Fine or compensation order made against the parent

Where a court finds a child under 17 guilty of an offence and considers a fine or compensation order to be appropriate, it must order the parent to pay the fine or compensation unless it considers it would be unreasonable to do so having regard to the circumstances of the case.[25]

The court must give the parent an opportunity to be heard but if s/he fails to attend having been invited, an order can be made in the parent's absence.

In practice, there is no other way in which a parent can be held legally responsible for the criminal acts of his or her child.

8 Practical considerations on the use of criminal proceedings

The purpose of using criminal proceedings in the context of a racial harassment policy has four elements, which will usually overlap:

— to punish the offender;
— to deter the offender from committing the same or a similar offence;
— to deter others from committing similar offences;
— to provide immediate protection for the victim.

The maximum advantage is gained from a criminal prosecution if it is successful, maximum publicity is obtained, the offender gets a sentence appropriate to the seriousness of the offences, the court process is used to keep the offender away from the victim and witnesses before the trial and the sentence keeps the offender away from the victim after the trial, at least at times of maximum risk of further offences being committed.

Clearly, careful preparation and the skillful use of publicity are two important factors. The following points are relevant when seeking to protect the victim and attempting to obtain a sentence which adequately reflects the seriousness of the offence.

Asking the court for a warrant rather than a summons
If a warrant is obtained, either the police or the court can consider whether to keep the defendant in custody or release him or her on bail. When a summons is issued no such power exists until the first hearing which is usually several weeks ahead.

Warrants are unlikely to be issued for minor offences triable only in the magistrates' court. For any serious offence punishable by imprisonment which is part of a campaign of racial harassment an authority can argue for the issue of a warrant. The court must be told:
— of the need for a warrant to allow immediate bail conditions to be imposed to protect the victim;
— of the background to the offence so as to reveal its serious nature even though it may appear to be a relatively minor offence. The background will include the motive of the offender and the pattern of previous offences which it is believed have occurred.
All offences that are prosecuted under the Protection from Eviction Act 1977 are likely to be sufficiently serious for a warrant to be appropriate.

Asking that the warrant should not be backed for bail
Magistrates can require the police to grant bail to defendants arrested under a warrant. In most cases, this will be undesirable since bail conditions to protect witnesses are less likely to be imposed by the police than by the court. An authority should therefore argue that the warrant should not require the defendant to be released on bail by the police, but that the defendant should be brought before the court who can then consider any bail application and either keep the defendant in custody or impose strict bail conditions.

Asking the police not to grant bail or to impose appropriate conditions
Even if the court does not require bail to be granted on the warrant, the police still have a discretion to grant bail once the defendant has been arrested under a warrant. They should be asked not to do so for the protection

of the victim and witnesses, or else to impose conditions for the protection of the victim or witnesses. It is worth explaining to the police in detail the reasons why bail should be refused and confirming these in writing.

Asking the court to refuse bail
The relevant grounds on which a court can refuse bail are given above. An authority will need to provide evidence that further offences are likely to be committed or witnesses likely to be interfered with. Circumstantial or hearsay evidence that the defendant is responsible for other criminal acts of racial harassment against the same victim can be provided by council officers. If combined with the close proximity of the victim's home to that of the defendant, there may be a strong argument for remand in custody or, more likely, for strict bail conditions.

It is advisable to obtain details of the defendant's previous convictions from the police. A police objection to bail in addition to the local authority's may considerably strengthen the latter's request.

Asking for bail conditions which protect witnesses and victims
There is no limit on the court's powers to impose conditions that are necessary to protect witnesses (which will almost certainly include the victim unless s/he is too young to give evidence: see p243) and to prevent further offences.

In one case involving racial harassment in which the police prosecuted for a serious assault, the perpetrator had a bail condition imposed that he did not enter the housing estate where he lived until the trial.[26] Effectively, he was evicted pending trial in order to protect witnesses and prevent further offences. The court must be informed of other accommodation available for the defendant. A bail hostel or relatives might be appropriate. Relatives can usually be expected to co-operate if the alternative is a possible remand in custody.

Examples of other conditions that might be appropriate include:
— exclusion from certain roads and shopping areas used by witnesses;
— exclusion from an area around the school attended by the victim's children;
— a curfew between 6pm and 8am or other appropriate times;
— staying the night at relatives and keeping off an estate or out of a particular road between 6pm and 8am;
— keeping a certain distance away from a particular pub, club, community centre, playgroup etc.

Bail conditions can be used in the private and public sector effectively to obtain an immediate eviction by banning the defendant from his or her home. The conditions can continue until the trial. If the defendant lives in local authority accommodation, the period before the trial can be used to obtain a possession order. In this way, criminal and civil remedies can be combined to prevent a perpetrator ever returning home following arrest for a criminal offence.

Asking for a bind over at the first available moment
Even if the court is reluctant to remand a defendant on bail it may be prepared to bind him or her over, given the risk of further incidents. There is no reason why the prosecution cannot ask for a bind over to be imposed on the first occasion that the defendant is before the court.

Choosing the appropriate court for trial
Where an offence is triable either way the prosecuting authority may seek a Crown Court trial. The choice of venue will depend considerably on local circumstances and the experience of dealing with the particular magistrates and judges sitting at the local courts.

Some of the possible advantages of a Crown Court trial are:
— the availability of greater powers of imprisonment and fining;
— the possibility that the Crown Court might impose a heavier sentence which more adequately reflects the seriousness of the offence;
— the greater publicity generated by a Crown Court trial;
— the fact that the Crown Court appropriately reflects the seriousness and importance of the case.

However, in the majority of cases, a perpetrator is unlikely to receive a sentence greater than the maximum that can be imposed by the magistrates. It should also be noted that a Crown Court trial is considerably more expensive.

When the police are prosecuting, there are advantages in having a trial in the magistrates' court as the defendant is more likely to be convicted. This advantage may not apply when local authorities are prosecuting because the local magistrates' courts tend not to treat a prosecution by a local authority with the same degree of seriousness or accept the evidence of local authority officers quite so readily as they may accept that of police officers.

It is not possible to lay down hard and fast rules about the choice of court. Experimentation is necessary. If an authority decides to seek a Crown Court trial, the arguments in favour of this must be put forward during the "mode of trial" procedure referred to above (see p163).

9 Presentation of the case

The attitude taken by the courts to a particular offence can be significantly altered by the way in which the case is presented by the prosecution. For this reason, it may be useful and important for an authority to observe prosecutions by the Crown Prosecution Service of perpetrators of racial harassment to ensure that the case is presented in the appropriate way.

Trials following a plea of not guilty
(a) *Opening speech* When the defendant pleads not guilty the prosecution often opens a case by outlining the facts. At this stage only facts relevant to the particular offence which can be proved may be mentioned. Thus, it is not usually permissible to refer to other offences that have been committed

by the perpetrator. This means that the offence cannot be set in context as part of a sustained campaign of racial harassment.

However, there is one offence where this rule will not apply. Where a prosecution is being brought under the Protection from Eviction Act 1977 s1, it is the whole campaign of harassment that constitutes the offence. This is a major advantage of this provision as it allows evidence of any acts committed by the perpetrator to be given in evidence whether they are major (eg assault, criminal damage) or minor (eg dogs urinating). In an opening speech, it is permissible to make the allegation that the defendant is motivated by racism if there is evidence which will be produced at the trial to back up this assertion.

(b) *Prosecution evidence* This chapter and Appendix 6 list offences that might be committed as part of a campaign of racial harassment. With the exception of the offences involving incitement to racial hatred, none of them require proof of a racial motive. It is not necessary to prove a racial motive to obtain a conviction and the prosecution can present its case without mentioning the racial motive. Nevertheless, the motive of a defendant is a relevant fact that helps to support the prosecution's case as it makes it more likely that the defendant committed the offence. Evidence of racial motive should therefore be introduced if it is available.

The racial motive of the defendant should also have a significant effect on the likely sentence imposed as it will contribute to the seriousness of the offence.

Sentencing after a plea of guilty or conviction
If a defendant pleads guilty, the prosecution usually outlines the facts of the case and the defendant's representative then makes a plea in mitigation.

The prosecution does not suggest a sentence but it is wholly appropriate for it to mention the following:
— the racial motive behind the criminal acts;
— the continuing nature of the harassment;
— the effect on the victims;
— the number of similar problems within the area;
— the continuing fears of the victim after the case;
— the fact that a child's parents have done nothing to stop their child committing the offence.

These factors should also be mentioned by the prosecution before sentencing after a conviction following a trial, if they have not already been dealt with in evidence.

The court frequently obtains reports from the probation service or social services department before sentencing. It is important that an authority draws to the attention of the officer responsible for preparing the report the factors referred to above, since these are relevant to the recommendations that are likely to be made. Some sentences provide a greater degree of long-term protection for victims than others and an officer may recommend the use of a more appropriate sentence if provided with all the relevant information.

It may be the social services department of the prosecuting local authority which is preparing the report for the court. If so, the department staff are operating as officers of the court and owe their duty to the court to present the facts as they see them. The prosecuting and reporting roles of the authority should be kept entirely distinct. It would be inappropriate for an authority to take any steps to adopt policies which interfered with the ability of the social services staff to make the recommendations they thought were most suitable for the particular case. That should not prevent the prosecuting department drawing the attention of the social services department to the relevant facts.

B. OFFENCES FOR WHICH LOCAL AUTHORITIES HAVE POWER TO PROSECUTE

The Protection from Eviction Act 1977 s1

This offence is not arrestable and is triable in either the magistrates' or Crown Court. Under the Protection from Eviction Act 1977 (PFE) it is an offence if a person:
"with intent to cause the residential occupier of any premises-
   (a) to give up the occupation of the premises or any part thereof; or
   (b) to refrain from exercising any right or pursuing any remedy in respect of the premises or part thereof;
does acts calculated to interfere with the peace or comfort of the residential occupier or members of his household."[27]
District councils and London boroughs are given power to prosecute for offences under the Act.[28] Clause 27 of the Housing Bill before Parliament at the beginning of December 1987, if enacted, will create a new additional offence of harassment, but this can only be committed by a landlord or a landlord's agent.

1 Definitions

Who is a residential occupier?
A residential occupier is defined as a person occupying the premises as a residence either:
— under a contract; or
— under a right given by statute; or
— under a "rule of law" giving the right to remain in occupation or restricting the right of others to recover possession.
This will certainly include:
(a) any tenant, whether council, housing association, housing co-operative or private sector;
(b) any licensee including lodgers, those living in hostels, or children or elderly people living in a council home, whose licence is still in force;

174 Criminal proceedings

(c) any tenant where a notice to quit has expired if the landlord must get an order for possession;
(d) any leaseholder under a long lease.[29]

It can also be argued that it includes an owner occupier.[30] It appears likely that squatters are not residential occupiers for the purposes of the Act.[31]

Who can be guilty of harassment?
Anyone can be guilty of harassment under the Act. The offence is not limited to landlords or neighbours.

The intent
To obtain a conviction for harassment, an authority must prove that the intention of the perpetrator is either to get the victim to move or to deter the victim from exercising a particular right relating to the premises or from pursuing a remedy. Evidence will therefore be required both of the act of harassment and the intention behind the act. Although the provision refers to "acts" the courts have held that one act will suffice for an offence.[32] The words "calculated to" in the definition of the offence have been interpreted as meaning "likely to".[33]

The maximum penalty in the Crown Court is two years' imprisonment.

2 Use of the provision

Authorities should consider prosecuting under this provision in all cases of racial harassment where the necessary proof exists, rather than relying on the use of LGA 1972 s222 and prosecutions for other offences, for the following reasons:

(a) there is no doubt that authorities have power to prosecute;
(b) the police will almost certainly not prosecute under the PFE so there is no argument that it is more appropriate for the police to prosecute;
(c) the penalties available under this provision are sufficiently great to be equivalent to what a perpetrator might receive for a relatively serious assault and are considerably higher than those for other offences where an authority has express power to prosecute;
(d) authorities should already be familiar with the procedure under the PFE in dealing with harassment in the private sector;
(e) almost any act of racial harassment relating to the home will constitute an offence under this provision (provided it can be proved);
(f) because the whole campaign of harassment against different members of the same household constitutes the one offence, evidence can be produced relating to all the acts that form part of the campaign. This allows the prosecuting authority to ensure that the court sees the whole matter in the proper context and that the seriousness of the offence is adequately reflected in the evidence. See p242 and Appendix 3.

3 Proving the intent behind the acts

In many cases of racial harassment the intention of the perpetrator will be to persuade the victim to move out or to prevent or deter the victim from using a staircase, playground, community hall etc. Where the perpetrator is identified, there will often be evidence of the motive, eg graffiti on the victim's home or comments made when abusing the victim. Comments made to housing officers may reinforce this evidence (eg "I've got nothing against them, I just don't want them living here").

If the natural effect of the harassment is to persuade the victim to move out and the perpetrator knows this, or the only explanation for the perpetrator's behaviour is that s/he intended the victim to be driven out, this will be sufficient to prove the necessary intent for the offence.[34]

Harassment of a tenant by a neighbouring tenant, by someone from outside the borough, or by an owner occupier or squatter is covered by the Act, as is harassment by an occupier of bed and breakfast accommodation or hostel by another occupier, someone from outside, the landlord or staff.

Situations where the intention of the perpetrator might be to deter the victim from exercising a right or pursuing a remedy relating to the premises might include harassment where the perpetrator intends to deter a tenant from:
— using a common staircase;
— using common facilities on the estate, eg lifts, parking spaces or playgrounds;
— taking action against the perpetrator for nuisance.

This provision will not apply to prospective tenants being shown a new flat who are met by a hostile "reception committee" as the victims will not be residential occupiers.

Public Health Act 1936 and Control of Pollution Act 1974

1 Breach of notices

Authorities possess powers to serve notices under the provisions dealt with in Chapter 9 relating to:
— the abatement of statutory nuisances (p153);
— the abatement of noise nuisances (p155);
— the method of rubbish collection (p158);
— the removal of rubbish that has been dumped (pp158 and 159).

Breach of any of these notices is a criminal offence. The procedure was discussed in Chapter 9. None of the offences are arrestable and all can be tried only in the magistrates' court.

2 Dumping rubbish

In addition, under the Control of Pollution Act (CPA) 1974 it is a criminal offence to dump household waste on any land.[35] This offence is not arrestable and can be tried either in the magistrates' or Crown Court. Household waste is not defined and the interpretation of the expression will be one for the court.

The penalty for the offence where it is prosecuted in the Crown Court can be up to two years' imprisonment and an unlimited fine.[36] If the household waste:

(a) is poisonous, noxious or polluting; or
(b) is such that its presence is likely to give rise to an environmental hazard; or
(c) is deposited in circumstances that it may assumed to have been abandoned then the maximum penalty is increased to five years' imprisonment.[37]

The types of acts that would amount to an offence under this provision include emptying the contents of dustbins outside victims' homes or into a victim's garden, or leaving soiled nappies or clothes outside the victim's home.

The Highways Act 1980 s137

"If a person, without lawful authority or excuse, in any way wilfully obstructs the free passage along a highway, he is guilty of an offence." Only police officers can arrest for this offence, and it can be tried only in the magistrates' court.

The HA 1980 does not explicitly give local authorities power to prosecute for this offence. However, as mentioned on p44 authorities have powers to assert and protect the rights of the public to use the highway. This should be sufficient to give them power to prosecute for obstruction.

For an act to amount to an obstruction under this provision:

(a) it must amount to an unreasonable use of the highway. Whether a particular use of the highway is reasonable is a question of fact;[38] and
(b) the highway must be obstructed even though, in the event, no individual may have been obstructed because no one was using the highway at the time;[39] and
(c) the person committing the act must have been aware that his or her acts would obstruct the highway.[40]

In practice, therefore, the court will have to decide in each case whether a particular act amounts to an obstruction of the highway.

The offence is punishable by a fine of up to £50. Where an obstruction of the highway has occurred, an authority should consider prosecuting for public nuisance for which the possible sentences are unlimited. If the offence is likely to be repeated, it should consider seeking an injunction (see p23).

The offence under the Highways Act 1980 will usually also be an offence under either the Metropolitan Police Act 1839 or Town Police Clauses Act 1847 and also a public nuisance. (See below for public nuisance and Chapter 11 for the other offences.)

In racial harassment cases obstruction of the highway might include:
— hanging around on the street outside victims' homes shouting abuse, throwing stones or simply waiting for the victims to come out;
— waiting outside school gates to abuse, obstruct or jostle school children as they leave or to hand out racist leaflets;
— deliberately blocking the way of victims as they walk along the street so that they have to push past, cross over or walk in the road to continue.

Where deliberate harassment is taking place it is difficult to see how the use of the highway for these purposes can be reasonable.

Leaving litter

It is an offence to drop or deposit litter in a place in the open air to which the public is entitled or permitted to have access.[41] The open air includes places that are covered but open on one side and available for public use.[42] The offence is not arrestable and is triable only in the magistrates' court. The maximum penalty is a £400 fine[43] and, when sentencing, the court must have regard to the nature of the litter and any resulting risk of injury or damage.[44]

County and district councils or London boroughs may prosecute for an offence.

This offence will be relevant to racial harassment probably only when litter is being dumped outside victims' homes. The gardens of victims' homes will clearly not be public places, but the landings of council estates may be for the purposes of this provision if the court is satisfied that the public are permitted to have access.

Offences for leaving litter may overlap with offences under the CPA 1974 (see p175 above).

Breach of byelaws

No statute expressly gives authorities power to prosecute for breaches of byelaws. Nevertheless, it is clear that a power to prosecute is implied by LGA 1972 s111. A breach of byelaws is not arrestable and is triable only in the magistrates' court. The maximum penalty is £100.

The matters that can be covered by byelaws are dealt with in other chapters. Where byelaws create new untried offences, the validity of the byelaws under the principles discussed on p45 can be raised as a defence in criminal proceedings in the magistrates' court.[45]

Public nuisance

A public nuisance is a criminal offence. It is not arrestable and is triable either in the magistrates' or Crown Court.

Authorities are not given express power to prosecute for public nuisances but there is little doubt that they have the power by virtue of LGA 1972 s111 and their statutory powers in relation to highways, planning, education, housing, environmental health etc. The definition of a public nuisance is given on p43 above, and public nuisances in relation to obstruction of the highway are discussed on p44).

The period of imprisonment or the fine that can be imposed on conviction by the Crown Court is unlimited. The most common form of public nuisance is obstruction of the highway. Because the court's powers are so limited on a prosecution for obstruction under the Highways Act 1980, it may be advisable to prosecute for public nuisance so that the court has greater sentencing powers, particularly when the offence involves serious racial harassment which is unlikely to be deterred by the maximum £50 fine available for obstruction.

It appears that a single act may amount to a public nuisance.[46] For an obstruction of a highway to amount to a public nuisance, the requirements are essentially the same as those for the offence under the Highways Act 1980 (see p44).

Causing or permitting a nuisance or disturbance on educational premises

This offence was considered on p149. It is triable only in the magistrates' court and is not arrestable, but any authorised person or a police officer can remove the person concerned from the premises. The maximum penalty is a £100 fine. Any education authority including ILEA may prosecute for an offence under this provision.

C. POWERS OF LOCAL AUTHORITIES UNDER LGA 1972 s222

It is not possible in a book of this nature to cover all the relevant criminal offences involved in acts of racial harassment. This part of this chapter will be restricted to considering the detail of a few selected offences. They are chosen either because they are particularly relevant, are relatively obscure or unknown, or are commonly-used offences where particular points need to be made as to their use in racial harassment cases.

Appendix 6 contains a fuller list of possible criminal offences for which s222 may authorise prosecutions in appropriate cases.

Criminal damage

Destroying or damaging property belonging to someone else is criminal damage. Where damage or destruction is caused by fire, the offence is arson. Criminal damage and arson in the context of racial harassment will include:
— damage to doors or windows of the victim's property whether s/he is a squatter, tenant or owner unless the perpetrator owns the property;
— smashing of milk bottles;

— tearing up of newspapers and letters;
— causing injury to dogs, cats or other pets (this may also amount to a separate offence of cruelty to animals);
— writing graffiti on walls, doors, hoardings or elsewhere;
— damage to cars;
— putting lighted newspaper through a letter-box and damaging a doormat (arson).

There is no separate offence of writing graffiti except in London (see p195).

A minor amount of damage may be evidence of a very serious offence. Pouring petrol through a letter-box and unsuccessfully trying to light it will cause minor damage to the doormat or carpet. However, such an action constitutes the serious offence of attempted arson, or may be an attempted murder.

Affray

The definition of affray is new, having been introduced by the Public Order Act 1986 s3. The offence is committed if a person:
— uses or threatens unlawful violence towards another person; and
— the conduct is such as would cause a person of reasonable firmness present at the scene to fear for his personal safety.[47]

There are various points to be made concerning this offence:

(a) a threat by words alone is insufficient — there must be some threatening gestures, or conduct;[48]
(b) there is no need for a person of reasonable firmness to be present. The test is merely whether such a person would understand the behaviour to be threatening and would be frightened if s/he happened to be present;[49]
(c) the offence can be committed by one person. If there are two or more people it is their joint conduct that is considered;[50]
(d) unlike the offence of threatening behaviour, affray can be committed in a private or public place.[51]

The requirements for the offences of violent disorder and riot are similar but require a specified number of people to be involved in the threats or use of violence (see Appendix 6).

If violence is actually used, it will usually constitute the offence of assault or assault occasioning actual bodily harm. The following behaviour might amount to the offence of affray:
— holding sticks, knives, bottles or stones in a position showing an intention to use them to attack;
— pinning a victim in a corner and surrounding him or her, even if not actually making physical contact;
— lining up across a pathway, stairs etc to prevent a victim passing;
— throwing a punch or aiming a kick at a victim;

— chasing a victim down the street even if the victim escapes;
— throwing a stone, bottle or some other object at a victim which falls short.

Incitement to racial hatred

There are a number of offences in the Public Order Act 1986 Pt III which deal with the stirring up of racial hatred. All the offences can be tried either in the magistrates' or Crown Court. The offence of using threatening words or behaviour is arrestable.[52]

The offences relevant to racial harassment are:
— using threatening, abusive or insulting words or behaviour;[53]
— publishing or distributing threatening abusive or insulting written material;[54]
— possessing written material which is threatening abusive or insulting with a view to publication or distribution.[55]

"Racial hatred" is defined as "hatred against a group of persons in Great Britain defined by reference to colour, race, nationality (including citizenship) or ethnic or national origins".[56] A person is guilty of an offence under the 1986 Act only if s/he intends to stir up racial hatred by the words, behaviour or written material or if racial hatred is likely to be stirred up by them.[57]

Various defences are available, enabling the person responsible to show that s/he did not intend to stir up racial hatred and was not aware that his or her conduct was likely to do so. A prosecution for any of the offences requires the consent of the Attorney-General.[58] The maximum penalty is two years' imprisonment or an unlimited fine or both.

Distributing racist leaflets or newsletters, organising a petition to remove black tenants from an estate, or holding a meeting at which tenants are encouraged to force black tenants off an estate, might all constitute offences under these provisions.

Common assault and assault occasioning actual bodily harm[59]

There are two separate offences of common assault and assault occasioning actual bodily harm.

1 Matters common to both offences

Both offences require a common assault to have been committed. The terminology relating to assaults is confusing. Technically, an assault occurs when a person deliberately causes another person to fear an attack. When there is physical contact that is a "battery". Most attacks are both an assault and a battery.

A "common assault" has been committed where there is either an assault or a battery. Common assault is often referred to merely as "assault". In the case of both offences, the court may bind over the defendant in addition to imposing a penalty (see p168).

2 Common assault

The Offences Against the Person Act (OAPA) 1861 s42 provides that magistrates may hear a complaint "by or on behalf of the party aggrieved" by any assault. This provision has been interpreted as preventing a police officer appearing as prosecutor for common assault in the assumed capacity of a person acting on behalf of the party aggrieved, ie the victim of the assault.[60] This does not appear to be correct. It seems that common assault is an offence triable either in the magistrates' or Crown Court that can be prosecuted by the police or any other person in the usual way.[61] The OAPA 1861 s42 does not prevent prosecution by anybody for common assault. Its only effect is in relation to any prosecution by the victim. This is considered further in Chapter 12.

The maximum sentence in the Crown Court is one year's imprisonment.[62]

3 Assault occasioning actual bodily harm

The offence is arrestable and triable either by the magistrates' or Crown Court. The words "actual bodily harm" appear to have their ordinary meaning. It has been said that they include any hurt or injury calculated to interfere with the health or comfort of the victim. The injury need not be permanent and an injury to the state of a person's mind may be sufficient, such as causing a nervous or hysterical condition.[63] It is probable that hurt feelings or distress do not amount to actual bodily harm.

The maximum penalty is five years' imprisonment or an unlimited fine or both.

A common assault does not require physical contact by the attacker. Many instances of an assault may also be an affray. Examples of common assaults include:
— dropping a brick or other object from a balcony onto someone;
— drawing a knife;
— setting a dog on to a person;
— getting a dog to pin someone in a corner so that s/he is fearful of attack;
— throwing an object at someone even if the object misses.

Actual physical contact constituting a common assault, but not assault occasioning actual bodily harm, would include pushing, shoving, slapping, smacking, or jostling.

Where a deliberate blow is actually inflicted, some kind of bodily harm will often result. This might be bruising or a small cut or swelling. The harm may have occurred indirectly from the physical contact. Pushing someone over so that they bruise their arm falling to the ground constitutes assault occasioning actual bodily harm. Similarly, if a person is injured escaping from a chasing dog which has been set on him or her, that might amount to an assault occasioning actual bodily harm.

Burglary

Burglary is arrestable and triable either in the magistrates' or Crown Court. Burglary is not limited to theft from buildings. The offence of burglary for our purposes is committed if a person:
— enters a building or part of a building as a trespasser; and
— has an intention either to:
   (a) steal something;
   (b) inflict grievous bodily harm on someone inside;
   (c) rape a woman inside; or
   (d) damage some property inside.

The maximum penalty is 14 years' imprisonment.

It can be seen that there are two essential requirements for the offence, the entering and the intent.

If a local authority were to fit entry-phones to a stairway or landing so that only those people given permission to enter by the tenants were authorised to enter, then any other person would be a trespasser. Any person entering would then be committing burglary if s/he intended to:
— paint graffiti on a door or wall;
— smash milk bottles outside a tenant's house;
— smash a window or damage a door opening off the landing;
— steal washing from a line;
— attack any victims and cause them grievous bodily harm.

By restricting the use of parts of their estates to tenants, authorities can make other persons trespassers. Any perpetrator who enters with the necessary criminal intent, commits burglary even if s/he is prevented from carrying out the theft, criminal damage etc.

Intimidation, persistent following or watching or besetting premises

It is an offence:
— to use violence to or intimidate any person or to injure his or her property;
— persistently to follow any person about from place to place;
— to watch or beset the house or other place where any other person resides or works, or carries on business or happens to be, or the approach to such house or place;
— to follow any person with two or more other people in a disorderly manner in or through any street or road.[64]

The offence is not arrestable and is triable only in the magistrates' court.

To constitute an offence, one of the above acts must be committed with intent "to compel the victim to abstain from doing or to do any act which the victim has a right to do or abstain from doing".[65] In addition, it appears that the act must amount to a tort before it becomes a criminal offence.[66] Torts are civil wrongs and the relevant torts are considered further in Chapter 12.

"Beset" means to surround with hostile intentions or to beseige or to occupy so as to allow no one to go out or in.

The maximum penalty is £100 fine or three months' imprisonment.

1 The intention

The criminal intent for this offence would include seeking to force victims to leave their home and go elsewhere, or seeking to prevent victims from:
— accepting a tenancy of a particular flat;
— accepting a job;
— taking their children to school;
— going shopping;
— using particular community facilities;
— using their garden.

2 The acts

The type of acts that might constitute an offence under this provision include:
— hanging around in a group outside a victim's home in an intimidatory fashion waiting for him or her to come out;
— following children to school or women to the shops on a regular basis;
— forming a hostile "reception committee" for tenants viewing a flat in an attempt to put them off accepting the tenancy;
— damaging a victim's property or threatening the victim's family. This may also constitute other offences.

False imprisonment

It is an offence falsely to imprison any other person. This means intentionally preventing him or her from moving away from a particular place. To constitute false imprisonment, a person must be prevented from going in any direction, at least without taking an unreasonable risk.

The offence is not arrestable and is triable either in the magistrates' or Crown Court.

Situations which might amount to false imprisonment include preventing a person from:
— leaving a lift;
— leaving their flat or house;
— escaping, having cornered or surrounded them against a wall;
— leaving a block of flats, community hall or playground.

1 Police and Criminal Evidence Act 1984 s24(4).
2 Ibid s24(5).
3 *Walters v WH Smith & Sons Ltd* [1914] 1 KB 595.
4 Magistrates' Courts Act 1980 s6.
5 Ibid s17.
6 Ibid s19.
7 Ibid s19(2).

8 Ibid s21.
9 Ibid s20.
10 Ibid s38.
11 Ibid s32.
12 Ibid ss1 and 2.
13 Police and Criminal Evidence Act 1984 s47.
14 Magistrates' Courts Rules 1981 SI No 552 r4.
15 Magistrates' Courts Act 1980 s1.
16 Ibid s13.
17 Bail Act 1976 Sch 1.
18 Ibid s6.
19 Ibid s3(6).
20 Ibid s7.
21 Ibid s3(7).
22 For the full range of sentences available to the magistrates' and juvenile courts and the limitations on their powers, see the current edition of *Stone's Justices' Manual*.
23 *Bond v Chief Constable of Kent* [1983] 1 All ER 456.
24 See *Stone's Justices' Manual* 1987 para 3-131.
25 Children and Young Persons Act 1933 s55 as amended by Criminal Justice Act 1982.
26 *R v Finnerty* (1987) February, Highbury Corner Magistrates' Court.
27 Protection from Eviction Act 1977 s1(3).
28 Ibid s6.
29 For a fuller list see Arden and Partington *Quiet Enjoyment* Legal Action Group, 2nd edn, 1985.
30 Since the law regards owner occupiers as tenants of the Crown who only hold the land as long as their heirs survive.
31 But see Arden and Partington, op cit, for the argument that the Criminal Law Act 1977 s6 may make a squatter a "residential occupier" for the purposes of the Protection from Eviction Act 1977.
32 *R v Evangelos Polycarpou* (1978) 9 HLR 129, CA.
33 *R v AMK (Property Management) Ltd* [1985] Crim LR 600, CA.
34 *R v Moloney* [1985] 1 All ER 1025, HL and see *R v AMK (Property Management) Ltd* n33.
35 Control of Pollution Act 1974 ss3(1)(a) and 30.
36 Ibid s3(2).
37 Ibid s3(3).
38 *Nagy v Weston* [1965] 1 All ER 78.
39 *Gill & Carson v Nield* [1917] 2 KB 674.
40 *Arrowsmith v Jenkins* [1963] 2 All ER 210.
41 Litter Act 1983 s1.
42 Ibid s1(2).
43 Ibid s1(3).
44 Ibid s1(4).
45 *R v Reading Crown Court ex p Hutchinson* (1987) *Independent* 5 August.
46 Per Denning LJ in *A-G v PYA Quarries Ltd* [1957] 2 QB 169, CA at 192.
47 Public Order Act 1986 s3(1).
48 Ibid s3(3).
49 Ibid s3(4).

50 Ibid s3(2).
51 Ibid s3(5).
52 Ibid s18(3).
53 Ibid s18.
54 Ibid s19.
55 Ibid s23.
56 Ibid s17.
57 Ibid ss18(1), 19(1) and 23(1).
58 Ibid s27.
59 Offences Against the Person Act 1861 ss42-47.
60 See the editions of *Stone's Justices' Manual* up to the early 1980s. This comment has been deleted from more recent editions.
61 See *R v Harrow Justices ex p Osaseri* [1985] 3 All ER 185 per May LJ at 190 and quoting *Bentley v Brudzinski* (1982) 75 Cr App R 217 per Donaldson LJ at 226.
62 Offences Against the Person Act 1861 s47.
63 *R v Miller* [1954] 2 All ER 529.
64 Conspiracy and Protection of Property Act 1875 s7.
65 Ibid.
66 See Scott J in *Thomas v NUM* [1985] 2 All ER 1 preferring *Ward Lock & Co Ltd v Operative Printers' Assistants' Society* (1906) 22 TLR 327 to *J Lyons and Sons Ltd v Wilkins* [1899] 1 Ch 255, both Court of Appeal cases.

CHAPTER ELEVEN

Police and Crown Prosecution Service Powers and Duties

The police have extensive powers and limited duties in respect of investigating crime. These are explained and the legal remedies for a police failure to tackle racial harassment are also discussed. The Crown Prosecution Service, now responsible for most criminal prosecutions begun by the police, has a discretion to take over the conduct of proceedings referred to it by local authorities and victims.

Although this book is primarily about the powers and duties of local authorities, it is important to be aware of the powers and duties of other organisations to deal with racial harassment.

Of all the authorities that have power to tackle racial harassment it is the police who have the most useful powers. Most incidents of racial harassment escape unpunished because the perpetrators cannot be identified. Although a local authority can devote resources to identifying perpetrators and can be assisted by community organisations and the victims themselves, it is the police to whom the law gives the necessary powers to identify and obtain evidence against those responsible for the criminal offences which are involved in a campaign of racial harassment. There is no substitute for the use of these powers in any attempt to eradicate racial harassment.

A. POLICE POWERS TO INVESTIGATE CRIME

Stop and search

A police officer has power to stop a person and search him or her or to stop and search a vehicle if the officer has reasonable grounds for suspecting that the person has:
— stolen articles;
— an offensive weapon;
— an article for use in burglary or theft;
— firearms.[1]

The power can be exercised in any public place or place to which people have ready access but cannot be exercised in a dwelling. Thus a search can be made in the common parts of a housing estate, a playground or the street.

Entry and search of premises

A police officer can always enter and search premises with the permission of the occupier. Additionally, an officer has a right to enter and search premises in certain circumstances outlined below.

1 With a search warrant issued by a magistrate under a particular statutory power

A warrant can be issued by a magistrate under a number of statutory powers. The grounds for the issue of a warrant which are relevant for our purposes include:

(a) where there is reasonable cause to believe that a person has an article which there is reasonable cause to believe has been used or is intended to be used for criminal damage including arson,[2] eg catapult, airgun, crowbar, brick, paint or petrol;

(b) where any explosive, dangerous or noxious thing is suspected to be kept for the purpose of offences under the Offences Against the Person Act 1861;[3]

(c) where there is reasonable cause to believe a person has stolen goods in his or her possession.[4]

2 With a search warrant issued by a magistrate under the Police and Criminal Evidence Act 1984 (PACE)[5]

A warrant can be issued under PACE by a magistrate if the magistrate is satisfied:

(a) that a serious arrestable offence has been committed; and

(b) that there is material on the premises which is likely to be of substantial value to the investigation of the offence and which is likely to be relevant evidence; and

(c) that a warrant is justified because entry will not be given voluntarily or the purpose of the search will be frustrated or seriously prejudiced unless the police can gain immediate entry, eg because the evidence will be destroyed.

Murder, rape, firearms offences and causing explosions are all serious arrestable offences.[6] Other arrestable offences that are relevant for our purposes will be serious only if the offence has led or was intended or likely to lead to any of the following consequences:[7]

— serious harm to public order, eg riot, affray, violent disorder;
— serious injury or death to any person, eg grievous bodily harm or wounding;
— serious financial loss to any person, eg criminal damage or arson.

If the offence in question involves the making of a threat, the making of the threat is a serious arrestable offence if carrying it out would lead to

3 Without a search warrant in certain circumstances

To make an arrest
A police officer may enter and search premises to make an arrest of someone named in an arrest warrant issued by the magistrates' court. For example, an authority applies for a warrant to start criminal proceedings; a warrant is issued; the police may enter premises to search for the person named and take him or her to the police station and subsequently to court.

Police can also enter and search premises to arrest someone for an arrestable offence (see below under "Arrest" and Chapter 10 and Appendix 6), or a person who has committed an offence under the Public Order Act 1986 s4 (threatening abusive or insulting words or behaviour) or the Criminal Law Act 1977 s6 (using violence to gain entry to premises).[9]

To save life or limb or prevent serious damage
A police officer may enter premises to save life or limb or prevent serious damage to property.[10]

To search for evidence
A police officer may search premises in which someone has just been arrested or which is occupied or controlled by a person under arrest to look for evidence of the offence or some other connected or similar offence.[11]

Seizure of property found

A police officer can seize anything found on premises if s/he has reasonable grounds for believing either that it has been obtained as a consequence of an offence, or that it is evidence in relation to an offence and it must be seized to prevent its being hidden, lost, damaged or destroyed.[12] Examples of items the police could remove under this power include:
— items they believed had been stolen;
— weapons they believed had been used in an attack;
— tools they believed had been used to damage property or break in to a home;
— clothes worn by a suspect which might have blood, hair, soil etc on them.

Arrest

1 Arrest with a warrant

A police officer may arrest a person named in a warrant of arrest, usually issued by a magistrate. Thus, where an authority begins criminal proceedings by obtaining the issue of a warrant of arrest from a magistrates' court, a police officer may arrest the defendant and take him or her to a police station.

2 Arrest without a warrant

Arrestable offences
The powers described in Chapter 10 p161 apply equally to police officers as to private citizens (and see also Appendix 6).

The police have two additional powers relating to arrestable offences.[13] When a police officer has reasonable grounds for suspecting that an arrestable offence has been committed s/he may arrest any person whom s/he has reasonable grounds for suspecting to be guilty of the offence. Similarly a police officer may arrest anyone who is about to commit an arrestable offence or whom s/he has reasonable grounds to suspect is about to commit an arrestable offence.

Offences which are not arrestable[14]
A police officer can arrest for offences which are not arrestable in certain circumstances. The officer must have reasonable grounds for believing that a non-arrestable offence has been committed or attempted or is being committed or attempted. The officer can then arrest anyone whom s/he has reasonable grounds for suspecting of having committed or attempted the offence or of being in the course of committing or attempting the offence, provided one of the following apply:

(a) the name of the person whom the officer suspects is unknown and cannot be readily ascertained; or
(b) the officer has reasonable grounds for doubting the name given; or
(c) the suspect has failed to give a satisfactory address for service of a summons; or
(d) the officer has reasonable grounds for doubting whether an address given is satisfactory for service; or
(e) the officer has reasonable grounds for believing that arrest is necessary to prevent the suspect from:
   • causing physical injury to some person; or
   • causing loss of or damage to property; or
   • causing an unlawful obstruction of the highway; or
(f) the officer has reasonable grounds for believing that arrest is necessary to protect a child or other vulnerable person from the suspect.

Where the police are called out to an incident, for example, where racial harassment has occurred involving violence, damage or threats, one or both of the last two conditions allowing arrest for any offence is likely to be satisfied. In those circumstances, arrest is authorised even for the most minor offence, eg causing harassment and alarm under Public Order Act 1986 s5.

Breach of the peace
Any individual including a police officer may arrest anyone:
— whom s/he sees breaching the peace;
— who has committed a breach of the peace and whom s/he reasonably believes will repeat the breach;
— whom s/he reasonably believes is about to commit a breach of the peace.[15]
The belief must be honestly held.[15] This will include a situation where there has been a breach of the peace and the person reasonably believes that it will recur if s/he leaves without arresting the person responsible.

A breach of the peace has been defined as arising whenever "harm is actually done or is likely to be done to a person or in his presence to his property, or a person is in fear of being so harmed through an assault, an affray, a riot, [violent disorder] or other disturbance".[16] This definition may cover many confrontations that occur in racial harassment cases.

Having arrested a person for breach of the peace, a police officer may either decide to charge the person with an offence, or may take the person before the court to be bound over.

Detention

Having arrested a suspect, the police may detain him or her for a limited period if there are reasonable grounds for believing that the suspect's detention is necessary to secure or preserve evidence relating to the offence for which the suspect was arrested or to obtain such evidence by questioning the suspect.[17] Thus the police can detain a suspect for questioning. They can also keep a suspect in custody while they go and search his or her home (see "Entry and search of premises" above).

The time limit on detention is 24 hours for most offences. For serious arrestable offences (see definition above) the initial time limit is 36 hours but applications may be made to the magistrates' court to extend this to a maximum of 96 hours from the original time of detention.[18] As soon as the police have sufficient evidence to justify charging a person in their custody with an offence, they must do so.[19]

Questioning

The police may interview a suspect held in custody. Records must be made of the interviews.[20] In most cases, those in custody must be given access to legal advice and have the right to have someone informed of their arrest. Where a serious arrestable offence has been committed these rights may be restricted in certain circumstances.[21]

Since the police are authorised to detain a person to obtain evidence from him or her by questioning, it follows that a failure to answer police questions can lead to a longer period of detention. For this reason, many people agree to be interviewed by police officers because they are anxious to be released from the police station.

Samples and fingerprints

The police have a variety of powers to obtain extra evidence which will help prove that the person in custody committed the offence.

1 Fingerprints[22]

The police may fingerprint a person in custody:
— if s/he has a previous conviction;
— if s/he has been charged or is being reported for most offences;
— if a superintendent authorises fingerprints to be taken because it is believed that the fingerprints will tend to confirm or disprove the person's involvement in the offence.

Fingerprints may be useful where a burglary or an assault using a weapon which has fingerprints on it had been committed, or criminal damage or arson has occurred and some instrument was used, eg a milk bottle or petrol can on which fingerprints were found.

2 Intimate samples[23]

When a person is arrested for a serious arrestable offence, the police may take samples of blood, urine, saliva or other similar samples from a person in custody with the person's consent, or if a superintendent authorises the sample being taken because there are reasonable grounds for believing the sample will confirm or disprove involvement in the offence. The sample must be taken by a doctor.

If the person in custody refuses consent, the court can be told of the refusal in any subsequent trial. Examples of situations where intimate samples might be relevant include:
— criminal damage or burglary where the perpetrator's blood is left on a smashed window;
— assault with a knife where the attacker cut him or herself and left blood on the weapon or on the ground.

3 Non-intimate samples[24]

Where a person is arrested for a serious arrestable offence, the police may take samples of hair, samples from under fingernails, or of footprints, or similar impressions without the consent of the suspect if this is authorised by a superintendent. The superintendent must have reasonable grounds for believing that the sample will tend to confirm or disprove the suspect's involvement in the offence.

Examples of situations where non-intimate samples might be taken include:
— where a jumper or hat has been left at the scene of the crime which had hairs attached which can be compared with those of the suspect;
— where a footprint has been found outside a ground-floor window which was used to gain entry;

— where a victim has been seriously scratched and it is believed that the perpetrator may have some of the victim's skin or blood under his or her fingernails.

Identification parades and identification by witnesses[25]

There are several methods by which witnesses can be asked to identify suspects at a police station.

1 Identification parades

This is the best method. The suspect stands with at least eight other people who as far as possible resemble him or her. The suspect may stand wherever he or she wishes in the line. The witness is brought into the room and asked if s/he can see the person who committed the offence in the line of men or women. In some circumstances, those people on the parade can be asked to move in a particular way, speak or adopt a particular posture. The suspect must agree to take part in the parade but if s/he refuses, the witness may be allowed to confront the suspect alone (see below) and the court may be told about the refusal.

2 Group identification

If a suspect refuses to take part in a parade the police should try and arrange for the witnesses to see the suspect in a group of people. Obviously, all the others should not be police officers in uniform! Group identifications are carried out in a similar manner to identification parades.

3 Confrontation

If a group identification is impossible the suspect may be confronted with the witness. The witness is shown the suspect and asked if s/he is the person who committed the offence.

4 Photographs

The police have sets of photographs of persons arrested or convicted for criminal offences. Where a perpetrator has not been identified but the witness would recognise him or her from a photograph, s/he may be shown folders of photographs at a police station and asked if s/he recognises any of the persons shown. If any individual is recognised, other witnesses should be asked to attend an identification parade.

Police bail

Once a person has been arrested there are three ways in which s/he can be dealt with. First, s/he may be kept in custody and taken to court immediately. The court then decides whether to remand in custody or on bail. Second, the person may be released without bail because no charges are likely, or, last, s/he may be released on bail.

If a person is arrested under a warrant issued by the magistrates which instructs the police to grant bail (a warrant "backed for bail") they must grant bail as instructed by the court. In the remainder of cases the police must grant bail unless:

(a) they doubt that the address given is the suspect's real address;
(b) they have reasonable grounds for believing detention is necessary to:
- the person's own protection;
- prevent the person causing physical injury to any other person;
- prevent loss of or damage to property;
(c) they have reasonable grounds for believing that s/he will not appear in court or will interfere with witnesses or evidence.[26]

Bail can be granted on the same conditions as those that the magistrates' court can impose (see p165).[27]

Tracing telephone calls

Technical facilities are available which enable the police to trace the origin of any calls to a particular number. In order to do this they may require a warrant from the Home Secretary though this is not absolutely clear. The law requires a warrant when a phone line is "intercepted".[28] If a warrant is required, it may be issued if the trace is required to prevent or detect serious crime, which is defined as crime involving the use of violence or where there is conduct by a large number of persons in pursuit of a common purpose and where the offence is punishable by more than three years' imprisonment.[29]

The main purpose of the Interception of Communications Act 1985 is to prevent a person's phone being tapped without their knowledge. In racial harassment cases, by contrast, the victim will be requesting the trace in order to identify the perpetrator. This may make it easier to obtain a warrant, if required. Senior officers of the local police should be contacted to make the necessary arrangements.

A warrant will not be granted to trace abusive phone calls since the maximum penalty is too low. However, where the words spoken amount to a threat to kill, or are evidence which would lead to the identification of a perpetrator who has committed offences of violence such as assault occasioning actual bodily harm, then a warrant may be available. Similarly, if attacks are being made by racist groups which include a serious offence such as arson, a warrant may be available because the members of the group are involved in crimes in pursuit of a common purpose. The offences therefore fall under the definition of "serious crime" and a warrant may be issued.

Other police powers

1   Power to apply to the magistrates' court to destroy a dog

Like local authorities, the police can apply for a dog to be destroyed (see Chapter 4 p46).

2   Power to impose conditions or ban marches and assemblies

The police may impose conditions on any procession in a public place, or on any assembly of people numbering over 20 in the open air in a public place.[30] The conditions can be imposed if the police reasonably believe that the procession or assembly:
— may result in serious public disorder, serious damage to property or serious disruption to the life of the community; or
— is organised to intimidate others with a view to compelling them not to do something they are entitled to do or to do something they have a right not to do.

Conditions can include directions as to the route of a procession, prohibiting entry to particular areas or restricting the number of people attending an assembly.

If the police do not consider that the powers to impose conditions are sufficient to prevent serious public disorder they may ask the district council to ban a march.[31] The powers may be exercised only by the chief police officer or his or her immediate deputies except on the day of the march or assembly, when the powers may be exercised by the senior officer on the scene.

3   Prosecuting for common assault

It has already been mentioned that, despite suggestions to the contrary, it appears that the police have power to prosecute for common assault (see p181).

4   Power to remove persons from school premises

Where persons are causing a nuisance or disturbance on school premises there is a power available to the police to remove them. This power is dealt with on p149.

B.   THE DUTIES OF THE POLICE

The Town Police Clauses Act 1847

Outside London, a police officer has a duty to arrest anyone who, in his or her view, in the street, to the obstruction, annoyance or danger of residents or those using the street:
(a)   allows an unmuzzled ferocious dog to be at large;

(b) sets or encourages a dog to attack, worry or put another person in fear;
(c) causes an obstruction to any public footpath or thoroughfare;
(d) uses obscene language or sings any obscene song;
(e) sets off a firework;
(f) throws a stone or other missile;
(g) deliberately disturbs an inhabitant by ringing door bells or knocking on the door;
(h) throws any item from a house or building.[32]

The maximum penalty is £300 fine or 14 days' imprisonment. The offence is triable only in the magistrates' court.

In London, the Town Police Clauses Act does not apply and there is no *duty* to make an arrest. There is however a *power* of arrest for the following offences committed in any thoroughfare or public place in view of a police officer by virtue of the Metropolitan Police Act 1839 s54:
— the offences described in (a), (b), (c), (e), (f), (g) above;
— without the consent of the owner or occupier of any building, wall or fence
 • flyposting it; or
 • writing on or marking it; or
 • destroying or damaging it.

Thus, both inside and outside London there is power to arrest for these offences committed within the view of an officer. Even if the offences are not committed in any officer's view, the powers described on pp189-190 may apply (offences which are not arrestable and breaches of the peace).

The offences outside London must be committed in the street; there will therefore be no offence when these acts are committed on a local authority housing estate. In London, an offence is committed if the acts are done in a public place, so the common parts of a housing estate are probably covered.

It should be noted that the penalty for obstruction of the highway under this provision is greater than that under the Highways Act 1980 (see p176).

An advantage of prosecuting under the Town Police Clauses Act 1847 is that it is necessary only to prove that other people have been obstructed, annoyed or put in danger. For example, if X throws a stone at Y this is an assault. To prove assault, it is necessary to prove that X intended to hit Y, or that Y thought he would be hit. Under the Town Police Clauses Act, it is necessary only to show that throwing the stone would put residents or those on the street in danger or would annoy them.

Under the Metropolitan Police Act, it is not even necessary to prove obstruction, annoyance or danger. Merely committing the act, whatever its effect, is an offence. Writing graffiti in the London area is a separate offence. Outside London, it is necessary to rely on the offence of criminal damage.

The duty to preserve the peace and prevent offences

When they become police constables, officers make a declaration which includes the words:

> "I will to the best of my power cause the peace to be kept and preserved and prevent all offences against the persons and property of Her Majesty's subjects and . . . I will to the best of my skill and knowledge discharge all the duties . . . according to the law."[33]

Individual police officers have a duty to preserve the peace, to protect the public and to arrest offenders and bring them to justice.[34] Whether these duties can be enforced is considered in part C below.

The duty to enforce the law

The police as a whole have a general duty to enforce the law.[35] Decisions about the allocation of resources to particular lines of enquiry or to the investigation of particular types of offence are within the discretion of each chief constable. Chief constables may not decide that certain laws will not be enforced. If they do the courts will be prepared to interfere.[36]

In practice, however, chief constables can, if they wish, decide to devote so few personnel and equipment resources that few, if any, successful arrests and prosecutions are made for particular offences. It is most unlikely that any form of legal challenge to operational decisions of this nature about the allocation of resources would succeed.

C. LEGAL REMEDIES FOR POLICE FAILURE TO TACKLE RACIAL HARASSMENT

There are few legal powers available to challenge police operational failures. The remedies that exist relate primarily to failures by individual officers and are only exercisable by individual victims. The only formal mechanism for local authorities is through their membership of the police authority (outside London) or by making representations using the procedures set up for obtaining the views of the community on policing, under PACE.

In the absence of any effective legal powers, local authorities must rely on obtaining the support of public opinion and negotiating to change police practices and allocation of resources. Assistance may be gained by authorities or victims mounting successful prosecutions in cases where the police have declined to prosecute and by presenting statistical evidence to the police of the level and seriousness of racial harassment in their area.

MPs may have influence with the police. In London, MPs can contact the Home Secretary who is the police authority and ask questions and make protests, though these will not necessarily be effective.

Requesting reports to the police authority

The police authority in London is the Home Secretary. Outside London, police authorities consist of one-third magistrates and two-thirds local councillors.[37] Police authorities must receive a report at the end of each year on policing in their area from the chief constable.[38] In addition, the police authority may, at any time, request a written report from the chief constable on any matter relating to policing. If the chief constable considers that the information should not be disclosed or is not needed for the discharge of the police authority's functions, s/he may require the police authority to refer the request to the Home Secretary who decides whether it is appropriate.[39]

This power can be used to seek reports on the number of offences reported, investigated and prosecuted concerning racial harassment. Offences which amount to "racial incidents" should be recorded as such by the police so that statistics are available.[40] In this way, deficiencies in recording methods or in the way in which enquiries are pursued may be brought to light. However, the information that can be obtained may be too general to achieve this object.

Making representations through the police consultative process

Under PACE s106, police authorities outside London are obliged to set up arrangements for obtaining the views of people in their area about matters concerning policing. Within London, the Commissioner of Police must make the arrangements under guidance from the Home Secretary. Where arrangements have successfully been established, authorities may be in a position to use the consultative process to try to influence police policies and practices. The ability to do this will depend on local circumstances.

By-passing the police and using the Crown Prosecution Service

This strategy is discussed below in part D.

Liability for failure to arrest a criminal

The Court of Appeal has decided on public policy grounds that a police officer is immune from legal action for negligence for failing to arrest a criminal who then commits further offences.[41] So unless and until the House of Lords decides otherwise, a victim cannot sue the police because they have not acted on the victim's previous complaints when further offences are committed by the same perpetrator.

Prosecution for misconduct in public office

If an individual officer deliberately fails to perform his or her duty s/he may be prosecuted for the criminal offence of "misconduct in public office".[42]

In 1979, a police officer, who saw an assault where a man was kicked to death and took no steps to intervene and merely drove away, was successfully prosecuted for misconduct in public office.[43] It seems likely that a prosecution for misconduct in public office will succeed only where an offence is committed in the presence of an officer, who deliberately fails to take any action to prevent it.

Submissions to the Inspector of Constabulary

The Inspector of Constabulary makes an annual report to the Home Secretary on the "efficiency" of each police force.[44] Authorities that have widespread evidence that police procedures are not being properly followed or that racial incidents are not being properly recorded or offences not being investigated could make submissions to the Inspector in the hope that s/he will take note of them and include them in the report.

Complaints against police officers

These are covered in Chapter 12 (p218).

D. THE CROWN PROSECUTION SERVICE

Referring cases to the Crown Prosecution Service

The Crown Prosecution Service (CPS) is now responsible for most criminal prosecutions begun by the police. The majority of the staff who appear in court are solicitors or barristers. The Service has largely replaced the prosecuting solicitors' departments previously operated by some police forces.

The CPS has a duty:
— to take over the conduct of almost all criminal proceedings begun by the police;
— to take over the conduct of all binding over proceedings begun by the police;
— to begin or have conduct of criminal proceedings in any case where it appears to it that:
  • the importance or difficulty of the case makes it appropriate that proceedings should be begun or conducted by the CPS; or
  • it is otherwise appropriate for proceedings to be begun or conducted by the CPS.[45]

Where the CPS has no obligation to take over the conduct of criminal proceedings, it still has a discretion to do so.[46] A code for crown prosecutors provides guidelines on decisions relating to prosecutions.[47]

If a local authority has evidence which is or may be sufficient to begin criminal proceedings, it may refer the case to the CPS, which may receive cases direct either from local authorities or victims. Until such time as this has been attempted it is not possible to predict the attitude of the CPS to direct referrals of this nature.

Since the CPS was set up to prosecute the types of offence described in Appendix 6 it would appear appropriate that it accepts referrals for prosecution of those offences from any source. It is less likely that it will accept referrals of the types of case listed in Chapter 10 part C, where a local authority is the most appropriate agency to prosecute. There is no objection to making a referral to both the police and the CPS at the same time. Each may then consider whether it will begin proceedings.

As a matter of practice, the CPS will be accustomed to receiving statements of evidence in the form set out in Appendix 3 Document 3. This is the form the police use in all cases. If the statements are not in that form, all the witnesses will have to be re-interviewed, resulting in considerable extra work. It is therefore advisable to provide statements both to the police and the CPS in the form that can be used in criminal proceedings shown in Appendix 3 Document 3.

1 Police and Criminal Evidence Act 1984 (PACE) s1 and Firearms Act 1968 s47.
2 Criminal Damage Act 1971 s6(1).
3 Offences Against the Person Act 1861 s65.
4 Theft Act 1968 s26.
5 PACE s8.
6 Ibid s116.
7 Ibid s116(6).
8 Ibid s116(4).
9 Ibid s17(1).
10 Ibid s17(1)(e).
11 Ibid s18.
12 Ibid s19.
13 Ibid s24.
14 Ibid s25.
15 See *R v Howell* [1981] 3 All ER 383, CA at 389 per Watkins LJ.
16 Ibid.
17 PACE s37(2).
18 Ibid ss40-44.
19 Ibid s37(7).
20 Code of Guidance issued under PACE para 11.3.
21 PACE ss56-58.
22 Ibid s61.
23 Ibid s62.
24 Ibid s63.
25 Code of Guidance issued under PACE Pt D.

26 PACE s38.
27 Ibid s47.
28 Interception of Communications Act 1985 s2.
29 Ibid ss2(2)(b) and 10(3).
30 Public Order Act 1986 ss12 and 14.
31 Ibid s13.
32 Town Police Clauses Act 1847 s28.
33 Police Act 1964 s18 and Schedule.
34 *R v Dytham* [1979] 3 All ER 641, CA.
35 *R v Metropolitan Police Commissioner ex p Blackburn* [1968] 1 All ER 763, CA.
36 Ibid.
37 Police Act 1964 ss2 and 2A.
38 Ibid s12(1).
39 Ibid s12(3).
40 *Racial Attacks - Guiding Principles* Association of Chief Police Officers, 1985, recommends a common definition to be used for recording, effective from 1 January 1986.
41 *Hill v Chief Constable of West Yorkshire* [1987] 1 All ER 1173, CA.
42 N34.
43 N34.
44 Police Act 1963 s38(2).
45 Prosecution of Offences Act 1985 s3.
46 Ibid s6(2).
47 (1986) 83 LS Gaz 2308.

CHAPTER TWELVE
Remedies Available to Victims

This chapter looks at the remedies available to victims, the advantages and disadvantages of the various courses of action and examples of situations where they might be appropriate. It also indicates sources of financial assistance and remedies against local authorities or the police for failing to act.

A. PAYING FOR LEGAL HELP

Legal advice

Some victims may be able to obtain free legal advice from a law centre, citizens advice bureau or other advice centre offering free services. A few solicitors' firms now offer free diagnostic interviews.

Those who are not within reach of such free facilities may be eligible for free legal advice under the green form scheme. This is means tested and anyone in receipt of income support automatically qualifies on the ground of income, but must also fall within specified capital limits. Others on low incomes will also qualify for free legal advice and those on higher incomes may qualify for advice after paying only a small, fixed contribution. The solicitor consulted is able to calculate financial eligibility on the spot, and any solicitors' firm that does legal aid work can operate the green form scheme.

Some private practice solicitors provide a first interview for a fixed fee of £5. The local citizens advice bureau and library should have a list of local solicitors in the legal aid scheme and this list will indicate those that offer a fixed-fee interview.

Legal representation in court proceedings

Law centres may be able to assist victims in taking legal action against perpetrators free of charge or at limited cost. Alternatively, victims may be eligible for legal aid to take proceedings.

1 The proceedings covered by legal aid

Legal aid is not available to prosecute in the magistrates' court. Victims cannot therefore apply for legal aid to take proceedings for any of the criminal offences referred to in Chapter 10 and Appendix 6.

Legal aid is available for all types of civil proceedings referred to below. Before legal aid is granted it will be necessary to show:
(a) that there is a reasonable prospect of success; and
(b) that the victim is financially eligible for legal aid; and
(c) that it is reasonable to take proceedings.

The last condition causes difficulties in some cases. The criteria often used to decide whether it is reasonable to take proceedings are the financial cost of the case, the likelihood of the perpetrator having the finances to pay the costs and the probable level of compensation payable to the victim. This ignores other important reasons why the victim may wish to take legal action. The victim's legal advisers will be able to assist on this point.

2 Financial eligibility for legal aid

The financial conditions for eligibility for legal aid are more generous than those for the green form scheme. The usual capital limit is £3,000 but can be higher in some circumstances.

B. DIRECT ACTION

The law allows a person to take certain steps to protect his or her home or family. However, the boundaries of what is allowed are strict but frequently unclear. Any steps beyond the boundaries of what is permissible could result in a victim being charged with committing a criminal offence or being sued by the perpetrator.

Self defence

Self defence can be pleaded as a defence to any criminal prosecution for violence, eg assault, grievous bodily harm or even murder. Self defence may also be used as a defence to a civil action for damages in tort. A person may use reasonable force to defend him or herself or any other person from attack and to protect his or her property.[1]

The degree of force that is reasonable in any particular circumstances is impossible to predict and that is what makes self defence an inadvisable remedy unless there is no alternative. However it seems that what the victim honestly and instinctively thought was necessary in the heat of the moment is an important factor in assessing whether the degree of force used was reasonable.[2] In practice, a victim who uses self defence may well be prosecuted and it will be a Crown Court jury of 12 unknown men and women who decide whether the force used was reasonable.

Certain factors are relevant to the degree of force that may be reasonable:
(a) The more serious the attack the greater degree of force justified, eg it seems unlikely that any force is reasonable if a perpetrator were about to smash a flowerpot on the doorstep of the victim's house. On the

other hand, it would probably be reasonable permanently to cripple a perpetrator who was about to stab a person to death.
(b) The use of force will be more reasonable when the victim has attempted to retreat and get away without resorting to force or has at least shown that s/he does not want to use force. Retreat is not essential.[3]
(c) Force may be justified if an attack is reasonably and honestly believed to be imminent.

Examples of reasonable measures in self defence are:
— throwing stones at a mob attacking a house with petrol bombs;
— warding off a person wielding a knife with a chair or stick;
— kicking an attacker in the shins or groin to allow an escape.

Making an arrest or preventing crime

Reasonable force may be used to make a lawful arrest or to prevent crime. This includes an arrest made for breach of the peace.[4] Again, the use of reasonable force will be a defence to a criminal prosecution for assault or other offence of violence or to a civil action for compensation, provided the arrest was lawful.

The circumstances in which an ordinary citizen has power to arrest a person who is committing or who has committed an offence or for breach of the peace were discussed on pp161 and 190. If the power of arrest exists, anyone may use reasonable force to make the arrest. It will rarely be sensible to make an arrest but it may, in some circumstances, be necessary to use reasonable force to do so in order to prevent a crime being committed.

The degree of force that would be reasonable to prevent a crime will be decided on the same basis as that for self defence. For example, if a person were pouring petrol through a letter-box it would probably be reasonable for four or five people to rush out of the door, grab the person and pin him or her to the floor. S/he could be held there until the police arrive.

Removing a trespasser

Reasonable force may be used to evict a trespasser. Where the trespass is peaceful it seems that the person should be asked to leave and given a reasonable time to comply before force is used. Where the trespasser is violent no request need be made.

Retaking goods that have been stolen

If a perpetrator steals goods belonging to the victim, the victim can enter the perpetrator's home and take the goods back. The extent of the remedy is extremely unclear but it appears likely that the victim will be immune from an action for damages by the perpetrator either for retaking the goods or for trespass in the perpetrator's home.

However, this remedy will not provide a defence to a prosecution under the Criminal Law Act 1977 s6 which makes it an offence to use violence to gain entry when some other person is present who resists entry. The use of this remedy should therefore, in practice, be restricted to circumstances where the victim can recover the goods without using any force. For example, if the property belonging to the victim is in the perpetrator's garden or beside an open window, the victim could climb over the fence and recover it.

C. ACTION IN THE CRIMINAL COURTS

The general law allows anyone to prosecute for a criminal offence. Thus a victim could prosecute, or a special organisation set up specifically to prosecute for criminal offences involved in a racial harassment campaign, or a law centre, provided the constitution of the organisation gives it power to prosecute. A victim can prosecute for the offences listed in Appendix 6 or those listed in Chapter 10. Prosecutions for some of the offences require the consent of the Attorney-General.

In practice, a victim will not prosecute for any of the offences involving breaches of local authority notices since s/he will have no control over the service of such notices. However, special procedures allow court action by victims for statutory nuisances and noise nuisances (see below).

Costs in criminal cases

The big disincentive for victims to prosecute are the costs involved. It has already been said that legal aid is not available to prosecute. Therefore the victim must either represent him or herself, pay a solicitor for representation, or rely on some free legal service such as a law centre.

The defendant, ie the perpetrator, will be able to apply for legal aid to defend the proceedings. The perpetrator may therefore have legal representation for which s/he does not have to pay.

The Prosecution of Offences Act 1985 prevents an order for costs being made against the victim if s/he is unsuccessful save in exceptional circumstances.[5]

Common assault and aggravated assault

The definition of common assault and the distinction between a common assault and an assault occasioning actual bodily harm were discussed on pp180-181. As with other offences, a prosecution for common assault can be brought by the victim. However, special provisions apply when a victim prosecutes for common assault which restrict the powers of the court and the usual right of the defendant to insist on the right to trial by jury in an offence that is triable either way. The special provisions apply when a prosecution is brought "by or on behalf of the party aggrieved". This would appear to be the victim of the assault. In the case of a child, it might be a parent or guardian.

A common assault is usually tried in the magistrates' court. If the magistrates accept jurisdiction and the victim is prosecuting, the defendant has no right to elect trial by jury. However, if the magistrates consider that the assault or battery is appropriate to be prosecuted in the Crown Court, they must hold committal proceedings as with other offences triable either way.[6]

If common assault is tried in the magistrates' court the maximum penalty is two months' imprisonment or a fine of £400.[7] Where the assault is on a child under 15 or a woman, the magistrates can impose a penalty of up to £1,000 or six months' imprisonment if they consider that the ordinary sentencing powers are insufficient because of the serious nature of the assault or battery. Such an assault is known as an "aggravated assault".[8] In both cases the court may bind over the defendant in addition to or instead of imposing a penalty (see p168). If the case is tried in the Crown Court the maximum penalty is one year's imprisonment.[9] If a victim prosecutes for common assault and the defendant is acquitted or is convicted and pays a fine or serves his or her sentence, this prevents any civil action for compensation for the same assault.[10]

In practice, individual victims who take out summonses for common assault are usually unrepresented and the magistrates generally decide to bind over both parties. The circumstances in which a party can be bound over are outlined on p168. It is often within the court's powers to require the victim of an assault to agree to be bound over despite the fact that s/he has committed no offence. However, even if the victim is bound over, the magistrates must still proceed to hear his or her prosecution if the victim wishes.

Obtaining a bind over of the perpetrator

Instead of prosecuting for common assault, victims can take out a complaint at the magistrates' court seeking just a bind over of the perpetrator in an attempt to prevent further attacks (see p168 above). The court may decide to bind over the victim as well.

Action to prevent statutory nuisances

Anyone who is affected by a statutory nuisance (see p153 above) may take action against the person responsible in the magistrates' court.[11] However, if the person responsible cannot be found, action may be taken against the owner or occupier of the premises on which the statutory nuisance exists.[12] If the nuisance is on the common parts of a housing estate, the local authority is owner and occupier and action can be taken against it, requiring it to remove the nuisance or prevent its recurrence.

The procedure is identical to that where the local authority takes action for a statutory nuisance except that no preliminary notice has to be served by the victim. If the magistrates are satisfied either that the nuisance exists at the time of the hearing or that it existed and is likely to recur, they may:
— order the nuisance to be removed;
— prohibit its recurrence;
— fine the defendant up to £1,000.[13]

The proceedings are criminal. It will therefore be necessary to prove beyond reasonable doubt, both that a statutory nuisance exists and that the defendant is the person responsible in order to obtain a conviction.

No legal aid is available for these proceedings. However, unlike most criminal proceedings, the victim is entitled to have his or her legal costs paid by the defendant provided s/he can show:
— that the defendant is the person responsible for the nuisance or that the person responsible cannot be identified and the defendant is the owner or occupier; and
— that the nuisance existed at the time the proceedings were begun even if it has ceased by the time of the hearing.[14]

The court has no discretion to refuse payment of costs in those circumstances.

Noise nuisances

An occupier of premises who is affected by a noise nuisance may take action in the magistrates' court.[15] Action must be taken against the person responsible for creating the noise nuisance. If that person cannot be found, action can be taken against the owner or occupier of the premises from which the noise originates.[16]

If the magistrates are satisfied that a noise nuisance has occurred and is likely to recur they may make an order prohibiting the recurrence of the nuisance. They may not impose a fine immediately.[17] A person who contravenes an order prohibiting a recurrence of the nuisance commits an offence which is punishable by a fine of up to £2,000 and there may be a daily fine of £50.[18]

Legal aid is not available for this procedure. There is no provision similar to that for statutory nuisances entitling a person who takes action to his or her costs. It is therefore in the court's discretion whether to award costs and how much, and victims who use this procedure risk having to pay some or all of their own legal costs even if they are successful.

Compensation in criminal proceedings

If a person is convicted of a criminal offence, a victim may claim compensation for any injury, loss or damage resulting from the offence (see p166). Where a child is convicted of an offence, the court must usually order any appropriate compensation to be paid by the parent (see p168). The provision applies to the magistrates' court or Crown Court, and a victim does not have to be prosecuting to claim compensation; s/he can do so when the police or local authority are prosecuting. Injury or loss resulting from the offence can include the terror, anxiety or distress it caused (see p166).[19]

Generally, the court requires some evidence of the injury or loss suffered. If the victim does not wish to attend court s/he must provide the prosecutor with some evidence of the loss or injury suffered. However, when only a small sum is sought to cover anxiety or distress it seems that proof may not be necessary.[20] In any event, it appears that the normal strict rules of evidence do not apply to a decision about the level of compensation.

Seeking an order for compensation in criminal proceedings against a child is usually the only method by which a victim can recover compensation from the child's parent. This is because in civil proceedings, almost without exception, it is the person responsible for the tort, ie the child, who must be sued, and it is usually impossible to enforce a court judgment for money against a child.

A victim will be able to claim compensation for any offence involving violence including common assault. The provision also applies to damage to property. However, if the victim is a tenant, it is the landlord and not the victim who can claim the cost of repairing windows and doors. Evidence of the loss or injury might include a medical report, estimate or bill for repairs, or a statement in the form shown in Appendix 3 Document 3, ie a written statement for use in criminal proceedings.

The police will usually assist a victim to make a claim if requested, but frequently omit to advise the victim of the possibility of making a claim.

D. ACTION IN THE CIVIL COURTS

A victim may take action in the civil courts against a perpetrator for an injunction and for damages. If the victim is under 18 his or her parent or guardian must take action on behalf of the child. The action will usually be for a tort (civil wrong).

The liability of children and their parents

The person responsible for a tortious act is liable to pay damages to the victim. This is true whatever the age of the perpetrator. However, in practice, an award of compensation against a child is likely to be unenforceable as a child will not usually have any money or assets.

It is by no means clear what remedy is available to the court to punish a child for breach of an injunction if the child is acting on his or her own intitiative.

1 Action against the parent

A victim can only claim damages against a parent for a tort committed by his or her child if:
— the parent authorised the tort;
— the child committed the tort because the parent was negligent in failing to exercise proper control;[21]
— the tort was a nuisance committed from the premises occupied by the parent.

Authorisation
Any instruction to a child or encouragement to commit a tort will make the parent liable to the victim in damages and an injunction may be obtained against the parent.

Negligent supervision
This is most likely to arise where a child has a weapon of some kind of which the parents are aware and which they fail to ensure the child uses only for a proper purpose. Examples might include a child who has:
— a catapult and breaks a window with a stone;
— a firework which is let off and injures someone;
— an air pistol which s/he fires at people, windows or animals.
It is not sufficient to show that there was inadequate supervision. It is necessary to show that this led to the child committing the tort. The fact that a tort has been committed before and is repeated by the child will add considerable weight to the argument that the parent is responsible, provided s/he knew about the first occasion.

Nuisance committed from premises occupied by the parent
The occupier of premises is liable for nuisances committed from the premises. Thus where a nuisance committed by a child is carried out from the parent's premises the latter will be liable. Examples include:
— a child throwing stones from a garden;
— noise nuisance by a child from within the home;
— firing an air pistol or catapult from the window of a house or flat.

2 Criminal compensation orders

A compensation order is available against the parent if a child is found guilty of a criminal offence (see p168).

Injunctions

In most cases a claim for an injunction must be linked to a claim for damages. Thus the victim must claim at least a nominal amount of damages if s/he wishes to seek an injunction. Like local authorities, victims may obtain a perpetual or an interlocutory injunction. The factors taken into account by the court when considering whether to grant such injunctions are covered on pp70–72. One important factor is whether damages would be an adequate remedy. Unlike the situation for local authorities, damages for victims may be substantial. However, it should still be possible to show that it is necessary to grant an injunction to protect the victim from further harassment.

Damages

Damages for a tort are usually intended to place the victim in the position s/he would have been in if the tort had not been committed; they are intended to compensate the victim. Damages for all torts may be awarded for:
— loss or damage to property;
— physical or mental injuries;
— other financial loss, eg loss of earnings due to injury or medical expenses.
Mental injuries for these purposes must amount to a clinical condition. In addition, damages will be recoverable for annoyance, inconvenience and discomfort for the torts of private and public nuisance (see below).

For certain other torts, the manner in which the tort was committed can be taken into account if it was done in such a way as to injure the victim's dignity or pride. The court can then award damages known as "aggravated damages" to compensate for grief or distress and the victim's damaged dignity or pride. This rule applies to :
— assault;
— trespass to land;
— interference with goods;
— false imprisonment;
— nuisance.[22]
It may also apply to unreasonable harassment but there has been no reported case in which a court has had the opportunity to assess damages for this tort.

The types of civil action available

A claim for an injunction or damages against a perpetrator may be brought by a victim for any of the following torts:
1 unreasonable harassment;
2 assault;
3 trespass to land;
4 private nuisance;
5 false imprisonment;
6 interference with goods;
7 public nuisance;
8 breach of Control of Pollution Act 1974.

1 Unreasonable harassment
That such a tort might exist appears to have first been suggested in a case

arising from the miners' strike. It may be a tort to "unreasonably harass" another person.

In *Thomas v NUM (South Wales Area)*[23] the High Court held that it constituted a tort of unreasonable harassment to picket a place of work with 50 to 70 men hurling abuse. An injunction was granted prohibiting the union from encouraging pickets to congregate in numbers exceeding six and in any way otherwise than to persuade people peacefully not to work. The judge commented that the tort of nuisance (see below) protected the use or enjoyment of land. He saw no reason why the rights of non-occupiers of land should not be similarly protected. He therefore considered that people using the highway or attempting to go to work should be protected from unreasonable harassment. No appeal was lodged against this decision.

In a more recent case, the Court of Appeal has stated that no tort of harassment exists and the issue as to whether there is a tort of unreasonable harassment must therefore be open to question until it is further tested in the courts.[23A]

If this tort exists, it provides great potential for use in racial harassment cases. It is difficult to predict what might constitute unreasonable harassment. It will depend on all the circumstances of the case. It seems far more likely that the courts would allow the use of this tort when there is an organised campaign of racial harassment by a group of individuals. However, the judge in *Thomas v NUM* gave an example of what he considered would amount to unreasonable harassment. His example was of an individual persistently following another person on a public highway, "making rude gestures or remarks in order to annoy or vex". The judge therefore clearly envisaged a remedy being available for action by one individual.

If the courts are prepared to protect someone entering or leaving their place of work then it would surely be even more appropriate to protect people entering or leaving their home or school. The remedy might therefore be available to prevent perpetrators lying in wait for victims near their home or school or other community facility.

The use of this remedy might be particularly appropriate where a number of neighbours are ganging up together to wage an organised campaign of racial harassment against a victim. Using this tort, it might be possible to combine a court action against all of them at the same time rather than attempting separate court actions for assault, nuisance etc each based on one incident of harassment. In this way evidence of the whole campaign could be put before the court in one action, making proof considerably easier.

2   Assault and battery

Assault and battery are torts as well as crimes. A perpetrator can be sued by the victim as well as prosecuted. A perpetrator cannot be sued if a criminal prosecution has been begun and the case has been dismissed or if s/he has been prosecuted and has paid any fine imposed or served any sentence of imprisonment.[24]

Assault is the appropriate tort for any offence of violence. Thus, for example, even though the act amounted to the criminal offence of causing grievous bodily harm, the victim sues for assault. All that will change will be the level of compensation payable.

3 Trespass to land

An owner or tenant of land can take action in trespass. A licensee cannot.[25] Trespass was covered on p42, 70 and 113. Trespass includes not only entering a person's land or building without permission but also damaging the property. Clearly an owner occupier, council or housing association tenant or private tenant can take action in trespass. Licensees in bed and breakfast accommodation, nursing homes, children's homes, women's refuges or homeless people's accommodation cannot take action in trespass. Any action in trespass for these groups must be taken by their landlords.

4 Private nuisance

Private nuisance was defined on p41. The occupier of land who is the owner or a tenant can sue in nuisance; a licensee cannot, just as for trespass, above. Private nuisance actionable by a victim might include:
— deliberately making a noise to harass the victim;
— urinating on the victim's property;
— dumping rubbish on the victim's property or just outside;
— watching or besetting the victim's home in an intimidating fashion (see p182);
— throwing stones at the victim's home.

5 False imprisonment

False imprisonment was defined on p183 and examples given.

6 Interference with goods

The tort of interference with goods includes damaging, destroying or removing the victim's goods either permanently or temporarily. "Goods" includes any property other than land or buildings. An animal is property for these purposes and it is therefore a tort of interference with goods to poison a victim's dog or cat. But to pull down a fence or damage a door is not covered by this tort — these acts are trespasses to land and not interference with goods.

7 Public nuisance

Public nuisance is discussed on p43. An individual can only claim damages or seek an injunction to prevent a public nuisance if s/he has suffered or is suffering damage or loss which is appreciably different from that suffered by the rest of the public.[26] An individual victim might be able to show that s/he has suffered particular loss or damage different from the general public in the following instances:

— where many children are intimidated on their way home from school or many adults leaving a housing estate but one person is attacked and injured (this will also amount to the tort of assault);
— where a dog harasses many people but bites one;
— where a house is attacked from the street, anyone who lives there will be able to take action.

8 Breach of Control of Pollution Act 1974

It is a criminal offence to dump household waste on land (see p175). Where damage is caused by any poisonous, noxious or polluting waste any person committing the criminal offence is also liable for the damage.[27] "Damage" includes an injury to a person.

E. OTHER REMEDIES

The Criminal Injuries Compensation Scheme[28]

A victim who is injured in certain circumstances may seek compensation through the Criminal Injuries Compensation Scheme. Compensation is payable if injury is caused to a person:
— by a crime of violence; or
— while s/he is trying to stop someone committing a crime; or
— while s/he is trying to arrest a suspect after a crime; or
— while s/he is helping the police arrrest someone.

Compensation is payable under the scheme even if the perpetrator is unidentified, or is identified but is not prosecuted, or is too young to be prosecuted (eg a nine-year-old child). The victim must have reported the incident to the police without delay, and have given every assistance to the police to help them identify the perpetrator and prosecute.

When deciding whether to award compensation the Criminal Injuries Compensation Board (CICB) takes account of the character and way of life of the victim. Anyone who has him or herself been convicted of a crime of violence is unlikely to recover compensation. In addition, the CICB may refuse or reduce compensation if the victim was responsible for or involved in the incident in any way. Compensation is assessed on the same basis as a claim for personal injury in the courts and is only payable if the injury is serious enough to merit payment of at least £400. It should be noted that compensation is only payable for injuries. It is not payable for damage to property or inconvenience, distress or hurt feelings.

Injuries serious enough to merit an award of at least £400 usually involve an injury whose effect lasts for at least a few months. Any broken limb or wound requiring stitches will probably qualify, as will some severe bruising or a bad sprain.

The advantage of the scheme is that compensation is payable out of public money and the perpetrator is unlikely to be involved or even to know that an application has been made. Any risk of intimidation is therefore considerably reduced, if not removed. A victim who is injured in a scuffle in which the victim also hits the perpetrator may find it difficult to recover any compensation. The CICB might also refuse compensation to a victim who had an opportunity to run away but did not do so.

In order to qualify, victims should consider reporting any violent incident to the police regardless of whether or not the police are likely to identify the perpetrator. An application is made on a standard form available from the CICB (10-12 Russell Square, London WC1).

Rating revaluation[29]

Any ratepayer can apply for a revaluation of their home. It might be possible to obtain a revaluation on the ground of racial harassment. Rating law is extremely complicated and no application for revaluation should be attempted without legal advice. Any tenant or owner may apply for a revaluation of their home on the ground that the present valuation is too high.

Valuation for rating purposes is based on a hypothetical yearly rent that would be paid for the premises based on certain assumptions. Thus, in theory, any factor that might affect the rent is relevant to the rateable value. Factors which make the home less desirable to any potential tenant or which reduce the number of potential tenants should reduce the hypothetical rent. There has been one reported case in which the rateable value of a home has been reduced because of harassment.[30] However, in that case the occupier had to pass through the flat of the person responsible for the harassment and the harassment was not racial.

Because rateable value works on the basis of how much a hypothetical tenant would pay for premises, racial harassment of one family by one other family is unlikely to be taken into account to reduce a rateable value. The hypothetical tenant might not suffer such harassment. However, if racial harassment is widespread in an area, in a street or on an estate and affects the decisions of black people about where they wish to live, there might be grounds for obtaining a reduction in valuation. The more evidence that can be produced about black people who have refused offers of accommodation in the area, the greater are the chances of success.

Referring papers to the Crown Prosecution Service for prosecution

Victims as well as local authorities can refer cases direct to the Crown Prosecution Service for prosecution if they have collected evidence themselves and the police do not wish to prosecute (see p198).

Preventing abusive phone calls

Several options are available. The police have facilities for identifying the origin of abusive calls (see p193).

1 Arranging interception of calls by the operator

British Telecom will intercept calls free of charge when a customer is receiving abusive phone calls. The operator will answer every call and will ask the caller for their name, where they are calling from and whom they wish to speak to. The customer is then rung and asked whether they wish to speak to that person. Three potential problems exist:
— genuine friends and relatives may be put off from calling;
— the operator may take a long time to answer;
— sometimes the operator does not ask all the necessary questions and callers get put through without being properly vetted.

However, in racial harassment cases it is probable that the caller is frightened of being identified and will ring off if calls are intercepted.

2 Changing the phone number

British Telecom will usually change a phone number reasonably quickly where there are abusive calls. It will charge for the change.

3 Ex-directory

Any subscriber can ask not to be included in the phone directory. This will obviously only be of use once a number has been changed.

Obtaining a mutual exchange

Tenants with a secure tenancy have a right to enter into a mutual exchange with another secure tenant with the consent of their respective landlords. The other tenant need not be a tenant of the same landlord.[31] Most tenants of local authorities, housing associations and charitable housing trusts are secure tenants. They can therefore exchange with other tenants of any local authority, housing association or charitable housing trust.[32]

The landlord can refuse consent on very limited grounds but only if objection is lodged within 42 days. Where there are rent arrears or some breach of the tenancy agreement, the landlord's consent can be given subject to a condition that the arrears are cleared or breach rectified.

The local authority should have a leaflet providing details of the National Mobility Scheme and a registration form. It should also have available for inspection a list of tenants who wish to move into its area. Using these facilities, tenants may be able to find another tenant who wishes to exchange homes and can then make arrangements to move out of the area into alternative council accommodation.

Opposing pub licences and music and dance licences

Local authorities have a power to oppose pub licences (see p53). Individuals can also oppose such licences and may oppose the issue of music and dance licences when these are being considered by the local authority. In practice, opposition by a single victim is unlikely to be effective unless supported by the local authority. Action by local residents' or tenants' associations is likely to achieve greater success.

F. ASSISTANCE FROM LOCAL AUTHORITIES WITH COURT PROCEEDINGS

There is no power in LGA 1972 s222 to assist victims with financing court action. There are, however, four ways in which authorities can assist with legal action by victims.

Funding court action by an individual victim

A local authority may be able to fund court action by an individual victim using its powers under LGA 1972 s137 (see p36). The authority must be satisfied that funding is "in the interests of [its] area or some or all of its inhabitants". The statutory requirement of LGA 1972 s137 is less restrictive than that in s222, and it should be possible to justify funding private prosecutions under it. Funds would be used to pay a private practice solicitor to act for the victim in a prosecution.

It seems unlikely that it would be possible to justify funding civil action by a victim since civil proceedings relate only to the individual and there is no recognition of the public interest in such proceedings. Legal aid is, in any event, available for civil action.

Funding a voluntary organisation to act for victims

A local authority can fund a voluntary organisation to assist or represent victims in private prosecutions or in civil actions. If the organisations are to provide representation they must employ at least one solicitor who would have to obtain a waiver of the solicitors' practice rules from the Law Society. Law centres already meet the conditions set out by the Law Society and have solicitors on their staff. In areas where law centres are established, authorities could fund additional law centre staff to deal specifically with racial harassment cases on behalf of victims.

Appearing in proceedings brought by victims

This is discussed on p27.

Seconding staff to organisations assisting victims

Authorities could second staff to voluntary organisations assisting victims to take court action. The salaries of such staff would probably have to be funded using the powers in LGA 1972 s137 if the staff were lawyers from the legal department. Such organisations would still be unable to represent victims in court unless they employed at least one solicitor who had obtained a waiver of the practice rules from the Law Society.

G. REMEDIES AGAINST LOCAL AUTHORITIES OR THE POLICE FOR FAILURE TO ACT

The major disadvantage of any direct or court action by a victim against a perpetrator is the major risk of aggravating an existing situation, leading to further intimidation and increased racial harassment. This risk still exists when local authorities or the police initiate proceedings where the victim is a witness, but, when the authority institutes proceedings, it is more likely that *it* will be perceived as the major source of threat rather than the victim and some of the perpetrator's anger may be directed at the authority rather than the victim. In addition, there are many legal remedies which, in practice, are only available to local authorities or the police either because a victim has insufficient legal powers or has insufficient resources.

It is therefore important to a victim that both the police and the local authority use their available powers. This part of this chapter looks briefly at the legal powers that victims have to influence the practices of the police and the local authority.

Remedies against the local authority

1 Judicial review

If a local authority fails to comply with any of the statutory duties set out in Chapters 4 to 9 or fails to comply with the requirements of administrative law when reaching a decision, a victim may be able to take proceedings for judicial review. The court has power to quash a wrongly made decision or to order the authority to carry out its duty in accordance with the law.

In practice, many duties are imprecisely defined and leave great scope for local authority discretion and the opportunity for judicial review proceedings will accordingly be rare. Legal advice will always be required, preferably from someone experienced in administrative law. Legal advice will be available under the green form scheme, but legal aid may be difficult to obtain if there is no direct benefit to the victim which will be achieved by such proceedings. For example, in Chapter 4 it was argued that local authorities might have a duty to establish and operate a policy on racial harassment in some circumstances by virtue of their duty under RRA 1976 s71. If so, a failure to operate such a policy would afford a victim the opportunity to challenge the authority's failure by judicial review. A court would merely order the authority to establish a policy but would not direct what it must contain. The victim might therefore obtain no direct benefit.

2 Action for discrimination

Where the complaint by a victim is that a local authority has discriminated against him or her on racial grounds, the victim can take action in the county court seeking compensation. Before doing so, it is useful to serve a questionnaire on the authority asking it specific questions about the way in which the victim's case has been dealt with and how it compares with other cases. The Commission for Racial Equality can advise on procedure and may be prepared to assist the victim by funding the case.

Where authorities fail to make offers of housing in certain areas to black applicants because of racial harassment this will amount to unlawful discrimination. Where allegations of nuisance or harassment by white tenants are treated differently from similar allegations by black tenants this may amount to unlawful discrimination. For example, authorities may deal severely with tenants responsible for general nuisance but fail to act at all against perpetrators of racial harassment.

3 Complaint to the Commission for Racial Equality

The CRE has a statutory duty "to work towards the elimination of discrimination, to promote equality of opportunity and good relations between persons of different racial groups and to keep under review the workings of the Race Relations Act 1976 and when necessary submit proposals to the Secretary of State for amendment."[33] In addition, it has powers if it thinks fit to conduct a formal investigation for any purpose connected with the carrying out of these duties.

The CRE clearly has a responsibility to tackle discrimination which it does by assisting individual complainants, by initiating its own investigations and by other means. However, its role extends to reviewing the operations of the RRA 1976. It could therefore justify an investigation into the workings of a local authority to see if and how it complies with its statutory duties under s71 in order to assess whether amendments to the RRA 1976 are necessary.

Victims affected by racial harassment who consider that their local authority is failing in its obligations under s71 could ask the CRE to mount a formal investigation.

4 Action for breach of covenant to repair

An authority which is a landlord owes a contractual duty to its tenants to carry out repairs (see p93). Where the authority fails to comply with its contractual obligation, the tenant may take proceedings for damages and in some circumstances seek an interlocutory injunction to ensure that the repairs are done.[34]

5 Action against the authority for nuisance
This is discussed on p95.

6 Complaint to the Secretary of State
If an authority fails to comply with its duties under the Public Health Act 1936 (statutory nuisances, see p153) or Control of Pollution Act 1974 (see p158), a complaint can be made to the Secretary of State. The Secretary can direct the authority what action it should take to comply with its statutory obligations. If it fails to comply, the Secretary of State can then carry out the authority's responsibilities and charge it for the costs of doing so.[35]

Remedies against the police
The limited scope for court action by a victim against the police is considered in Chapter 11 (pp196-198).

1 Individual complaints against the police
An individual victim may make a complaint "about the conduct of a police officer".[36] Complaints cannot be made about the general direction or control of the police force.[37] An individual's ability to complain is therefore limited to a single act of misconduct by a police officer. A complaint might be possible where:
— an officer fails to carry out instructions (eg where a local senior officer has received instructions from his or her superiors to allocate staff resources to detecting racial harassment but fails to do so, or where an individual officer has been ordered to investigate a particular crime but fails to do so);
— an officer fails to act when a crime is committed in his or her presence, (eg the police are called to an incident by the victim. While they are still there the perpetrator attacks the victim but the police do nothing to stop the attack).

It can be seen that the scope for complaints is limited. In the first example, access to police force instructions or information about what particular officers have been instructed to do, would be necessary.

2 Other methods of complaint
Individuals may be able to voice their complaints about police policies and procedures through the police consultative process or by speaking to members of the police authority (see p197). MPs who take up issues on behalf of their constituents may receive a better response from the police than might other sources of support to victims.

1 See *R v McInnes* [1971] 3 All ER 295, CA.
2 Ibid citing *Palmer v Reginam* [1971] 1 All ER 1077.
3 See n1.
4 Criminal Justice Act 1967 s3.

5 Prosecution of Offences Act 1985 s17.
6 Offences Against the Person Act 1861 s46.
7 Ibid s42.
8 Ibid s43.
9 Ibid s47.
10 Ibid s45.
11 Public Health Act 1936 s99.
12 Ibid s93.
13 Ibid s94.
14 Ibid s94(3).
15 Control of Pollution Act 1974 s59.
16 Ibid s59(3).
17 Ibid s59(2).
18 Ibid s59(4).
19 *Bond v Chief Constable of Kent* [1983] 1 All ER 456.
20 Ibid.
21 See, eg, *Gorely v Codd* [1966] 3 All ER 891 and *Newton v Edgerley* [1959] 3 All ER 337.
22 See *Guppys (Bridport) Ltd v Brookling* (1984) 269 EG 846, CA. This case concerned exemplary damages but suggests that a court would award aggravated damages for nuisance.
23 [1985] 2 All ER 1.
23A *Patel v Patel* (1987) *Times* 21 August, CA.
24 Offences Against the Person Act 1861 s46.
25 See, eg, *Allan v Liverpool Overseers* (1874) LR 9 QB 180 at 191-2 per Blackburn J and *Masters v Brent LBC* [1978] QB 841 where this point appears to have been assumed.
26 See cases cited at *Halsbury's Laws* 4th edn, Vol 34, para 370.
27 Control of Pollution Act 1974 s88.
28 See Bailey and Tucker *Remedies for Victims of Crime* Legal Action Group, 1984.
29 See generally *Ryde on Rating* and Forbes "General Rates on Residential Accommodation: Valuation" January 1987 *LEGAL ACTION* 23. Legal advice on revaluation is essential.
30 *Black v Oliver* [1978] 3 All ER 408, CA.
31 HA 1985 s92.
32 Ibid s80.
33 RRA 1976 s43.
34 For further details see Jan Luba *Repairs: Tenants' Rights* Legal Action Group, 1986.
35 Public Health Act 1936 s322 and Control of Pollution Act 1974 s97.
36 PACE s84.
37 Ibid s84(5).

CHAPTER THIRTEEN
Local Authority Policies and Practices

For a local authority to develop a long-term, comprehensive policy in respect of racial harassment, effective co-ordination between departments is essential, and the role of the legal department is particularly important. These two factors are also crucial in any legal action taken against perpetrators by local authorities.

This book is primarily concerned with the legal powers available to local authorities to tackle racial harassment. Considerable research has already been carried out into local authorities' policies, and other research is nearing completion which deals with the policy issues and suggestions for good practice in greater detail.[1] In this chapter the discussion will therefore be limited to issues that arise from the points made in previous chapters and those which relate to the use of legal action against perpetrators.

Racial harassment presents a challenge to local authorities. It is a problem that requires imaginative long-term measures as well as rapid reaction to particular incidents; it requires a response that is unconstrained by departmental boundaries, a degree of liaison with the voluntary sector that is frequently lacking, the imaginative use of legal powers and, often, different skills within the local authority's legal department from those required in much of its other work.

A. DEPARTMENTAL ORGANISATION

This book has shown that the powers of local authorities to tackle racial harassment extend to most, if not all, departments. It follows that a comprehensive racial harassment policy should embrace all departments of an authority. In order to achieve this aim the following recommendations should be considered.

Developing a comprehensive policy

Rather than developing policy solely within departmental boundaries which are artificial and may hinder attempts to be comprehensive, authorities should consider developing policy in four areas. Although the areas overlap, they provide a more logical and useful way of evolving a racial harassment policy than any attempt along departmental lines can achieve. Within each of these areas authorities should consider the role that could be played by community groups and other voluntary sector agencies in developing the most effective measures and gaining the greatest degree of public support.

1 Long-term measures

The long-term measures that authorities can adopt to eradicate racism and racial harassment, using their available legal powers, is one area in which policy should be developed. Examples are:
— the development of anti-racist teaching by an education authority;
— the design of new buildings;
— the lighting of streets;
— the inclusion of security measures in any redevelopment scheme;
— the use of vandal-proof paint or paint from which graffiti can be more easily removed in any redecoration programme;
— the adoption of measures to encourage or force other local organisations or firms to adopt policies and practices aimed at eradicating racism and racial harassment.

2 The protection of victims

The development of any comprehensive racial harassment policy should take into account the package of measures that can be adopted to provide protection to individual victims who remain in their own homes, permanently or pending rehousing, both in the private and public sector. These measures might include:
— physical protection measures such as locks, entryphones etc;
— protection by the use of legal action against perpetrators;
— support systems for the family being harassed;
— grants to owner occupiers.

3 Allocation procedures

The allocation procedure for transfers of racial harassment victims, both from the private sector and from other local authority housing, and the package of measures that the authority can adopt to assist in rehousing, should form part of any policy.

This policy includes the type of housing that is offered and the length of time before rehousing. The measures might include the payment of removal expenses and other costs of rehousing and support systems for victims after they have been transferred to avoid isolation in their new home. The role of housing associations in providing rehousing should also be considered.

Within this package the policy to be adopted in the allocation of the dwelling vacated by the victim should be considered. The recent CRE report on racial harassment discusses this issue.[2] Authorities should record and monitor the level of rejections of offers of accommodation due to the likelihood of racial harassment.

4 Procedures for taking legal action

The procedures for taking legal action against perpetrators in both public and private sector, should be developed within the framework of an overall policy on racial harassment. This is dealt with below.

Co-ordination of policy

Clearly, any attempts at developing policies on a council-wide basis will require a strong co-ordinating role. Co-ordination may be required both at officer and member level. Each authority will decide its own method of ensuring that policy development is properly co-ordinated. It may best be achieved either by one department assuming primary responsibility as the lead department or by central co-ordination in all areas by the department of the chief executive. If the "lead department" model is adopted, different departments might assume responsibility for different aspects of the policy. For example, responsibility for co-ordinating:

— long-term strategy might be taken by a central policy team within the chief executive's department;
— measures to protect victims within their homes and to provide rehousing might be taken by the housing department;
— legal action against perpetrators might be taken by the legal department.

Inter-departmental working parties, chaired by an officer from the co-ordinating department and with representatives from the voluntary sector, will probably be required to develop and monitor the policy. A similar committee or sub-committee may be required at member level, again with voluntary sector involvement.

Some authorities have already set up racial harassment panels which monitor the operation of the racial harassment policy and discuss the progress of particular cases. There is no reason why similar panels could not be involved in the development of council-wide policies and procedures.

1 The role of the legal department

The role of the legal department of a local authority is crucial in two areas — the development of policies and legal action against perpetrators. Legal action is dealt with below. Here, the role of the legal department in the development of policy is discussed.

For legal departments to play a proper role in the development of local authority policies on racial harassment four things are required:

(a) the availability of suitably knowledgeable and experienced lawyers within the department;
(b) that the legal advisers are involved in the policy development at all stages and therefore understand the objectives, rather than being consulted at the end of the process and asked to give a red or green light to proposals that they have had no part in developing;
(c) that local authority officers alter their narrow view of the legal department's role;

(d) that the legal department is alert to the way in which changes in the law or the development of case law affects the ability of the authority to carry out its desired policies.

These four issues will be dealt with in turn.

(a) *The availability of knowledgeable and experienced lawyers*
To advise an authority on a racial harassment policy requires knowledge of all aspects of law relating to local authorities, together with the rules of evidence and court procedure. In addition, since most of the powers available to local authorities are not designed to tackle racial harassment, legal advisers should be able and prepared to provide firm advice on uncharted areas of law. This advice should be available without constant recourse to counsel's opinion which should be unnecessary in most cases.

(b) *Involving legal advisers at all stages*
In order to advise an authority properly on the legal avenues available, a legal adviser must understand what the authority is seeking to achieve. Local authority lawyers frequently complain that they are consulted too late. Involving lawyers at an early stage may prevent time being wasted both by attempting to implement policies which are unlawful and by not having to wait for legal advice when the policy is completed and ready to implement.

A representative of the legal department should therefore be a member of all working parties involved in the development of local authority policies and practices for dealing with racial harassment.

(c) *Adopting a broad view of the role of the legal department*
The role of the legal department in policy development can be seen in two different ways. One view of its role is its negative aspect: to stop the authority doing anything illegal. The other view of its role is its positive element: to find some legal power to enable an authority to do what it wants to do. Some officers in local authorities appear to adopt a narrow and negative view of the role of the legal department in the development of policy.

This occurs in two ways. On the one hand, departments seeking legal advice ask very specific questions that invite narrow answers rather than asking open-ended questions. For example, a legal department might be asked whether the Land Compensation Act 1973 could be used to authorise payment of compensation to racial harassment victims. The short answer is that it cannot. Advice from the legal department which says that it cannot is perfectly correct and answers the question posed. Negative advice saves the authority from doing something illegal. On the other hand, legal departments often answer only the narrow question posed rather than attempting to find out what the instructing department is trying to achieve and assisting them to achieve it. For instance, in the previous example, it is clear from the question being asked that the housing department is trying to find a legal power to pay compensation to victims. Adopting the broad view of the role of the legal department, its advice should be that the Land Compensation Act cannot be used but there are other available powers under LGA 1972 s111 and HA 1985 s21 which could be used to make payments similar to those under the Land Compensation Act 1973.

Positive advice enables the authority to carry out the policy it wished to implement by finding other legal powers to do so lawfully.

To some extent, this problem would be resolved by involving legal advisers in the policy development so that they are present during discussions about the purpose of the policy. Where legal advisers are not present, requests for advice should be framed as open-ended questions, eg "Can we use the Land Compensation Act to make payment of compensation to victims and, if not, what other powers are available to enable us to make similar compensation payments?"

In all cases, those providing legal advice should ensure that they are aware of the objects which the department seeking advice is trying to achieve. Where necessary, this must be discovered by obtaining further instructions. The advice provided should then, not only answer any specific questions that have been asked about legal powers, but also provide guidance on other legal powers that are available and the advantages and disadvantages of each. Such advice will enable the instructing department to reach a decision on the best way to proceed and the best legal power to use.

(d) *Being alert to the effects of new law or developing case law*
The law is never static. Significant decisions are made in the courts which lead to a different interpretation being put on the powers or duties in a particular statute. New statutes affecting local authorities are passed each year. For example:

- the Tower Hamlets case on the duties of social services authorities under the Child Care Act 1980[3] in August 1987 which is now in the process of appeal should clarify and may alter the interpretation of that statute;
- Shell has begun a court challenge against a decision of Lewisham council to boycott its products because of its connections with South Africa. This case may affect the interpretation of the powers provided by the RRA 1976 s71;
- the Criminal Justice Bill before Parliament in December 1987 contains proposals to amend the rules relating to prosecutions for common assault (see p204). Government has announced proposals to alter the offence of "harassment" in the Protection from Eviction Act 1977.

Developments in the law may extend or narrow the ability of local authorities to implement policies on racial harassment. Legal departments should be alert to and understand the effect of these developments. They can only do so if:
— there are adequate procedures for ensuring that legal department staff are aware of new statutes and court decisions; and

— the legal department has been involved in policy development so that it is aware of the purposes sought to be achieved by particular aspects of the policy.

2 Resolving conflicts between departments

Many of those responsible for racial harassment are children or are from families with children. The social services and education authorities have statutory responsibilities to such children which cannot be avoided. Potential conflict can be created within an authority by the different roles of departments. The housing department may be arguing that a family should be evicted to protect the victims of racial harassment. The social services department may consider that it is in the interests of the children who are part of the family perpetrating the harassment that they should remain living where they are. In some cases, perpetrators may even seek to call social workers as witnesses for the defence in court proceedings. If they are witness summonsed, they cannot avoid giving evidence and must give their honest opinion.

Authorities should recognise the inevitable conflict that arises even if officers with different responsibilities are fulfilling them in a thoroughly professional way. Steps should be taken to ensure that staff from different departments understand the duties of their colleagues within the authority, and recognise that others may be working towards a different objective because of their professional duties and not because they are attempting to undermine the authority's position.

Authorities should ensure that inter-departmental policies and procedures are developed which identify possible areas of conflict and reduce the likelihood of conflicting objectives to a minimum. In particular, social services and education department officers should not be invited to case conferences discussing legal action against perpetrators if their role at such conferences is to represent the interests of the perpetrator or their family.

Legal action against perpetrators

The scope for legal action against perpetrators exists within each department. In any particular case, an authority should make use of the most appropriate and effective legal remedy for the objective it wishes to achieve. This requires consideration of the potential legal action available to all departments of the authority.

Legal action is not necessarily effective even if it is successful. Perpetrators can ignore court orders and can evade detection. Those who are prosecuted may be punished but very little long-term legal protection for victims is provided, even if a perpetrator receives a prison sentence. Publicity gained from a case may in some cases cause additional racial harassment by racist groups and individuals. Any policy on legal action should consider first the objectives that are sought from legal action against a perpetrator. These might be:

(a) to provide immediate protection of some kind for the victim;
(b) to provide longer-term protection to the victim, eg by a perpetual injunction, custodial sentence or eviction of the perpetrator;
(c) to deter racial harassment by others by making an example of the particular perpetrator;
(d) in some cases, to compensate the victim for distress and loss caused by racial harassment;
(e) to punish the individual perpetrator;
(f) to make racial and ethnic minorities feel safer by showing that the local authority and the courts are able and willing to provide assistance and support.

These objectives are not mutually exclusive. In any policy in which the needs of the victim are the first and paramount consideration, the first two objectives will be the priorities when considering legal action in a particular case. The third objective, though highly desirable, must be a secondary consideration if racial harassment victims are not to be used by a local authority for its own wider political purposes. It can only be a primary objective if the witnesses and victim share that objective and agree to become involved in court proceedings on that basis.

In addition to considering the objectives of court proceedings, authorities should consider the possible side-effects. The undesirable side-effects might include:
— increased harassment of the victims by the perpetrator or others;
— harassment or intimidation of witnesses who were not previously victims;
— an overall rise in racial harassment due to increased activity by local racists.

However, as a result of court proceedings victims and witnesses might be encouraged to come forward.

Having considered these issues, several very important points should be made about the policies and procedures to be adopted to enable effective legal action to be mounted.

1 Speed

Where legal proceedings are being used to provide immediate protection for a victim, the purpose of the proceedings is to transfer power. Until legal proceedings are begun the perpetrator is in control. S/he is under no threat. Once legal action is begun, the perpetratror is put on the defensive and may modify his or her behaviour.

Legal proceedings can be begun very quickly indeed. In exceptional circumstances, injunctions can be obtained within hours. They can more usually be obtained within a few days. Once it is decided that legal action is appropriate, it should be begun immediately and steps should be taken to obtain some element of protection for the victim from the court as soon as possible. Methods by which this can be achieved are considered in Chapters 5 and 10.

Legal department organisation
The legal department needs to be in a position to take legal action immediately. Where it is proposed to obtain an injunction this will involve interviewing witnesses and drafting court papers. Other work will need to take second place for both the lawyer involved and any administrative and secretarial back-up staff. Typing facilities may need to be available out of office hours to ensure that all the necessary paperwork can be prepared for a hearing early the following day.

Legal departments need to review their current practices to ensure that they can provide the necessary lawyers and administrative back-up to enable legal action to be commenced at very short notice.

Delegated authority for decision making
If rapid court action is to be begun, the decision to take proceedings must be delegated to officers who are available whenever necessary to make that decision. It is unlikely that members can meet sufficiently quickly to make the decision. Clearly, the chairperson of a committee cannot make the decision because powers cannot be delegated to a single councillor.

At present, many authorities require committee or sub-committee approval for court proceedings against perpetrators. That is wholly inappropriate if proceedings are to be used to provide immediate short-term protection to victims, though it may be appropriate for longer-term measures.

Authorities should therefore review the extent of delegated authority to take court proceedings, and delegate appropriate powers to enable proceedings to be commenced rapidly.

Collecting and preserving evidence
Evidence should be collected as soon as possible for reasons explained in Chapter 14. This may include such matters as the taking of photographs of damage before it is repaired or of injuries before they have healed.

2 The role of the legal department

Racial harassment cases are likely to be very different from any other type of case handled by a legal department with the exception of possession proceedings for nuisance or annoyance. Possession proceedings for racial harassment bear no resemblance to proceedings for rent arrears in terms of evidence, preparation and presentation. The different nature of racial harassment cases will require a completely different approach by the legal department.

Similarly, many of the procedures that work satisfactorily for rent arrears cases are unlikely to be appropriate for racial harassment cases. For example, that certain tasks in rent arrears cases might be carried out by the housing department, eg the drafting of notices of intention to seek possession, does not mean that this is appropriate to a possession action based on racial harassment.

The legal department should, itself, develop procedures for dealing with legal action against perpetrators in addition to any procedures in service departments. There are key responsibilities to be carried out in any legal action:
— identifying and interviewing witnesses;
— collecting other evidence, eg photos, plans, documentary evidence;
— obtaining the confidence of witnesses, keeping them informed and ensuring that they attend on the day of any hearing;
— deciding whether witnesses require interpreters and selecting the appropriate interpreter;
— writing warning letters and drafting notices to be used in court proceedings;
— drafting court documentation;
— arranging court hearings and directing the speed and progress of the case;
— making decisions about the manner in which a case is to be presented;
— deciding which witnesses will be called;
— presenting the case in court.

All of these tasks require training and expertise. Lawyers within the legal department should already have the training and expertise and should be used to accepting responsibility for all these tasks which are part of the day-to-day work of any litigation lawyer.

All of these tasks must be carried out correctly and at the proper time if legal action is to succeed. Mistakes or delays may mean that legal action fails for technical reasons. One London authority recently had a possession action dismissed within a few minutes because the notice of intention to seek possession was defective. These types of mistake should not happen in any case, but it is particularly important that they do not occur in racial harassment cases where there may be increased physical danger to witnesses and victims if a case fails completely.

All these tasks would usually be carried out by a lawyer responsible for litigation. Authorities which wish to assign responsibility for any of these tasks to departments other than the legal department should consider what advantage is gained by so doing. Even if tasks are assigned to service departments, the legal department should check that they have been satisfactorily completed, and this is a duplication of effort.

If it is decided that responsibility for some of these tasks should be assigned to departments other than the legal department, considerable training should be given on the law, procedures and practical aspects of the task. None of these responsibilities are suitable for delegation to service departments unless all the appropriate officers have received adequate training. In the following three areas, this is particularly important.

Notice of intention to seek possession
These notices are crucial to possession proceedings. If they are defective, ie incorrectly drafted, the case is likely to be dismissed on a technicality. Many authorities presently authorise notices to be served by the housing department. The only way to remove any risk of serving a defective notice is to include in the notice all the allegations which are contained in the particulars of claim. Shortened versions may succeed but may not.

Contact and liaison with witnesses
Liaison with witnesses is a key responsibility. Witnesses are entitled to be kept informed of the progress of the case. They will have greater confidence if they are able to establish a working relationship with one officer. It is desirable that the officer concerned should have a detailed knowledge of court procedure and rules of evidence, is the person responsible for ensuring that witnesses attend and for deciding which witnesses should be called, and is intimately involved with progressing the case to trial. Ideally, that role should be taken by the person responsible for the case within the legal department.

Advising on evidence
If the legal department is asked to advise on whether there is sufficient evidence to proceed with a case, it will in many cases be impossible for it to do so without interviewing the available witnesses (including the victim). Clearly, where there are no witnesses, there is no possibility of successful proceedings. Where there is even one witness, properly considered advice can only be given after some assessment has been made as to whether s/he can give sufficient evidence to obtain a successful result.

Authorities should ensure that legal departments are not asked to advise on the prospects of legal action without adequate information.

3 Deciding strategies in legal action

Decisions about the way in which a case is presented are usually taken by a client, solicitor and barrister jointly. In racial harassment cases brought by local authorities, some key decisions about presentation can be made in advance. The "client" is, strictly speaking, the service department on whose behalf the legal department is bringing proceedings. However, if the case is brought with the objective of providing short- or long-term protection for an individual victim, then s/he is likely to be a key witness in the case and, unlike local authority officers, will be personally affected by the result of the proceedings.

The way in which the case is presented, who is called to give evidence, the types of proceedings that are taken and whether proceedings are taken at all or stopped (eg after an initial injunction) are all key decisions which affect the victim and could affect witnesses. Victims of racial harassment should therefore be involved in regular meetings with those responsible for legal action within an authority to decide on the strategies to be adopted at different stages of the proceedings. Wherever possible, s/he should have separate advice and support from voluntary agencies which should also attend such meetings.

Where the authority is to be represented by counsel, the barrister should be involved in such meetings as soon as possible, to ensure that s/he is aware of the discussions that have taken place and the strategies that have been agreed, and so that his or her point of view can be put forward.

4   Liaison with the voluntary sector and support groups

Support groups and other voluntary sector groups can provide considerable assistance during the course of a legal action. They will often have a far better idea of what is happening on the ground and be more closely involved in the local community than the local authority officers. Such groups should therefore be involved in any legal action, if they support the authority's action and are prepared to provide support and assistance to the victims and witnesses. Where appropriate, they should be invited to attend the meetings at which strategies are discussed and developed.

5   Investigation team

One reason why authorities take so few racial harassment cases to court is the difficulty of identifying the perpetrators and of persuading witnesses to give evidence, particularly when witnesses have been rehoused.

In areas where racial harassment is particularly prevalent, authorities might set up investigation teams, which encourage relevant departments to take a more active role in identifying perpetrators. Alternatively, authorities might consider funding a voluntary organisation for this purpose.

6   Publicity

Publicity may be a useful weapon in a campaign against racial harassment and is usually essential if a successful court case result is to be used to deter others from committing racial harassment. Authorities should consider a publicity campaign to coincide with any successful legal action. When doing so they must take into account the following points:

(a) It may not be in the interests of the particular victims for there to be any publicity at all. The victim should be consulted and precautionary measures taken to ensure that there are no adverse effects from publicity (see Chapter 14).

(b) Once a publicity campaign is under way, it may be difficult to stop if the result is unsuccessful. Thus, negative publicity may be created.

(c) The press may present a successful racial harassment case as hounding of the perpetrator by the authority. This is what occurred in one of the first possession cases for racial harassment in Newham.

Authorities should therefore consider these points when developing a publicity campaign and ensure that the staff responsible for such a campaign, and officers or members who might be asked to make statements, have the skills and expertise to gain the maximum benefit from the publicity. Those responsible for public relations should be constantly available to journalists and the media and provide information on a regular basis. This is the only way to outflank any racist organisations that attempt to make use of press and media attention surrounding a racial harassment case.

7 Record-keeping

The importance of making proper records of interviews, conversations, telephone calls and observations is discussed in Chapter 14. Authorities should ensure that all staff who have contact with either victims, potential witnesses or perpetrators in racial harassment cases should keep full records of any conversations, and that officers who observe relevant facts such as physical damage or injuries should make records of such observations.

8 Expert witnesses

The success or failure of many types of legal action involving racial harassment depends on the discretion of the court. Most judges and magistrates know very little about racial harassment or racism. To succeed in such cases it may be necessary to provide an explanation of the background to racial harassment or racism in the area and to explain the purpose behind the authority's racial harassment policy and the importance of achieving a successful result. The effect of racism on the people against whom it is directed should also be explained.

Judges may measure the importance that an authority attaches to a case by the seniority of the witnesses and of those present in court to watch the proceedings. If the case is regarded as important, the director of the relevant service department and the head of the legal department would be present, if not throughout the case, then at least at crucial stages. The director of the department concerned would give evidence to justify the authority's policy and why the remedy being sought is the appropriate one. Presenting a case relying solely on evidence from the same estates officer who gave evidence on the previous twenty cases for rent arrears is unlikely to convince a judge of the importance the authority attaches to racial harassment cases.

Teachers are often ideal witnesses to explain the effect of racism on children whom they see every day. Racial harassment may affect the behaviour of children both in the classroom and the playground. No other professionals are likely to have the same degree of contact with child victims.

Where it is proposed to explain the background and importance of racial harassment, a judge would expect a good expert witness to give evidence. Senior police officers might be the best witnesses to give evidence of racial violence in an area if they have kept adequate records. A senior officer from the Commission for Racial Equality might give evidence about racial harassment nationally, and the difficulties that authorities face in dealing with it, and the importance of success in this case.

Authorities should provide the most senior witness available to give evidence in support of authority policies and should not expect junior staff to do so. They should consider what other professional witnesses should be produced to justify the remedy being sought and the policies adopted. They should never assume an understanding of racism and racial harassment by judges.

B. SUMMARY OF RECOMMENDATIONS

1 That local authorities develop a comprehensive policy for tackling racial harassment using all available legal powers and involving all departments.

2 That authorities consider developing policy under four practical heads. The roles of different departments should be co-ordinated in developing and implementing policies under each of these heads. These four heads to be:
— long-term measures;
— measures to protect individuals in their own homes;
— a package of measures for rehousing;
— action against perpetrators.

3 That the role of the voluntary sector be considered in the development of all policies for tackling racial harassment.

4 That authorities record and monitor rejections of offers of accommodation due to the likelihood of racial harassment.

5 That an officer be responsible for co-ordinating the development of council-wide policy and for the work of all the departments. Co-ordination might be central or on the basis of a "lead department".

6 That the voluntary sector be consulted and involved in the development of policy.

7 That consideration be given to setting up inter-departmental working parties chaired by the officer responsible for co-ordinating policy development.

8 That authorities consider setting up an equivalent committee or sub-committee of members from different standing committees.

9 That voluntary sector representatives be invited to join any such members' committees or sub-committees.

10 That authorities ensure that they have sufficient, suitably qualified staff in their legal department to develop and implement any policy.

11 That the legal department be involved in all policy development.

12 That authorities review the role of their legal department in policy development and ensure that all officers take a broad view of the department's role.

13 That legal departments be alert to developments in the law and their effect on the implementation of local authority policies.

14 That authorities ensure that inter-departmental policies and procedures are developed which identify possible areas of conflict between departments and reduce the likelihood of conflicting objectives to a minimum. In particular, social services and education department officers should not be invited to case conferences discussing legal action against perpetrators if they attend to represent the perpetrators or their families.

15 That authorities ensure that officers recognise the different legal and professional responsibilities of colleagues in other departments.

16 That social services and education authorities widen their consideration of children's interests to consider the interests of the victim's children as well as those of the perpetrator's children when deciding on their approach to cases of racial harassment.

17 That authorities consider what objectives they wish to achieve by legal action against perpetrators.

18 That, in each case, consideration be given to the type of legal action most likely to achieve such objects, and to the possible negative effects of such action.

19 That the objective of deterring would-be perpetrators from committing racial harassment be a secondary objective of legal action. The primary objective should be the needs of the individual victim.

20 That legal action be begun immediately once it has been decided upon, in order to shift the balance of power and put the perpetrator on the defensive.

21 That, once legal proceedings have been commenced, the measures to provide immediate protection for victims and witnesses discussed in Chapters 5, 10 and 14 be considered and used.

22 That the legal department develops procedures for dealing with legal action against perpetrators.

23 That authorities ensure that the legal department is so staffed, trained and organised that lawyers and administrative personnel are available to enable legal action to be commenced at very short notice.

24 That decisions to commence proceedings for the immediate protection of victims be delegated to officers who are readily available at short notice.

25 That authorities obtain and preserve available evidence as soon as possible after incidents of racial harassment.

26 That authorities exmine what advantages are gained by assigning responsibility for tasks relating to court proceedings to departments other than the legal department.

27 That where such tasks are assigned to other departments, adequate training in the law, procedures and practical aspects is provided to all relevant staff.

28 That authorities ensure that legal departments are not asked to advise on the prospects of legal action without adequate information.

29 That special care is taken in the drafting of notices of intention to seek possession in racial harassment cases.

30 That the legal department be responsible for liaising with witnesses and keeping them informed of progress in the case.

31 That victims of racial harassment and any organisations whom they have consulted and who are providing support to them should be involved in regular meetings to discuss strategies in court proceedings, and in particular the type of legal action commenced, the manner in which the case is presented, whether the case should proceed to trial and the type of evidence produced.

32 That if an authority is to be represented by counsel in proceedings, s/he be involved in such meetings at as early a stage as possible.

33 That authorities consider setting up an investigation team or funding a voluntary organisation to assist in the identification of perpetrators.

34 That authorities consider the use of publicity to gain maximum advantage from a successful case but should take into account the potential difficulties that might arise. The first consideration should always be the protection of the individual victims and witnesses from further harassment or intimidation.

35 That officers responsible for publicity campaigns, and officers and members who might be asked to make statements on behalf of the authority, be properly briefed and have the skills to obtain the maximum benefit from any publicity.

36 That officers responsible for public relations be constantly available to journalists and the media, and provide information on a regular basis to prevent racist organisations from taking advantage of press and media attention surrounding racial harassment cases.

37 That all relevant staff be instructed to record any facts that might become relevant in proceedings for racial harassment.

38 That authorities call their most senior officers as witnesses in any proceedings, to underline the importance of the case and to explain the need for their policies, the need for backing from the court and the day-to-day effects of racism.

39 That authorities consider calling other expert witnesses to emphasise the need for support from the court.

40 That presentation of any case involving racial harassment does not assume any knowledge or understanding of racism or racial harassment by the judiciary.

1 *Living in Terror* CRE, 1987. *Racial violence and harassment in local authority housing* Brunel University, Centre for the Study of Community and Race Relations, forthcoming. *Racial harassment on local authority housing estates* The London Race and Housing Forum, 1981.
2 *Living in Terror* CRE, 1987.
3 *R v LB Tower Hamlets ex p Monaf and Others* (1987) 19 HLR 577.

CHAPTER FOURTEEN

Collecting Evidence and Interviewing

The rules governing the admissibility of evidence are explained, together with the implications for the preparation of a case. The chapter describes in detail how to record and preserve evidence and interview witnesses.

A. RULES OF EVIDENCE

In civil cases, plaintiffs must prove their case on the balance of probabilities, ie it must be more likely than not that what the plaintiff claims happened did actually happen.

In criminal cases, the prosecution must prove all the requirements of the offence beyond reasonable doubt, ie the court must be sure that the defendant committed the crime. Where the offence requires proof of intention or motive this, too, must be proved beyond reasonable doubt. It is therefore much easier to discharge the burden of proof in a civil case than in a criminal case. In addition, the rules of evidence are less strict in civil proceedings.

It is of paramount importance that evidence is collected and information recorded at the earliest possible time, thereby substantially increasing the prospects of success in any civil or criminal case. Only those rules of evidence considered of most relevance to racial harassment cases are discussed. The rules are illustrated by reference to an example which is given in Appendix 3. It is assumed that all the witnesses listed are happy to give evidence.

Many of the rules of evidence are the same for both civil and criminal courts though certain rules differ. Here, under each heading, the rules that are common are considered first, followed by those that are specific to civil cases and ending with those that apply only to criminal proceedings.

Types of evidence and requirements for their use

1   Oral evidence (civil and criminal)

The most important type of evidence is oral evidence, ie the witness taking the oath and stating from the witness box what happened. Oral evidence may be of direct experiences, for example, what the witness saw (eg, "I saw excrement smeared on the door"), what the witness felt or feels (eg "I am too frightened to go out of the front of the flats in case someone drops something on me"), sounds the witness heard (eg, "I heard a loud smash and a milk bottle had landed a few yards away"), or what the witness said (eg, "I warned A and his mother that they would be evicted if any further acts of racial harassment occurred"). Oral evidence cannot always be given of what other people have said because of the hearsay rule.

2 The hearsay rule (civil and criminal)

A witness, X, cannot usually repeat what Y has said if the words are reported to prove that what Y said was true. Thus, any statement which X could begin with "It must be true because Y told me . . ." will be hearsay. The purpose of the hearsay rule is to prevent the use of second-hand evidence which is considered less reliable. Only direct evidence is allowed, so Y must attend court and give evidence of what s/he saw or did.

> **Example**: *Mrs C cannot give evidence of what F told her about issuing A and his mother with a warning. Mrs C would effectively be saying "It must be true that F issued a warning because she told me she had". F must attend court and give direct evidence of the warning she gave A.*

Similarly, it is not usually possible to produce a written document as evidence to prove that what is written in it is true.

> **Example**: *Mrs C could not produce a letter or statement she had obtained from a neighbour which said it was A who threw the brick through the window. She would be saying "It must be true because it is written in this letter . . ."*
>
> *The neighbour would have to come to court to give direct evidence.*

3 Situations where the hearsay rule does not apply

There are certain important circumstances where the hearsay rule does not apply. Eleven are relevant for our purposes.

Reported words or a written document, produced to show the intention of the perpetrator or the effect on the person hearing the words (civil and criminal)
These are admissible because the evidence is not hearsay.

> **Example**: *Mrs C: "The letter said, 'If I see you on this block again you will get more than bruises'."*
>
> *Mrs C can produce the letter itself as written evidence.*

This statement and the letter are being produced in evidence to prove the harassment, nuisance or annoyance, namely the effect on Mrs C and her family and the intention of the perpetrator. It is not repeated by Mrs C in order to show the truth of the statement, ie that the family will get more than bruises next time.

The rules of evidence generally require the original of every document to be produced. A copy can be used in civil proceedings if:
— the defendant agrees (which will usually occur if the validity of the letter is not challenged); or

— a notice called a "notice to produce" the original document is served on the defendant who fails to produce the original at court.

Because words reported to show the intention of the perpetrator or effect on the victim are not hearsay, words spoken by others will be allowed to be repeated on a charge of threatening words or behaviour or incitement to racial hatred. Whether the threats are true will not be relevant. It is the effect of the words that is the important constituent of the offence in each case.

To show that a witness has been consistent and has not just made up his or her story a short while before (civil and criminal)
If a witness is accused of making up a story a short time ago, then anyone to whom the witness has recounted the story may be able to give evidence that the witness has been consistent.

> **Example**: *The possession action gets to trial in six months and L gives evidence of the assault on herself. She is accused of making the story up weeks after the assault occurred. Her mother can give evidence that she complained about the assault only minutes after it happened.*
>
> *If the council solicitor or housing officer interviewed L on the day after the assault, the council officer can also give evidence of what L said in her interview.*

Statements by a victim spontaneously after an attack (civil and criminal)
Generally, if a victim X tells Y that he was attacked by Z, Y cannot give evidence of what X had said. However, Y can give evidence of what X has said if X does so "in conditions that are sufficiently spontaneous and sufficiently coterminous with the event to preclude the possibility of concoction or distortion".[1] To be sufficiently spontaneous, the words have to be so closely associated with the event which excites the statement that the victim's mind is still dominated by the event.

> **Example**: *Mrs C:* "*My daughter L came running upstairs and told me A had dropped a milk bottle on her. She was distraught.*"

It is up to the court to decide whether these statements are sufficiently spontaneous. If Mrs C can repeat the statement made to her by her daughter this may avoid any need for the daughter herself to give evidence. Statements made to the police some time after an attack have been considered sufficiently spontaneous.[2]

Written business records (civil and criminal)
Records made by local authority officers can be produced in evidence in certain circumstances, provided that the person who originally supplied the information in the records had personal knowledge of the information.[3]

If the person who supplied the information is available to give evidence the records cannot be produced, but if s/he is unavailable for specified reasons then the record can be used. The most important specified reasons are that the person is dead, abroad, is unfit to attend due to physical or mental condition, cannot be identified with reasonable diligence, cannot be found with reasonable diligence or cannot reasonably be expected to recollect the circumstances recorded.[4]

Example: *F's written notes can be produced of what she did, heard or saw if she is away on holiday, abroad at the time of the hearing or has moved jobs and no one knows where she has gone.*

Example: *Suppose it is important to obtain evidence from the housing works department of the date a window was repaired. The operative will not remember; s/he probably repairs 10–20 windows each week. The authority's records can be produced of the date the work was carried out.*

If local authority officers are instructed to take details of incidents or complaints from victims and other witnesses and to keep records of these interviews, the interview record itself may be used in evidence if the original witness is unavailable for one of the specified reasons.

Example: *F is instructed to take statements from witnesses. She interviews N and makes a note of what she said. This is kept in the file. N dies shortly afterwards. The record of the interview can be used as written evidence.*

Civil court rules require special notices to be served on the other party before business records can be used under this provision in civil cases.

Admissions (civil only)
An admission is a statement made by a party to court proceedings or some other person who is on the same side which is against that person's interest.

Example: *Mrs A: "I know he knocked over and kicked N the other day but he was only messing about."*

This statement is an admission by Mrs A that A assaulted N. She is on the same side as A and the admission can be used in proceedings against Mrs A or in civil proceedings against A.

Statements of unavailable witnesses (civil only)
Written statements of any witnesses can be used in evidence in civil proceedings if the other party agrees. There is no formal process to follow. In addition, such statements may be used if the witness who made the statement is unavailable for the same specified reasons as above.[5] Notice that if the statement is to be used it must be served on the other party not more than 21 days after the trial date is fixed.

Example: *P meets F on the landing. She tells F that she found N lying on the ground and took her home. She also says she saw A leaving the block shortly before she found N. F takes a written statement from P.*

Suppose P dies, moves away and cannot be traced or goes senile. Her statement to F can be used in evidence. She may be an elderly person with a lapsing memory. When the case comes to trial she cannot remember what happened.

Example: *P meets F on the landing and tells her the same as above. F fails to ask P's name. It turns out that P does not live on the estate and no one knows where she lives. Her oral statement to F can be allowed in evidence because P cannot be identified.*

A statement produced under this provision may not be given as much weight by the court as evidence from someone who attends and is cross-examined but the procedure is only used where the alternative is to lose the evidence altogether.

Computer records (civil only)[6]

Computer records are unlikely to be as useful in racial harassment cases as they are in rent arrears cases. However, one important circumstance where computer records might be crucial is to prove that a tenant has been served with a notice of variation of tenancy. If its computer records are to be used in evidence an authority will have to show:
— that the computer has been operating properly throughout the relevant period or that defects did not affect its accuracy;
— that the computer was regularly used to store and process information by the authority of a similar nature to the record to be used in evidence;
— that the computer was regularly given the information it required to produce the record to be used in evidence;
— that the record to be produced in evidence has been derived from information provided to the computer.

Example: *Suppose the authority wished to show that Mrs A had been served with a notice of variation of tenancy on 1 January 1987. Notices were printed by the computer and posted. The computer can confirm that it was instructed to send notices to all existing tenants at 1/1/87 and that Mrs A was a tenant at that time. It deduces that it sent her a notice and produces a written statement to that effect. This statement can be used as evidence of service of the notice.*

The court rules require special notices to be served on the other party before computer records can be used under this provision.

Affidavits and affirmations (civil only)[7]

An affidavit is a written statement made under oath on the Bible, Koran or equivalent for other religions. An affirmation is a written statement containing a declaration as to its truth and can be made by a person of any religion or who has no religious beliefs. Affirmations are allowed in evidence in the same circumstances as affidavits. Both affirmations and affidavits have to be signed and declared or sworn in the presence either of a solicitor or an authorised court officer.

Affidavits and affirmations are primarily used in evidence in interlocutory proceedings. For our purposes, this means they are used for any application for an interlocutory injunction. The general rule is that affidavits must contain only information that a person can confirm from his or her own personal knowledge and which the rules of evidence would allow that person to state in evidence from the witness box. However, affidavits in interlocutory proceedings can contain statements made "to the best of a person's knowledge or belief", provided the source of information is disclosed.

> **Example**: *In an application for an interlocutory injunction F could provide an affidavit saying that she believed that A assaulted L and N because the girls told her so and as far as she knew they had no reason to lie.*
>
> *F could not give evidence of this belief at the final hearing but may do so at the interlocutory hearing.*

Evidence of belief is not as reliable as direct evidence of observations and experiences. For this reason, if time permits, it is preferable to produce affidavits from those with direct experience wherever possible.

Confessions (criminal only)
If the words were spoken by the person being prosecuted and amount to a confession then a witness can give evidence of what was said.

> **Example**: *F: "I saw A the day after the incident. I asked him why he had beaten up Mr C and what he had against Mr C's family. A smiled and said 'We've got our reasons. You'd better find him somewhere else to live pretty quick.'"*

Although the words do not amount to a direct confession, A does not deny the attack, and the smile and subsequent words can certainly be taken by the court to amount to a confession.

Written statements accepted by the defence (criminal only)
To be allowed in evidence, statements by witnesses must:
— be signed by the person who made the statement;
— contain a declaration in the form beginning the statement in Appendix 3, Document 3;
— be served on the defendant with a notice stating that it is proposed to use it in evidence.[8]

If the defence agrees the use of the statement or does not object within seven days, the statement can be used as evidence unless the court decides otherwise. In practice, using the statement will require the agreement of the defence.

Committal proceedings are usually carried out by considering the written statements only. These must also be in the form shown in Appendix 3, Document 3. Therefore, all statements for use in criminal proceedings should be produced in the standard form shown in Document 3. For this reason this form is always used by the police in their witness statements.

Example: *Document 3 shows Mr C's statement in the necessary form for use in evidence. In practice, the defence will not allow his statement to be used because it could not agree the contents without A pleading guilty to the charges.*

The defence may agree to allow written statements by G, H, I, Dr J, and K because these do not identify A and contain only background information.

Depositions from child witnesses (criminal only)[9]
To avoid child witnesses (for these purposes under 17) having to appear in person and give evidence at committal proceedings, evidence can be taken from them independently of the committal hearing, by a magistrate. The written statement taken is known as a deposition. This rule only applies to some offences. The relevant ones for our purposes are any offences involving physical injury to the child, eg common assault or assault occasioning actual bodily harm.

Before depositions are allowed, the magistrate must be satisfied "that attendance in court would involve serious danger to [the child's] life or health".[10] This danger must be proved by evidence from a doctor. The meaning of "serious danger" will be a matter for the court. In these circumstances, depositions taken from children can be used in evidence in criminal proceedings provided the defence has had an opportunity to cross-examine the child.[11] The cross-examination will take place before the magistrate who is taking the deposition.

4 Real evidence (civil and criminal)

Real evidence includes material objects, people's appearance, eg the look of hatred on A's face as he looks at Mr C in court, the bruises on Mr C's face, the look of fear on L's face as she gives evidence in court, the site of the incident if inspected by the court, and fingerprints.

5 Evidence of criminal convictions (civil only)[12]

If the defendant or a member of the defendant's family has been convicted of a criminal offence and the same incident forms part of the authority's claim for possession, the authority can produce evidence of the conviction which will usually be an extract from the register of the appropriate court. If an authority proposes to rely on a conviction, this should be stated in the particulars of claim.

6 Previous harassment by the perpetrator (criminal only)

As a general rule, no evidence can be given of previous criminal offences or harassment by the perpetrator. This is because the evidence is considered to prejudice a fair trial on the incidents for which s/he is charged. However, evidence can be allowed if it shows a similarity or uniqueness of conduct.[13]

This will be true in many cases of racial harassment so the exception may be extremely important.

Example: *It is possible that evidence of the two previous assaults on Mr C's daughters would be allowed if the circumstances surrounding those assaults show them to be part of a general campaign to drive the family off the estate.*

One of the major advantages of prosecuting for an offence under the Protection from Eviction Act 1977 is that all the incidents of harassment against the same household form part of the single offence and so evidence relating to the whole campaign is relevant and can be produced. See Appendix 3.

7 Other evidence (civil and criminal)

Sound recording, photographs or videos
These are evidence, provided that someone can verify when they were made or taken and in what circumstances.

Example: *Mrs C can produce a photograph she took of her daughter's bruises and of the broken window.*

Plans
A plan of a site may be produced in evidence. However, such a plan must not include any comments or markings to show the position of the various parties or their movements during an incident. The plan must merely show the fixed physical objects.

Example: *Mrs C can produce a plan she has drawn. However, if she shows on her plan the spot at which L was attacked her plan will not be allowed in evidence. L can use the plan in court to describe where she was standing when the bottle fell.*

Children as witnesses

1 In civil proceedings

Children can give evidence in civil proceedings if the court considers that they understand the nature and consequences of an oath. In contrast to the rules in criminal proceedings, children cannot give evidence without taking an oath or affirming. The desirability of calling children to give evidence is considered below.

2 In criminal proceedings[14]

Children can give evidence in criminal proceedings if the court considers that they understand the duty of speaking the truth and are sufficiently intelligent to justify the use of their evidence.

Generally, children must take an oath to tell the truth just like an adult, unless the court considers that they are too young to understand the meaning of an oath. In that case, they may give evidence without taking an oath. A special rule applies to the evidence of children who have not taken an oath. Their evidence must be backed up by some other, independent evidence which shows that what they are saying is more likely to be true. This other evidence is known as "corroboration".

Witnesses using notes when giving evidence (civil and criminal)

A witness may refresh his or her memory from notes when giving evidence in certain circumstances. The notes must have been made at a time when the events were still fresh in his or her memory. If the notes were not made by the witness, they must have been made under his or her supervision or have been read to him or her at the time s/he had a recollection of the facts.

> **Example:** *If Mrs C made notes of what happened shortly after her daughter L ran home crying, she could refresh her memory from these notes when giving evidence.*
>
> *If Mrs C did not make notes but recounted the story to F the following morning, and she wrote down her exact words or read back what she had written and Mrs C agreed it, it is possible that the court might allow Mrs C to use F's notes to refresh her memory when giving evidence.*
>
> *F can certainly use her notes of what she saw and heard to refresh her own memory if made at the time.*

Practical points on evidence

1 Choice of witnesses and type of evidence to be produced

There are many factors to be considered when deciding how to prove a case.

Proving the legal requirements
A decision about which evidence to use requires consideration of the facts that need to be proved as a matter of law to obtain the remedy sought. In possession proceedings, ,,,this will often be (a) that X has committed a nuisance or annoyance to neighbours and (b) that it is reasonable to order possession. Thus, it is necessary to decide what factors are likely to make a judge order possession.

Anticipating the defence
It is also advisable to consider what defence is likely to be raised and the facts that may need to be proved to defeat any such defence.

For example, in possession proceedings this will involve consideration of the arguments that the defendant is likely to try to use to dissuade a judge from ordering possession. Evidence will then be needed to support the authority's arguments as to why the defence should not succeed. Some factors that will be relevant in possession proceedings are suggested on p65.

Collecting all the evidence
Part C below deals with interviewing witnesses and recording information. Evidence should be collected as shortly as possible after each of the events that is being relied upon in the proceedings. Some evidence will disappear. Memories will fade. Witnesses may move and become impossible to trace. In most cases, the authority should have a good idea what evidence is available before proceedings are begun or, at least, very shortly afterwards.

A party is not obliged to call all the evidence it possesses. In particular, it has no obligation to produce evidence that will help the other side, although it must not dishonestly conceal such evidence either.

It is advisable to collect all the evidence available at an early stage even if it is decided later not to use it. For example, a child witness should be interviewed even though s/he may not be called for other reasons. If no statement is taken from the child, s/he may have forgotten some crucial facts if it is decided to call him or her as a witness at a trial several months later.

Deciding which evidence to use
This may be a very difficult decision to make. Whether or not a witness should be called will depend on, among other things, whether:
— there is an alternative method of proving what the witness was going to say;
— the evidence of the witness is crucial to winning the case;
— the court is likely to believe the witness;
— the witness will give useful evidence;
— the witness will be so intimidated by the court hearing that s/he will forget his or her evidence;
— the witness's memory is reliable;
— the witness is able to communicate satisfactorily what s/he is trying to say;
— the witness should be put through the ordeal of giving evidence;
— the witness is at risk of intimidation after giving evidence;
— the court will be assisted by having the evidence repeated, where one witness duplicates evidence given by another;
— it is considered desirable to call a child as a witness so as to avoid press publicity (see p253 below).
Some of these points will be considered in turn.

(a) *Alternative method of proof* Often the decision whether or not to call a particular witness will depend on whether there is some alternative method of proof. Other methods of proof might include:

— another witness who is preferable for other reasons, eg an adult rather than a child or a witness who has made a record rather than one who is relying on memory alone;
— a written statement which may be admissible;
— an affidavit which might be accepted by the defence (in practice, the defence will not accept affidavits unless it accepts the evidence contained in them);
— written or photographic evidence.

(b) *Whether the evidence of the witness is crucial to winning the case* In possession cases it is often difficult to predict whether a particular witness is crucial. For example, no one factor need necessarily be crucial to prove that it is reasonable for a possession order to be made, but each factor supporting the reasonableness of the order will strengthen the case. Leaving out any one factor by deciding not to call evidence may be fatal.

Whether the risk of deciding not to call all the available evidence is worth taking, will depend on the weight of the other factors. Where the incident is minor, other factors such as protecting a child from the court ordeal may be more important.

(c) *Whether the court is likely to believe the witness* Only a person who has personally interviewed a witness can give an opinion as to whether s/he is likely to be believed. As explained in part C below, an interview of a witness for court proceedings will usually involve a degree of cross-examination. This is because the witness will be cross-examined in court and the story needs to be tested properly before it is decided whether to call the witness at all.

In general, if the person who interviews a witness for the authority does not believe the witness, it is unlikely that the witness will be believed in court. However, it is important to be alert to the possibility that the interviewer him or herself is affected by personal prejudices when forming a view of the reliability of a particular witness.

The court may not believe a witness for all sorts of reasons, all entirely subjective. What counts in the end is the opinion of the judge, magistrates or judge and jury hearing the case. Witnesses who exaggerate or who contradict themselves during an interview, or change their story, may not be believed.

Witnesses who have recorded facts shortly after incidents and repeated them to others, eg housing officers or solicitors, are more likely to be believed, since there will be less opportunity for them to concoct their story.

(d) *Whether the witness will be so intimidated by the court hearing that s/he will forget his or her evidence* This must be recognised as a factor. It can be overcome if a witness makes an immediate record of incidents as they occur. In that way, even if the memory fails standing in the witness box, there is a written note to assist (see part C below).

(e) *The reliability of a witness's memory* People's memories vary considerably. Many people are vague about times and dates. In court, the inability to remember these minor details can often cast doubt on the more important facts. This factor can also be overcome by proper record keeping by all witnesses.

(f) *How well the witness is able to communicate what s/he is trying to say* Where the first language of a witness is not English, s/he should be able to give evidence through an interpreter (see below).

Even where a witness does speak English, not everyone is equally capable of expressing his or her meaning. To give evidence well requires ability to understand what factors are relevant and the purpose behind the questions being asked, and an accurate memory. If the witness is not capable of this, his or her evidence will often be presented in an illogical and confusing fashion and may be less useful. A good witness needs to be able to perceive the purpose behind the questions being asked by the defence advocate in cross-examination and to have sufficient confidence to be able to correct misleading impressions that his or her answers may be giving.

People who may have no difficulty in expressing themselves in day-to-day life may find the court atmosphere sufficiently intimidating to become incomprehensible and confused. Remember that giving evidence is a form of public speaking which few people have experienced before.

(g) *Whether the witness should be put through the ordeal of giving evidence in court* Giving evidence will involve reliving experiences that may be extremely distressing or even damaging to a witness in a racial harassment case. The witness will usually have to face the perpetrator in court in addition to having to undergo the strain and anxiety of giving evidence in the intimidating formality of a court room.

The stresses of giving evidence, likely to be suffered by a particular witness, will have to be balanced against other factors such as the availability of alternative evidence and the need to prove particular facts to win with the case (see (a) and (b) above). All these factors will need to be discussed with the witness at the earliest possible stage in the proceedings.

Giving evidence is far worse for a person who is unreliable or confused or whose memory is poor than it is for a good witness. These are the witnesses who will be heavily cross-examined and may be made to look inadequate or stupid. The judge may even state when giving judgment that s/he does not believe the witness's evidence. It is therefore in the interests of the witness, as well as the authority, that the individual is properly tested before s/he comes to give evidence.

(h) *Whether the witness is at risk of intimidation after giving evidence* Many witnesses in racial harassment cases will be at risk of intimidation after giving evidence. Measures to protect witnesses are considered below.

Professional witnesses who are employees of the authority are far less likely to risk intimidation. It will therefore be preferable to call a professional witness rather than a victim when the evidence they can give is the same.

(i) Whether a witness repeats evidence given by another At the beginning of a case it is difficult to say whether evidence that repeats that of other witnesses will be useful.

> **Example:** *Suppose four people are walking home and are attacked. Each may be able to give evidence. If one gives evidence and the defence does not seriously challenge that person's evidence, there is probably little point in calling the other three witnesses. On the other hand, if the defence accuses the witness of lying, the other three witnesses can be called to back up the story.*

2   Evidence from witnesses who cannot give evidence in English

The general rule is that witnesses who are able to should give evidence in English. Where a witness does not speak English or does so only very little, s/he must give evidence through an interpreter.

A difficult point may arise where a witness speaks English but does not feel at ease in the language and finds it difficult to express him or herself adequately in English. In those circumstances the court should also allow an interpreter to be used. A relevant factor in possession proceedings for racial harassment is the genuine fears and anguish of the victims. These feelings may be difficult to explain for someone whose first language is not English and it is very important that the feelings come across. Often the only way in which this can be done is by using an interpreter.

Who can interpret?
A person used as an interpreter in a court must take an oath to interpret accurately. The requirements for an interpreter are as follows:
— s/he must be able to speak English fluently;
— s/he must be able to speak the language of the witness fluently including any relevant dialect;
— wherever possible, s/he should have had experience of interpreting in court before;
— s/he must be independent of any party to the proceedings.
From this last point it will be apparent that a local authority employee or relative of a witness cannot interpret in court proceedings.

The interpreter must be sufficiently fluent to be able to intrepret the exact words used in a question and the exact words and expressions of a witness in reply. S/he must not translate the meaning into his or her own expressions.

Precise interpretation may be crucial. Let us look at an example.

> **Example:** *Question from advocate: "Was the defendant in the vicinity?"*
> *Translation to witness: "Was the defendant next to you?"*
> *Answer from witness: "No".*
> *Translation to judge: "No".*

The witness heard a question and gave an honest reply. The judge heard a reply to the original question asked by the advocate which was different from the question heard by the witness. No one except the interpreter knows that there was a slight difference in the question which might have affected the answer.

Where an interpreter is not sufficiently fluent, the witness is likely to come across as either lying or confused and therefore unreliable.

Presenting the evidence
Evidence through an interpreter takes far longer than evidence in English. It is important that sufficient court time is allowed. If it is not, the judge may get impatient and it may be the witness who unjustifiably gets the blame.

It is important that a witness understands that s/he must not enter into a dialogue with the interpreter while in the witness box. The witness may ask the interpreter to explain a question s/he does not understand. This request for information should be retranslated back to the questioner. The interpreter should not be told anything by the witness which is not translated to the court. Witnesses must be advised of this before giving evidence. If a witness and an interpreter do enter into a dialogue in the witness box this will seriously undermine the evidence being given. The judge is unlikely to understand the exchange and may conclude that the witness is asking for guidance from the interpreter or that the interpreter is not accurately translating what is being said.

Interviewing witnesses
Witnesses who need an interpreter to give evidence, have also to be interviewed, and the same points can be made about the importance of accurate interpreting, as it is necessary to test the reliability of the evidence and its relevance and usefulness. Interviewing can be done using an authority employee. Wherever possible, family members should be avoided as they inevitably add their own recollections to those of the witness for whom they are interpreting.

Interpreters who will be used at court should always meet the witnesses before the hearing to ensure that the witness and the authority are happy with the interpreter's ability to translate. If an interpreter is used for preliminary interviews with witnesses, his or her impartiality may be challenged, since there will be some risk that s/he will translate answers based on what was said at a previous interview rather than the answer given in court. There is no clear rule as to the degree to which the practice may be allowed, since the decision whether the interpreter is sufficiently impartial is a matter for the judge at the trial. To some extent, the degree of risk will depend on the experience of the interpreter. The use of the same interpreter at a preliminary interview should therefore be avoided, if possible, though it must be borne in mind that some authorities will have no other way of carrying out an interview.

3 Protection and assistance for witnesses

Practical measures
Chapter 6 sections B and C contain examples of measures that can be taken to protect victims, including assistance with rehousing and physical security measures in the home. All these measures should be considered for lay witnesses in racial harassment cases who may become victims in the future.

In addition, special measures may be necessary. These might include:
— having emergency accommodation available at the time of the trial;
— providing transport and an escort to and from court;
— obtaining secure waiting space at court to allow the authority's witnesses and the perpetrators to wait separately;
— providing escorts at lunch time and adjournments;
— providing a child care service for children of witnesses;
— increasing security on the estate during the period of the trial;
— providing premises for a support group in close proximity to witnesses' homes.

When the trial is completed, the need for protection of witnesses will not cease. If the case is unsuccessful, the need will increase substantially and rehousing may be necessary.

Protection by the court
The court has various powers to protect witnesses.

(a) *Interlocutory injunction* A court will grant an interlocutory injunction preventing the intimidation of a witness.

(b) *Committal for contempt of court* It is a contempt of court to intimidate a witness both before s/he gives evidence and after.[15] No injunction is necessary. Perpetrators can therefore be warned that any harassment of witnesses will lead to an application for their committal to prison for contempt.

(c) *Perpetual injunction* It is not clear whether the court's powers extend to issuing a perpetual injunction to protect a witness when it is likely that intimidation will take place after the trial. Since the court can commit for contempt, it would seem logical that it does have power to protect a witness by injunction.

(d) *Allowing witnesses to leave addresses out of affidavits* The court rules state that unless the court orders otherwise every affidavit must state the place of residence of a witness.[16] This implies that the court has power to allow a witness, giving evidence by affidavit, to withhold his or her address in an appropriate case.

In some courts, it is the practice to require a separate affidavit to be prepared which sets out the reasons why the witness wishes to withhold his or her address. This point is then considered separately by the judge before the other affidavit is admitted as evidence. This power will be useful in injunction proceedings where evidence is provided by affidavit. The court's permission will be needed at the commencement of the hearing before the affidavit is used.

It will be appropriate to use this power where the victim has been rehoused and does not want the perpetrator to know his or her new address, or where a witness is unknown to the perpetrator.

The reason why witnesses are usually required to give their address is so that they can be clearly identified. It is therefore important that the affidavit provides other details of identification to substitute for omitting the address. For example, a victim's affidavit should state the address s/he previously lived at.

A witness is unlikely to be allowed to omit the address if it is crucial to his or her evidence. For example, a witness who saw an attack from his or her bedroom window will have to disclose the address since the defendant needs to know how good the view was etc, in order to ask appropriate questions to challenge the evidence.

(e) *Allowing witnesses giving oral evidence to omit their address* There is no provision in the court rules requiring witnesses to give their address. However, as explained above, witnesses must sufficiently identify themselves to the court. Courts have power to regulate their own procedure so far as this is necessary in the interests of the administration of justice.[17] This should give a court power to allow a witness to withhold his or her address from the other party in appropriate circumstances.[18] In domestic violence cases, courts may allow parties to withhold their address and this practice should be extended to racial harassment cases where a witness has a genuine and reasonable fear of intimidation if his or her address is disclosed. The witness will usually be asked to write his or her address on a piece of paper and hand it to the judge. The defendant will not see the address. See (d) above for the circumstances in which this power might be available.

(f) *Banning publication of name or address* Even if the court has no power to allow a witness to withhold his or her address, it does have power to allow the witness to provide the name and address only to the court and the defendant, without announcing it publicly in evidence.[19] The court can then ban newspapers from publishing any information which would lead to the witness being identified.[20] Although it will usually be the perpetrator from whom a witness wishes to keep his or her address, there may be circumstances where the threat of intimidation or attack comes from local racist groups which might discover the name and address of a witness from the local newspapers. In such a case, this provision might be useful.

(g) *Protection of child witnesses* Whatever its other powers, a court definitely has power to direct that no newspaper report reveals the name, address, school or other information which will enable a witness under 17 to be identified.[21]

Where a child giving evidence is a member of the victim's family, this will mean that the whole family gains protection from publicity if the child gives evidence, since any identification of a member of the family is likely to lead to identification of the child. This may be a relevant factor when considering whether to call a child as a witness. In addition, the court definitely has power to order that the court should be cleared of members of the public while a child under 17 is giving evidence. Only the parties, court officials and bona fide press reporters are allowed to remain.[22]

(h) *Sitting in camera* The general rule is that court proceedings are held in public. However, it appears that the court has power to decide to sit in camera (ie behind closed doors) if this is necessary in the due administration of justice.[23] Where the court sits in camera the press will be excluded as well as the public. Only the parties, court officials and the witness giving evidence will be present in court.

Assistance and encouragement to witnesses
The prospect of giving evidence is daunting. When it is compounded by the fear of intimidation, both before and afterwards, it may be overwhelming. The reasonable and genuine fears of witnesses can be partially allayed by making use of the measures described above. However, in addition, it is absolutely crucial to consider the following points.

(a) *Explaining the court procedure and layout* Most witnesses have never been to court before. It is important that they understand who the personnel are, where they will sit or stand, and how the hearing will proceed.

(b) *Preparing the witness for cross-examination* As explained in part C below, a good interview will involve a degree of cross-examination. Some pressure must be exerted on the witness in order to test the reliability of the evidence. The ability to do this without leaving the witness feeling humiliated or hostile is one of the major skills of interviewing. Too much pressure leads the witness to think that the interviewer is on the opposite side. Too little pressure, and the story is not properly tested. Once in the witness box, under real cross-examination, the story may fall apart and the witness made to look dishonest or a fool.

It is in the interests of the witness that s/he is tested before the trial. A witness who cannot remember events without prompting, eg from a member of the family, will not perform well in the witness box and should not be called if this can be avoided. The statement of a witness should be believable and rational. If the interviewer does not think it is, the judge is unlikely to. Inexperienced interviewers are often reluctant to tell a witness that what s/he is saying cannot be correct or to point out that the witness has contradicated him or herself or changed the story. This is a big mistake, for these points will certainly be put to the witness in court.

Witnesses will accept a greater degree of pressure from a person they know and trust than from a person they have just met. For this reason, it is advisable that the same person carries out all interviews and deals with the case, so that the witnesses can gain confidence in that person.

(c) *Getting results* One of the quickest ways to gain a person's confidence is to achieve results. An authority which says it will obtain an injunction within a few days, and does so, is more likely to find its witnesses turning up at court than an authority which fails to get an application into court at all.

(d) *Keeping witnesses informed* A month or two months may not seem long to lawyers or others who are regularly involved in court proceedings. For a witness, the prospect of giving evidence may be constantly on his or her mind. Anxiety makes time drag, nothing appears to be happening, and perhaps the racial harassment is continuing.

It is essential that the person dealing with the case maintains regular contact with the witness. If that person is a lawyer in the legal department s/he must be the one who keeps witnesses informed on progress. Second- or third-hand information, or contact with a housing officer who knows nothing because s/he has not been kept informed by the legal department, will reduce the confidence that the witness has in the authority and reduce the chances of that witness appearing in court. The more daunted, intimidated or frightened the witness, the more frequent the contact that is necessary.

(e) *Choosing witnesses* It is those witnesses whose evidence is least reliable or most confused who will receive the hardest treatment in cross-examination in court. In addition, judges are sometimes rude to or irritable with witnesses whom they do not believe or who have difficulty expressing themselves. Judges may also state in their judgments that they do not believe the evidence of a particular witness. This kind of treatment can be very hurtful and distressing. It may therefore not be in the interests of a witness to be called to give evidence.

Legal protection for witnesses by other court proceedings
The legal measures described in this book for the protection of victims can also be used for the protection of witnesses. For example, a criminal prosecution and the imposition of bail conditions protecting witnesses or the use of separate proceedings to obtain a perpetual injunction might be considered.

4 Children

Several of the factors relating to the choice of witnesses will have special relevance to children, particularly the need to protect children from the ordeal of court proceedings. It is, however, worth considering two points. First, if the evidence of a child is necessary for the case to succeed, the child's interests may be more damaged by a failed case than by having to give evidence. Second, evidence from a child can be extremely effective because a judge may be more likely to believe an innocent child.

5 Summonsing witnesses

A party to court proceedings can obtain a witness summons requiring any witness to attend who has relevant evidence to give. Once present, a witness must answer questions truthfully or s/he commits perjury.

In practice, it will rarely, if ever, be wise to force a lay witness to attend, since witnesses who are forced to attend unwillingly, frequently do not give the answers that are expected from them. Provided an authority has shown that it can achieve results and has considered and discussed the other measures described above, a witness summons should not be necessary. One effective way of helping to ensure that a witness attends on the hearing date is to offer him or her a lift to court and to arrive half an hour earlier than expected to help calm the nerves.

6 Preventing witnesses attending

The defendant can witness summons any person who has relevant evidence to give. This may include the family's social worker, school teacher or other local authority employee. It is a contempt of court either to prevent a person attending court who has been witness summonsed or to punish a witness for attending court.[24] A social worker employed by the landlord local authority who has been witness summonsed is obliged to attend and answer questions truthfully. Any attempt to discipline the social worker for giving evidence will be a contempt and the officers responsible could be committed to prison.

7 Witness expenses

Local authorities may compensate witnesses for attending court. As a matter of good practice they should certainly pay travel expenses and the cost of subsistence. Travel should be by taxi where this is necessary for the protection of the witness. Witnesses who are in work may lose pay or be forced to take annual leave. As a matter of good practice they should therefore be compensated for each day on which they attend.

Witnesses who are forced to attend by witness summons are entitled to be paid travel expenses in advance.

B. RECORDING AND PRESERVING EVIDENCE

Keeping notes of incidents and observations

Part A dealt with the rules of evidence in civil and criminal proceedings. These show how important it is for local authority employees, victims of racial harassment and other lay witnesses and representatives of community groups to keep full and accurate notes of every relevant thing that takes place. In civil proceedings this is important for the following reasons (in criminal proceedings similar reasons apply):

(a) where a note is made while events are fresh in a person's mind these notes can be referred to in court to refresh the memory. This can substantially improve the quality of evidence given;
(b) notes of conversations with the perpetrator may provide evidence of admissions;
(c) notes of conversations with witnesses may subsequently be used to show that the witness has been consistent;
(d) if a comment made by a witness is noted down, a written statement can be submitted if the witness subsequently dies, goes abroad or cannot be traced;
(e) evidence can sometimes be given of statements made by victims immediately after an attack in which they might identify those responsible;
(f) evidence can be given of a person's observation of real evidence such as racist graffiti, broken windows, a weapon, bruising or blood-staining.

The greater the detail of records, the less likelihood there is of memories failing in the witness box and crucial facts being lost. The more evidence that can be provided by local authority employees or representatives of tenants' associations or community groups using their notes, the less burden will fall on other witnesses and victims to recall what occurred.

1 The form of notes

There is no essential form in which notes should be made; a note on the back of an envelope will suffice if nothing else is to hand. To act as a useful reminder and to assist with filing, authorities might provide pre-printed forms for notes. These might be in a format along the lines of Appendix 8.

This form can be provided in languages other than English. There is no obligation for the records to be in English. They are only for the use of the person who kept them.

2 Safe-keeping of notes

Authorities must adopt some system for safe-keeping of records. A note on the back of an envelope is of no use unless someone keeps the envelope and is able to produce it at the appropriate time.

3 Use of notes

In some cases, it may be possible to make use of notes to provide a written statement to the court. More often, the person who made the note will have to give oral evidence in the witness box. The original note must be given to the witness so s/he can refresh his or her memory.

4 What to record

Unfortunately, it is impossible to predict what evidence might eventually be needed in a racial harassment case. However, certain ground rules for recording information can be made for guidance.

All conversations with potential perpetrators should be recorded in full. Where possible the exact words used should be noted. This should preferably be done while the conversation is in progress, but if this is not possible, it should be recorded immediately afterwards while events are still fresh in the mind. A note should then be made of how long after the conversation the note was made.

All conversations with potential witnesses should be recorded even if the witnesses say they do not want to attend court, and, where it is known that damage or injury has been sustained, attempts should be made to make direct observations and to record such observations. Notes of observations that might be useful evidence should be made, for example, signs of activity by racist groups or the presence of individuals known to be connected with racist groups on an estate.

5 Practical steps

Anyone who complains of racial harassment should be advised of the importance of keeping notes and given a form for completion. Any incident that appears as if it might be relevant should be recorded either as it is occurring or immediately afterwards. From the first contact with an authority any potential witnesses should be asked to make their own note of everything they can recall for their own use. They should also be given a form for completion.

Where community groups, other organisations, tenants' associations or individuals such as representatives of religious denominations are supporting victims, they should also be asked to assist by keeping notes of relevant observations. In some circumstances of course, victims' conversations with such people may be confidential.

Authorities should instruct all their staff to keep records when racial harassment is occurring in a particular area or when staff are dealing with a racial harassment complaint.

Preserving evidence

If evidence exists, it is important that it is preserved until any subsequent court hearing. The types of evidence that should be preserved include written threats or abuse and items used as weapons or to cause damage, eg a stick or brick.

In some cases, preservation of evidence will not be possible. As a substitute, it may then be possible to use a photograph of the item in question. Examples include:

— a damaged car which the victim wants to have repaired;

— a broken window;
— items that are perishable such as rubbish that has been dumped, dead animals or dog excreta.

Authorities should ensure that officers who make initial investigations of racial harassment are instructed to take items of evidence into safe custody and that facilities exist for obtaining photographs where appropriate.

C. INTERVIEWING

Many authorities make use of pro-forma questionnaires for officers to obtain initial information about racial harassment complaints. These ensure that, in all cases, key information is obtained for record-keeping and statistical purposes. The same forms can also be helpful reminders to officers of the procedures that must be followed.

Such questionnaires are extremely useful but if there are any witnesses (including the victim) who can give direct evidence, the information obtained on a form will rarely prove adequate by itself to enable a legal department to advise on whether sufficient evidence exists to take action against a perpetrator, let alone to commence proceedings. For legal action, detailed statements are needed from all available witnesses. Pro-formas are inappropriate for such statements but they provide guidance as to the essential information required.

Preparing for an interview

Before beginning any interview, the interviewer should have read and absorbed all the other statements which have been made in the case and made a mental or written note of the questions that must be asked of the particular witness to be interviewed. The interviewer should have considered and understood the factors that will need to be proved in any court proceedings.

It is apparent from the points considered below that an interview with a witness involving incidents over a period of months or years may take a considerable amount of time. Adequate time must be made available.

Preliminaries

It should, perhaps, be obvious that the first stage of any interview is to put the person being interviewed at ease and explain who is present, why they are present and what is to occur.

Before taking any statement from a witness, it is often best to allow him or her to make a statement without prompting. S/he will often have made a mental note of points to mention and will be put at greater ease if allowed to raise such points at the beginning. All these points may not be very significant for any legal action but they may be important to the witness.

Essential information that must be recorded at an early stage is as follows:
— full name;
— address;
— correspondence address if there are any difficulties about correspondence at home or if the witness is likely to move shortly;
— telephone number if any;
— date of birth and age;
— occupation.

Illiciting relevant information

A court wishes to hear evidence from witnesses in a sensible order. Generally the most logical order is the chronological sequence in which events occurred. One way of taking a statement is, therefore, to go back to the very beginning of the events connected with the racial harassment and go through them one by one, collecting all the details. Where the witness is a victim, the date on which s/he began living on the estate will be important.

For every incident, as much information as possible must be obtained. This will include:
— when it occurred: time and date or day;
— where it occurred;
— who was present either as a perpetrator, witness or victim;
— what happened exactly, including conversations and physical actions;
— to whom the incident was reported (including family members);
— what effect the incident had (eg headache after assault, sleepless nights etc);
— what action was taken after the incident (eg visit to hospital, window was mended following day etc).

At this stage no consideration needs to be given to whether any of the statement is admissible in evidence. The more information that can be obtained the better.

Where the perpetrator is unidentified, questions should try and establish:
— whether s/he has been seen before or since and if so where and when;
— a physical description of the perpetrator;
— whether the same person has been involved in a series of incidents.

As much information as possible should be obtained about other potential witnesses. This includes children, however young they may be. Young children may have a vivid recollection of what occurred and might be useful to interview even though there is no possibility of calling them at court to give evidence. They may help with information that leads to the identification of other witnesses or of the perpetrators.

Jogging the memory

Inevitably, people rarely remember the time and date of things that happened some time before. The exact time and date is often unimportant, provided that the events can be put in some kind of realistic order and the witness has some idea of relative time-scales. Witnesses are often drastically inaccurate in their perceptions of dates. In the author's experience they tend to be more accurate about the time of year at which events occurred, the day of the week or the time of day. A good interviewer gives witnesses assistance to jog their memory. For example, a witness may state that an incident occurred at Christmas time, but be vague as to which year. Reference to the birth of the youngest child leads him or her to remember that the child had been born when the incident occurred but that it was before a close relative died. The exact dates of both events are easily checked and may pinpoint the year in which the incident occurred.

Although some prompting may be helpful, it is important that a witness is not made to feel that an answer is so important that s/he makes one up. A witness who can recall an incident, but admits that s/he has no idea when it happened, will be far more believable than a witness who claims to remember exact dates and time, from several years ago. Witnesses are only likely to pinpoint dates with such accuracy when they have kept notes or diaries.

Testing the evidence

1 Inconsistencies in a statement

Inconsistencies in a statement may mean either that a witness cannot properly remember what happened or that s/he is lying. The real reason needs to be established during the interview, because part of the statement cannot be true. It is important to explain to a person being interviewed why it is that what s/he has said cannot be right and to ask why s/he got it wrong. This needs to be done sensitively but firmly. An interviewer who does not challenge a witness about inconsistencies is not being helpful to him or her, because those inconsistencies will be examined far more forcefully in court by the defence or the judge.

If the reason is that the witness cannot remember, s/he should be advised to state only what s/he can remember and admit that s/he cannot recall the rest. If a witness is lying, there will usually be a good reason. For example, s/he may not completely trust the interviewer, may be lying to protect some family member or may feel under pressure to say what s/he thinks the interviewer wants to hear.

2 Conflict with other evidence

Witnesses may state facts which conflict with what other witnesses have said or seen. The interviewer should be aware of the conflict from having read all the previous statements that have been made by other witnesses. These inconsistencies in the overall evidence must also be tested. Obviously in this situation either the current witness or one of the previous witnesses must be mistaken or lying.

3 Facts that belie common sense

Witnesses may state facts which common sense suggests must be wrong. They will not always be wrong, however unlikely they may be but some may be totally impossible. For example, a witness cannot have run between two places one mile apart in two minutes! Other facts may be extremely unlikely and an interviewer may feel very sceptical. In fact, the witness may be mistaken or lying. However, it is also possible that the witness is telling the truth. An interviewer who shows disbelief may lose the witness's confidence if the facts are actually true.

Great care must therefore be taken to establish the truth. If the interviewer is initially sceptical, it is fair to say that a court will probably also be sceptical. This should be explained to the witness and s/he should be asked what other evidence exists to support such a statement. For example, it may turn out that a witness who says that s/he ran one mile in five minutes is a championship runner! When statements are made that are difficult to believe but are true, this can cause considerable difficulties. Not least amongst these are:
— the risk that the assessment of the evidence is based on the subjective views and/or prejudices of the interviewer and that an honest witness is being unfairly disbelieved;
— the reality of court proceedings in which so much depends on the subjective views and prejudices of the judge who is obliged to decide whether to believe or disbelieve a witness.

Perhaps the most satisfactory way to resolve these difficulties is to explain to the witness that what s/he says will sound unlikely to a judge and unless some other supporting evidence can be produced s/he may be disbelieved even if the evidence is true. That is part of the lottery of court proceedings.

Explaining the procedure and future intentions

It is important that the interviewer has had experience of court procedure so that the witness can be rehearsed in the way in which proceedings are conducted. S/he might be advised to go and watch a case before the trial. In addition, interviewers should explain:
— what steps the authority proposes to take;
— what further information is expected from the witness (if any);
— the likely time-scale before further contact and until the hearing;
— the need to keep records of further incidents or observations;
— the need to report any further harassment immediately;
— the steps the authority will take to protect the witness before and after court proceedings.

These matters are in addition to those of advising victims of the options in respect of court proceedings, the advantages and disadvantages of each and seeking their views on what action should be taken. These latter points may be discussed at the interview or at some other stage.

D. SUMMARY OF RECOMMENDATIONS

1 Authorities should consider providing pre-printed forms for their officers and other witnesses to keep contemporaneous notes of incidents, conversations and observations.

2 Authorities should adopt a system for safe-keeping of original notes made by relevant witnesses for use by a witness at a hearing.

3 Authorities should issue guidance to staff and other witnesses on relevant information that should be noted, and should issue instructions to staff to note such information.

4 Any person who complains of racial harassment and any potential witness should be advised to make their own note of what has already occurred as soon as possible.

5 Any complainant and potential witness should be provided with a form and advised to keep notes of future incidents, conversations with the perpetrator and observations, either as they occur or immediately afterwards.

6 Authorities should advise other individuals who may be involved with potential witnesses or active on an estate (eg tenants' associations, community groups etc) to keep appropriate notes.

7 Authorities should issue guidance and instructions to staff on the steps that should be taken to preserve evidence or to obtain evidence by photographs.

8 Authorities should ensure that only staff who have received suitable training take responsibility for the detailed interviewing of witnesses.

1 See *R v Andrews* [1987] 1 All ER 513, HL.
2 Ibid.
3 Civil Evidence Act 1968 s4 and Criminal Evidence Act 1965 s1.
4 Civil Evidence Act 1968 s8 and Criminal Evidence Act 1965 s1.
5 Civil Evidence Act 1968 s2.
6 Ibid s5.
7 RSC Ord 41 and CCR Ord 20 Pt II.
8 Criminal Justice Act 1967 s9.
9 Children and Young Persons Act 1933 s42(1).
10 Ibid.
11 Ibid s43 and see Spencer and Tucker "The evidence of absent children" NLJ 28 August 1987 p816.
12 Civil Evidence Act 1968 s11.
13 *DPP v Boardman* [1974] 3 All ER 887.
14 Children and Young Persons Act 1933 s38(1).
15 *Chapman v Honig* [1963] 2 All ER 513 and see *Rowden v Universities Co-operative Association Ltd* (1881) 71 LT 373 and *Giles v Fox* July [1987] 7 CL 317.
16 RSC Ord 41 r1.

17 See, eg, *R v Malvern Justices ex p Evans* (1987) 137 NLJ 757 and *A-G v Leveller Magazine* [1979] 1 All ER 745, HL.
18 *R v Evesham Justices ex p McDonagh* (1987) 137 NLJ 757
19 See *A-G v Leveller Magazine* n17.
20 Contempt of Court Act 1981 s11.
21 Children and Young Persons Act 1969 s39.
22 Ibid s37.
23 See, eg, *A-G v Leveller Magazine* n17 and *Scott v Scott* [1913] AC 417, HL.
24 See the cases at n15.

CHAPTER FIFTEEN
Proposals for Change

As the previous chapters show, the existing law imposes some duties on local authorities, and provides them with various powers, which are of relevance to racial harassment. Nevertheless, the existing law is unsatisfactory for a number of reasons:

(a) the law does not recognise racial harassment as a problem, much less as the serious problem it represents for many black people;

(b) the duties imposed on local authorities and the police are often unclear, insufficient or unenforceable;

(c) the extent of the powers available to local authorities are often unclear and insufficient to enable them to tackle racial harassment effectively, particularly when it occurs elsewhere than in local authority housing;

(d) there is no obligation on the government of the day to recognise and to tackle racial harassment.

It is therefore clear that changes in the law are necessary to remedy these defects.

The Commission for Racial Equality has a duty to make proposals for necessary changes in the RRA 1976. Measures designed to tackle racial harassment could fall within the remit of that Act. It is hoped that the proposals in this chapter will stimulate debate about additional measures required to tackle racial harassment.

These proposals are put forward on the following basis:
- that they should strengthen the ability of local authorities and the police to tackle racial harassment and go some way to ensuring that they do so;
- that they can be fitted into the existing legal framework of institutions and procedures and do not require radical reform going far beyond the remit of this book. They could therefore be implemented by a single Act of Parliament;
- that they will strengthen the individual remedies available to victims of racial harassment;
- that they will demonstrate to both victims and perpetrators that racial harassment is to be taken seriously by the relevant authorities and will not be tolerated;
- that where it is rational to do so the suggested reforms are restricted to racial harassment. Inevitably, many cannot be so restricted and have implications in other fields since racial harassment does not fit into a watertight legal compartment isolated from all other areas of law.

A. GENERAL POWERS AND DUTIES

1 *Duty on local authorities to take steps to eradicate racism and racial harassment*
Proposal: Impose a statutory duty on local authorities to use their available powers to eradicate racism and racial harassment.
Implementation: By amendment to the RRA 1976.
Purpose: To ensure that all local authorities including local education authorities adopt a strategy for the long-term eradication of racism and racial harassment and do not merely react to individual cases.

2 *Duty on local authorities to monitor racial harassment and to adopt procedures for tackling it*
Proposal: Impose a statutory duty on local authorities to:
— monitor and record incidents of racial harassment in their areas;
— adopt and implement procedures for taking action to protect victims and deal with perpetrators using all their available powers;
— publish annual reports giving details of the complaints received, the extent to which the number recorded is considered by them to reflect the true number of incidents and the action taken by the authority and other agencies to deal with incidents reported.
Implementation: By amendment to the RRA 1976.
Purpose: To ensure that all authorities record incidents of racial harassment and implement procedures for dealing with reported cases. To ensure that authorities adopt a multi-departmental response to incidents. To ensure that authorities inform the public of the steps they take to tackle racial harassment.

3 *Duty on the government to ensure minimum standards in local authority practices*
Proposal: Impose a statutory duty on the Home Office and Department of Environment, after consulting the Commission for Racial Equality, to issue a statutory instrument which lays down minimum requirements for local authorities when complying with proposal 2. Local authorities to be under a duty to comply.
Impose a statutory duty on the Home Office and Department of Environment (or Department of Education and Science for local education authorities), after consulting the CRE, to issue a code of guidance to local authorities on how best to carry out their duties under proposal 1.
Implementation: By amendment to the RRA 1976.
Purpose: To ensure that local authorities comply with minimum standards and some element of uniformity is achieved. To guarantee that the government's primary responsibility to ensure that local authorities tackle racial harassment is recognised. To ensure that discussion occurs at national level on the best methods of eradicating racism.

4 *Power for CRE to enforce local authority duties*
Proposal: Extend the powers and duties of the CRE to include responsibility for monitoring the policies and practices of local authorities and other agencies responsible for tackling racial harassment. Provide the power to issue mandatory notices to agencies in default.
Implementation: By amendment to the RRA 1976.
Purpose: To ensure that all agencies responsible for tackling racial harassment comply with their statutory responsibilities.

5 *Power for individuals to make a complaint*
Proposal: Allow individuals to make a complaint to the county court for an agency's failure to comply with its statutory duty in the same manner as a complaint can currently be made of discrimination.
Power for the CRE to assist the complainant.
Implementation: By amendment to the RRA 1976.
Purpose: To allow individuals affected by breaches of statutory duty to take action for compensation against the agency responsible.

6 *Duty on the government to take account of the extent of racial harassment and measures to eradicate racism and racial harassment when assessing the financial needs of local authorities*
Proposal: Require the government to consider the needs of local authorities for financial resources to take steps to eradicate racism and racial harasment whenever grants are made from central to local government and to include extra resources for these purposes in central government grants, eg grants to local education authorities, block grants.
Implementation: Since grants are made for different local authority functions under different statutes a general responsibility could be imposed by an amendment to the RRA 1976.
Purpose: To ensure that a factor taken into account in all central government grants is the finance required for measures to eradicate racial harassment and racism and that this need is recognised as essential in all areas of central and local government activities and is not marginalised.

7 *Wider power for local authorities to prosecute for criminal offences*
Proposal: Allow local authorities to prosecute when they consider it to be in the interests of some or all of the inhabitants of their areas.
Implementation: By amendment to the Local Government Act 1972.
Purpose: To extend the circumstances in which local authorities can prosecute beyond those allowed by the present wording of s222.

8 *Power to local authorities to take High Court proceedings to prevent racial harassment*
Proposal: Allow local authorities to seek injunctions in the High Court to prevent racial harassment if they consider that their other powers provide an inadequate remedy. This power will be similar to other powers, eg to

take proceedings to prevent a statutory nuisance under Public Health Act 1936 s100.
Implementation: By amendment to the LGA 1972.
Purpose: To provide a residual power to local authorities to use court proceedings to protect the victims of racial harassment and take action against the perpetrators, particularly where harassment occurs in private sector housing.

9 *Power to local authorities to provide funding to voluntary organisations to assist the eradication of racial harassment and racism or to assist the victims of racial harassment*
Proposal: Provide a specific funding power enabling grants to be made to voluntary sector organisations which are:
— involved in the long-term eradication of racism and racial harassment;
— providing practical assistance and support to victims;
— involved in identifying perpetrators and taking or assisting in legal action.
Implementation: By amendment to the LGA 1972.
Purpose: To avoid local authorities having to rely on the limited funds available under LGA 1972 s137 to fund such schemes, and to recognise the importance of local organisations and community groups in assisting any policy designed to eradicate racism and racial harassment.

10 *Power to local authorities to spend money on crime prevention*
Proposal: To allow local authorities to use resources for crime prevention measures.
Implementation: By a Racial Harassment Act or as an amendment to the LGA 1972.
Purpose: To recognise that local authorities have a role in crime prevention and need specific powers to clarify the existing law and to extend their powers.

11 *Power for local authorities to compensate victims for loss caused by racial harassment and to recover these losses from the perpetrator*
Proposal: To give local authorities powers to compensate victims for financial loss, personal injury, inconvenience, aggravation and distress caused by racial harassment including the inconvenience and cost of having to move and set up a new home. Local authorities to be entitled to recover such costs from the perpetrator who has caused the loss, standing in the place of the victim in such a claim. For local authorities in effect to have power to provide an insurance scheme for the victims of racial harassment. The authority could take out insurance for this liability if it saw fit.
Implementation: By amendment to the RRA 1976.
Purpose: To extend the existing powers of local authorities to pay compensation to their own tenants who are victims of racial harassment to cover all victims of racial harassment, and allow a public insurance scheme for racial harassment victims to ensure that they suffer no financial loss

by reason of racial harassment. To allow authorities to recover what they can from the perpetrators which may assist in discouraging racial harassment.

B. HOUSING

Powers and duties

12 *New mandatory housing grant for home security devices*
Proposal: Establish a new grant for home security devices which can be made to owner occupiers, long lessees and private and public sector tenants with necessary funds provided by central government. The Secretary of State to have power to issue codes of guidance on minimum standards that must be adhered to and to make regulations as to the amounts of grants that can be made.
Implementation: By amendment to the HA 1985.
Purpose: To clarify the existing law relating to the power of local authorities to make improvement grants for security devices and make security grants mandatory so that victims of racial harassment can obtain financial assistance to help make their homes less vulnerable to attack.

13 *Power to local authorities to operate schemes providing and fitting security devices*
Proposal: Local authorities to be able to purchase security devices wholesale and provide them to owner occupiers, tenants and other private sector occupiers as well as council tenants and to be able to set up an installation service.
Implementation: By amendment to the HA 1985.
Purpose: To allow authorities to purchase large quantities of security devices and apparatus and provide them at low cost to those in need. To ensure that the installation of devices is carried out by skilled and responsible operators. To extend the existing powers of local authorities beyond the provision of security devices for their own housing stock.

14 *Duty of local authorities to give substantial preference to those in danger of violence to person or property in the allocation of tenancies*
Proposal: That authorities should be under a statutory duty to give a great degree of preference in their allocation schemes for both temporary and permanent housing to those on the waiting and transfer lists who are in danger in their existing home or who have been provided with emergency accommodation due to homelessness caused by harassment.
Implementation: By amendment to the HA 1985.
Purpose: To ensure that racial harassment victims are given very high priority for rehousing in allocation policies for both temporary and permanent rehousing whether they are living in the private sector and seeking local authority housing or living in local authority housing and seeking a transfer.

To clarify the existing law to ensure that victims are given some preference if they request rehousing and to increase the degree of preference that is given. To ensure that this preference remains even after victims have been provided with temporary accommodation under the authority's duties towards the homeless.

15 *Include victims of harassment within the statutory definition of "homeless"*
Proposal: Extend the definition of "homeless" contained in HA 1985 Pt III to provide that a person is homeless if s/he has accommodation but it is probable that occupation of it is likely to lead to harassment involving the use or threat of violence to the person or to property. Extend the definition of "priority need" to include a person who has suffered harassment in his or her home. Extend the definition of "suitable accommodation" for the purposes of the duty to secure that accommodation is available, to include "freedom from the threat of harassment".
Implementation: By amendment to the HA 1985.
Purpose: To clarify the existing law and specifically require that victims of racial harassment be accepted as homeless and rehoused in accommodation where they will be secure from racial harassment.

16 *Amend code of guidance on homelessness*
Proposal: That the code of guidance issued to local authorities should advise that it is not considered reasonable for a victim of racial harassment to continue to occupy his or her home and that authorities should take into account the trauma associated with racial harassment when assessing whether a household is in priority need due to a member of that household being vulnerable.
Implementation: By the issuing of a revised code of guidance to local authorities following the amendments made by the Housing and Planning Act 1986.
Purpose: To encourage authorities to consider victims of racial harassment as homeless and in priority need under the existing law and rehouse them accordingly.

17 *Duty on housing associations to give preference to victims of racial harassment in the allocation of their tenancies*
Proposal: That housing associations should be obliged to assist the rehousing of victims of racial harassment by giving them preference in allocations or by making a reasonable proportion of voids available for housing victims.
Implementation: By amendment to the Housing Associations Act 1985. This proposal can to some extent be implemented immediately by the Secretary of State issuing directions to the Housing Corporation and local authorities imposing conditions on providing land to housing associations.

Purpose: To ensure that housing associations play a part in assisting the rehousing of victims of racial harassment.

18 *Duty on the Housing Corporation to require housing associations to adopt and implement policies for dealing with racial harassment as part of the proper performance of their functions*
Proposal: That the Housing Corporation should be given the responsibility for ensuring that housing associations adopt policies for tackling racial harassment in their housing and that they implement them.
Implementation: By a direction to the Housing Corporation by the Secretary of State under the Housing Associations Act 1985.
Purpose: To ensure that all housing associations have policies and procedures for dealing with racial harassment in their housing.

19 *Power of local authorities to buy owner-occupied housing from the victim of racial harassment at market value*
Proposal: Local authorities to have power to buy owner-occupied housing from racial harassment victims at market value and to have authority to borrow money for this purpose in addition to any authority to borrow money for other purposes, eg Housing Investment Programme.
Implementation: By amendment to the HA 1985.
Purpose: To allow victims of racial harassment who live in owner-occupied housing to move quickly by selling their homes to the authority at market value and not to have to advertise the fact that they are moving.

20 *Specific power of compulsory purchase of housing accommodation where there is harassment by a landlord or other occupiers*
Proposal: That compulsory purchase powers should apply specifically to housing accommodation where the landlord or one or more occupiers is harassing other occupiers and the landlord has failed to take reasonable steps to prevent harassment.
Implementation: By amendment to the HA 1985.
Purpose: To clarify the existing law and make clear that local authorities have compulsory purchase powers where a landlord is harassing tenants. To extend this power to inter-tenant harassment if the landlord fails to take steps to prevent it.

Grounds for possession

21 *Amend the present discretionary ground for possession based on nuisance or annoyance*
Proposal: Amend ground 2 of HA 1985 Sch 2 as follows:

(a) include "harassment" as a discretionary ground for possession as well as "nuisance or annoyance";

(b) to make tenants responsible for any nuisance etc by visitors and those staying temporarily in the dwelling;
(c) to define "neighbours" as meaning any person living on the same estate or in the same locality or who is affected or is likely to be affected by the conduct concerned, whether or not such person is a tenant of the same landlord;
(d) specifically to include nuisance, annoyance or harassment committed against neighbours or their families wherever they may be, eg at school.

Purpose: To ensure that the courts and the public are aware that harassment can constitute grounds for a possession order; to extend the responsibility of tenants for visitors and those temporarily staying in the dwelling; to provide a definition of "neighbour" and to ensure that nuisance etc committed against a neighbour can be taken into account wherever it occurs.

22 *Include "racial harassment" as a mandatory ground for possession*
Proposal: To provide a mandatory ground for possession where a tenant or any person residing in or visiting a dwelling-house has been guilty of racial harassment against neighbours.
Implementation: By amendment to the HA 1985.
Purpose: To ensure that where racial harassment occurs, the perpetrator and family can be evicted in order to protect the victim.

23 *Allow possession proceedings to be commenced before the expiry of any notice of intention to seek possession*
Proposal: That proceedings for possession may be commenced solely for the purposes of obtaining an injunction in cases involving nuisance, annoyance, harassment or racial harassment. The proceedings to be stayed once an injunction is obtained until the notice has expired.
Implementation: By amendment to the HA 1985.
Purpose: To allow landlords to obtain immediate injunctions to protect victims without having to wait four weeks for any notice of intention to seek possession to expire or to issue separate injunction proceedings.

24 *Landlords to be legally liable for acts of tenants which are within their control*
Proposal: That where a landlord is entitled to enforce a covenant against a tenant or is entitled to seek possession against a tenant for nuisance etc but fails to do so, another tenant of the same landlord should be able to take action against the landlord if s/he suffers any inconvenience, loss or damage resulting from the landlord's failure to enforce the covenant or to seek possession.
Implementation: By amendment to the Landlord and Tenant Act 1985.
Purpose: To clarify the existing law and provide a direct remedy for tenants whose landlord fails to act to prevent racial harassment when s/he has power to act.

C. PLANNING

25 *Powers to local authorities to serve notices for the removal and prevention of offensive graffiti*
Proposal: Planning authorities should have power to serve notices on the owners or occupiers of premises requiring them to remove offensive graffiti.
Implementation: By amendment to the Town and Country Planning Act 1971.
Purpose: To provide authorities with clear powers to act to have graffiti removed by owners or occupiers.

D. EDUCATION

26 *Powers for local education authorities to take steps to ensure the safety of children on their way to and from school*
Proposal: That local education authorities should have a specific power to take steps to ensure the safety of children on their way to and from school.
Implementation: By amendment to the Education Acts.
Purpose: To clarify the existing law to make clear that the powers of the education authority do not end at the school gates.

E. CRIME

27 *Make a racial motive an aggravating factor in all crimes*
Proposal: That any offence committed by any person wholly or partly because of the colour, race, nationality or ethnic or national origin of the victim should be considered to have been committed under aggravating circumstances and the court should be obliged to take that factor into account when sentencing.
Implementation: Immediately, by clear guidance from the Court of Appeal that a racial motive to any offence is an aggravating factor, and practice guidance to the Crown Prosecution Service that a racial motive in any case should be drawn to the court's attention. In the longer term, by an amendment to the Powers of the Criminal Courts Act 1973.
Purpose: To provide official recognition that a racial motive makes offences more serious and to ensure that the criminal law recognises that many offences are committed because of racism and that the courts should condemn such acts and the motives behind them.

28 *Make "racial harassment" a separate criminal offence*
Proposal: Create a new offence of racial harassment defined as follows:

(a) "harassment" for the purposes of such offence to be defined as:

two or more criminal acts each of which is committed against at least one of the following:
- the same person; or
- persons who form part of the same household or family; or
- the property of any of such persons; or
- the home of any of such persons;

where at least one of such acts amounts to an offence which involves the use, threat of use or attempted use of violence against any person or property or an offence under s4 or s5 of the Public Order Act 1986.

(b) "Racial harassment" to be harassment which is committed by a person wholly or partly because of the racial origin of any of the persons mentioned above.

Where the perpetrator has been previously prosecuted for an offence involving the use or threat or attempted use of violence against any person or against the property of the same family or for an offence under the Public Order Act 1986 of which any member of the family was the victim, the requirement to constitute an offence of racial harassment should be reduced to allow any subsequent criminal offence to amount to racial harassment if committed because of the colour, race, nationality or ethnic or national origin of any of the persons mentioned above.

Implementation: By a Racial Harassment Act.

Purpose: To ensure that, when several offences are committed against the same family or household which might appear relatively minor when considered in isolation, they can be dealt with and considered by the court as one serious offence and an appropriate sentence imposed. To ensure that this new offence can be used even if the perpetrator has already been convicted of one offence which forms part of the racial harassment campaign.

29 *Amend the provisions relating to harassment in the Protection from Eviction Act 1977*

Proposal: Extend the 1977 Act to all harassment which is intended to drive any person from their home so that it is specifically intended to include harassment outside the context of landlord and tenant.

Extend definition of a residential occupier to include any owner occupier or any other person who originally went into occupation with the licence or permission of a person with authority to give it or was subsequently given licence or permission by such a person.

Redefine the offence in s1(3), "harassment" to read as follows:

"any person who causes or who intends to cause the residential occupier of any premises-

(a) to give up occupation of the premises or any part thereof; or

(b) to refrain from exercising any right or pursuing any remedy in respect of the premises or part thereof;

by doing any act or acts which interferes with the peace and comfort of the residential occupier or members of his household or by withdrawing or withholding services required for occupation of the premises shall be guilty of an offence."

If the accused is not shown to have intended to cause the residential occupier to give up occupation or to refrain from exercising any right or pursuing any remedy, it should be a defence to prove that the defendant did not intend his or her acts to cause one of those results.

To make harassment under the Protection from Eviction Act an arrestable offence and specifically to authorise the police as well as the local authority to prosecute.

Implementation: By amendment to the Protection from Eviction Act 1977.

Purpose: To overcome some of the difficulties with the present definition of "harassment" in the 1977 Act which make it unworkable and to extend the remit of the offence under the Act specifically to cover harassment of people in their homes whatever their housing tenure. To allow the police to arrest an offender and encourage them to prosecute by expressly stating that they have power to do so.

30 *Remove the requirement for the Attorney-General's consent to a prosecution under the Public Order Act 1986 Pt III*

Proposal: Remove the need to obtain the consent of the Attorney-General before any prosecution can be brought for offences involving incitement to racial hatred.

Implementation: By amendment to the Public Order Act 1986.

Purpose: To allow prosecutions to be more easily brought under this provision.

31 *Create an offence of allowing or permitting a child to racially harass*

Proposal: That a parent or guardian commits an offence if s/he permits or allows a child to commit racial harassment. "Child" meaning anyone under 14 even if under the age of criminal responsibility. Racial harassment to be defined as in 29 above.

Implementation: By a Racial Harassment Act.

Purpose: To ensure that parents prevent young children from committing acts of racial harassment and take responsibility for their children's behaviour if acts of racial harassment are committed and the parents were able to take steps to prevent them.

32 *Create an offence of causing criminal damage by graffiti which is threatening, abusive, insulting or offensive*

Proposal: That writing graffiti which is offensive should be an offence separate from the offence of criminal damage.

Implementation: By an amendment to the Public Order Act 1986.

Purpose: To ensure that the criminal law acknowledges that there is a significant problem of racist graffiti in some areas and to provide powers to deal with those responsible.

33 *Extend the powers of the courts to award compensation in criminal proceedings*
Proposal: Extend the powers of the courts to award compensation to allow substantial sums to be awarded for inconvenience, distress and injury to feelings caused by a criminal offence.
Implementation: By amendment to the Powers of the Criminal Courts Act 1973.
Purpose: To allow victims of racial harassment who may have suffered substantial distress and psychological damage to obtain appropriate compensation which properly reflects their suffering through the criminal courts without having to take separate proceedings.

34 *Provide the criminal courts with power to make perpetual injunctions to protect witnesses from retaliation*
Proposal: Provide the criminal courts with powers to make orders against those found guilty of offences, for the protection of witnesses whom the court considers are likely to be in danger of physical violence.
Implementation: By amendment to the Powers of the Criminal Courts Act 1973 or a Criminal Justice Act.
Purpose: To enable the criminal courts to provide some form of protection to witnesses after the proceedings have ended.

35 *Extend legal aid for prosecutions*
Proposal: Extend legal aid to cover private prosecutions for offences of violence or damage to property where the police or Crown Prosecution Service have been asked to prosecute but have not taken action within a reasonable time.
Implementation: By amendment to the Legal Aid Acts and Regulations.
Purpose: To enable victims of criminal offences to prosecute.

36 *Impose a duty on the prosecution to advise the court of the effects of an offence on the victim*
Proposal: That prosecutors should be under a professional duty to draw the court's attention to the effect of the offence on the victim.
Implementation: By instructions to the Crown Prosecution Service issued by the Director of Public Prosecutions.
Purpose: To ensure that courts consider the effect of an offence on the victim when deciding upon an appropriate sentence.

F. POLICE POWERS AND DUTIES

37 *Duty on the police to monitor racial harassment*
Proposal: Impose a statutory duty on the police to keep records of complaints, investigations and prosecutions for offences which are or may have been committed because of the racial origin of the victim, the intended victim or any member of the victim's family. An annual report to be published giving details of the numbers recorded, the result of any investigations and of any prosecutions. The report also to include proposals for future action to tackle racial harassment.
Implementation: By amendment to the Police Act 1964.
Purpose: To ensure that adequate records are kept of complaints involving racial harassment and that the public is provided with information relating to these complaints and the manner in which they have been dealt with. To ensure that the police each year examine the way in which their efforts to tackle racial harassment can be improved.

38 *Duty on the Crown Prosecution Service to monitor cases of racial harassment*
Proposal: Impose a statutory duty on the Crown Prosecution Service to keep records of cases involving racial harassment and the action taken and to publish an annual report.
Implementation: In part by directions made by the Attorney-General to the CPS under Prosecution of Offences Act 1985 s8. By amendment to the Prosecution of Offences Act 1985.
Purpose: To ensure that the CPS keeps separate records of prosecutions for offences amounting to racial harassment and provides public information of the action it has taken to deal with such cases.

39 *Duty to prosecute in certain circumstances*
Proposal: That the police and Crown Prosecution Service should be under a duty to prosecute for any offence of violence where the victim requires them to do so and there is sufficient evidence.
Where there is considered to be insufficient evidence, the victim to be informed in writing why this is considered to be so.
Implementation: By amendment to the Prosecution of Offences Act 1985.
Purpose: To allow victims of racial harassment to insist on prosecution if there is sufficient evidence, and to consider a private prosecution (with the assistance of legal aid if appropriate) if the CPS is not prepared to prosecute.

40 *Duty to provide information regarding an investigation to the victim or any other person at the victim's request*
Proposal: That the police and CPS should be under a duty to keep a victim informed of the progress of an investigation of any criminal offence if requested to do so.

Implementation: By amendment to the Police and Criminal Evidence Act 1984 and Prosecution of Offences Act 1985.
Purpose: To ensure that a victim is kept informed about the investigation of any offence committed against him or her.

41 Duty on individual police officers to prevent racial harassment
Proposal: That individual police officers should be under a duty to prevent racial harassment in the same manner as they have a duty to prevent breaches of the peace.
Implementation: By amendment to the declaration made by police officers when taking office to include a specific undertaking to prevent racial harassment.
Purpose: To draw the attention of individual police officers to the fact that they are under a duty to prevent racial harassment.

42 Provide powers for the civil courts to include a power of arrest on any injunction where it is necessary to protect the person or property of the party in whose favour the injunction is made
Proposal: Provide the civil courts with powers to include a power of arrest for police officers for breach of any injunction where this is necessary to provide protection for a party to the civil proceedings to avoid violence or damage to property. The police to be obliged to take the person arrested before the court which made the injunction.
Implementation: By amendment to the Supreme Court Act 1981 and County Courts Act 1984.
Purpose: To give the police powers to provide additional protection and assistance to those who have used the civil courts, and to provide a speedy and effective method of bringing a person who has breached an injunction back before the civil courts.

G. OTHER CHANGES IN THE CIVIL LAW

43 Allow the civil courts to award substantial damages for inconvenience, distress and hurt feelings
Proposal: That the law should recognise a specific head of damages for inconvenience, distress and hurt feelings which can be awarded for any tort or breach of statutory duty and that the sums that can be awarded should properly reflect the degree of damage that has occurred.
Implementation: By a Civil Damages Act.
Purpose: To allow the courts properly to compensate distress caused by torts or breaches of statutory duty, particularly in cases involving discrimination, racial harassment and similar matters where there may be no personal injury or financial loss but the psychological effect of the acts may be very substantial.

44 *Make racial harassment a tort*
Proposal: That racial harassment should be an actionable tort. "Racial harassment" to be defined as harassment committed against a person wholly or partly because of the racial origin of that person or any member of that person's family. To be defined so that separate acts of racial harassment against the same family or household are considered to be a tort against all members of the family and any family member can take action on behalf of other members.
Implementation: In a Racial Harassment Act.
Purpose: To allow victims to take action for racial harassment committed against the family in one civil action and obtain injunctions to protect any member of the family and damages to compensate any member of the family.

H. COURT PROCEDURE

45 *Protection for victims and witnesses giving evidence*
Proposal: That both civil and criminal courts should have specific powers:

(a) to allow a witness to give evidence without disclosing his or her present address where the address is not necessary to allow any other party to test the reliability or accuracy of the evidence; and

(b) to allow the court to ban the press from publishing the name and address of any witness or any information by which they might be identified;

in both cases if it is necessary to do so to protect the witness from a likelihood of intimidation or violence by any person whether or not a party to the proceedings.

Implementation: For addresses, by amendment to rules of court. For press publicity, by amendment to the Contempt of Court Act 1981.
Purpose: To clarify the existing law relating to the confidentiality of witnesses' addresses and to publicity, to ensure that witnesses are not identified if they would be in danger.

APPENDIX ONE

Suggested Clauses for Tenancy Agreements

These clauses are numbered in terms of an addition to an existing clause no 8 in a tenancy agreement.

"8A(1)(a) The tenant and any person living on the premises whether permanently or temporarily and any visitor to the premises must not commit on the premises or on any part of the common parts or in the vicinity or neighbourhood of the premises or the common parts any acts which cause a nuisance, annoyance or disturbance to any person or any acts of harassment (whether racial, sexual or otherwise) of any person.

8A(1)(b) 'Harassment' includes but is not limited to:
a) violence or threats of violence towards any person;
b) abusive or insulting words or behaviour;
c) damage or threats of damage to property belonging to another person including damage to any part of a person's home;
d) writing threatening, abusive or insulting graffiti;
e) any act or omission calculated to interfere with the peace or comfort of any other person or to inconvenience such person."

Comment: This clause covers harassment committed against any person in the area of the premises. It will include harassment of council employees and potential tenants viewing property for allocation. Racial harassment is not defined since any definition is likely to be restrictive. To avoid any doubt, an authority might define the vicinity or neighbourhood by naming the estate, streets etc though this would involve considerable extra work completing each tenancy agreement correctly. The "common parts" must be defined elsewhere in the agreement.

"8A(2) The tenant and any person living on the premises whether permanently or temporarily must not at any time or in any place commit any acts which cause a nuisance, annoyance or disturbance or which amount to harassment (whether racial, sexual or otherwise) of other tenants of the council or members of their household or of members or employees of the council."

Comment: This clause covers racial harassment by any person living on the premises committed against other council tenants or their families, eg children on their way to school, adults shopping, youth clubs etc, or of council staff or councillors, eg staff in the housing office. An attempt to extend this clause to non-council tenants wherever they may be, would probably be outside the powers of a housing authority.

"**8A(3)** The tenant and any person living on the premises whether permanently or temporarily and any visitor to the premises must not commit any breach of the authority's byelaws."

"**8A(4)** The tenant and any person living on the premises whether permanently or temporarily and any visitor to the premises must not cause damage to any property owned by the council and must not deface or damage any wall, door, fence or other part of any premises owned by the council by graffiti or any other means."

"**8A(5)(a)** The tenant shall not permit, incite or allow any person living on the premises nor any visitor to commit any act which is in breach of clauses 8A(1) to (4) above.

8A(5)(b) In addition to the requirement of clause 8A(5)(a):

i) The tenant shall be held responsible for the behaviour of any person living on the premises whether permanently or temporarily.

ii) The tenant shall be held responsible for the acts of any visitors to the premises while present on the premises and while entering or leaving the premises or the common parts for the purposes of his or her visit.

Any act by persons living with the tenant or visitors in breach of clauses 8A(1) to (4) shall be considered to be a breach of this agreement by the tenant.

8A(5)(c) For the avoidance of doubt this clause applies to adult children, lodgers, licensees, sub-tenants and other adult members of the tenant's family or household as well as to children under 18.

8A(5)(d) The tenant shall upon demand reimburse the council for the cost of making good any loss or damage caused by the acts of any persons in breach of clauses 8A(1) to (4)."

Comment: Clause 8A(5)(a) is designed to enable an injunction to be obtained if the tenant is in breach. A wider clause requiring a tenant to stop any member of the household, of any age, committing racial harassment would probably be impossible to enforce by injunction since it would be extremely difficult to specify with sufficient precision what action was required of the tenant. Clause 8A(5)(b) is wider than 8A(5)(a) to enable a council to obtain possession for racial harassment by visitors and those living with the tenant even if the tenant was not in breach of clause 8A(5)(a), eg independent action by an adult living with the tenant. It will still be necessary to show that it is reasonable to order possession.

"**8A(6)** The tenant shall not keep a dog or allow any dog to be kept on the premises without the permission of the council. The council may grant permission subject to such conditions as it sees fit and may alter such conditions from time to time and may withdraw such permission if it considers that the conditions have not been complied with."

Comment: This clause allows the council to draw up rules and regulations about dogs, covering some of the points mentioned on p 58. These can then be altered without following the procedure laid down in the HA 1985. The tenant can be asked to sign a copy of the conditions. If they are breached, the authority can withdraw permission allowing the dog to be kept. The tenant must then remove the dog or be in breach of the tenancy agreement. A breach could be the subject of injunction proceedings to have the dog removed, or possession proceedings for breach of tenancy agreement.

Example of clause making a local authority landlord responsible for taking action against neighbours causing a nuisance annoyance or harassment

"If so required by the tenant, the council will enforce the conditions identical to those contained in clause 8A hereof contained in tenancy agreements entered into or to be entered into by the tenants of other flats on the estate of which the premises form part."

APPENDIX TWO

Notices Required to Vary a Tenancy Agreement

Document 1: Preliminary notice of landlord's intention to change the tenancy agreement

To:
The Tenant,
22, Anyestate,
Somewhere.

1st March 1987

Dear Tenant,

Variation of tenancy conditions

We are proposing to serve a notice of variation on you which will vary the terms of your tenancy by including the following clause:

"**8A(1)(a)** The tenant and any person living on the premises whether permanently or temporarily and any visitor to the premises must not commit on the premises or on any part of the common parts or in the vicinity or neighbourhood of the premises or the common parts any acts which cause a nuisance, annoyance or disturbance to any person or any acts of harassment (whether racial, sexual or otherwise) of any person."

[For reasons of space, clauses 8A(2)-(4) are omitted.]

"**8A(5)(a)** The tenant shall not permit, incite or allow any person living on the premises nor any visitor to commit any act which is in breach of clauses 8A(1) to (4) above.

8A(5)(b) In addition to the requirement of clause 8A(5)(a):

i) The tenant shall be held responsible for the behaviour of any person living on the premises whether permanently or temporarily.

ii) The tenant shall be held responsible for the acts of any visitors to the premises while present on the premises and while entering or leaving the premises or the common parts for the purposes of his or her visit.

Any act by persons living with the tenant or visitors in breach of clauses 8A(1) to (4) shall be considered to be a breach of this agreement by the tenant.

8A(5)(c) For the avoidance of doubt clause 8A applies to adult children, lodgers, licensees, sub-tenants and other adult members of the tenant's family or household as well as to children under 18."

The effect of this clause is that you must not cause any nuisance, annoyance or disturbance to anyone else on your estate or in the area of the estate and you must not harass any such person in any way. If you do you will be in breach of your tenancy agreement and could be evicted.

In addition, the clause makes clear that you must ensure that anyone living in your home or visiting you does not cause any nuisance, annoyance or disturbance to anyone or harass anyone on the estate or in the area of the estate. Since you are responsible for the behaviour of anyone living with you or visiting you, you could also be evicted if they breach this clause.

The reasons why the council considers the new clause to be necessary are discussed in the enclosed leaflet.

Before we make a final decision about whether or not to vary your tenancy conditions you are invited to make comments on the proposed variation.

Any comments you wish to make should be sent to your estates officer, Ms F, the Housing Office, Housing Department, Somewhere to arrive by the 1st April 1987.

Yours faithfully,
R
Director of Housing

Document 2: Notice of variation of tenancy

To:
Mrs A,
22, Anyestate,
Somewhere.
1st May 1987

Variation of tenancy conditions
With effect from 15th June 1987 the terms of your tenancy are hereby varied by the inclusion of the following clause:
   [*Repeat clauses 8A(1) and (5) from Document 1 above.*]
It is council policy to ensure that its tenants do not racially harass others living or working in the area, or council employees. The council therefore intends to enforce this clause against any tenant who breaches it or who does not prevent visitors or others from breaching it, by means of possession proceedings. This policy and the reasons for it, together with the action you should take if you consider you are being racially harassed, are explained more fully in the accompanying leaflet.

Dated 1st May 1987

Signed
R
Director of Housing

Note: Additional information informing you of the meaning of this variation is contained in the papers delivered with this notice.

This is the notice, a copy of which was delivered by me to the tenant named in the notice, together with additional explanatory information and racial harassment leaflet, this 6th day of May 1987.

Signed:
   A. Caretaker

APPENDIX THREE
Sample Case Studies

A. CIVIL CASE

The facts of a case in which an authority seeks an order for possession and an injunction. The facts contained in the statement of Mr C, in section B below, form part of the same campaign of racial harassment.

Witnesses who can give evidence in court:

Mrs C: Confirms her daughter's story of the milk bottle and the daughter who was attacked outside the lift, tells of finding the note and the dog excrement and seeing a man's shadow outside the window. Tells of seeing A disappear into his flat. Tells of the continuing distress of her two daughters following the attacks on them and the effect on the family.

Mr C: Tells of seeing A disappearing into his flat.

Miss L: The older daughter who tells of the attack on herself.

M: The teacher of L who tells how suddenly L's behaviour at school changed and she did unexpectedly badly in her exams.

Miss N: The younger daughter who tells of the attack on herself.

P: The lady from another flat who found N.

F: The housing officer who saw the excrement on the door, the writing, the broken window, the glass in the courtyard outside the flats and the bruise on N's leg and who warned A orally that further harassment would lead to eviction.

Q: The Area Housing Manager who wrote a warning letter to A's mother, the tenant.

R: The Director of Housing who can confirm that there have been eight complaints of racial harassment by different black tenants on that estate but it has not been possible to identify the perpetrator; that there are so far a total of 98 recorded instances of racial harassment in the authority's housing in the borough this year; that black tenants will not accept tenancies on this estate because of its reputation for harassment; that this estate is one of the best in the borough and that in his opinion, an order for possession is essential to make an example of A's family and to protect the C family.

Document 1: Statement of Mrs C

25, Anyestate, Somewhere

Age: 41   Occupation: Mother

I make this statement about the harassment of our family by A.

On the 22nd May my daughter L left home to go to school. She is 14 years old and in the third year at school. As she walked out of the bottom of our flats, a milk bottle landed on the ground about five yards away. It was thrown by A from the fifth floor. My daughter saw him up there when she looked up. It shattered and bits of glass flew everywhere. Fortunately my daughter was not hurt but she burst into tears, ran back into the block and returned to our flat. She refused to go to school that day. Since then she has been too frightened to go to school unless I take her. She never goes out of the flat on her own and she will only leave the communal entrance if I or my husband go out first to make sure no one is going to throw anything at her. I have spoken to her teachers who say that she burst into tears in her exam on the 29th May and she only just passed when they would have expected her easily to get an 'A' because she had been doing so well all year.

On the 8th July my daughter N was coming home from school at about 3.45pm. She is 10. The primary school is only about 300 yards away and she can come home on her own because there are no roads to cross. She came into the front entrance of the block and called the lift. It came down and the door opened. A was standing in the lift. He walked out of the lift and pushed N so that she fell over. He said to her "You'll not be living here long. I'll make sure of that". He kicked her in the leg and walked off. A lady from another flat came into the entrance and saw N crying on the floor holding her leg. She asked her where she lived and brought her home. N is now too frightened to go to school on her own. She will also no longer go out and play with her other friends on the estate playground just behind our block where there are swings and a roundabout. Before this attack she would go out every evening for an hour or so before her tea. The day after the attack she had a large bruise on her leg where she had been kicked and a graze on her elbow where she had fallen over when pushed.

Our housing officer, F, told me she went to see A and his mother on the 14th July and warned them that further harassment of our family would lead to eviction. She told me that Mrs A said to her, "I know he knocked N over and kicked her the other day but he was only mucking about." A said, "Why did you put them on this estate? We don't want them here."

On the 15th July at 8am there was a note on our doormat which had been put through our letter box. It said, "If I see you on this block again you will get more than bruises. You've been telling tales. Signed, You know who."

On the 25th July, I opened the front door in the morning to find dog excrement smeared all over it. Someone had written on the door, "You were warned."

On the 10th August at 10.30pm, a brick was thrown through our front window from the balcony. I saw a man's shadow outside and it disappeared. My husband rushed onto the balcony but he had gone. A few seconds later we saw A disappearing into his flat at No 22, one floor below. We can see his door from ours because it is along the side of the block. No one went out of the main entrance of the flats.

B. CRIMINAL CASE

The facts given below provide an example of a situation where a prosecution could be brought for three offences:
(a) criminal damage to Mr C's car;
(b) assault occasioning actual bodily harm on Mr C;
(c) harassment under the Protection from Eviction Act 1977 of Mr C.
For the reasons explained on pp174 and 243, prosecution for harassment is preferable whenever possible. In this example, the previous assault on N could be included as part of the harassment relied upon constituting the one offence. It may also be possible to provide evidence relating to the assault on L. It would probably not be possible to introduce evidence relating to either of the assaults on the girls if A were charged only with assault occasioning actual bodily harm or criminal damage.

An example of the form of statement required to be laid before magistrates on oath to obtain the issue of a warrant to begin proceedings under the Protection from Eviction Act 1977 is contained in Appendix 7.

In case the local authority is unable to prove the specific intent required to obtain a conviction under the Protection from Eviction Act 1977 it would be advisable to bring proceedings for criminal damage and assault occasioning actual bodily harm at the same time.

Witnesses who can give evidence in court:

Mr C: The victim.
D: The neighbour who found Mr C on the landing and whom Mr C told that A had attacked him.
E: The neighbour who saw A with a brick 15 minutes before the attack.
F: The housing officer who saw the damage to the car, picked up the brick used to damage the car, saw the blood on the landing and interviewed A.
G: The laboratory technician who collected a sample of blood from the landing and from Mr C and confirmed that they were the same blood.
H: The photographer who took a photograph of the damaged car, Mr

C's bruises, the courtyard, flats and landing where the assault occurred.
I: The architect who prepared a sketch-plan of the flats, courtyard and landing.
Dr J: The doctor who treated Mr C at hospital.
K: The car mechanic who repaired the car.

The story is recounted by Mr C in a full statement. The initial statement includes evidence that would not be allowed in court because it is hearsay. However, it is important to record the points made by Mr C because he refers to several other witnesses who should be interviewed. For use in court proceedings the solicitor prepares a statement containing only admissible evidence. This is shown as Document 3. It is in a form which allows it to be used in committal proceedings.

Document 2: Initial statement of Mr C

Name: Mr C
Address: 25, Anyestate, Somewhere
Date of birth 1/1/47
Occupation: Works foreman

I live at 25 Anyestate, Somewhere. It is a three-bedroomed flat on the sixth floor of a council block.

On Thursday the 20th August at about 6.30pm I was coming home from work, I parked my car in the courtyard a short distance from the entrance to my block as usual and locked it.

I walked towards the block where I live. As I approached it I heard a loud crash behind me. I turned round quickly and saw a brick bouncing off my car on to the ground. There was a large dent in the roof of the car. I looked up and I saw a youth leaning over the balcony on the fifth floor. He was immediately above me and he was laughing. I recognised him as one of the occupants of a flat on the fifth floor which I now know is No 22 Anyestate. I know the youth well as he is often hanging around the estate and I see him regularly. His name is A.

A shouted at me, "The next one will be on your head. You've got three days to get out or we'll burn you out. We don't want your kind on our estate."

I rushed into the block to go up to my flat to phone the police. I went into the entrance hall and pressed the button for the lift. After a while it came and I went up to the sixth floor. The door opened and A was on the landing immediately outside the lift.

I left the lift and walked towards the balcony on which my flat is situated. I did not say anything to him.

A said to me: "Where do you think you're going?" He grabbed hold of me and swung me round so that I crashed into a wall with my left shoulder. He then punched me very hard in the stomach and again in the face. I fell to the ground and he kicked me in the back several times and then ran off.

I lay there for several minutes unable to move. Then the woman from No 24, D, came along the balcony. I told her that A from No 22 had attacked me. She saw that I was injured and called my wife. Together they helped me home and called an ambulance. I had a cut on my right cheek which bled until the ambulance officer put a dressing on it. I was taken to hospital and had X-rays. I was then discharged. I still have painful bruises on my shoulder, back and face.

The next day my wife met E from No 21 Anyestate. He told her that on the evening in question he had seen A on his landing on the fifth floor at about 6.15 the same evening. A had a brick in his hand. He took no notice of it at the time.

The morning after the attack the housing officer, F, came to see us because my wife had rung her. She saw the bruises on my face. She went out on the landing and saw a blood stain and my wife showed her the brick which was still lying where it fell and the dent in my car.

F went to see A. She asked him why he had beaten me up and what he had against us. F said that A just smiled and said, "We've got our reasons. You'd better find him somewhere else to live pretty quick."

My family has been harassed and taunted by A and the rest of his family for about nine months. The details of all the incidents are on our tenancy file. We have reported two previous assaults on my daughters to the police. The police advised us to take a private prosecution.

Signed: ....

Date: 22nd August 1987

Document 3: Statement for use in committal proceedings containing only admissible parts of Mr C's evidence

FULL NAME: Mr X Y C
Address: 25, Anyestate, Somewhere
Age/Date of birth: Over 21   Occupation: Works foreman

WHO STATES: This statement consisting of one page signed by me is true to the best of my knowledge and belief and I make it knowing that if it is tendered in evidence I shall be liable to prosecution if I have wilfully stated in it anything which I know to be false or do not believe to be true.

Dated 31st August 1987   ....(Signed)
                                   Mr C

I live at 25 Anyestate, Somewhere. It is a three-bedroomed flat on the sixth floor of a council block.

On Thursday the 20th August at about 6.30pm I was coming home from work. I parked my car in the courtyard a short distance from the entrance to my block as usual and locked it.

I walked towards the block where I live. As I approached it I heard a loud crash behind me. I turned round quickly and saw a brick bouncing off my car on to the ground. There was a large dent in the roof of the car. I looked up and I saw a youth leaning over the balcony on the fifth floor. He was immediately above me and was laughing. I recognised him as one of the occupiers of a flat on the fifth floor which I now know is No 22 Anyestate. I know the youth well as he is often hanging around the estate and I see him regularly. His name is A.

A shouted at me, "The next one will be on your head. You've got three days to get out or we'll burn you out. We don't want your kind on our estate."

I rushed into the block to go up to my flat to phone the police. I went into the entrance hall and pressed the button for the lift. After a while it came and I went up to the sixth floor. The door opened and A was on the landing immediately outside the lift.

I left the lift and walked towards the balcony on which my flat is situated. I did not say anything to him.

A said to me: "Where do you think you're going?" He grabbed hold of me and swung me round so that I crashed into a wall with my left shoulder. He then punched me very hard in the stomach and again in the face. I fell to the ground and he kicked me in the back several times and then ran off.

I lay there for several minutes unable to move. Then the woman from No 24, D, came along the balcony. I told her that A from No 22 had attacked me. She saw that I was injured and called my wife. Together they helped me home and called an ambulance. I had a cut on my right cheek which bled until the ambulance officer put a dressing on it. I was taken to hospital and had X-rays and I was then discharged. I still have painful bruises on my shoulder, back and face.

Signed: ....
        Mr C
Witnessed: ....

APPENDIX FOUR

Documents for Civil Proceedings

The examples that follow are based on the following:
1. that clauses 8A(1) to (6) shown in Appendix 1 have been incorporated into the tenancy agreement using a notice of variation, part of which is shown as an example in Appendix 2;
2. the facts contained in the case studies in Appendix 3.

Document 1: Notice of intention to seek possession

It is not proposed to reproduce the entire notice here. There is a prescribed form contained in the Secure Tenancies (Notices) Regulations 1987 SI No 755 Pt I which must be used. The form contains notes of explanation for tenants. The important clauses are nos 3 to 5, examples of which are given below.

3 Possession will be sought on grounds 1 and 2 of Schedule 2 to the Housing Act 1985 which read:
Ground 1: [*Enter the wording of ground 1*]
Ground 2: [*Enter the wording of ground 2*]

4 Particulars of each ground are as follows:
Ground 1. You are in breach of clause 8A of your tenancy agreement in that you are responsible under clause 8A(5) for the following acts committed by your son A who lives with you which amount to a nuisance, annoyance or disturbance or to harassment and which are in breach of clauses 8A(1), 8A(2) and 8A(4) of your tenancy agreement which came into effect on the 15th June 1987.

PARTICULARS OF NUISANCE, ANNOYANCE DISTURBANCE OR HARASSMENT

(1) On the 8th July 1987 A assaulted N, the daughter aged 10, of the tenant at 25 Anyestate, causing bruising on her leg and a graze on her arm;
(2) On the night of the 14th to 15th July 1987 A delivered a threatening note to the tenant at 25 Anyestate;
(3) On the night of the 24th to 25th July 1987 A smeared dog excrement on the door of 25 Anyestate and wrote "You were warned";
(4) On the 10th August 1987 A threw a brick through the window of 25 Anyestate;
(5) On the 20th August 1987 A dropped a brick from the fifth floor of Anyblock, Anyestate on to a Ford Escort motor car owned by Mr C who is the tenant of 25 Anyestate causing a dent in the roof;

(6) On the 20th August 1987 A assaulted Mr C on the sixth floor of Anyblock causing a cut on the cheek and bruising on the shoulder, back and face.

Ground 2: Your son who lives with you has been guilty of the following conduct which is a nuisance or annoyance to neighbours:
    (1) On the 22nd May 1987 A dropped a milk bottle from the fifth floor of Anyblock, Anyestate which landed approximately five yards from L, who is the daughter, aged 14, of the tenant at 25 Anyestate and who lives at that address;
    (2) The council will rely on the list of incidents numbered (1) to (6) above.

5 The court proceedings will not be begun until after the 21st September 1987.

Signed A.N. Officer
on behalf of Somewhere Borough Council
Address and telephone number
Dated this 21st day of August 1987.

Document 2: Claim for possession and a perpetual injunction

Note that the court may order that the claim for possession against Mrs A and the claim for trespass against A should be separated (see County Court Rules Ord 5 r2).

IN THE SOMEWHERE COUNTY COURT   Case No

BETWEEN:

SOMEWHERE BOROUGH COUNCIL	Plaintiff
and	
MRS A	First Defendant
and	
A	Second Defendant

PARTICULARS OF CLAIM

1 The Plaintiff is a local authority and is the freehold owner and entitled to possession of premises known as 22, Anyestate, Somewhere.

2 By a written agreement made between the Plaintiff and the First Defendant on the 1st April 1977 the said premises were let by the Plaintiff to the Defendant on a weekly tenancy commencing on the 5th April 1977, together with the use of the common parts of the Anyestate for the purposes only of access to and exit from the premises or for other purposes authorised by the Plaintiff.

3   The rateable value of the said premises and common parts is £300.
4   By written notice dated the 1st May 1987 the terms of the said agreement were varied in accordance with the provisions of section 102 of the Housing Act 1985 with effect from the 15th June 1987. From the 15th June there were express terms of the said tenancy that (inter alia):
[*Repeat the relevant clauses shown in Appendix 1 and referred to in the notice of intention to seek possession ie clauses 8A(1), (2), (4) and (5).*]
5   At all material times the First Defendant has lived in the said premises with her son A, the Second Defendant.
6   In breach of clauses 8A(1), (2) and (4) of the said agreement with effect from 15th June 1987 referred to in paragraph 4 above, the Second Defendant has committed acts of nuisance, annoyance or disturbance and/or harassment on the Anyestate.

PARTICULARS OF NUISANCE, ANNOYANCE, DISTURBANCE AND/OR HARASSMENT

[*Repeat verbatim the list of incidents 1 to 6 contained in the notice of intention to seek possession under ground 1 (see Document 1).*]

7   The First Defendant has permitted, incited or allowed the Second Defendant to commit the acts of nuisance, annoyance, disturbance or harassment referred to in paragraph 6.
8   Further or in the alternative by 'virtue of clause 8A(5) of the said agreement referred to in paragraph 4 the First Defendant is responsible for the acts of the Second Defendant specified in paragraph 6 and the First Defendant has broken an obligation under the said agreement.
9   Further or in the alternative A has committed nuisance or annoyance to neighbours within the meaning of ground 2 of Schedule 2 of the Housing Act 1985.

PARTICULARS OF NUISANCE OR ANNOYANCE

(1) On the 22nd May 1987 A dropped a milk bottle from the fifth floor of Anyblock, Anyestate which landed approximately five yards from L, who is the daughter aged 14 of the tenant at 25 Anyestate and who lives at that address;
(2) The council repeats the particulars in paragraph 6 above.

10   On the 14th July 1987 the First and Second Defendants were orally informed by a housing officer, F, employed by the Plaintiff, that further harassment of the C family would lead to eviction. On the 21st July the Area Housing Manager of the Plaintiff, Q, informed the First Defendant that further incidents of nuisance, annoyance or harassment by her son would lead to the Plaintiff taking possession proceedings against her and seeking her eviction. Notwithstanding the said warnings the nuisance, annoyance or harassment continued. The Plaintiff will rely on the said warnings (inter alia) as to the reasonableness of an order for possession.
11   On or about the 21st August 1987 the Plaintiff served on the First Defendant a notice seeking possession of the premises complying with section 83 of the Housing Act 1985.

12 The said tenancy is a secure tenancy within the meaning of Part IV of the Housing Act 1985 and possession is claimed under grounds 1 and 2 of Schedule 2 of the said Act.
13 Further the Plaintiff is and was at all material times the owner in possession of the common parts of the estate known as Anyestate and of the block of flats known as Anyblock on that estate of which 22, Anyestate forms a part.
14 On the 14th July the Plaintiff's housing officer, F, orally informed the Second Defendant that he was not permitted to use any of the common parts of the said Anyblock other than the walkway and landing on the fifth floor together with the stairway to the ground floor and the ground-floor passage and exit door.
15 The Second Defendant has wrongfully used the common parts of the said estate in excess of the authority given by the said tenancy agreement or otherwise for purposes other than of access to and exit from the property at 22, Anyestate.

PARTICULARS OF TRESPASS

The Plaintiff repeats the particulars in paragraphs 6 and 9 above.

16 Further the Second Defendant has wrongfully entered the common parts of Anyblock from which he was specifically excluded by the Plaintiff through their housing officer, F, on the 14th July 1987.

PARTICULARS OF TRESPASS

(1) On the night of the 14th to 15th July 1987 A went to the sixth floor of Anyblock to deliver a threatening note to the tenant at 25 Anyestate;

(2) On the night of the 24th to 25th July 1987 A went to the sixth floor of Anyblock to smear dog excrement on the door of 25 Anyestate and to write "You were warned";

(3) On the 10th August 1987 A went to the sixth floor of Anyblock to throw a brick through the window of 25 Anyestate;

(4) On the 20th August 1987 A went to the sixth floor of Anyblock to assault Mr C.

17 Further the Second Defendant has damaged and/or defaced property belonging to the Plaintiff.

PARTICULARS OF DAMAGE

(1) On the night of the 24th to 25th July 1987 A damaged and/or defaced a door at 25, Anyestate belonging to the Plaintiff by smearing dog excrement on it and writing "You were warned";

(2) On the 10th August 1987 A damaged a window of 25, Anyestate belonging to the Plaintiff by smashing the glass with a brick.

18 By reason of the matters referred to in clause 17 the Plaintiff has suffered loss and damage.

PARTICULARS OF LOSS AND DAMAGE

(1) Repair to door and repainting:	£25
(2) Reglazing window:	£25
Total loss:	£50

AND THE PLAINTIFF CLAIMS:
Against the First Defendant:
(1) Possession of the premises at 22 Anyestate, Somewhere;
(2) Rent and/or mesne profits at the rate of £25 per week from the date hereof until possession be delivered up;

OR IN THE ALTERNATIVE:
(3) An order against the First Defendant that by herself, her servants, agents, members of her family or otherwise she shall not:
   a) cause any nuisance, annoyance or disturbance to or harass the tenant at 25 Anyestate or any member of his family or household wherever they may be or any visitor to his home and in particular shall not assault molest or otherwise interfere with such persons or use threatening or abusive or insulting words or behaviour to such persons or deliver threatening abusive or insulting written material to the premises at 25 Anyestate;
   b) permit, incite or allow her son A to cause any nuisance, annoyance or disturbance or to harass the tenant at 25 Anyestate or any member of his family or household or visitor to his home or to assault, molest or otherwise interfere with such persons or to use threatening, abusive or insulting words or behaviour to such persons or deliver threatening or abusive or insulting written material to the premises at 25 Anyestate;
   c) damage or deface council property and in particular any part of the premises at 25 Anyestate or forming part of Anyblock on the Anyestate or permit, incite or allow her son A to do so;
   and in either case
(4) Costs;

Against the Second Defendant:
(5) Damages for trespass limited to £50;
(6) Interest pursuant to statute;
(7) An order that the Second Defendant by himself, his servants, agents or otherwise shall not:
   a) enter any part of the Plaintiff's property known as the Anyestate, Somewhere provided that the Second Defendant may enter the following parts of the estate for the purposes only of entering to or leaving from the premises at 22, Anyestate but for no other purposes whatsoever:
      i) the fifth floor of Anyblock;
      ii) the stairway leading from the fifth floor to the ground floor of the block;
      iii) the entrance hall on the ground floor of the block;
      iv) the passage to the exit door from the block;
      v) the paved walkway leading from the exit door of Anyblock to the roadway at Anyroad;
   b) cause any damage to or deface any property belonging to the Plaintiff;
(8) Costs.
Dated this 22nd September 1987.

Document 3: Interlocutory injunction

An interlocutory injunction obtained ex parte on the morning of 23rd September 1987 and expressed by the court to remain in effect until the 28th September 1987.

Note that the aspects of the particulars of claim shown in Document 2 that relate to trespass by the second defendant could have formed the basis of an application for an injunction considerably earlier, since the council could take proceedings for trespass before the notice of intention to seek possession had expired.

Heading as in document 2.

ORDER

Upon hearing the solicitor for the Plaintiff and upon reading the affidavits of Mr C and F and upon the Plaintiff undertaking by its solicitor to abide by any order this court may make for the payment of damages in case this court shall hereafter find that the Defendants have sustained any loss or damage by reason of this order
NOW IT IS HEREBY ORDERED as follows:
1. The First Defendant by herself, her servants, agents, members of her family or otherwise shall not:
   a) cause any nuisance, annoyance or disturbance to or harass the tenant at 25 Anyestate or any member of his family or household wherever they may be or any visitor to his home and in particular shall not assault, molest or otherwise interfere with such persons or use threatening or abusive or insulting words or behaviour to such persons or deliver threatening, abusive or insulting written material to the premises at 25 Anyestate;
   b) permit, incite or allow her son A to cause any nuisance, annoyance or disturbance to or to harass the tenant at 25 Anyestate or any member of his family or household or visitor to his home or to assault, molest or otherwise interfere with such persons or to use threatening, abusive or insulting words or behaviour to such persons or deliver threatening abusive or insulting written material to the premises at 25 Anyestate;
   c) damage or deface council property and in particular any part of the premises at 25 Anyestate or forming part of Anyblock on the Anyestate or permit, incite or allow her son A to do so.

2. The Second Defendant by himself, his servants, agents or otherwise shall not:
   a) enter any part of the Plaintiff's property known as the Anyestate, Somewhere provided that the Second Defendant may enter the following parts of the estate for the purposes only of entering to or leaving from the premises at 22, Anyestate but for no other purposes whatsoever:
   (i) the fifth floor of Anyblock;

(ii) the stairway leading from the fifth floor to the ground floor of the block;
(iii) the entrance hall on the ground floor of the block;
(iv) the passage to the exit door from the block;
(v) the paved walkway leading from the exit door of Anyblock to the roadway at Anyroad;
b) cause any damage to or deface any property belonging to the Plaintiff.

This order shall continue in effect until the 28th September 1987 at 10.30am when the court shall further consider the matter.
Costs reserved.
Dated this 23rd day of September 1987.

Signed: A Judge

TO THE FIRST DEFENDANT: Mrs A, 22 Anyestate, Anytown
AND TO THE SECOND DEFENDANT: Mr A, 22 Anyestate, Anytown.

TAKE NOTICE that unless you obey the directions contained in this order you will be guilty of contempt of court and will be liable to be committed to prison.

Signed: A Registrar

Document 4: Application for an interlocutory injunction

An application for an interlocutory injunction lasting from the 28th September 1987 until the final hearing to replace the ex parte injunction which lapses on that date.

Heading as in document 2.

NOTICE OF APPLICATION

TAKE NOTICE that the Plaintiff intends to apply to the Judge at this court at The Court House, Anystreet, Somewhere on the 28th September 1987 at 10.30am for an order that until the trial of this action:
[*Repeat the terms of the ex parte injunction in Document 3 above.*]
and that the costs of this application be the Plaintiff's in any event.
Dated this 23rd day of September 1987.

Document 5: Application to commit to prison for contempt

Heading as in document 2.

To: A
of 22, Anyestate, Somewhere.

TAKE NOTICE that the Plaintiff will apply to this Court at 10.30am on Monday the 5th October 1987 for an order for your committal to prison for having disobeyed the order of this court made on the 28th September 1987 restraining you from:

a) entering any part of the Plaintiff's property known as the Anyestate, Somewhere provided that you were permitted to enter the following parts of the estate for the purposes only of entering to or leaving from the premises at 22, Anyestate but for no other purposes whatsoever:
i) the fifth floor of Anyblock;
ii) the stairway leading from the fifth floor to the ground floor of the block;
iii) the entrance hall on the ground floor of the block;
iv) the passage to the exit door from the block;
v) the paved walkway leading from the exit door of Anyblock to the roadway at Anyroad;
b) causing any damage to or defacing any property belonging to the council;

by:
(1) Entering the landing on the sixth floor of Anyblock at approximately 5.00pm on the 28th September 1987;
(2) Defacing a wall of the ground-floor entrance hall to Anyblock on the 29th September 1987 by writing the words "You will pay for this";
(3) Entering the parking area of the Anyestate at approximately 3pm on the 30th September during the course of which you assaulted Mr C.

AND FURTHER TAKE NOTICE that you are required to attend court on the first mentioned day to show cause why an order for your committal should not be made.

Signed:
    Court officer

APPENDIX FIVE

Case Reports on Possession Proceedings Involving Racial Harassment

Note: The cases referred to below are those of which the author has details as at 1 December 1987. County court possession actions do not create precedents and the details given are extracted from judgments and other documents which in some cases provide poor or inadequate information. They are included here only as illustrations of some of the issues that may arise.

1 LB Newham v McDonnell, Bow County Court, HHJ Dobry, 23 November 1984

Source of information: Particulars of claim and copy of the judgment.

Grounds: The council claimed possession under grounds 1 and 2 of the HA 1985 Sch 2. There was an express clause in the tenancy agreement prohibiting nuisance or annoyance and making tenant responsible for friends, relatives, lodgers and sub-tenants.

Allegations: The council alleged that there were frequent late-night parties held by the tenant's sons, associated with violence, noise, racial abuse, racist graffiti and the smashing of milk bottles; fouling of common parts by dogs; racial abuse to one neighbour. The victim had been rehoused but was still in fear of harassment.

Court hearing: The council provided evidence that it was unable to rehouse black tenants on that estate. A police witness confirmed noisy parties and nuisance by dogs. The tenant was unrepresented and declined to give evidence.

Decision: Possession order in 14 days and £100 costs. The judge said he accepted the authority's version of the facts and that the nuisance was racial. He also accepted that the tenant was legally responsible for the acts of her sons which were very serious. The behaviour was an annoyance within ground 2. The housing management problems of trying to allocate housing to black families were taken into account.

Comments:
i) After initial complaints the victim was supplied with an incident form which he kept very fully and which must have considerably improved his evidence.

ii) It is difficult to know what effect there would have been if the tenant had been legally represented.
iii) Note that the victims had already been rehoused.

2 LB Camden v Walsh, Bloomsbury and Marylebone County Court, HHJ Martin, 10 April 1986

Sources of information: Copy of the judgment, particulars of claim and report to Housing Management Committee of LB Camden 11/8/86.

Grounds: The council claimed possession under grounds 1 and 2. There was an express clause in the tenancy agreement prohibiting racial harassment. The claim for possession was expressly based on a campaign of racial harassment against neighbours. Tenant's children were 20, 18, 16 and 15.

Allegations: The council made 18 allegations against the Walsh family, including two incidents when Bengali men were shot with an air rifle. The tenant's 17-year-old son was convicted of assault occasioning actual bodily harm for one of the attacks. The council alleged that the tenant knew her son had the gun and allowed its use. Other incidents including cutting of telephone wires, threats of violence, abuse, assaults, damage to property, dumping rubbish and urinating outside neighbours' homes. Seven of the incidents were against Asians. Seven were against a neighbouring tenant, Mrs Whelan, who had, until recently, been friendly with the defendant.

Court hearing: The tenant admitted that the tenancy agreement contained a clause prohibiting racial harassment (contrast with case 3 below). The tenant denied almost all the allegations, claiming several of the incidents were two-sided fights. The tenant's representatives made play of the fact that no warning had been given.

Decision: Possession ordered, suspended as long as the tenant or any person residing with her committed no further act of nuisance or annoyance against anyone on the estate and no weapon was kept on the premises.

The judge said he considered racial harassment "an emotive phrase" and said that the tenant's motive was not relevant. He accepted that nuisance and annoyance had been caused but stated that there was no evidence of a campaign of racial harassment. Many of the acts complained of were against one white neighbour. The acts had all occurred within a period of a few weeks and he was not convinced that eviction was the best solution. He accepted that there was fear amongst other tenants on the estate particularly Bengalis. The judge considered that the tenant should have been given a warning.

Comments:
i) It cannot be correct that the motive of the tenant is irrelevant. It must certainly be a factor to be taken into account when deciding whether it is reasonable to order possession. In addition, if the motive for an attack

is racism, this makes it considerably more likely that attacks will occur against other innocent victims.

ii) The last incident of harassment occurred in July/August 1985 but proceedings were not issued until early 1986. The authority had received advice that its case would be improved by a conviction in criminal proceedings of one of the tenant's children. While a conviction may improve matters, the consequent delay and opportunity for the court to decide that the problem has resolved itself will outweigh any advantage from a conviction in most circumstances.

iii) The independence of the council's interpreter was successfully challenged on the first day and eventually a council officer had to interpret. This case shows how important it is for an authority to arrange for proper interpreters.

iv) Warnings form an important part of any authority case. The sooner they can be issued the better.

v) The authority took steps to protect witnesses, including:
- increased caretaker patrols every day;
- keeping emergency rehousing available in case required;
- installing telephones and providing officers' phone numbers at home;
- informing police and asking for increased vigilance;
- alerting the authority's mobile security patrol;
- providing transport for witnesses to and from court.

3 LB Camden v Hawkins, Clerkenwell County Court, HHJ Burkett-Baker QC, 6 November 1986

Sources of information: Copy of the judgment and particulars of claim.

Grounds: The council claimed possession under grounds 1 and 2. There was an express clause in the tenancy agreement prohibiting racial harassment.

Allegations: The council alleged that the tenant had assaulted a neighbour and been convicted of assault; the tenant's son, aged 17, had assaulted another neighbour, had smashed windows, spat at visitors and shouted racist and other verbal abuse; that the tenant had kept a dog in breach of a court order and that a council workman had been abused. The council also sought possession for rent arrears but this aspect of the claim was discounted at an early stage.

Court hearing: The tenant called two Afro-Caribbean witnesses to give evidence that she was not racially prejudiced and argued that the express clause relating to racial harassment had not been properly incorporated into her tenancy agreement.

Decision: No order for possession. The council to pay the tenant's costs. The judge accepted that racial harassment could amount to nuisance or annoyance. He discounted the assault on the neighbour by the tenant because it had happened five years before. The judge did not accept much of the evidence of the main Asian witness, saying, "The interpreter was clearly uncomfortable." The judge concluded that the allegations were largely a short-lived feud between the tenant's son and a neighbouring family and that the tenant could not be expected to control the behaviour of her 17-year-old.

Comments:
i) The council could not prove that it had followed the procedure for varying tenancy conditions set out in the HA 1985 so the court ruled that the old conditions still applied which did not refer to racial harassment.
ii) The judge's comments suggest that poor interpretation adversely affected the result.
iii) The judge's view that he could not expect the tenant to control her 17-year-old son must be incorrect as the statute clearly intends tenants to be responsible for the behaviour of those living with them however old they may be.

4 LB Islington v Isherwood, Mr Recorder Montlake, Clerkenwell County Court, February 1987

Sorces of information: Judgment and particulars of claim.

Ground: The council claimed possession based on ground 2.

Allegations: The council alleged nine acts against one neighbouring black family including assaults, abuse and threats; four acts of general nuisance to all tenants in the area and two incidents involving other families. The tenant was responsible for some of the incidents but many of them were carried out by the tenant's children.

Court hearing: The tenant argued that the notice of intention to seek possession was invalid as it did not contain sufficient particulars.

Decision: Order for possession in 28 days. The judge accepted most of the council's evidence and held the tenant responsible for her children's behaviour. The judgment makes no reference to "racial harassment" and dealt with the case on the basis of nuisance. The judge held that the notice of intention to seek possession was valid since the tenant was aware of what was complained of because there had been separate proceedings by a neighbour in which a comprehensive affidavit had been filed.

Comments:
i) The council called the 13-year-old daughter of one of the tenants to give evidence on its behalf because the defence challenged an attempt to give hearsay evidence. The judge accepted that girl's evidence.
ii) If there had been no previous proceedings between the tenant and a neighbour the council's notice of intention to seek possession might have been held to have been invalid, in which case the case would have been dismissed.

5 Ealing Family Housing Association v Taylor, HHJ Barr, Brentford County Court, 17 March 1987

Source of information: Copy of judgment (two-thirds of a page).

Ground: The Housing Association claimed possession under ground 2.

Allegations: The Association claimed one incident of assault on a visitor and incidents of obscene language and racial abuse. The victims were two Asian girls living above the defendant, a single man in a house converted into two flats.

Decision: No order for possession. The judge found the evidence called on the Association's behalf to be exaggerated and was not satisfied that there had been a nuisance at all or only a slight one. The judge stated at the commencement of the hearing that he would be very reluctant to deprive the defendant of his right to a discount which would be a considerable amount because he was a long-standing tenant.

Comment: The loss of a discount is clearly a factor which affects the reasonableness of an order for possession but the statute still intends that possession can be granted where it is appropriate, even if the defendant might lose a discount. In this case, the defendant appeared to intend to exercise the right to a discount in the near future.

6 LB Islington v Connor, HHJ Lipfriend, Westminster County Court, 25 March 1987

Sources of information: Judgment and briefing to Islington Housing Management sub-committee dated March 1987.

Grounds: The council claimed possession based on grounds 1 and 2. There was an express clause relating to racial harassment in the tenancy agreement.

Allegations: The council alleged damage to property, racial and other abuse and threats and intimidation of many Bangladeshi children. Almost all the incidents were committed by the tenant's son, aged 10. Harassment had continued even after the court proceedings were begun. The council stated that it would rehouse the tenant if she were evicted.

Court hearing: The council called teachers from the local school to give evidence, who were able to add substantial weight to the allegations of racial harassment and its effect on the Bangladeshi children.

Decision: Immediate order for possession. The judge accepted that the tenant's son was responsible for racial harassment and that the tenant should have controlled him.

Comments:
i) The judge accepted evidence of the racial nature of the harassment and this formed the basis for the order for possession.
ii) The evidence from teachers of the racial nature of the harassment seemed to be crucial.
iii) The council's offer to rehouse the tenant if she were evicted obviously influenced the decision.

iv) The council, ILEA staff and local community groups took measures to protect witnesses, including:
- setting up a phone network with telephones or two-way radios for all vulnerable families;
- providing a flat on the estate for a support group;
- reinforcing doors and windows;
- installing fireproof letter boxes;
- agreeing increased caretaker patrols (never provided, in fact);
- undertaking to rehouse immediately any family under serious threat;
- play-scheme for children of vulnerable families;
- separation of witnesses at court from the defendant and her witnesses;
- transport to and from court;
- an escort service for children to and from school.

7 LB Hackney v Towart, HHJ Stucley, Shoreditch County Court, 27 August 1987

Source of information: LB Hackney legal department.

Ground: The council claimed possession based on ground 2. There was no express clause relating to racial harassment in the tenancy agreement.

Court hearing: The court heard that the allegations made against the tenant had already been the subject of separate proceedings brought by the victim and an injunction was still in force against the tenant Mr Towart.

Decision: The judge considered that an outright possession order was inappropriate when the tenant was already restrained from further harassment by an injunction, but indicated that he was prepared to make a suspended possession order. The council declined to accept this, insisting on outright possession. This was refused and no possession order was made.

Comment: The case suggests that it may be difficult to get an outright order for possession if an injunction is already in force, unless there has been further harassment since the injunction was made.

APPENDIX SIX

Criminal Offences

List of criminal offences that may be relevant to cases of racial harassment (excluding those covered in Chapter 10 part B)

The requirements of the offences are paraphrased. Unless otherwise stated each offence:
— is arrestable by a police officer;
— can be tried in the Crown Court;
— is such that the maximum sentence includes an unlimited fine or a term of imprisonment exceeding five years.

1 *Criminal damage* (destroying or damaging property belonging to another): Criminal Damage Act (CDA) 1971. Triable only in the magistrates' court if the value of damage is less than £400 and damage is not caused by fire. See p178.

2 *Arson* (destroying or damaging property belonging to another by fire): CDA 1971 s1(1). See p178.

3 *Destroying or damaging property with intent to endanger life or reckless whether life would be endangered:* CDA 1971 s1(2).

4 *Threats to destroy or damage property belonging to any person:* CDA 1971 s2.

5 *Possessing anything with intent to destroy or damage property:* CDA 1971 s3.

6 *Riot* (12 or more people threatening or using violence for a common purpose which would cause a reasonable person to fear for his or her safety if such a person were present): Public Order Act (POA) 1986 s1. Prosecution requires the consent of the Director of Public Prosecutions.

7 *Violent disorder* (three or more people using or threatening violence which would cause a reasonable person to fear for his or her safety if such a person were present): POA 1986 s2.

8 *Affray* (using or threatening violence which would cause a reasonable person to fear for his or her safety if such a person were present): POA 1986 s3. Maximum sentence 3 years' imprisonment on Crown Court trial. See p179.

9 *Threatening, abusive or insulting words or behaviour causing fear of violence or provoking or likely to provoke violence by any person:* POA 1986 s4(1)(a).

Triable only in the magistrates' court. Maximum sentence 6 months' imprisonment or £2,000 fine or both.

10 *Displaying or distributing any writing, sign or other visible thing that is threatening, abusive or insulting and causing fear of violence or provoking or likely to provoke violence by any person:* POA 1986 s4(1)(b). Triable and sentencing as for 9 above.

11 *Threatening, abusive or insulting words or behaviour or disorderly behaviour within the hearing or sight of a person likely to be caused harassment, alarm or distress:* POA 1986 s5(1)(a). Triable only in the magistrates' court. Maximum sentence £400 fine. No imprisonment powers. A police officer may only arrest if s/he has warned the offender to stop and the offence is repeated shortly afterwards.

12 *Displaying any writing, sign or visible thing which is threatening abusive or insulting within the hearing or sight of a person likely to be caused harassment, alarm or distress:* POA 1986 s5(1)(b). Triable, arrestable and sentencing as for 11 above.

13 *Using threatening abusive or insulting words or behaviour or displaying written material which is threatening abusive or insulting intending to stir up racial hatred:* (see p180).

14 *Publishing or distributing written material which is threatening abusive or insulting intending to stir up racial hatred:* (see p180).

15 *Possessing written material which is threatening abusive or insulting with a view to its being distributed or published and intending to stir up racial hatred:* (see p180).

16 *Possession of an offensive weapon in a public place:* Prevention of Crimes Act 1953 s1. Maximum sentence on Crown Court trial is two years' imprisonment or unlimited fine or both.

17 *Common assault:* (see pp180 and 204).

18 *Aggravated assault:* (see p 205).

19 *Assault occasioning actual bodily harm:* (see p181).

20 *Wounding with intent to do grievous bodily harm:* Offences Against the Person Act (OAPA) 1861 s18.

21 *Malicious wounding or grievous bodily harm:* OAPA 1861 s20.

22 *Threats to kill:* OAPA 1861 s16.

23 *Causing an explosive substance to explode or sending or delivering an explosive substance or any other dangerous or noxious thing to any person or throwing any corrosive, explosive or destructive substance at any person with intent to burn, maim, disfigure or cause grievous bodily harm:* OAPA 1861 s29.

24 *Using or threatening violence to a person or to property in order to gain entry into premises when some person is present inside the premises who is opposed to entry:* Criminal Law Act (CLA) 1977 s6. Triable only in the magistrates' court. Maximum sentence is 6 months' imprisonment or £2,000 fine or both.

25 *Trespassing with a weapon of offence:* CLA 1977 s8. Triable only in the magistrates' court. Maximum sentence is 3 months' imprisonment or £2,000 fine or both.

26 *Rape:* Sexual Offences Act 1956 s1.

27 *Murder.*

28 *Manslaughter.*

29 *False imprisonment:* (see p183).

30 *Robbery:* Theft Act (TA) 1968 s8.

31 *Blackmail* (an unwarranted demand with menaces with a view to gaining property or money): TA 1968 s21.

32 *Burglary:* (see p182).

33 *Aggravated burglary* (burglary with an offensive weapon or explosive): TA 1968 s10.

34 *Possession of articles for use in the course of a burglary:* TA 1968 s25. Maximum sentence on Crown Court trial is 3 years' imprisonment.

35 *Causing explosion likely to endanger life:* Explosive Substances Act (ESA) 1883 s2. Prosecution requires consent of Attorney-General.

36 *Attempting to cause explosion or possession of explosive with intent to endanger life or cause serious injury:* ESA 1883 s3. Prosecution requires consent of Attorney-General.

37 *Possession of explosive substance for unlawful object:* ESA 1883 s4. Prosecution requires consent of Attorney-General.

38 *Publishing an obscene article:* Obscene Publications Act 1959 s2.

39 *Posting an indecent or obscene document through the post:* Post Office Act 1953 s11(b). Maximum sentence on Crown Court trial is 12 months' imprisonment. The offence is not arrestable.

40 *Posting an explosive, dangerous, noxious or deleterious article or any filth which is likely to injure postal staff:* Post Office Act 1953 s11(a). Penalties as in 39.

41 *Making grossly offensive or indecent, obscene or menacing phone calls:* Post Office Act 1969 s78. The offence is not arrestable. It is triable only in the magistrates' court and the maximum penalty is a £400 fine.

42 *Cruelty to animals including poisoning:* Protection of Animals Act 1911 s1. The offence is triable only in the magistrates' court and the maximum sentence is 3 months' imprisonment or a fine of £1,000 or both.

43 *Intimidation, persistent following or watching or besetting premises:* (see p182).

44 *Misconduct in public office:* (see p198).

45 *Offences in the street of obstruction of the highway, obscene language, discharging a firework, throwing a stone and other similar offences:* Town Police Clauses Act 1847 s28. Outside London only (see Chapter 11).

46 *Offences in a public place of obstruction of highway, flyposting or writing graffiti, discharging fireworks and similar offences:* Metropolitan Police Act 1839 s54. Greater London only (see Chapter 11).

Note that in addition to the above offences, it will usually also be an offence:
— to conspire to commit the offence (Criminal Law Act 1977 s1);
— to attempt to commit the offence (Criminal Attempts Act 1981 s1);
— to incite others to commit the offence;
— to aid and abet the offence.

APPENDIX SEVEN

A Specimen Information

This specimen information to start criminal proceedings is based on the facts given in the statement of Mr C in Appendix 3. Separate informations would be required for offences of criminal damage and assault occasioning actual bodily harm.

BEFORE THE   MAGISTRATES' COURT
INFORMATION UNDER PROTECTION FROM EVICTION ACT 1977 s1(3)
(Magistrates' Courts Act 1980 s1; Magistrates' Courts Rules 1981)

DATE:

ACCUSED: A

ADDRESS: 22, Anyestate, Somewhere

ALLEGED OFFENCE: That with intent to cause Mr C, the residential occupier of premises at 25, Anyestate, Somewhere, to give up the occupation of the premises, the accused has done acts calculated to interfere with the peace or comfort of Mr C or members of his household.

THE INFORMATION OF: Mr E. Ficient, Solicitor to the council on behalf of the Somewhere Borough Council.

ADDRESS: Town Hall, Somewhere.
Who states on oath that the accused committed the offence of which particulars are given above.

....
Justice of the Peace/Justices' Clerk

APPENDIX EIGHT

Suggested format for keeping contemporaneous notes

Somewhere Borough Council   Ref:

　　Please return this form to: Ms F, Estate Officer, Housing Office, Anyestate

Issued to: Mr A and family, 25 Anyestate

Date	Time	Details of incident	Noted by

Index

ABUSE, 43, 44, 46, 177, 180, 210, 279
ACCOMMODATION
  alternative, 120, 121, 128, 143, 170
  temporary, 88, 89, 91, 101, 108, 109, 121, 124, 127, 128, 135, 267
ACTION
  positive, see POSITIVE ACTION
ADJOURNMENT, 76, 77, 78, 165
ADMINISTRATIVE LAW, 6, 20, 21, 22, 23, 24, 87, 91, 112, 125, 128, 216
AFFIDAVIT, 72, 80, 81, 83, 240-241, 246, 250
AFFRAY, 179-180, 181, 187, 190, 305
AGREEMENT
  tenancy, see TENANCY AGREEMENT
AID
  legal, see LEGAL AID
ALLOCATION
  housing, of, 26, 27, 86-88, 92-93, 102, 108, 109, 110, 115, 221, 267, 268
ARREST, 82, 83, 150, 161, 164, 188-190, 195, 203, 212, 276
ARSON, 3, 89, 178, 179, 187, 305
ASSAULT
  common, 23, 28, 168, 180, 181, 194, 204-205, 306
ATTORNEY-GENERAL, 19, 22, 23, 24, 25, 27, 180, 204, 273, 275

BAIL, 164, 165, 169, 170, 192-193
  condition of, 142, 164, 165-166, 168, 170, 193
BAILIFF, 79, 83
BED & BREAKFAST, 99, 102, 119-123, 124, 175, 211
BIND OVER, 28, 139, 168, 171, 180, 190, 205
BREACH OF THE PEACE, 83, 150, 161, 168, 190, 203, 276
BUILDING SOCIETY, 51, 52, 53, 98, 102, 103, 107
BYELAW, 45, 112-113, 128, 129, 159
  breach of, 16, 45, 46, 59, 129, 159, 177

CAMERA
  video, 36, 40, 110, 243
CARE PROCEEDINGS, 136-139, 161
  order in, see ORDER
CENTRE
  law, see LAW CENTRE
CHILD
  witness, as, see WITNESS
CLAIM
  particulars of, see PARTICULARS OF CLAIM
COMMISSION FOR RACIAL EQUALITY, 32, 67, 115, 217, 231, 263, 264, 265
COMMITTEE
  reception, see "RECEPTION COMMITTEE"
COMMUNITY GROUP, 4, 5, 36, 38, 47, 186, 221, 230, 254, 255

COMPENSATION, 43, 202, 203, 207, 211, 212, 217, 223, 224, 226, 266
  see also DAMAGES
  order, *see* ORDER
COMPULSORY PURCHASE ORDER *see* ORDER
CONSULTATION, 16, 49, 62, 96, 97, 98, 112, 197, 218
CONTEMPT
  court, of, 73, 82, 83, 250, 298
CONTRACT
  breach of, 19, 25
  compliance, 13, 16, 48
CO-OPERATIVE
  housing, 52, 53, 57, 97, 117-118, 119, 173
  management, 101, 102, 118-119
COSTS, 21, 75, 96, 204, 206, 299, 301
COUNTY COURT *see* COURT
COURT
  county, 18, 66, 75, 80, 83, 124, 141, 217, 299
  Court of Appeal, 11, 134, 197, 210, 224
  Crown, 18, 43, 162, 163, 171, 173, 174, 175, 176, 177, 180, 181, 182, 183, 202, 205, 207
  High, 11, 18, 80, 141, 154, 156, 265
  House of Lords, 11, 197
  juvenile, 138-139, 142, 163-164, 168
  magistrates', 18, 28, 43, 53, 129, 143, 144, 154, 155, 156, 159, 162, 163, 164, 168, 169, 171, 173, 175, 176, 177, 178, 180, 181, 182, 183, 188, 190, 193, 194, 201, 205, 206, 207
  order *see* ORDER
CRIMINAL OFFENCE *see* OFFENCE
CROWN PROSECUTION SERVICE, 21, 198-199, 213, 275

DAMAGE
  criminal, 23, 43, 178-179, 187, 195, 274, 287, 305
DAMAGES, 57, 70, 71, 80, 95, 162, 207, 208, 209, 211, 276
  see also COMPENSATION
DECISION-MAKING
  authorisation of, 9, 28, 61, 74, 227
  delegation of, 8, 91, 134
DEFENCE
  self, 202-203
DEPARTMENT OF ENVIRONMENT, 45, 87, 264
DIRECTOR OF PUBLIC PROSECUTIONS, 19
DISCRETION
  fettering of, 9, 91, 95
DISCRETIONARY FACILITIES, 38, 111, 140, 143, 266
  withdrawal of, 13, 14, 111
  withholding of, 11, 13, 14, 46, 47, 49, 111, 142, 266
DISCRIMINATION
  racial, 7, 11, 13, 26, 31, 32, 33, 92, 115, 146, 217
  indirect, 31
DOGS
  harassment by, 43, 46, 58, 59, 113, 155, 181, 194, 195, 212
DUTY
  statutory,
    obstruction to, 26, 70, 115

ENVIRONMENT
  Department of, *see* DEPARTMENT OF ENVIRONMENT
ENVIRONMENTAL HEALTH OFFICER, 54, 123, 126, 157
EQUAL OPPORTUNITIES, 11, 27, 146
  policy on, 13, 14, 16, 48, 50, 112

EVICTION, 79, 87, 90, 91, 92, 116, 127, 141, 170, 226, 270,
EVIDENCE
rules of, 166, 207, 223

FINE, 45, 69, 154, 156, 159, 161, 163, 166, 168, 171, 176, 178, 180, 181, 183, 195, 205, 206
FINGERPRINTS, 191

GRAFFITI, 19, 42, 51, 52, 59, 65, 93, 94, 149, 158, 179, 182, 195, 271, 273
GRANTS
conditions imposed in, 16, 47, 50, 101, 109, 112, 118, 127, 143, 266
GROUP
racial, 32, 33, 93, 97, 148, 180

HARASSMENT
non-racial, 1, 7, 16, 18, 93, 95, 116, 121, 122, 172, 174, 175, 189, 269-270, 272, 287
racial,
policy on, 6, 7, 12, 13, 15, 18, 30, 31, 33, 34, 35, 37, 50, 94, 98, 112, 118, 143, 146, 155, 220-222, 264, 265, 269
unreasonable, 209-210
HIGH COURT see COURT
HIGHWAY, 40, 44, 54, 149, 158, 176
obstruction of, 25, 44, 176, 178, 189, 195, 308
unreasonable use of, 43, 44, 70, 149, 176
HOME HELP, 15, 48, 140, 143
HOME OFFICE, 37, 67, 264
HOMELESS
intentionally homeless, 10, 26, 64, 87, 88-92, 110, 121, 134, 135, 268

HOSTEL
local authority, 48, 123, 124, 143, 211
HOUSE IN MULTIPLE OCCUPATION, 39, 122, 123-126
HOUSING ASSOCIATION, 16, 50, 52, 53, 57, 63, 86, 90, 96, 97, 98, 99, 100, 101, 102, 106, 117-118, 173, 214, 221, 269
co-operative, 97, 117-118
HOUSING CO-OPERATIVE see CO-OPERATIVE
HOUSING TRUST, 52, 57, 96, 97, 117-118, 214

IDENTIFICATION
group, 192
parade, see PARADE
IMPRISONMENT
false, 183, 209, 211, 307
INCITEMENT
racial hatred, to, 1, 19, 180, 238, 306
INJUNCTION, 20, 23, 24, 25, 26, 40, 41, 46, 57, 61, 65, 69-73, 80, 82, 83, 113, 115, 116, 117, 141, 148, 149, 154, 156, 176, 208-209, 211, 226, 250, 274, 277, 292
breach of, 73, 83, 207, 276
interlocutory, 71, 72, 73, 78, 80-83, 208, 217, 241, 250, 296
INTEREST
public, see PUBLIC INTEREST
INTERPRETER, 77, 228, 248-249, 301, 302

JUDGE, 65, 68, 69, 72, 73, 79, 90, 141, 171, 210, 231, 232, 235, 246, 247, 249, 250, 252, 253, 254, 260, 299-304
JUDICIAL REVIEW, 6, 216-217

LANDLORD, 41, 52, 173, 174, 175, 207, 211, 269, 270

LAW
  administrative, *see*
    ADMINISTRATIVE LAW
  centre, 36, 50, 201, 204, 215
LEGAL AID, 21, 72, 73, 78, 96,
    201-202, 204, 206, 215, 216,
    274
LICENCE
  conditions imposed in, 15, 47,
    49, 101, 110, 111, 114, 127,
    128, 143, 266
  football club drinking, 54
  music and dance, 54, 55, 215
  public house, 53, 54, 215
LICENSEE
  hostel, 16, 48, 125, 143, 173,
    175, 211

MAGISTRATES' COURT *see*
    COURT
MANAGEMENT
  co-operative, *see* CO-OPERATIVE
  housing, 14, 19, 26, 27, 39, 40,
    49, 58, 65, 66, 67-68, 96, 99,
    100, 104, 105, 106, 107, 109,
    112
MOBILITY
  Scheme, 98, 102, 214
MOTIVE
  racial, 8, 41, 65, 69, 71, 147,
    169, 172, 300

NOMINATION
  rights of, 50, 101, 102, 111
NOTICE
  notice of intention to seek
    possession, 73-75, 228, 229,
    270, 291, 302
  service of notice requiring
    information, 39, 52, 123,
    124, 156
  suspension of, 126, 156, 157,
    159
NUISANCE, 3, 8, 16, 19, 25, 40,
    41, 44, 57, 58, 63, 69, 71, 93,
    95, 115, 116, 126, 128, 129,
    148, 149, 150, 178, 209, 211,
    218, 227
  noise, 25, 155-157, 175, 204,
    206
  public, 19, 20, 25, 27, 40, 43,
    44, 45, 70, 149, 151, 176,
    177-178, 209, 211-212
  recurring, 66, 71, 154-155, 176,
    206
  statutory, 25, 153-155, 175, 204,
    205-206, 218

OCCUPIER, 39, 41, 42, 52, 86, 154,
    155, 156, 157, 158, 159, 175,
    187, 195, 205, 206, 208, 211,
    269, 272-273
OFFENCE
  criminal, 7, 23, 27, 59, 66, 70,
    77, 113, 124, 137, 138, 139,
    149, 154, 156, 157, 159, 161,
    175, 204, 206-207, 265, 271-
    272, 273, 305-308
ORDER
  attendance centre, 167
  care, 167, 168
  community service, 167
  compensation, 139, 149, 166,
    168, 207, 208, 274
  compulsory purchase, 126-127,
    269
  control, 87, 125-126
  court,
    breach of, 81, 82, 83, 141,
      154, 156, 157, 159, 165,
      276, 298
    suspended, 73, 79, 83, 116,
      167, 300, 304
  nuisance, 154, 155
  possession,
    reasonableness of, 59, 60, 61,
      64, 65-66, 72, 75, 79, 122,
      126, 244, 246, 303
  probation, 167
  supervision, 138, 142, 167-168

ORGANISATION
   voluntary, see VOLUNTARY ORGANISATION
OWNER OCCUPIER, 25, 41, 45, 53, 58, 64, 86, 99, 102, 106-107, 126, 174, 175, 211, 213, 221, 267, 269

PARADE
   identification, 192
PARTICULARS OF CLAIM, 74, 76, 77, 80, 83, 242, 292
PEACE
   breach of the, see BREACH OF THE PEACE
PERMISSION
   to enter,
      withholding of, 42
PERPETRATOR
   identification of, 16, 39, 41, 94, 109, 155, 175, 186, 192, 206, 212, 213, 230, 258, 285
PLAYGROUP, 16, 38, 47, 104, 112, 135, 140, 142, 144
POLICE, 4, 21, 23, 39, 54, 67, 82, 83, 137, 138, 150, 162, 164, 165, 174, 181, 212-213, 218, 231
   complaints against, 37
POSITIVE ACTION, 33
POSSESSION PROCEEDINGS, 19, 57, 60, 61, 63-69, 73, 80, 90, 91, 227, 270, 292, 299-304
PROBATION
   service, 139, 167, 172
PROCEEDINGS
   criminal
      awaiting the outcome of, 24, 77-78
      same offence, for, 23, 66, 161, 205, 210, 242, 243
   possession, see POSSESSION PROCEEDINGS
PROOF
   burden of, 77-78, 137, 154, 156, 206, 236

PROSECUTION
   private, 28, 36
PUBLIC INTEREST, 21, 22, 23, 28, 71, 215
PUBLICITY
   educational, 35, 61, 109, 112, 118, 142, 146-147
   media, 46, 169, 171, 225, 230-231, 234, 245, 251, 252, 277

QUALIFICATION
   genuine occupational, 33

RACIAL GROUP see GROUP
RATEPAYER, 7, 23, 49
RATES, 49, 50, 213,
"RECEPTION COMMITTEE", 115, 175, 183
RECOGNISANCE, 138, 168
RECORDING
   racial incidents, of, 4, 23, 38, 67, 69, 118, 119, 121, 123, 158, 196, 197, 198, 231, 254-256, 264, 275, 285, 310
   refusals of housing offers, of, 67, 92, 221
REGISTRATION, 124, 128-129, 143, 144
REHOUSING, 66, 67, 68, 87, 89, 98, 101, 102, 122, 126, 127, 128, 135, 136, 141, 221, 222, 250, 267, 300, 303
REMOVAL
   expenses of, 7, 66, 68, 99, 100, 101, 103, 135, 221, 266
REPAIR
   duty to, 93, 94, 217
REVIEW
   judicial, see JUDICIAL REVIEW
RIGHT TO BUY, 15, 16, 49, 52
RUBBISH
   dumping of, 42, 46, 113, 155, 158, 175-176, 177, 211, 212

SAMPLE, 191

SCHEME
Mobility, see MOBILITY SCHEME
SCHOOL, 41, 42, 45, 46, 48, 50, 54, 146-151, 183, 210, 270, 271, 279
  children, 25, 40, 42, 43, 44, 58, 146-151, 177, 271
SECONDMENT
  staff, of, 16, 35, 37, 140, 216
SECURITY
  devices, 36, 40, 94, 100, 104-107, 127, 135, 221, 250, 267
SERVICE
  proof of, 61, 62, 74, 81, 82, 83, 164
SOCIAL WORKER, 34, 35, 37, 140, 142, 157, 173, 225, 254
SQUATTER, 127, 174, 175, 178
STONE-THROWING, 43, 44, 46, 113, 177, 180, 181, 195, 203, 211
SUMMONS, 164, 165, 169, 205
  witness, 254

TELEPHONE CALLS
  abusive, 40, 193, 214
TENANCY AGREEMENT
  breach of, 63, 68-69, 70, 71, 116, 141, 214
  conditions imposed in, 15, 49, 51, 57-63, 101, 110, 111, 114, 116, 117, 127, 143, 266, 279-281
  enforcement of, 95, 96, 270, 281
  express clause in, 51, 57-61, 65, 68, 69, 70, 90, 114, 118, 279-281, 299
  variation of, 9, 61-63, 76, 240, 282-284, 302
TENANT
  ex-council, 15, 16, 49, 116
  lodgers of, 41, 58, 59, 64, 90
  private, 58, 64, 86, 99, 102, 106, 107, 173, 211, 267
  sub-tenant, 41, 58, 59, 64

  visitor of, 41, 42, 58, 59, 60, 90, 95, 114, 270
TENANTS' ASSOCIATION, 16, 47, 62, 97, 98, 111, 112, 215, 255
TRADE UNION, 16, 47
TRANSFER
  conditions imposed in, 15, 48, 49, 51, 116, 117
TRESPASS, 16, 19, 25, 40, 41, 42, 60, 70, 71, 82, 113, 114, 115, 148, 149, 150, 182, 203, 204, 209, 211, 292, 307

UNDERTAKING, 81, 82, 83

VICTIM
  protection of, 18, 67, 71, 72, 78, 104, 120, 122, 126, 128, 139, 143, 165, 166, 167, 169, 170, 172, 209, 222, 225, 226, 233, 234, 247, 270
  support group, 35, 36, 37, 98, 108, 109, 140, 230, 266
VOLUNTARY ORGANISATION, 34, 35, 36, 38, 135, 140, 143, 215, 221, 222, 230, 266

WARDSHIP, 19, 25, 121, 141-142
WARNING, 60, 65, 92, 109, 121, 126, 300, 301
WARRANT, 164, 165, 169, 188, 193
  possession, of, 79
  search, 187
WASTE, 63, 64, 65
WITNESS, 72, 76, 129, 162, 163, 166, 170, 225, 226, 228, 229, 231, 244-254, 257-260, 274, 277, 285, 287
  child, 242, 243-244, 245, 246, 251-252, 253-254, 258, 302
  expert, 67, 173, 225, 231-232, 247, 254

Other LAG Law and Practice Guides

Police Misconduct: Legal Remedies Harrison

A fully comprehensive guide to the remedies and procedures available in this often complex area; from court action to an application to the Criminal Injuries Compensation Board:

- police complaints
- civil actions against the police
- inquests
- European Convention on Human Rights
- police discipline
- judicial review
- wrongful convictions
- inquiries
- criminal proceedings
- legal aid

Appendices include levels of damages, police records, useful names and addresses and the police Codes of Practice. Fully tabled and indexed, this guide will be invaluable for lay advisers and solicitors alike.

Feb 1987   248pp   £12.00

Practice and Procedure in Industrial Tribunals: A Guide to Unfair Dismissal and Redundancy Clayton

This book comprises the series of articles by Richard Clayton first published in the LAG's monthly journal, *LEGAL ACTION*, between August 1985 and August 1986. The full texts of the Industrial Tribunals and Employment Appeal Tribunal Rules of Procedure are included, with comprehensive tables and index.

Detailed guidance and practical advice on tactics are provided for the employment law adviser, from first application through to the substantive hearing, costs, reviews and enforcement to appeals.

Oct 1986   142pp   £7.50

Immigration Emergency Procedures   Fransman and Webb

A companion to *The Emergency Procedures Handbook*, *Immigration Emergency Procedures* is a complete guide to dealing with the range of immigration emergencies which require immediate action to prevent a client's removal from the UK and/or to secure release from detention.

Additional appendices include official forms used by the immigration authorities which an adviser is likely to encounter, client questionnaire, visa requirements, charts indicating the administrative structure of the immigration authorities (with useful telephone numbers) and appeals and time limits, relevant organisations and bibliography. The Immigration Act 1971, as amended, is also provided.

"a useful and practical book" — *Solicitor's Journal*
"this is a book to be recommended" — *SCOLAG*

Mar 1986   198pp   £11.00

Homeless Persons   *third edition*   Arden

A new edition of Arden's popular guide. *Roof* described the first edition as "a fine phrase by phrase dissection, explaining the meaning of each part [of the legislation] in the light of decided cases and relating the parts to the whole with the usual Arden skills."

Fully up-to-date, *Homeless Persons* is revised to take account of the enormous wealth of case-law that has continued to grow since the first edition was published. *Homeless Persons* includes the full text of the Housing Act 1985 Part III and the revised Code of Guidance.

Forthcoming   £12.00

Quiet Enjoyment   *second edition*   Arden and Partington

The law relating to harassment and illegal eviction is particularly complex and technical. But speedy action is often needed to prevent tenants from becoming homeless. *Quiet Enjoyment* brings together all the relevant provisions and gives clear, practical advice on how to use both the civil and criminal law.

This fully revised edition includes step by step guidance to obtaining an injunction, detailed notes on damages awards, the forms used in civil proceedings and explanations of how to complete them, and the full text of the Protection from Eviction Act 1977.

"advisers should prepare themselves by obtaining at least one copy of this book — you will be glad of the company" — *Roof*

April 1985   132pp   £7.00

Repairs: Tenants' Rights   Luba

A guide to the diverse statutory and common law rights of tenants whose homes are in disrepair.

Successive chapters clearly explain the landlord's obligations and liabilities — and the tenant's remedies where these obligations are not met:

- the repairs problem
- contractual rights
- landlord's liability
- civil remedies
- using the Public Health Acts
- the Housing Act and bad housing
- displaced tenants
- related housing conditions

Right up-to-date, *Repairs: Tenants' Rights* takes account of the consolidating Housing Act 1985. Written by Jan Luba, highly respected for his work in this field, this guide will prove indispensable to housing advisers and to solicitors.

"gives a good, practical grounding for those helping tenants" — *Solicitor's Journal*

April 1986   164pp   £11.00

Sex and Race Discrimination in Employment
Palmer and Poulton

Sex and Race Discrimination in Employment is written "clearly and intelligently. . . . It is well presented, with simple headings and numerous cross-references. It contains a large body of accurate information about the statutes and the case law.
. . . This excellent book deserves a wide readership. It meets a real need as a practical and concise handbook for lawyers, and for trade unions and employers, in the continuing struggle to achieve genuine equality of treatment in Britain."
Anthony Lester, QC, from his foreword.

"A reference book which is reasonably priced, clearly written, thoroughly referenced and full of helpful and practical arguments to use in everyday cases." – *The Adviser*

September 1987   235pp   £14.00